Writing Permitted in Designated Areas Only

PEDAGOGY AND CULTURAL PRACTICE

Edited by Henry Giroux and Roger Simon

Recognizing that pedagogy begins with the affirmation of differences as a precondition for extending the possibilities of democratic life, the series analyzes the diverse democratic and ideological struggles of people across a wide range of economic, social, and political spheres.

4. *Writing Permitted in Designated Areas Only*, Linda Brodkey

3. *The Crisis of Meaning in Culture and Education*, David Trend

2. *Margins in the Classroom: Teaching Literature*, Kostas Myrsiades and Linda S. Myrsiades, editors

1. *The End of Education: Toward Posthumanism*, William Spanos

Writing Permitted in Designated Areas Only

Linda Brodkey

Pedagogy and Cultural Practice
V o l u m e 4

University of Minnesota Press
Minneapolis
London

Sections of "Poststructural Theories, Methods, and Practices" originally appeared as "Articulating Poststructural Theory in Research on Literacy" in *Multidisciplinary Perspectives on Literacy Research*, ed. Richard Beach, Judith L. Green, Michael L. Kamil, and Timothy Shanahan, 293-318, copyright 1992 the National Conference on Research in English and the National Council of Teachers of English, reprinted by permission; "Writing on the Bias" reprinted from *College English*, no. 56: 527-47, copyright 1994 the National Council of Teachers of English, by permission; "Modernism and the Scene(s) of Writing" reprinted from *College English*, no. 49: 396-418, copyright 1986 the National Council of Teachers of English, by permission; "Tropics of Literacy" reprinted from *Journal of Education*, no. 168: 47-54, copyright 1986, by permission; "On the Subjects of Class and Gender in 'The Literacy Letters' " reprinted from *College English*, no. 51: 125-41, copyright 1989 the National Council of Teachers of English, by permission; "Writing Critical Ethnographic Narratives" reprinted from *Anthropology and Education Quarterly*, no. 18: 67-76, copyright 1987, by permission of the American Anthropological Association; "Presence of Mind in the Absence of Body" reprinted from *Journal of Education*, no. 170: 84-99, copyright 1988, by permission; "Writing Permitted in Designated Areas Only" reprinted from *Higher Education under Fire: Politics, Economics, and the Crisis of the Humanities*, ed. Michael Berube and Cary Nelson, 214-37, copyright 1995 Routledge, by permission; "Telling Experiences" originally appeared as "Storytelling" in *The Oxford Companion to Women's Writing in the United States*, ed. Cathy N. Davidson and Linda Wagner-Martin, 854-56, copyright 1995 Oxford University Press, Inc., reprinted by permission; "Transvaluing Difference" reprinted from *College English*, no. 51: 597-601, copyright 1989 the National Council of Teachers of English, by permission; "Writing about Difference: 'Hard Cases' for Cultural Studies" reprinted from *Cultural Studies in the English Classroom*, ed. James A. Berlin and Michael J. Vivion, 123-44, copyright 1992 Heinemann-Boynton/Cook, by permission; poem from "Prologue by Carl Sandburg" in *The Family of Man*, ed. Edward Steichen, Museum of Modern Art, 1955, by permission; excerpt from Susan Griffin "Three Poems for Women," in *Like the Iris of an Eye*, published by Harper & Row, 1976, copyright Susan Griffin, by permission; selections from Beverly Slapin, *The Magic Washing Machine: A Diary of Single Motherhood*, Ide House, Mesquite, Texas, 1983, by permission.

Published by the University of Minnesota Press
111 Third Avenue South, Suite 290, Minneapolis, MN 55401-2520
Printed in the United States of America on acid-free paper

Library of Congress Cataloging-in-Publication Data

Brodkey, Linda.
Writing permitted in designated areas only / Linda Brodkey.
p. cm. — (Pedagogy and cultural practice ; v. 4)
Includes bibliographical references and index.
ISBN 0-8166-2806-8
ISBN 0-8166-2807-6 (pbk.)
1. Creative writing. 2. Creative writing—Study and teaching.
I. Title. II. Series.
PN181.B76 1996
808—dc20 95-44818

For

Jesse

Contents

Part IV. Teaching

Writing Permitted in Designated Areas Only is a collection of essays and papers on writing and writing pedagogy. The volume includes a selection of my published essays and unpublished papers, along with experimental essays written by students in a graduate seminar called Ethnographies of Literacy that I teach. I selected the material to gloss the curriculum vitae that professors update annually as part of their academic files. That vita, which formats, standardizes, and then reduces the intellectual lives of faculty to a list of professional activities acceptable to local institutions, substantiates the right of institutions to evaluate employees. There is no place for the personal pleasures, frustrations, joys, tedium, and sorrows of teaching and research in a standard curriculum vitae, where categories such as education, employment, grants and awards, publications, presentations, professional organizations, and courses establish the categories and fix the terms according to which institutions value faculty. These are not necessarily the terms, however, that teaching scholars would use to judge the quality of their intellectual labor.

Just by way of example, at the universities where I have worked, my teaching has always been evaluated in terms of a syllabus and student course evaluations. While these criteria are relevant, the quality of my teaching is ultimately in the writing students do. If any of them write to be read, after years of being graded but not necessarily read, then I consider myself to have done well by that class. For along with many others in my field, which is composition, I consider a desire to be read the sine qua non of writing. In fact, reading what students write—they are listened to and read while they are writing and provided written evidence of their words having been read when they have completed their essays—may be what distinguishes the best writing classes from other good college courses.

Many people who like the way I write presume that words come easily to me. They do not. It is true that I write often and that sometimes I write well. It is even true that I cannot imagine not writing. I like to believe I am most myself on the days I write. Certainly the self I like the best writes. I probably owe my patience as a writer and teacher to the fact that while my prose falls apart far more often than it comes together, the pleasures of writing are unlike the other pleasures of my life. It's not that others are any more or less pleasurable, but that the unexpected moments in writing when time becomes space literally and figuratively move me. For the duration of the convergence of time and space, I am in my body and the body of my text. The physical pleasure I take from the momentary location of myself in words that I have written is comparable to an experience many people have while reading, when they recognize themselves in words and say "That's me." It may also be comparable to an experience I have only heard about from people who talk about being *in* the virtual spaces of MUSEs (multi-user simulated environments located on the Internet). Although the sensation of being in my own text happens at the computer, I imagine the words to be *on*, not *behind*, the screen and can only hope someday to find myself in the monitor as well as in my text.

To write a recognizable self is perhaps the more satisfying in my case because I sometimes ride the fault lines of postmodernity in my writing. These verbal excursions onto the shifting terrain of the late twentieth century succor me when I approach utter despair over the naturalization of social and political inequities. There is nothing natural about widespread discrimination, poverty, hunger, unemployment, underemployment, hate crimes, hate speech, homelessness, rape, murder, abuse, incest, infant morbidity and mortality, illiteracy, and substandard housing, schooling, and health care. Nor, for that matter, is there anything natural about equality, disposable income, adequate food, employment, housing, schooling, health care, and so on. No one in this country understands better than the professional middle class that nothing social is natural. The class that in *Fear of Falling* Barbara Ehrenreich argues "discovered" poverty in the early 1960s is, however, also the class whose anxiety about its own professional credentials (the degrees and expertise that cannot be willed to its children) makes it desirous of social and political insularity and susceptible to what she calls the language of "critical discourse," language that rationalizes social inequality.

Critical discourse, according to Ehrenreich, is "the language of the academy and also bureaucracy" and can be "distinguished, above all, by its impersonal, and seemingly universal tone" and its indifference and even hostility to vernacular discourse as "weightless, fragmentary, unprocessed" (1989: 259). It is, in other words, a language that *naturalizes* indifference to actual people and their lives. While planned communities and the exorbitant cost of public and private postsecondary education support her case for professional class anxiety, the recent academic culture wars belie Ehrenreich's assumption that academics, let alone academics and other middle-class professionals, speak the same language. What Ehrenreich calls critical discourse, the language that denies any reality other than its own and that treats its own as unarguably true, is not the lingua franca of the academy. In fact, what she takes to be the language of an academic community, I have known instead as a perversely dominant, *uncritical*, modern academic dialect hostile to the *critical* discourses that have arisen out of postmodern and poststructural theories over the past quarter century. These theories challenge the validity of the modernist distinction between objectivity and subjectivity. The authority as well as authenticity of Ehrenreich's critical discourse rests on this distinction, which is ironically also a distinction she must herself accept in order to contrast the universality of critical discourse with the particularity of vernacular discourse. At stake in disputes between academic modernists and postmodernists is, first, the right to define reality and, second, the related right to cross disciplinary borders without an academic passport, the credentials that have traditionally discredited reports from anyone who is not a certified expert.

Postmodernism accounts for postmodernity by theorizing breaks with modernity. Yet the unpredictable aftershocks in some fields seem to have been even more devastating than the havoc wreaked by the comparatively brief theoretical upheavals of the late 1970s and early 1980s. Years later, postmodernists confront a virulent species of anti-intellectualism in the academy that has arisen in defense of the power if not the authority of modernism. While I am the subject of such a modernist campaign (Brodkey 1994a), the most persuasive and powerful modernist I confront is myself. The modernist me longs to be the objective, unbiased, neutral, disinterested, dispassionate, invisible, apolitical representative-witness-instrument-messenger of modern science. In the spiteful bellow of tracts calling for the restoration of one form or another of modernist common sense (tradition, standards, authority) in the garden of academe, it is tempting to ignore the residual modernism in postmodernism, let alone the sly presence of the modernist in the postmodernist.

If I do not renounce my modernist self, and I do not, it is because I have come to welcome my own discomfort with coeval contradictory selves as a signal of postmodern rumblings the more recognizable in the din of modernism. For in the cacophony I sometimes detect cadences of the "self-disengagement" and "self-invention" that John Rajchman argues constitute the ethic of Michel Foucault (1985: 9-41), which I take to mean that self-invention is animated in precisely such moments of self-disengagement, that a postmodernist is aroused not in the rejection but in the critique of the modernist self. The moment of critique may well give rise to the moment of self-invention in writing or reading that I referred to earlier as self-recognition. I regard most modernist in myself not just my desire but the sheer force of my desire to be innocent and to profess my innocence, for that seems to be a desire to deny my own complicity in discourses I consider dangerous to myself and others. Were I not implicated, however, in virtually every discourse I critique, I could not have written the essays and papers in this volume, nor would I have encouraged graduate students to invent themselves by disengaging themselves from their literate practices in writing.

"Modernism and the Scene(s) of Writing," "Writing Critical Ethnographic Narratives," and "Tropics of Literacy" in Part II were written not out of contempt for but under the influence of modernism. I am, moreover, as complexly entailed as everyone else who teaches writing by the middle-class discursive practices I identify, analyze, and critique in two other essays in the section, "On the Subjects of Class and Gender in 'The Literacy Letters' " and "Writing Permitted in Designated Areas Only." I say as much in Part I, in "Writing on the Bias," the essay that comes first but was written last. In the course of grounding cultural criticism in a narrative account of my own literacy education, however, I also realized that I turn to critique when I suspect that a prevailing discourse inhibits teaching and learning via the invidious modern habit of representing and publicizing a white middle-class practice as the standard by which to calibrate the "natural" worth of all other practices.

There is no doubt considerably more and even more disruptive white noise in writing classrooms than the shrill static that emanates from the narrow band of unreflective modernist practices I have noticed and whose volume I try to decrease in my teaching and scholarship. I focus on modernism's citadel of populist precepts because of its exclusive purchase on what counts as real and valuable in education. In composition, for example, the modernist distinction between objectivity and subjectivity warrants the polemics that pits theory against practice, research against practice, form against content, process against product, poetry against prose, and argument against narrative. I am using *polemics* as Michel Foucault defined it, shortly before he died, in an interview with Paul Rabinow: "polemics allows for no possibility of equal discussion: it examines a case; it isn't dealing with an interlocutor, it is processing a suspect; it collects proofs of his guilt, designates the infraction he has committed, and pronounces the verdict and sentences him" (Rabinow 1984: 382). It is the legacy of the polemics of common sense that makes a mockery of discussion—and, by extension, education—that I seek to interrupt in my work.

When a theoretical notion achieves the status of a natural fact among a group of people it is commonly thought to be unarguable. Many people, for instance, believe that form and content are literally, not just theoretically, separable, that there is something called an idea and something else called language or grammar or style. A good many people who teach and most who take composition classes seem to believe this. It is the intellectual basis of the split grade (one for form and one for content), which is in turn the commonsense warrant invoked by students to distinguish what content-area teachers may remark on in grading their essays from what writing teachers may mention. The separation of form from content is also a commonsense warrant invoked by those whose objections to multiculturalism are grounded solely in the desire to preserve the authority of disciplinary boundaries. Composition colludes, according to Susan Miller, writing in *Textual Carnivals*, in the institutional legitimation of high culture at the expense of writing and writing pedagogy, for the trivial topics students are traditionally asked to write on in composition classes verify and amplify the importance of the topics undertaken in literature and literary studies. Put another way, composition teachers are not paid to teach writing but to patrol the borders of language and literature.

Hired to police grammar, composition teachers transgress if they comment on content, for it follows, apparently as naturally as the night the day, that if the grammar police are not surveilling language they will police thought, which is the legitimate domain of historians, sociologists, scientists, and so on. Composition teachers who look on "content" as part of writing, and hence part of writing instruction, run the risk of being seen as illegally crossing the line and singled out as rogue cops. The rogues of one theory are another's teachers, however, and I count myself among the composition teachers whose refusal to police students—in the name of something called tradition, standards, excellence, discipline, or language—is theoretically as well as practically warranted by poststructural/postmodern accounts of language and reality. As I understand and teach it, language is reducible to neither grammar nor ideas, two notions so familiar that it is difficult (not impossible) to remember that they are just notions, not things. Modern structural linguistics proceeds on the *theoretical* separability of form and content (*langue* and *parole* in Saussure, competence and performance in Chomsky). Lingusitic theoretical explanations of structural variation in or across languages, however, are not offered and hence are not to be taken as descriptions of actual language use. For instance, arguing that the marked and unmarked terms in such familiar pairs as *man* and *woman*, *white* and *black*, *straight* and *gay* is linguistically arbitrary or neutral does not mean that they are also socially and politically neutral.

The variations that linguists treat as arbitrary can be and are used to naturalize institutionalized privilege. I am thinking of people who insist that generic "he" just sounds "natural," and I wonder, as I usually do in the face of this assertion, if there is not also an implication that changes in "natural" grammatical relations (form) signal unnatural changes in the social and political order (content). After all, if the order of the marked and unmarked terms in pairs like "he and she" were socially and politically as well as linguistically arbitrary, England would have passed no law in the mid–nineteenth century mandating the use of generic "he," and feminist efforts to replace that usage in the late twentieth century would be a matter of indifference (see Zuber and Reed 1993). It matters because something is at stake. It matters because we choose worlds with our words.

Many modernists could settle the argument by giving accuracy as the reason to replace generic "he" with some variant of "he or she" or even singular "they." A modernist can appeal to accuracy because in structuralism language is supposed to reflect a given reality, and the feminist challenge changed reality. Changes in language usage (form) reflect changes in reality (content). Such an argument has limited appeal to postmodernists, however, who take the position that language represents a discursive reality, rather than mirrors an empirical one. Unlike the empirical reality that is independent of language in modernism, language and reality are interdependent in postmodernism. Interdependency suggests an inquiry that explores the extraordinary sway of discourses over the language of "reality."

That inquiry would raise questions about what is at stake when the words used to represent a discursive reality are challenged and the challenges are met with the insistence that the familiar is natural, commonsense, plain as the nose on your face, unarguable, not subject to discussion, and, above all, not subject to change. Perhaps this modernist collocation of language and reality explains why, according to the *Chronicle of Higher Education*, 32.5 percent of the 1993 entering college class reported believing that "Realistically, an individual can do little to bring about changes in our society" (*Almanac* 1994: 17). It certainly suggests that students who have learned their modernist lessons will undergo a good deal of difficulty even considering the proposition that language plays a part in constructing the familiar social and political realities they regularly summon as "indisputable facts."

When a writing teacher challenges the words students use, a modernist is probably looking for a more accurate reflection of a given reality, and a postmodernist for a more complicated discussion of a discursive reality. In my work with student writers, discursive complications proliferate most readily and fruitfully in the face of difference, all the more so when representations of relations between self and other are posed in the context of a just world. I doubt that I could overestimate the critical importance of difference to my scholarship and teaching. I first spoke of its importance in 1989 at the Conference on College Composition and Communication in a paper published later the same year in *College English* as an opinion, "Transvaluing Difference," the first essay in Part III. As the unpublished papers in Part III indicate, I was later given more than ample opportunity to explore some of the practical, theoretical, and political ramifications of difference in public talks after the course syllabus "Writing about Difference" became the first casualty in what its opponents in the academy and the media represented, and mostly continue to represent, as a valiant battle against the forces of political correctness, thought control, and/or multiculturalism. Since I do not imagine myself to be in any army, I consider the syllabus for "Writing about Difference" and the students and teachers who would have used it to be collateral damage in what many academics would now call the culture wars. The relentless barrage of negative publicity about a composition course that professors in the English department at the University of Texas had given little thought, since it is taught by graduate students, is a stark reminder that there are no civilians in the war some modernists seem intent on waging against postmodernists in English studies and, sadly, no possibility for discussions in modernist polemics. The incivility of once-local battles in the humanities has lately reemerged in a decidedly polemical defense of modern science (Gross and Levitt 1994), which suggests that at least for some people the culture wars have only just begun.

Part IV opens with two essays on writing pedagogy, "Writing about Difference: The Syllabus for English 306" and "Writing about Difference: 'Hard Cases' for Cultural Studies." The first essay, written especially for this volume, introduces the materials developed for the course—writing assignments, writing and reading schedule, and table of contents for the course packet—by recalling how pedagogical decisions were made by the Ad Hoc Syllabus-Writing Group. I wrote the second essay with the chair of that committee, Richard Penticoff, who was then a graduate student at the University of Texas. The essay situates the "Writing about Difference" syllabus in the context of the program at Texas and then discusses its pedagogical and rhetorical grounding in relation to cultural studies. The five autoethnographic essays in Part III were written by graduate students who have studied with me over the past few years. Bear in mind that their papers were written under institutional constraints that distinguish them from essays written for publication. First, they were written in partial fulfillment of the requirements for a graduate seminar, Ethnographies of Literacy. In most cases, students were as unfamiliar with autoethnography as they were with the literature on ethnography and literacy when they entered the seminar. The course was taught in a five-week summer session at the University of Texas and in a ten-week quarter at the University of California, San Diego. I gave the writing assignment on the first day of class and required students to complete it by the last day. These are not conditions conducive to writing for publication, even taking into account the day set aside for peer response to work in progress near the end of both courses. The autoethnographies resemble a personal narrative or autobiography in that they concern the writer's life, but differ to the extent that personal histories ground cultural analysis and criticism. I selected these particular essays because I consider them interesting examples of what students make of writing assignments that call for a fair amount of intellectual integration and because I consider the essays to be a rare opportunity for those who do not teach and study literacy to consider what some of the most successful white middle-class students of a generation have to say about what else they learned when they learned to read and write.

To summarize, the essays in this volume document my efforts to teach and write at a time when theoretical upheavals continue to shift the terms of my authority as a teacher and scholar. In the preface to *Flexible Bodies: Tracking Immunity in American Culture from the Days of Polio to the Age of AIDS*, Emily Martin writes: "My fieldwork has made clear to me that the categories of social analysis that we once found useful to describe our lives—gender, race, class, work, home, family, community, state and nation, science and religion—are no longer sufficient to describe, let alone analyze, the phenomena of the contemporary metropolis" (1994: xvi). The categories Martin no longer finds sufficient were developed over the course of many years in many critiques of modernism, especially modern science. Writing something worth writing and reading arises in the course of complicating common sense by denaturalizing notions, including those that Martin mentions and that I use myself, without losing sight of the partial and provisional status of our claims to knowledge. My work as a teacher and program administrator, even more than my work as a scholar, leads me to suggest that when pedagogy invites students to complicate commonsense notions that arguably diminish people, categorization itself becomes suspect.

I would like to see composition set up a game of cat's cradle for itself on the order of the one Donna Haraway has recommended for science studies. In other words, I would like composition to call a halt to the old war games in which modernists and postmodernists regularly provide the easy entertainment of polemics in lieu of pursuing difficult discussions about writing and writing pedagogy at the end of the twentieth century. Haraway's cradle consists of what she calls "intersecting and often coconstitutive threads of analysis—cultural studies, feminist, multicultural, and antiracist theory and projects, and science studies—because each of them does indispensable work for the project of dealing with sites of transformation, heterogeneous complexity, and complex objects" (1994: 63). I would like to believe that such a complex weaving of threads is possible in composition because discussions along these lines are already in progress—prominently in the work of Susan Miller, Sharon Crowley, and Lester Faigley—and suggest that the institutional future of composition is in the moments when a piece of common sense is dislodged and along with it the presumption that it goes without saying that the familiar is natural. I would also like to think that my work has contributed something to that discussion, for I would not have bothered to write, much less publish, essays and give papers on writing and pedagogy, nor would I have continued to teach, if I believed the polemics of the present have already destroyed even the possibility of discussing the future of writing in the field of composition. It is to that discussion, which is not necessarily a part of institutional evalutions of faculty productivity, that I hope to contribute with *Writing Permitted in Designated Areas Only*.

I turn now to the pleasures of acknowledging the generosity of friends and colleagues at the three institutions where these essays were written. To begin, I have had the good fortune to meet a good many people whose intellectual commitments to teaching and scholarship intersect with mine wherever I have worked. That I single out people here whose counsel I sought does not mean that I have not adjusted and even altered my thinking based on the hundreds of conversations, drafts, working papers, and manuscripts that punctuate my life. The person whose advice I regularly seek is Michelle Fine. We met on our first day as assistant professors at the University of Pennsylvania, where we soon developed a practice of checking in with one another that is now the signal habit of our friendship. I cannot overestimate the importance of having in my life someone who is not only willing but eager to talk with me when I am half convinced that what I'm thinking may not even be worth mentioning, let alone pursuing. Michelle, who has never failed to see potential in even my most tentative musings, is always there, even when articulation is beset by the inevitable complications. I also worked with several students at Penn who have since become friends with whom I discuss work in progress. Mark Clark, Pat Johnston, and Frank Sullivan also read and provided invaluable comments on several of the essays and papers in this volume.

When I moved to the University of Texas, I added some new colleagues to my list of friends and readers, notably Lester Faigley, Sara Kimball, and John Slatin, whose friendly readings I cherish as much as friendships that endured even "the troubles" at Texas. I also met and worked with several graduate students I now consider friends, including Rick Penticoff, with whom I wrote one of the essays in this collection and who listens as well as he reads. The graduate students who wrote the essays included in this book are but a few of the extraordinary students I have had the good fortune to work with over the past fifteen years. Since moving to San Diego, I have made more new friends of colleagues generous enough to read and discuss work in progress. Barbara Tomlinson and George Lipsitz have advised me often and well. Roddey Reid—whose work on Michel Foucault I admire and whose advice on what to read in Foucault's long list of publications has been as generous as discussions of our respective writing projects have been fruitful—has been a good friend and colleague. I also thank John Herschel and Robert McDonell of the Warren College Writing Program. Robert's unstinting support has included discouraging me from writing with one finger on delete, reading and discussing more ideas and drafts than I care to remember, and scanning more articles than either of us cares to remember. Gail Shatsky, also of the Warren College Writing Program, patiently copyedited many of the pieces included here.

Because there are usually only a handful of composition scholars in a university, most of us find it difficult to discuss our work in our local departments. In the few short years since I met Susan Miller, I have grown accustomed to asking for her advice and soliciting her comments on drafts. She is a reader whose judgment I value whether or not we agree. Patricia Irvine and I began talking about our writing when we were graduate students at the University of New Mexico. Although we rarely meet face to face these days, over the years I have come to so treasure her intellectual sense of the politics of writing that sooner or later I get around to asking for her comments. Since my sister Mary Archer is not an academic, I do not usually discuss the intricacies of my research with her. But during the two years that I worked on the essay "Writing on the Bias," which concerns her childhood as well as mine, I often sought and always received her help.

When I began writing about writing and writing pedagogy for publication, my son, Jesse, was a young child. Over the years he has provided me mounds of material about his writing, including his frustration with school writing, but a child is not much interested in what his mother writes. Now that he's an adult who also writes, however, he often asks what I'm working on and even offers to read drafts. Because Jesse is a student rather than a teacher of writing and considers all my statements about teaching and learning from that critical vantage point, he reminds me, as no one else probably could, that there is no student who is not also a Jesse, no student who is not also immensely more complicated, that is, than any representation I or anyone else could write. For as Jesse is quick to remind me, a student is not only a student, just as my son is not only my son.

POSTSTRUCTURAL THEORIES, METHODS, AND PRACTICES

In February of 1990, the National Council of Research in English, in collaboration with the National Council of Teachers of English, sponsored a conference to which a number of scholars were invited to explain their approach to research on literacy to a gathering of educators in the United States. The proceedings were later published as a volume of essays called Multidisciplinary Perspectives on Literacy Research, *edited by the organizers, Richard Beach, Judith L. Green, Michael L. Kamil, and Timothy Shanahan. In their introduction to that collection, the editors explain that the papers given at this second conference on literacy, convened fifteen years after the first, "represent a dramatic broadening and revision of disciplinary and methodological perspectives" (1992: 2). That I was invited to talk about poststructuralism is one such example of the range of disciplinary and methodological perspectives the editors had in mind. Whereas "linguistics, rhetoric, and cognitive science . . . shaped the papers' definition of problems and methods" at the conference in 1976 (1), a good many of us who spoke were invited in 1990 because our theories and methods were not those that had organized earlier research on literacy, but were instead new approaches that the audience, which was familiar with our publications but not necessarily with our theoretical and methodological concerns, wanted to discuss.*

I used the occasion to talk about how I came to the particular version of poststructuralism that brought me to the attention of the conference. To that end, I spent a fair amount of time distinguishing poststructural language theory from structural language theory and then explaining why I preferred Foucauldian to Lacanian poststructuralism in my own research on literacy. Since writing "Articulating Poststructural Theory in Research on Literacy," my contribution to both the conference and the volume, I have often wished I could revise not so much the argument as some of the claims in light of my ever shifting understanding of the problems that attend the articulation of theory into research and practice. In the course of tinkering, however, I could not resist adding some new material to replace deleted text or to elaborate on themes that on reflection seem more or less complicated. I offer as the introductory essay of this volume such a substantially revised version of "Articulating Poststructural Theory in Research on Literacy" that readers familiar with the first might well say it should be called "Rearticulating Poststructural Theory in Research on Literacy." I think of it as yet another bout of tinkering.

Let me set the record straight before I try to explain how I conduct research on literacy. I am not a social scientist. The best that can be said of me (which in some circles would be the worst) is that I have a penchant for social theories of language. I have spent my intellectual life tinkering with language theories in hopes of becoming a good writer and teacher of writers. I think of myself as a tinker because tinkers are both curious and arrogant enough to try to fix almost anything. That is a fair description of how I work with theories. I try to make particular theories work, since theories are all I have to work with when my experiences of writing and teaching baffle me. While I hope I have become a better theorist over the years, some theories seem to have fallen apart in my hands. No amount of ingenuity on my part seemed enough, for instance, to recycle speech act theory for classroom use. My failures notwithstanding, since it is theories, not methods, I have worked at the hardest, and theories, not methods, I understand best in relation to literacy research and practice, by now I articulate my interest in research and practice more precisely in the theories than in the methods I use.

In one way or another the theories I tinker with consider language to be a form of social action. That I see writing and speaking as social action does not mean that I am foolish enough to see words as substitutes for actions. I have heard and read enough political promises in my lifetime to know what "just rhetoric" means, and to be sickened by the abuse of language that fecklessly destroys word as bond. And so along with many others, I have altered my definition of social action over time to include social activism, which has meant, among a good many other things, coming to see that my own interest in words is not a simple academic curiosity about language. Mine is rather a desire to understand the awful power of language, for I was a child who recited "Sticks and stones may break my bones, but words will never hurt me" as a frenzied incantation against the pain of being named. And I am an adult who fully recognizes the extraordinary privilege of living among people for most of whom the threat of words, and only on occasion the violence of words, has been both more imminent and more consequential than the threat or fact of physical violence.

While it may seem naive to say so, literacy is the trope of my desire for political equity. I equate literacy with democracy, and suspect all definitions of literacy that either exclude writing or subordinate writing to reading of eroding everyone's civil liberties and civil rights by barring most citizens from access to publication, one of the most important public forums for sustained critique of government in any participatory democracy. In light of my conviction, I view the writing and recovery of slave narratives and other writing by people of color, along with the writing and recovery of women's texts, as invaluable critiques of official history. By way of example, I consider Geneva, the imaginary interlocutor in Derrick Bell's *And We Are Not Saved*, to be largely responsible for the critical force of his trenchant allegory on the African-American struggle for legal equity, an invention made possible by such recovery projects. I see Jane Marcus's afterword to Helen Zenna Smith's *Not So Quiet . . .*, published first in 1930 and recently republished by the Feminist Press, as another effort to rewrite history. Marcus takes the occasion of the republication of this novel about middle-class British women who had to pay to drive ambulances in World War I to complicate a chapter in the history of women's suffrage in the early twentieth century:

> The study of World War I and its effects on women in England begins with the acknowledgment that all wars destroy women's culture, returning women to the restricted roles of childbearing and nursing and only that work that helps the war effort. The struggle for women's own political equity becomes almost treasonous in wartime. . . . Any account of women's wartime energetic and responsible performance of social labor must recognize that that performance in the public sphere came from the previous struggle against an immensely hostile state to win the elements of education, knowledge, and skills that any democracy customarily grants its citizens, but which, in Edwardian England, were systematically denied to half the population. (Marcus 1989: 249)

These and similar multivocalic literary projects are commonly seen as extraordinary rather than ordinary examples of literacy. Yet literacy campaigns in this country and around the world are all arguably warranted by struggles for the education and knowledge routinely denied slaves, women, and unwelcome immigrants by governments indifferent at best and hostile at worst to their well-being. Hence all are potentially liberating.

Literacy as Discursive Practice

As wonderful an invention as I find Derrick Bell's Geneva, she necessarily modulates his voice, which can only speak out on behalf of those silenced by laws forbidding slaves to read and write, just as Helen Zenna Smith's characters reveal only the plight of upper-middle-class white women in her novel. Literacy is the trope of my desire for political equity not because I believe that literacy is in itself liberating, but because I would like to hear from every Geneva who has a story to tell. If my work has been motivated by the coincidence of literacy and liberation, my writing has been an attempt to account for our failure as educators to make literacy an offer that just cannot be refused. There are any number of reasons why people might resist literacy, not least among them the unattractive ways reading and writing are taught in school. But people put up with even the most outlandish tedium if they believe there is something in it for them (amateur and professional athletes, bodybuilders, would-be-licensed drivers, aspiring dancers and musicians, to name a few). That far too many who *could* do not learn to read and write suggests that they fail to see anything of value in most definitions of literacy. And when I think about some of the reasons given for teaching reading and writing, I too begin to wonder what is in it for most people. The sad fact is that in too many quarters literacy is defined as reading, and reading as a matter of learning to comprehend and then follow instructions. Need I say that writing enters into this definition of literacy only as a measure of a reader's comprehension of the instructions? That doesn't strike me as much of an offer, unless the prospect of following orders thrills you or, more realistically, the prospect of requiring others to do so does.

We need to examine and evaluate the version of literacy offered to most people—in the name of education—first because many of us do not believe it is anywhere near the best offer we can make, and second because literacy defined as reading and following instructions makes it easy to think of those who do not read as outlaws, to accept without comment representations of illiterates as an economic liability or a criminal threat to literates. Literacy does not literally defend people against unemployment. Mexico is attractive to businesses not because the labor force is literate, but because Mexicans work for a fraction of what companies would have to pay unionized or even nonunionized workers in the United States—about a dollar a day, according to letters in the *New York Times* protesting the "free trade agreement" (Olenick 1992; Gartman 1992). Literacy is no defense against crime. I would venture to guess that the folks who brought us the savings and loan frauds read above the fourth-grade level.

While illiteracy may not be the cause of crime or unemployment, illiterates are convenient political fetishes of middle-class anxieties about social and economic inequity. Illiterates keep company with the fetishes of gays and lesbians, feminists, gangs, pregnant teens, welfare mothers, working mothers, the homeless, people with AIDS, Willie Horton, rap musicians, Robert Mapplethorpe, Murphy Brown, and cultural elites (the list seems and probably is endless) that threaten fetishes of literates in the bosom of the happy American family, people who read the classics, fly the American flag, and otherwise defend the nation from all manner of threats to Western civilization. Fetishes of illiterates as "the problem" displace public interest in egregious systemic inequities in schooling, not to mention distracting us from examining and discussing the educational policies and programs that have historically produced illiteracy. If fetishized illiterates are the problem, the solutions are ridiculously simple: *they* don't speak English (English Only); *they* can't function in an advanced technological society (functional literacy); *they* don't know what educated people know (cultural literacy).

Fetishized illiterates are radically disconnected from fetishized literates in these so-called solutions. In much the way that the fetishized stranger-rapist is easier to villainize than acquaintances, friends, or husbands who rape, the fetishized illiterate is a convenient political scapegoat for a complexly troubled middle class. Accustomed to sentimentalized caricatures of the occasional adults who beat the odds and learn to read with the help of a dedicated tutor, we are apt to forget that illiterates personify class terrors. The British mystery writer Ruth Rendell spells out the threat to literates in the chilling opening sentence of *A Judgement in Stone:* "Eunice Parchman killed the Coverdale family because she could not read or write" (1981: 1). As Rendell tells the story, "Eunice was arrested—because she could not read" (2). As is often true of her mysteries, the plot is meticulous, which makes it all the more difficult to remember that Rendell is not recounting an event but telling a story of her own making, in which a housekeeper kills her conservative, literate employers because their liberal daughter, who discovers her illiteracy and offers to teach her to read, threatens to destroy what Rendell sees as the complacency of her illiteracy. The impenitent illiterate, who possesses "the awful practical sanity of the atavistic ape disguised as twentieth-century woman" (1), assaults civilization itself when she kills off the entire literate family while they are watching an opera on television. The stakes are high:

> Literacy is one of the cornerstones of civilization. To be illiterate is to be deformed. And the derision that was once directed at the physical freak may, perhaps more justly, descend upon the illiterate. If he, or she, can live a cautious life among the uneducated, all may be well, for in the country of the purblind the eyeless is not rejected. It was unfortunate for Eunice Parchman, and for them, that those people who employed her and in whose home she lived for ten months were peculiarly literate. Had they been a family of philistines, they might be alive today and Eunice free in her mysterious dark freedom of sensation and instinct and blank absence of the printed word. (1)

Rendell's projection of seemingly fathomless middle-class terrors onto an illiterate working-class housekeeper equates literacy with civilization even as it confounds both with an upper-middle-class family's knowledge of and taste for opera.

I do not dismiss *A Judgement in Stone* as a reactionary fantasy, though I see it as one, for its success in the marketplace surely rests on Rendell's having tapped a wellspring of disturbing middle-class anxieties. The piece of the fantasy that concerns me is the presumption that what impoverished "illiterates" hate and fear most about wealthy "literates" is their literacy rather than, say, their wealth or power or leisure. Represented as a criminal or economic threat, the predatory illiterates roaming the landscape of Rendell's mystery and the long unemployment lines in the print and electronic media, academic studies, and government reports endanger not themselves or other illiterates, but the middle class, which in these accounts, at least, is synonymous with civilization itself.

Education is not likely to make literacy an offer even worth considering unless we begin to think more about how to represent writing and reading as discursive practices and less about them as a set of skills or abilities or competencies that "we" have and "they" want, to be taught by "us" and learned by "them." To conceptualize literacy as discursive practice is to link the "literacy events" that Shirley Heath has studied on the local level (in families, communities, classrooms, churches) to more remote and less visible but critical historical and sometimes even historic circumstances (acts of Congress and acts of war, economic indicators, voter registration campaigns, computer technologies), which also determine the social, economic, and political meaning and value of literacy. This is by way of saying that the political events that impinge on the meaning and value of literacy events also shape, and in some cases even dictate, the educational policies that ground curriculum, pedagogy, programs, and research. And it is also by way of saying that the macro- as well as micropolitics surrounding education alter the boundaries of the social context of literacy, for in addition to the usual suspects—students, teachers, parents, administrators, textbooks, curriculum—we shall also need to consider legislators, legislation, and legislative histories, not to mention political action committees, think tanks, school boards, foundations, corporations, the media, and government bureaucracies that also have a stake in literacy. Even this preliminary list is, I think, enough to suggest that the people who make up the far-flung network involved in literacy programs, education, and research will not be evenly committed to a single definition of literacy, let alone to its meaning and value.

That politics figure in literacy seems obvious to me. That we can ignore them, on whatever grounds, in theory and research and practice does not mean that we have rid ourselves of politics. It means instead that they operate covertly rather than overtly in our programs, classrooms, and studies. To think of literacy in terms of discursive practice means trying to identify and account for the political dimensions of literacy in theory, research, and pedagogy, and is a matter of becoming as suspicious as the mother, in Bertolt Brecht's play *The Mother*, of the imperious teacher who finally agrees to write "class struggle" on the board only to break faith with the students by saying, "Be sure to write in a straight line, and not over the edge. Whosoever overwrites the margin also oversteps the law" (1965: 78). I would like to think that we, like Brecht's mother and workers, recognize the following refrain from "Praise of Learning" as the proper response to a cynical teacher who would disguise the political and economic privileges of the literate in spurious law:

> Study, man in exile!
> Study, man in the prison!
> Study, wife in your kitchen!
> Study, old-age pensioner!
> You must prepare to take command now!
> Locate yourself a school, homeless folk!

Go search some knowledge, you who freeze!
You who starve, reach for a book:
It will be a weapon.
You must prepare to take command now. (79)

However uncomfortable I am made by the hyperbole, the mother's position is, I hope, also mine. I know that I would not be a scholar today had I taken such rules to heart, and I would like to think that a good many educators are willing, and that some of us are even quite eager, to write in the margins, to encourage students to do the same, to see empty margins as the unlawful borders defending print against readers who write back. In any event, my dreams for a universally literate and critical citizenry are probably most visible on the margins of texts, where anything from Brecht's mother to Bell's Geneva to Smith's ambulance drivers—and who knows what else—can happen.

I am not sure that the contradictions I write about in "Tropics of Literacy" or in "On the Subjects of Class and Gender in 'The Literacy Letters' " or in "Transvaluing Difference" or in "Writing Permitted in Designated Areas Only" or in "Writing on the Bias"—contradictions between the literacy we define for ourselves and the literacy we define for others, or contradictions between our professed educational goals and our teaching practices—technically qualify me as a critical theorist. I am attracted to language theories that allow me to critique as well as analyze programs and policies and practices that reproduce, knowingly or unknowingly, inequitable social arrangements, and my work is critical of theories and studies that ignore politics and insist on locating literacy education on some supposedly neutral terrain where the political arrangements contributing to literacy and illiteracy are deemed moot. While I am decidedly critical, I have constructed most of my studies as well as my arguments from poststructural theories of language and discourse, none of which were available to the founding members of the Frankfurt school, which, until recently, was synonymous with critical theory. Moreover, Jürgen Habermas, the most influential contemporary theorist of the Frankfurt school, dismisses Michel Foucault, the theorist whose work has most influenced mine, as a neoconservative who summarily rejects the modern world. I do not think of either Foucault's work or my own as either culturally or politically conservative, although I am more than a little wary of modernist assumptions (the writer in the garret) that function as truisms or common sense in literacy research and pedagogy.

The Hegemony of Naive Empiricism in the Study of Language

While not wishing to ignore the importance of the early Frankfurt school on my thinking (see "Writing Critical Ethnographic Narratives"), and in particular the notion of negative critique (Horkheimer, *Critique of Instrumental Reason* and *Critical Theory*), I have been considerably less interested in the Frankfurt critique of the politics of positivism than in the poststructural critique of the politics of empiricism. At issue in both instances, however, is the *hegemony* of positivism or empiricism over what counts as real or worthwhile in research and practice. The Frankfurt theorists mostly objected to the positivist hegemony over social inquiry via the valorization of formal logic at the expense of what they saw as the human desire to remember the past and to envision a future and better world. At the end of the century, positivism no longer reigns supreme in the academy or elsewhere, but I would not credit the Frankfurt school with single-handedly routing the exclusive value of positivism in the sciences and social sciences. At least, I would guess the proliferation of theories and qualitative methodologies in the social and human sciences to have even more to do with widespread misgivings about the indiscriminate use of positivism to describe and explain human events.

The hegemony that poststructural discourse theories specifically counter may sometimes be called positivism but is probably better characterized as naive empiricism, which I take to be the belief that scientific method guarantees the objectivity of the researcher along with the research (see Brodkey 1987a: 82-94; Brodkey 1987d: 26-32). Historian of science Donna Haraway argues in "Situated Knowledges" that only nonscientists seem actually to believe in the "doctrine of disembodied scientific objectivity—enshrined in elementary textbooks and technoscience booster literature" (1988: 376) and, further, that that version of objectivity is neither desirable nor possible for a number of reasons she links to literal and figurative human vision. First, vision, our literal and figurative perception of reality, is limited to what can be seen/"seen" from a particular vantage point. Although Haraway dismisses any possibility of transcendent scientific objectivity, her argument is a dismissal of neither science nor objectivity. It is instead a case for scientific modesty, a long overdue recognition that any and all knowledge, including that arrived at empirically, is necessarily "situated knowledge." Second, that we view the world from a particular vantage point also means that what can be seen by either a human eye or a human theory is necessarily partial, that is, both an *incomplete* and an *interested* account of whatever is envisioned.

The importance of Haraway's argument on the positioning and partiality of theories cannot be overstated, if only because it means that researchers should be as wary of relativizing as of totalizing claims, both of which she calls

> "god tricks" promising vision from everywhere and nowhere equally and fully, common myths in rhetorics surrounding Science. But it is precisely in the politics and epistemology of partial perspectives that the possibility of sustained, rational, objective inquiry rests. (584)

To my mind, the empirical naïveté that besets those of us who study and teach writing and reading is just such a trick, and the assumption too often taken as *fact* in theory, research, and practice is the belief not only that language can be studied independent of thought and reality, but that language is actually only a tool for reflecting a given reality and translating thought.

The structuralist separation of language, thought, and reality is a theoretical convenience (like the separation of form and content), not an empirical fact but simply a way to organize, regulate, and evaluate linguistic research on language. The structural argument concerning the arbitrary or neutral relationship between language and reality is an account of linguistic structural variation, an explanation that does not, as far as I can see, even attempt to describe and explain the structure of the social, political, and historical circumstances under which people speak and write. Structural linguistic theory is an attempt to explain not language, but only those parts of language that the theory finds linguistically interesting: in this instance, that since phonological and morphological variation in the word, say, for "cat," in languages where such a word appears, is not linguistically meaningful, the relationship between sound and sense is arbitrary.

While it may be true that the linguistic marking of "woman" and "black" in such familiar binary pairs as "man and woman" and "black and white" is arbitrary or neutral, I doubt whether many women or black people live in a world where the logic of linguistic markedness overrides the logic of, say, institutional racism and sexism. Linguistic arbitrariness is the kind of situated knowledge that Haraway would see as contingent on the positioned and partial vision of structural linguistics. Its limitations as an explanation for literacy practices have less to do with linguistics, however, than with our losing sight of the partiality of linguistics as a theory of language. At the risk of stating the obvious, it's naive to expect a theory that was designed to describe internal linguistic relationships to provide a vantage point from which to view and examine the social and political relations linking language, thought, and reality in the production and reception of written or spoken texts.

Theory and Research

Earlier I introduced the conceit of the tinker, an image that seems increasingly more suitable as I try to explain the partiality of theory as it concerns my own attempts to conceptualize literacy as a set of social and political practices, rather than linguistic skills, abilities, or competencies. The theories I tinker with are all poststructural accounts of discourse, and the version of discourse I continue piecing together from my reading of Foucault, and only in passing from Jacques Lacan and Jacques Derrida, is decidedly critical rather than dismissive of empirical research. Over the years, it has become evident to me that at least some of my interest in Foucault's work has to do with his empirical tenacity in the face of nomothetical accounts of modernism (see Rajchman 1985). Despite my reservations about naive empiricism, which I am inclined to dismiss as scientific literalism or fundamentalism, my interest in empiricism has not waned. That is not to say, however, that it has not been tempered by feminist, poststructuralist, and antiracist accounts of the part language and discourse play in social constructions of reality. The absence of woman as a category in many experimental studies, for instance, has materially affected women's lives, including my own, so I am not likely to forget that far too many experimental studies claiming to be objective and empirical have ignored differences that matter (race, gender, class, ethnicity, age, nationality, ability, and sexual orientation, to name but a few) as scientifically or mathematically uninteresting. Yet the systematic erasure of these and other differences in social science research may be less a consequence of scientific method than a practice of social scientists, for many of the same differences that go unremarked in quantitative research are also ignored in qualitative studies (e.g., Brodkey 1987d), not to mention social theories. I think it's fair to say, however, that scientific objectivity has too often and for too long been used as an excuse to ignore a social and hence a political practice in which women and people of color, among others, are dismissed as legitimate subjects of research.

Nowhere are the consequences of this dismissal in educational research more clear to me than in the Department of Labor figures (*Time of Change*) that I included in "Tropics of Literacy" and from which I argued that the value of literacy is not absolute but contingent on race *and* gender: "[15 percent] of white male high school dropouts aged 22 to 34 live below the poverty line, compared to 28% of white females, 37% of black males, and 62% of black females" (Brodkey 1986a: 51). The gaps in these figures are dramatic enough to warrant a political theory of literacy, as well as studies and teaching practices, sensitive to the simple fact that race and gender confound the meaning and value of education in ways that are not accounted for when we study writing and reading apart from the historical and political circumstances that have so invariably discriminated against both the education and employment of minorities and women (most ruthlessly against black women, if we take the figures seriously) that they are among the classes singled out for protection under civil rights law.

Poststructuralism may not have spoiled my commitment to empirical research, but it has made me more aware of the theories that ground the analysis and interpretation of data. This is by way of saying that my interest in poststructural theory has had more effect on how I analyze and interpret data than on how I collect it. I plan to go on designing research projects based on what people say and do as writers and readers, on the stories told about literacy and illiteracy, and, given my long-standing fascination with anthropology, I am likely to continue collecting ethnographic data, that is, likely to concentrate on situational rather than experimental or quasi-experimental data. I see these choices as having to do with my education and talents, however, not as a principled objection to other ways of conducting research.

I think of discourses as physicists once thought of atoms, as conceptual rather than empirical objects. That means that my research has been an effort to discern empirical traces of discourses in texts in hopes that applied research on literacy will eventually catch up with theory in much the same way experimental physics eventually caught up with theoretical physics. When I look back over my work I see myself struggling to develop a method for interpreting data consistent with poststructural discourse theory, that is, a method that assumes language, thought, and reality to be *interdependent*. Among the advantages of working from such a self-conscious theory as poststructuralism is that it is difficult to forget that it *is* a theory. That a theory is only a theory sounds sensible enough, but one of the dangers all researchers as well as theorists face, if I understand Haraway's argument, is forgetting that a theory is only an account of something, not the thing itself. While I doubt that anyone remembers all the time that the theory they are working from is only an account, and a partial one at that, a theory that begins by assuming the nearly invisible influence of discourses over our ability to imagine and reflect on who we are in ourselves and in relation to others and the world is, to my way of thinking, difficult to forget as a theory.

Structuralism falls short of my needs for a lot of reasons, not least among them the commitment to a theory that ignores practice in favor of nomothetic accounts of linguistic universals (*langue* and *parole* in early versions, competence and performance in late ones). Some of the direct and indirect consequences of the structural commitment to underlying and invariant rules can be seen in the contemporary history of applied research on writing and reading over the past twenty years (error analysis and miscue analysis, sentence combining, research on reading as comprehension as well as studies of decoding, cognitive protocols and protocol analysis, models of composing, as well as research on style, coherence, cohesion, and so on). It is not that these notions are not interesting (at least I find them interesting), but that even this cursory list, which is far from complete, clarifies for me, as little else does, the extent to which most literacy researchers and practitioners have come to see language as structural linguistics represents it. And whatever else may be true of linguistics, what interests linguistics is not all there is to language. Literacy researchers who limit themselves to linguistics run the risk of confounding linguistics and language, of forgetting that an account of language, or anything else, is useful only so long as people remember that it *is* an account.

Discourse and Discursive Practice in Poststructural Theory

I have a penchant for narratives as well as theories, and so it is not all that surprising, to me at least, that I would be attracted to a theory grounded in a narrative that explicitly sets out to explain some of the problems in practice that have eluded or not interested either linguistic or literary structuralists. Even taking into account variation in theories, sooner or later a poststructural theory argues that it is the discourses (or worldviews or ideologies) we learn that teach us how to read and write the world as well as words. I do not take this to be a metaphysical assertion about reality, but see it instead as an assertion about what human beings can reasonably expect to know about reality. In other words, poststructuralism is best thought of as an epistemology: a theory of knowledge in which knowing is contingent on discourses.

One argument for the power of discourses over language is in Jacques Lacan's revision of the classical Freudian account of the division of the conscious from the unconscious. As I understand Lacan, when an infant (around eighteen months) first recognizes itself in a mirror, two things happen at once: it sees itself as *over there* in the mirror and it also sees itself as *separate* from its mother. This moment of split or divided consciousness, literally experienced as a trauma (the child who is here also sees itself as over there, and sees that it is not its mother), motivates the child to learn language, for only language (personal pronouns, specifically) promises to reunify the now divided self—as an "I." Lacan argues that the child learns what he calls the language of the "father," a term that means a powerful discourse or ideology, but that conflates the cultural power of the "father" and the syntactic power of language in the phallus. The fetishism of the phallus and the word in the West is aptly summarized in the seemingly outlandish Lacanian neologism *phallologocentrism* (*Ecrits*).

In sum, Lacan rewrites Freud's Oedipal narrative, also a psychoanalytic account of the separation of the conscious from the unconscious, in terms of discourse. In Lacan's version the male infant's unbridled lust for language is a desire to *be* the phallus, for it is the symbolic power of the phallus (discourse), not the physical fact of a penis, that promises unity. The female infant is also beset by desire, not to *be* but to *have* the phallus, for she too is driven by the same desire for the unity represented in the powerful language of the father. It's a fantastic story, that is, an incredible story (if you're not a psychoanalyst). Yet it is also an instructive story for those of us who wonder about the tenacity with which children acquire language, not to mention the faith that many of us still retain in language—to put things right—in the face of unbearable sorrows and unthinkable atrocities.

I have simplified the Lacanian narrative, which was written by a psychoanalyst for other psychoanalysts, in hopes of showing that the plot is familiar. It is a thoroughly modern romance, a quest—of the self for the self—in which the the grail is language qua discourse. Discourse, in this version, replaces the sense of being at one with self, other, and the world with a discursive practice that constantly maintains the illusion of a self unified as "I." The illusion is maintained in large part by the personal pronoun system, which grammatically regulates both person and number in more or less predictable ways. The discursive unity is only an illusion but a necessary (healthy) one, according to Lacan, if we are to survive the trauma of split or divided subjectivity.

The poststructural project is not to unmask discourses as false consciousness (that's a classical Marxist project), but to demystify the part they play in our constructions of self, other, and reality. So, if discourse is to function fruitfully as a concept for representing and distinguishing among ideologies or worldviews, we cannot continue to use the word *discourse* indiscriminately. I say this even though *discourse* has probably already achieved a ubiquity in the academy that is exceeded only by *paradigm* (Thomas Kuhn's nemesis). Like paradigm, however, discourse is a notion that loses much of its explanatory force when virtually everything is called discourse. By way of example, I think it is a serious mistake to call academic prose academic discourse. I say that in part because the variety in academic texts suggests not one but several discourses at work on academic writing practices and in part because it gratuitously collapses a useful distinction between texts and discourses. At least my understanding of poststructural theory tells me to examine texts for traces of discourses. In other words, I see my work on literacy as a matter of studying not discourse(s) but discursive practices, via the production and reception of written texts.

Discourses

At least some of what I would like to know about discursive practice in or out of the academy could be learned by tracing the influence of the five interdependent discourses of science, law, art, education, and religion/ethics that I proposed in "On the Subjects of Class and Gender in 'The Literacy Letters,' " a study that tracks the awkward maintenance of discursive hegemony in correspondence between teachers and students. My point then and now is that particular "dialects" of ideologies or worldviews or discourses have been institutionalized for such a long time that they are viewed as natural or proper ways of seeing and knowing and talking about such things as reality or the self. At issue in these letters is the extraordinary sway of a middle-class dialect of educational discourse over the teachers. Some of the problems working-class adults experience in school must surely have to do with the invisible presence of middle-class sensibilities in the educational discourse its fluent speakers unwittingly presume to be a classless lingua franca. So strongly does a middle-class propriety govern the educational discourse that authorizes teachers in the study that they ignored or changed the topic when their correspondents introduced such mundane working-class concerns as money or violence into their letters. The teachers' occasional and surprising violations of the conventions arguably governing storytelling in their personal correspondence—manifested in their linguistic lapses—suggest that teachers as well as students are at times overwhelmed by the very discourse that underwrites teaching.

In the course of summarizing the study, I wrote about the importance of difference to the critical examination of teaching:

> What is immediately challenged by the narratives is the rhetorical practice in which the privileges of one subject—to tell stories or decide what the topic is—materially diminish the rights of other subjects. What is ultimately challenged is the ideology that class, and by extension race and gender differences, are present in American society but absent from American classrooms. If that's true, it is only true because the representation by students of those concerns inside educational discourse goes unarticulated by teachers. (Brodkey 1989a: 140)

When I mentioned earlier that the poststructural project is not to dismantle but to demystify discourse(s), part of what I hoped to make clear is that the discursive practice of denying the differences introduced by the working-class women in their narratives is a *middle-class* variant of educational discourse. Denial is not, however, the only possible response to difference. Looking at the correspondence as discursive practices is, to my mind, a way not only of examining teaching practices, but also of changing them. Judging from letters that teachers who read the article wrote to me, I would say that class conflicts of the sort the correspondents encountered are not unusual and that some teachers who recognized themselves in the article also found in the critical analysis of the discursive practices of good teachers grounds for reevaluating some vexing problems in their own classrooms.

Jim Henry and I used the same five hypothetical discourses in our study of "voices" in a student paper written and revised for an undergraduate course on architecture, a field in which, we argued, the discourses of science and art are equally influential and in which traces of both discourses can be found in the discursive practices of architects and successful architecture students (Brodkey and Henry 1992). I won't go on at length about an essay you can read for yourself, except to reiterate here our explanation of what Stuart Hall calls articulation, which I see as a crucial notion for anyone attempting to apply poststructural theory to research on writing and reading practices:

> By *articulation* Hall means both utterance and connection, in the second definition trying to capture the fact that an articulated joint may or may not connect to another. Discourses may well *intend* to construct social identities, but a theory of articulation is needed to distinguish between hegemonic intentions and the uneven effects of discourse in practice. . . . Articulation is a construct for recovering at least some of the complexity

of what happens during attempts to identify and unify people as the subjects of discourse. (146)

Articulation is crucial to the empirical analysis of discursive tension in both "On the Subjects of Class and Gender" and "Voice Lessons in a Poststructural Key," for it allows a researcher to trace a cycle of production and reception, to coordinate a writer's representations of self, other, and reality in a text with readers' responses to these representations.

Henry and I argue that academic essays are situated, in the first instance, in educational discourse, which authorizes a writer to teach a reader something. Beyond that first discursive warranting, however, claims could be warranted by any and all of the discourses: science, art, law, education, and religion/ethics. The student, whose writing we studied in a series of drafts on which both Henry and the professor commented, "experiments" with voices grounded in science and art, but in his final essay "articulates" his claim in what Henry and I call the Voice of the Architect. In other words, he addresses himself to his teacher as if they shared the criteria for evaluating Buckminster Fuller, whose designs, the student writer concludes, "do not represent a balance between art and science" (159). We relate the articulation of this particular voice in the student's essay to both his teacher's use of a similar voice in his comments and Henry's advice to think of the essay as a conversation among architects. The student makes claims in at least three discourses—science and art and education—and he also calls on a number of voices in which to make them. The voice in which he finally articulates his argument against Fuller as an architect, however, is only one of several we were able to identify and trace in his drafts and is mostly important because it emerges as the dominant voice in his final essay.

Hall's essay on articulation limns an array of possibilities for empirical research on the production and reception of spoken and written texts. Among the texts that have most interested me are those that students write and teachers read. In that set, response and revision is a cycle of production and reception that most writing teachers wish they understood better, if only because it is a vexing chronicle of teaching and learning. On the one hand, we read and advise students on how to revise their essays; on the other, we are often unpleasantly surprised by what students make of our comments in their revisions. The value of articulation to poststructural theory has to do with making distinctions between the intentions of discourses (which have to do with positioning people as subjects) and the effects of discursive practices (which have to do with whether people identify themselves as the subjects of a discourse). The value of articulation to us as researchers and practitioners also has to do with the notion of a discursive cycle, for articulation demands that discursive practices be studied in terms of both writers/producers and readers/receivers of texts.

Literacy and illiteracy lend themselves "naturally" to this kind of research on the cycle of intentions and effects. Moreover, those of us who teach writing and reading have acquired a wealth of practical experience of articulation in our classrooms that lends a special credence to the notion itself. I would like to see teachers take articulation as an invitation to read poststructural theories, but to read them with research on literacy in mind. For it goes without saying, or should, that the promise of poststructural theories of discourse and applied poststructural research on literacy relies on practitioners, not practice, on researchers, not research, on theorists, not theories.

Thus far I have tried to explain why I find poststructural theory a more suitable account of language and discourse than structural theory. I have also tried to explain how I apply poststructural theory of discourse in my research on writing and reading as discursive practices. In these attempts to clarify relationships between theory, research, and practice in my own work, I have tried to make what I believe to be a powerful theory of practice more intelligible to teachers and researchers. It is conventional wisdom to say that theory and practice go hand in hand. That does not mean that we are necessarily aware of either our theories or our practices, however, or that we understand how they are related to one another. The relationship I would like to see more clearly articulated is one in which research *mediates* theory and practice. Most theorists imagine that practice follows from theory, or would, if practitioners would only pay attention to theory. Many practitioners complain, however, that theory is irrelevant to practice, which I would like to believe is a critique not so much of theory as of theorists, and in particular of their tendency to speak only to one another. The future of literacy education and research relies on teachers' knowing theories and assessing their value in research on literacy practices.

Poststructural theory of language and discourse is not made to order for research on literacy. At least I haven't found it so. I find I still approach every book and every article as a conversation overheard. I say that because it takes a good long while to catch even the gist of theoretical arguments, and longer still to begin reflecting on their relevance to research on practice. I am, however, a patient and persistent reader who has grown accustomed to the bold claims that are only later modified in most poststructural theories, and who has therefore grown accustomed as well to the awkward path of her own understandings. Fortunately, theory is not an IQ test, and learning to read it is largely a matter of desire, leisure, and experience. In my case, desire has been supported by both leisure in virtue of my academic appointments and experience in virtue of my education. Not many practitioners are as fortunate, however, for it is commonly assumed that they are being paid to impart rather than to make knowledge, and the material differences in our circumstances are meaningful. Yet I am nonetheless concerned that the separation of theory from research and practice in educational research does a good deal more damage to teachers and students than any of us realizes, and that only teacher-theorists can even hope to remedy the negative consequences of that division of intellectual labor (see Aronowitz and Giroux 1985). In the meantime, teachers might treat research that passes itself off as unencumbered by theory as a Haraway "god trick," for research that refuses to acknowledge its theoretical commitments is every bit as dangerous to practice as a theory that presumes to discipline practice without benefit of research.

Research on Discursive Practice

As attracted as I am to poststructural theories, they interest me only insofar as they clarify the part language plays in constructing social reality and hence the part teachers and students and researchers *could* play in constructing more equitable classrooms, schools, neighborhoods, communities, and towns and cities, not to mention boardrooms, courtrooms, and legislative chambers that, in one way or another, also influence research on educational policies and practices. If words constitute worldviews rather than simply restate reality in language, what teachers say and write matters and what students say and write matters. For those who see practice as a legitimate site of educational reform and who are inclined to conduct research on educational discursive practice, let me suggest three poststructural notions to keep in mind. I single out multiple discourses, multiple subjectivity, and shifting subjectivity not because they are necessarily the most important theoretical notions, but because I believe understanding them better could play a critical part in resisting discursive constructions so powerful as to appear implacable. Teachers who can identify, describe, and analyze discursive formations currently informing curriculum and pedagogy are even better poised to reconceptualize education if their plans for reform also entail a critique of the discursive practices that impede teaching and learning. In other words, a critical analysis poses the terms in which to demystify the status quo as neither natural nor immutable.

Multiple Discourses. The poststructural notion of multiple and interdependent discourses means that cultural hegemony in democratic societies (as opposed to the seemingly absolute hegemony of physical violence, or the threat of it, in police-driven states) is contingent on the struggle for domination among discourses. If people learn not one but several discourses along with whatever languages they learn, then absolute discursive hegemony is constantly frustrated, in principle, though not necessarily in the practice of individuals. We have all heard and probably even told stories about doctors who refuse to acknowledge patients as anything other than diseases and illnesses (a discursive practice presumably rooted in an absolute commitment to science as a discourse); we know stories about lawyers who transform all topics into legal arguments (a commitment to the superiority of law over all other discourses); and we know stories about teachers who see everyone as their students and treat every topic as an opportunity to lecture (a commitment to educational discourse commonly known as pedantry). Most if not all of us have been unfortunate enough to have had practical as well as theoretical experience of being on the wrong end of such single-minded and frustrating discursive practices, not to mention under the institutional authority of such boorish absolutists.

The notion of interdependent discourses provides at least a preliminary explanation of why such practices are abhorrent as well as tedious. It is not just that there is something perverse about the refusal to acknowledge constructions of people and events offered by other discourses, but that such exclusionary practices make a mockery of speech itself. At least I can see little point in talking to people who insist that some dialect of law or science or art or education or religion/ethics has exclusive rights to reality. If we imagine discourses to be interdependent ideologies or worldviews, then some of the marvelous complexities of spoken or written texts may be attributed to the influence of competing discourses on writers' discursive practice, as seems to be the case in many texts. And it may also be that the unwanted simplicity of some student texts could be attributed to the lack of multiple discursive influences. Some of the undergraduates I teach, for instance, state their claims about social problems in terms of religion. Given that in higher education, science usually has considerably more sway than religion, and given that students are often posing solutions to problems, such as abortion, in terms of legislation, proclaiming abortion to be a sin is tantamount to declaring that there is nothing to talk about, no reason to argue, for religion used in that way effectively moots arguments warranted in either science or law.

Multiple Subjectivity. Every discourse offers not only a worldview, but also an array of subject positions that I discuss in "On the Subjects of Class and Gender" as representing people in terms ranging from mostly satisfying or positive to mostly unsatisfying or negative. If we think of the earlier example from medicine as a discursive practice grounded in scientific discourse, it would be more satisfying to be the doctor than the patient, at least when medicine is being spoken and practiced. In addition to the obvious material fact that being in good health is simply better than being in poor health, it is better, at least on the face of it, to be the knowing rather than unknowing subject of medical discursive practice qua science, or, for that matter, to be the knowing subject of any discursive practice. There are doctors, however, whose practices at least resemble educational discursive practice, insofar as they treat patients as students, teach rather than pronounce diagnoses, and encourage rather than discourage questions. I see the promise of poststructural discourse theory for research in this and other mundane instances of multiple subjectivity in practice.

In principle, a discourse is attractive because its worldview and subject positions defend us against our experience of being at odds with ourselves, others, and the world. Earlier I read the psychoanalytic version of discourse as a story about the individual quest for a unified self. In the Lacanian narrative, discourse is thought to unify the self divided during infancy in the moment when the child first looks in a mirror and recognizes itself as at once in the mirror and separate from its mother. In a Foucauldian narrative, by contrast, discourse concerns not the internal relations of psychoanalysis, but external relations between self and other and self and the world that are arguably alienating. If Lacan is seen as writing a poststructural romance, then Foucault would be a poststructural novelist, in the sense that novels, albeit some more explicitly than others, narrate social and political conflicts between the individual and society (Balibar and Macherey 1980). I am not sure how far I can take, or even want to take, this conceit, but I think it is important to distinguish the multiply determined human subject in Foucault's work from the singly determined human subject in Lacan's.

Lacan is talking about an invariably traumatic process determined by a single psychological event, the separation of the unconscious from the conscious. Foucault, however, is talking about discourses that have historically singled out certain human behaviors (and hence certain humans) as dangerous to the modern state. At least as I understand his work on the power of discourse, particularly on sexuality, criminality, and insanity, Foucault is trying to document the conjunction of science and law in the construction and isolation of a set of human behaviors (and humans) as subject to the joint authority of science/medicine and the state. These discursive practices mark the onset of modernism as the hegemony of science and law over what counts as "deviance" and what happens to "deviants." He contrasts the interdependency of science and law in the modern era to earlier periods when "deviants" would have been subject to the joint authority of the church and the (prebourgeois) family, that is, when the authority of the discourses I call religion and education held considerably more sway over both the imagination and social life (Foucault 1973, 1979, 1980a).

The Foucauldian project is to demystify the power of discourse in order to better understand the discursive practices that construct our sense of self, other, and reality. One of the reasons I am more attracted to Foucault's narrative than to Lacan's probably has to do with my decided preference for novels with complicated plots, for I see endless possibilities for discursive resistance in the subplots that introduce but do not resolve social and political conflicts. In terms of at least one official narrative, for example, education is largely a matter of disciplining students by subjecting them to a series of lessons and examinations that monitor their progress toward "mastery" of a subject matter. Success is measured by the gradual policing of self that culminates, ideally, in autonomous, educated adults who know what their teachers know. The plot of the official educational narrative is not only complicated but contradicted in practice by one subplot or another. There are working-class students, for instance, who do not identify themselves as the middle-class subject of the plot, not to mention middle-class people—women, people of color, lesbians and gays—who do not; there are also teachers who for one reason or another do not articulate themselves as the subject of the plot. I, for one, would like to learn a good deal more about the intellectual lives of students and teachers who articulate themselves as the subjects in the unresolved subplots of official educational narratives.

The narrative plot produced from Foucault's considerably more complex arguments on discourse and discursive practice interests me because I am not only fascinated by the possibilities of socially constructed political reality, but also committed to the possibility of teachers and students resisting representations that demean them and their labor. I am talking about devising ways for teachers and students and researchers to identify and "interrupt" discursive practices that, for one reason or another, appear counterproductive to teaching and learning. I have in mind any statement of "the solution" that scapegoats a group of people as "the problem": pregnant teens, gangs, irresponsible parents, uneducated teachers, immigrants, administrators, unions. To my mind, at least, denying the middle-class underpinnings of educational discourse and insisting that educational discourse transcends class is dangerous to the extent that such a discursive practice reduces all who study and teach to one version of the good student and one version of the good teacher without benefit of discussion.

Shifting Subjectivity. In theory, a discourse represents all humans as subjects. In practice, however, some humans consistently fare worse than others in and across discourses, for some are commonly represented as diminished or objectified human subjects. That is to say that historically they have been consistently "othered" as unknowing or unknowable subjects in science, art, law, education, and religion or ethics. Some may see this dispassionate macro view of discourse and discursive representation as a serious limitation of Foucauldian poststructuralism. I do not. I see it instead as treating the crucial decision of what in practice is worth noticing and analyzing as a local matter. In my case, that has usually amounted to acknowledging that educational research advocates a politics of education along with its problems, methods, analyses, and conclusions. I would be more sanguine about literacy if more people assumed political responsibility for the educational realities (change is not possible, change is possible, change is needed, not needed, students can read, can't, can write, can't, teachers can teach, can't, parents should help, should leave teachers alone, the state should intervene, shouldn't under any circumstances) represented and in effect advocated by research.

In most of my work I ask first myself and then readers, "What's wrong with this picture?" I see that not as a matter of disrupting but of *interrupting* commonsense representations of self, other, and reality. Put another way, I want to change the topic, not stop the conversation. I look at "Tropics of Literacy" as my first effort to locate the devastating consequences of articulating an alienated and alienating subject by "othering," a process by which we "stipulate the political as well as cultural terms on which the 'literate' wish to live with the 'illiterate' by defining what is meant by reading and writing" (1986a: 47). Seen in this light, E. D. Hirsch's *Cultural Literacy* amplifies this negative articulation by confounding hegemony and consensus. Put another way, cultural literacy puts a bizarre spin on the Lacanian romance, since Hirsch projects onto the "other" a desire to be Hirsch (the father), which ignores, among other things, how thoroughly the projection conflates the institutional authority of a "Hirsch" with the power of the "father." A Foucauldian novelistic reading would consider Hirsch's dictionary to be an attempt to pass off cultural hegemony as cultural consensus. Consider, for example, the definition of AC/DC as "alternating current/direct current" (Hirsch 1987: 152). This not only represents a class consensus among those who make enough money to travel abroad, it also represents a hegemony of heterosexuality over bisexuality and homosexuality. For surely Hirsch must know that in some circles, AC/DC defines a good deal more than electricity. Perhaps cultural literacy is part of the same middle-class fantasy that in *Literary Theory* Terry Eagleton argues underlies Hirsch's literary theory, that is, perhaps adding the dictionary to the canonical texts is best seen as an expression of Hirsch's desire to insure the value of his intellectual property.

I suspect that the situations we find ourselves in as teachers and researchers resemble novels more than romances, that is, are more productively analyzed as Foucauldian than as Lacanian narratives, which is to say that we are in a position to represent literates and illiterates alike as both more complex and positive human subjects than those encountered in *Cultural Literacy* and Rendell's *A Judgement in Stone*. And I think, furthermore, that eductors are more likely to do that if we can teach ourselves to read (articulate) what students write not only as so much formal evidence of their illiteracy but also as evidence of a struggle to represent themselves and others as complex and even contradictory subjects. I try to reread students in "On the Subjects of Class and Gender," but I am more confident about my right to do so in "Writing on the Bias" because I am the site of the struggle for self-representation in that narrative.

Discursive practices that diminish human subjectivity reduce the possibility of imagining people as agents of their own lives, let alone as agents of social change. Even though I have witnessed some remarkable improvements in the representation of women as subjects, the effects are uneven and generally more consequential to professional women like myself. Yet even the lives of middle-class white women have been less altered than I thought. In the work Michelle Fine and I have done on sexual harassment narratives, for instance, women students at the University of Pennsylvania who reported being harassed by their professors did not write about harassment, but speculated instead on harassers' motives and on institutional reprisals that would follow reporting incidents (Brodkey and Fine 1988). These narratives are important for a number of reasons, not least that they were written by some of the most privileged and well-educated women in the United States, who cannot be written off as lacking the reading and writing skills, abilities, or competencies of working-class students. Their unexpected failure to describe what happened to them seems to be linked to their reluctance or inability to articulate themselves as female subjects in their own narratives.

Less surprising but more consequential, it is working-class women and men and women and men of color, especially African-Americans, who are historically the least positively represented subjects of discourse. One of the indisputable advantages of ethnic studies is the dramatic increase in representations of a host of "others," and particularly African-Americans, as complex and contradictory subjects in academic and popular texts. The complexity of representations in Hortense Spillers's "Mama's Baby, Papa's Maybe: An American Grammar Book" and in any of Toni Morrison's novels or essays, for example, contests the egregiously simplified and arguably stereotypical representation of African-American matriarchy in social science research like the "Moynihan Report" (Moynihan 1965). Similarly, Michelle Fine's ethnographic studies, *Framing Dropouts* and "Silencing in the Public Schools," along with Cameron McCarthy and Warren Crichlow's edited volume *Race, Identity, and Representation in Education*, effectively challenge the usefulness of categories like race in light of new theories and studies on the complex relations of students and teachers to schools.

Adolescents who drop out or even graduate without learning how to write and read mostly do so in silence (Fine 1990). But whether they leave quietly or create a brouhaha in the process, when they leave they not only forfeit the credentials but also cede a forum in which to interrupt the educational discursive practices that first construct and then represent them as functionally illiterate or semiliterate. I can think of no more important project for teachers and researchers than studying classroom discursive practices in relation to the part they play in alienating students from literacy by failing to articulate their representations of themselves as subjects who are different from their teachers. That would mean, of course, taking the position that literacy begins not in reading but in writing, and would in turn mean inviting students to begin writing back and supporting them while they hone critical discursive literacy practices in our classes. Ultimately, taking literacy seriously would constitute a decision to rewrite the subjects of educational discourse.

"Legal interpretation takes place in a field of pain and death," the critical legal scholar Robert Cover reminds readers in "Violence and the Word" (1986: 1601), for a legal sentence literally alters the material reality of plaintiffs and defendants. The view of discourses and discursive practices that I have been working out over the past few years sees those who rebel against the power of discourse with silence or violence as walking alone onto a field of pain and death, but those who critique a discursive practice as recognizing that "pain and death destroy the world that 'interpretation' calls up" (1601). Cover sets legal interpretation against literary interpretation as an argument against a literary theory of the social construction of reality for law. But interpretation is not the issue. The conjunction of violence and the word in a legal interpretation is grounded in the powerful discursive hegemony of the state, which confers on judges the authority to reconstruct the lives of plaintiffs and defendents with words. Legal discursive practice may be a powerful interpretive practice, but it is the authority of the state in the person of the judge that makes legal discursive practices (both legislative and juridical) consequential. And it is the authority of the state in the person of the teacher that makes educational discursive practices consequential.

Conclusion

The poststructural narrative on human subjectivity is all the more attractive to me because of the possibilities for discursive resistance suggested in the notion of articulation. In much the same way that theorists argue that the unity of discourse is a necessary illusion, I view resistance or interruption as a necessary illusion, if only because I need to believe that social change is possible and, further, that the possibility of shifting discursive positions and articulating positive representations of oneself is a more effective, a more inclusive and lasting, form of political resistance than either silence or violence. A world in which polemics masquerades as argumentation is a world in which there is no point in talking, no reason to keep the conversation going. For far too many people, the time for talking has long since come and gone. It is an extraordinary privilege to be someone whose life has more to do with altering discursive practices than finding food and shelter or maintaining constant vigilance against violence. Not many people on the planet, not to mention in the United States, live free of the kind of pain Cover is talking about in his essay on the violence of legal sentencing. For that matter, probably not enough of us understand that the privilege of discursive self-representation is not a right but an unwarranted liberty unless it extends to everyone. Teachers and researchers who abhor the systemic inequities of schooling are uniquely poised to advocate for extending the privilege of literacy in their own classrooms and institutions, to be sure, but even more importantly in their professional organizations. In other words, first we need to redefine literacy in terms of writing as well as reading and then teach ourselves and our students to see writing as an invitation to identify, analyze, and critique anything and everything that represents itself as unarguably true. Critical literacy is an approach to teaching that insists on the students' right to learn how to conduct themselves as writers of the world. That would entail, at the very least, learning how to lay out a case in support of a position in a variety of genres. Advocating on behalf of students means developing a literacy curriculum that supports critique in our own classrooms, it means learning to live with the consequences of animating critique, it means soliciting the scrutiny of our peers in professional meetings, and it will eventually mean taking on the additional burden of defending such curricular and pedagogical reforms against any and all educational policies that valorize reading by using writing to test students.

As intellectually exhilarating as I imagine such a literacy campaign would be, a critical pedagogy is likely to generate writing that will wound as well as delight its advocates. For while few young people are content with what they see, they view the world neither from a single vantage point, nor from the perspectives of their teachers. Bear in mind, however, that as Jonathan Kozol is reported to have told Phil Donahue, “Our injured feelings are not at issue here” (Levine 1994: 11). While Kozol was trying to explain that African-Americans are not obligated to absolve white Americans of their guilt, I am trying to say that critical literacy is not about soothing anyone’s sensibilities, least of all teachers’. Students should not be asked to write for us. We should, however, be able to ask and teach them to write to us. Poststructuralism is not the only story about human life that interests me, but to the extent that poststructural theory narrates a story, it tells a complex story about the power of discourse(s) over the human imagination. I read the history of literacy as just such a story, for there are no narratives more powerful than those that chronicle the shift from orality to literacy in modern democratic societies, and no narratives after that shift give us more to think about than those told from the vantage point of poststructural theories.

PART I

Education

Introduction to Part I

There is a world of difference between an educational history and the educational credentials that a curriculum vitae records. On the face of it, my vita is an argument for meritocracy. I am living proof, it would seem, that in America you don't have to go to the right schools or study with the right people to become a university professor. Even though I took my undergraduate degree at Western Illinois University and my graduate degrees at the University of New Mexico, I went on to work at the University of Pennsylvania, the University of Texas, and the University of California, San Diego. While I may believe myself to be deserving, individual merit fails to explain why so few whose educational credentials parallel mine are my colleagues, most of whom hold degrees from the institutions that have historically produced university professors. That people who can afford it pay the exorbitant tuition exacted by such institutions is not an argument for meritocracy. It may well be a case, however, for acknowledging that when the market value of education is calibrated by criteria as potentially meaningless as institutional reputation or as meaningful as low student-teacher ratios, one need not believe in meritocracy to vaunt the value of education for other people's children while carefully tending the educational credentials of one's own.

I wrote "Writing on the Bias" in memory of other people's children. I once was and sometimes still am one of those children, judging by the frequent appearances of the child I conjured for this narrative about my own education. She is the child of my memory, which is probably as reliable as anyone else's personal, cultural, and historical memory. It is not, however, her experience that I try to recall in "Writing on the Bias," but a story told by the persistence of memory, which is selective, to be sure, but none the less instructive for that. The result is a critical educational history in which everyone, children as well as adults, is implicated, not because people are inherently malicious but because education is rarely candid in the face of the tangled nexus of human desire. I did not set out to reconcile the two conflicting territories I occupy—that of the working-class child and that of the middle-class adult—in the essay. From where I stand, with a foot in both worlds, my lifelong preoccupation with writing and writing pedagogy, however, now seems to me an ambitious peacekeeping effort, an expression of my desire to preserve an uneasy alliance between the selves and worlds I literally and figuratively inhabit.

"Writing on the Bias" is truly an essay. Not only did I write it as an experiment, to find out what would happen; I also experimented with autoethnography, whose idiom I set out to teach myself by trial and error in the course of writing a narrative account of my own education. This relatively unfamiliar and admittedly ungainly term, *autoethnography*, was coined to describe a genre of autobiography that, Françoise Lionnet argues, "opens up a space of resistance between the individual (*auto-*) and the collective (*-ethno-*) where the writing (*-graphy*) of singularity cannot be foreclosed" (1990: 391). Anyone who has ever glimpsed the fleeting singular self that is constituted in social relations knows that dynamic and elusive self to be more what is meant by self than the one defined by the social categories of the individual and the collective. That a singular self is realized in writing that challenges received categories is no doubt part of my attraction to autoethnography, but it is ultimately the potential for social change rather than any psychological benefits that may accrue that attracts me as a writer and teacher.

For Mary Louise Pratt, the autoethnography is well suited to what she calls "contact zones," described as "social spaces where cultures meet, clash, and grapple with each other, often in contexts of highly asymmetrical relations of power" (1991: 24). Writing from the contact zone disputes representations of such social spaces as classrooms as communities by contending that the stakes in believing there to be social consensus are as unequally distributed as power among its denizens. Autoethnography is another quarter heard from. The view from that quarter is one of the many that needs to be taken into account, for the inhabitants of contact zones recognize differences among themselves, including power differences, to be a condition of social relations. There is limited tolerance there for teachers who disclaim their institutional power or for students who insist on their absolute powerlessness, and limited tolerance as well for unexamined presumptions of race, class, and gender privileges or unexamined accusations of elitism, racism, sexism, homophobia, radicalism, liberalism, conservatism.

Social identities are not labels to be flaunted in the contact zone. To know that a man is white and middle class or a woman black and middle class is to know too little and to believe too much about them. Social identities are the serious, impish, ridiculous, generous, wary, contradictory singular selves constructed and reconstructed in ludic, painful, hostile, prosaic relations of sociality. Autoethnographies are produced by people who acknowledge their multiple affiliations *and* realize that they are strategically poised to interrupt the negative effects of what passes for common sense. Such texts do not attempt to replace one version of history with another, but try instead to make an official history accountable to differences among people that communitarian narratives typically ignore. "Writing on the Bias" exposes commonsense notions that promote middle-class interests at the expense of writing and pedagogy. Equated with spelling, grammar, and punctuation, writing bears little resemblance to itself and far too much to testing. In this instance, the autoethnographic case counters the common sense that has prevailed over decades of failure with the uncommon sense of a writing theorist's narrative of her own childhood encounters with literacy. Viewed from this quarter, since there is little to attract children to writing taught solely as knowing and following the rules, there are sufficient grounds to warrant curricular and pedagogical reforms that absolutely ignore common sense.

Writing on the Bias

One of the pleasures of writing that academics rarely give themselves is permission to experiment. I have broken with tradition here because I wanted to document the experience of being my own informant as well as tell a story about a white working-class girl's sorties into white middle-class culture. I began working on the narrative in an effort to recall my childhood and adolescent experiences of literacy, and kept at it because the more I wrote the more uneasy I became about having forgotten that I had learned to write and read before I started school.

"Writing on the Bias" was written under the influence of all that I remember of what I have seen, heard, read, and written over the years. Yet not one of the thousands of texts that has influenced me is appended in a list of works cited, since no textual authority was summoned to underwrite the telling of the narrative. While I may not have depended on published texts while I wrote, I prevailed mercilessly on the generosity of family and friends, whose support I gratefully acknowledge here and whose advice contributed to none of the shortcomings of this text: my son, Jesse Brodkey, my sister Mary Archer, Mark Clark, Michelle Fine, Patricia Irvine, Sara Kimball, George Lipsitz, Robert McDonell, Susan Miller, Roddey Reid, and Barbara Tomlinson.

If you believe family folklore, I began writing the year before I entered kindergarten, when I conducted a census (presumably inspired by a visit from the 1950 census taker). I consider it a story about writing rather than, say, survey research because while it has me asking the neighbors when they were going to die, in my mind's eye I see myself as a child recording their answers—one to a page—in a Big Chief tablet. As I remember, my mother sometimes told this story when she and her sister were of a mind to reflect on their children's behavior. Since in my family the past provided the only possible understanding of the present, the story was probably my mother's way of talking about her middle daughter's indiscriminate extroversion and perfectionism. On the one hand, these inborn traits would explain my performance in school, for teachers like gregarious children who approach all tasks as worth their full attention. On the other hand, my mother, who claims to have found me engaged in conversations with strangers on more than one occasion, would have been worrried about such wholesale friendliness. Innocence was not first among the virtues my mother admired in her children. That I view the census story as my mother's does not erase faint outlines I also see of myself as a little girl who leaves her mother's house to travel the neighborhood under the protective mantle of writing.

Writing was the girl's passport to neighbors' houses, where she whiled away the long and lonely days chatting up the grown-ups when the older children were at school, and otherwise entertained herself with this newfound power over adults, who responded to her even if they did not also answer her question. As naive as the question may seem, as startling and by some standards even unmannerly, a child asking grown-ups when they were going to die was probably considered a good deal less intrusive in the white, working-class neighborhood in the small Midwestern city where I grew up than the federal government's sending a grown man to ask questions about income, education, and religion. Forty-some years later, stories are all that remain of that childhood experience. I remember nothing: not if I ever met an official census taker, not if I believed grown-ups *knew* when they would die, not if I was a four-year-old preoccupied by death, not even if I took a survey. And while it seems to me of a piece with other family narratives explaining human behavior as inborn, whether it is a "true" story interests me a good deal less than how it may have affected me and my writing.

I would like to think that the story of my preschool experience sustained me through what I now remember as many lean years of writing in school. Yet when I look back I see only a young girl intent on getting it right, eager to produce flawless prose, and not a trace of the woman who years later will write that school writing is to writing as catsup is to tomatoes: as junk food is to food. What is nutritious has been eliminated (or nearly so) in processing. What remains is not just empty but poisonous fare because some people so crave junk that they prefer it to food, and their preference is then used by those who, since they profit by selling us catsup as a vegetable and rules as writing, lobby to keep both on the school menu. Surely a child possessed of a Big Chief tablet would be having a very different experience of writing than the one who keeps her lines straight and stays out of margins, memorizes spelling and vocabulary words, fills in blanks, makes book reports, explicates poems and interprets novels, and turns it all in on time. In the neighborhood I was fed food and conversation in exchange for writing. At school I learned to trade my words for grades and degrees, in what might be seen as the academic equivalent of dealing in futures—speculation based on remarkably little information about my prospects as an academic commodity.

Lately I seem to have come full cycle, for I am sometimes reminded of the little girl whose writing seemed to make food appear and people talk when something I write appears in print or when I give a paper. I never think of her when I write annual reports on my research and teaching or revise my curriculum vitae (that's school all over again), but when someone writes back or talks back, I'm in the old neighborhood again, back where writing is playing is eating is visiting is talking, back where the pleasures of writing are many and school just another game I played. While the census may have taught me *to* write, taught me that writing is worth doing, I learned things about *how* to write in school. That some children who already see themselves as writers can appropriate skills that when they are presented *as* writing would arguably alienate most children from writing should not be construed as a testimonial for teaching writing as skills. Well into graduate school, I despaired of becoming a writer whenever a grade or a comment even hinted that I had not learned and meticulously followed all the rules of spelling, punctuation, and grammar. To this day, when a copyeditor invokes an in-house rule I feel shame, as if my not having mastered a rule that I could not have known even existed means I must not be much of a writer. As a child I trusted teachers and distrusted myself, as girls are known to do. And to make matters even worse, I was a child who lived by rules.

I suspect I loved rules because I loved the idea of controlling events. Step on a crack and break your mother's back. Hop over it and save her. You are safe from all harm as long as you cross only on green. Say a perfect act of contrition immediately before dying and you will go directly to heaven. Say it too fast or too slow, misspeak a word, forget one, or remember something you should have confessed, and you will go to directly to hell or, worse, languish in purgatory. Better yet, live such an exemplary life that confession will be moot. The new rules for spelling, grammar, and punctuation were simply added to injunctions against stepping on cracks in sidewalks and crossing against the light, not to mention the rules for saying a perfect act of contrition. Write perfectly spelled and punctuated, grammatically correct sentences and you are a writer. I fetishized the rules of grammar, spelling, and punctuation as I did the others, believing that if they governed me they also governed reality/eternity/writing.

Over the years, I have thought a good deal about why I succumbed so readily to what I now recall as senseless hours of tedious exercises, distracting at best and debilitating at worst. To this day, I police my own prose with a vigilance that ought to be reserved for writers who set out to deceive, say, for spin doctors who write off the indictable crimes of their bosses as peccadilloes. A tendency to fetishize rules at once fueled my childhood enthusiasms and threatened to extinguish the pleasure of the most powerful of my desires, to be a ballerina. My long affair with dance began where all my childhood enthusiasms with Art began—in the children's room of the public library, where in the summer of the fourth grade I found the holdings, as I now say, on dance. As I remember, these included biographies of dancers (Anna Pavlova and Maria Tallchief) and probably choreographers, and at least one illustrated book, which I studied and as a result of which forced my body to assume the positions illustrated until I could complete with relative ease my rendition of a *barre*. Above all else, what I seem to have learned from those hours of painstaking and excruciating self-instruction, in addition to a number of habits that later had to be just as painstakingly unlearned, is that dance is discipline, and discipline a faultless physical reenactment of an ideal. Perfect *barres*, perfect acts of contrition, perfect sentences. Without diminishing the importance of the *barre* to dance, prayer to religion, or grammar to writing, the danger of making a fetish of rules is in the illustrated book of ballet, the Baltimore Catechism, and English handbooks, in codifications that purport to instruct but as often as not ground a ritual fascination with rules, the perfection of which is in turn used as a standard against which to measure someone's devotion to dance, religion, or writing rather than their performances as dancers, *religieuses*, or writers.

In the mid-1950s when I was checking ballet books out of the children's library, I had seen ballet performed only on the *Ed Sulllivan Show*, that is, seen tiny dancers flit across a snowy screen. Other than that, there was the seemingly spontaneous, effortless, and flawless dancing in movies. But the dance I tried to recreate from the photographs in the book little resembled these professional performances or even the amateur recitals staged by local dance studios. Others who grew up in small Midwestern cities (Quincy, Illinois: population 41,450 according to the 1950 census; 43,743 according to the census taken in 1960) may have also attended recitals where top billing was given to adolescent girls adept at toe-tap, origins unknown to me. I consider it still a quintessential spectacle of white lower-middle-class female sensuality. The girl danced solo, and the din created by the plates on the points of her toe shoes was as riveting as it was raucous. For all I know, the plates were there to warn the weary women who usually operated dance studios that a child was not *en pointe*. Or perhaps since toe-tap recitals are as noisy as they are vigorous, the taps, which would disguise the noise of moving feet and creaking bones, were there to distract audiences and dancers alike from the painful reality of being *en pointe*, which is not unlike that of running in five-inch heels. I secretly admired the girls I publicly condemned, and in my mind's eye I see them flaunting their sexual independence before a captive audience of family and friends. As wildly different as toe-tap is from ballet, they are nonetheless alike in being performing arts, even if the flagrant sensuality of the one now seems to me a burlesque of the sexual sensibilities of the other. By contrast, the book I read illustrated ballet as a set of discrete skills to be learned and then routinely deployed in seemingly endless and sexless reenactments of tableaux—bodies transfixed in, rather than moving through, space.

When I finally studied dance—with the only teacher in town who disdained toe-tap—I learned the rules and followed them religiously. I loved the discipline of ballet with all the fervor of an S/M enthusiast, for I can recall making no distinctions between pleasure and pain. I cherished the grueling daily routine that disciplines students not to cut classes for fear of permanent injury; I learned to trust bloody toes and aching muscles as proof of progress; I fasted and dieted routinely, all so that I could, every once in a while, fly. Not incidentally, I also acquired the arrogance that dismisses toe-tap as shameless artistic pretense and that places New York City at the center of the cultural universe and displaces Hollywood to the hinterlands (this even though "my" New York was created by Hollywood). Inasmuch as ballet is discipline, I learned to be a reasonably good dancer. If I didn't fly as often as I wished, perhaps it was because I was a good Catholic girl who translated the discipline of ballet into ritual enactments, for my understanding of religion and dance alike was radically diminished by my experience of, and faith in, the absolute power of rules.

A child's confusing discipline with dance is understandable, for it can be traced to the order of things, an ordering produced by her reading, which represented dance as a natural progression from the *barre* to the stage. It's not so much that the child misunderstood the illustrations, but that she misread the book, which was not a manual for dancers, but one from which children who attended performances were to learn to appreciate ballet. Fortunately for me, my autodidacticism was modified enough by performance that I gradually revised my understanding of dance. And fortunately for me, my mother's narrative of my preschool writing as a social performance worth remembering and telling probably enabled me to learn rules and eventually to resist mistaking them for writing. Over the years, the schools have probably quelled a desire to write in a good many children by subjecting them to ritual performances of penmanship, spelling, grammar, punctuation, oraganization, and, most recently, thinking. Every generation mixes its own nostrums and passes them off as writing. The fetishes may change but not the substitution of some formal ritual performance for writing.

When I was in elementary school, before children were allowed to write, they were expected to learn to read, write cursive, spell, diagram sentences, punctuate them, and arrange them in paragraphs. The first writing assignment I remember was in the fifth grade—"Write about your favorite country"—and my essay on Africa was a compilation of sentences copied in my own hand from encyclopedia entries. Apparently neither the teacher nor I knew that Africa is not a country. And apparently neither of us noticed that the Africa in the encyclopedias was populated by precious goods and wild animals, not people. I would have produced that essay around the time that I gave up on the novel I was secretly writing, featuring the heroine Susan Saint, because while I wanted her to drive away in her roadster (she bore a striking resemblance to Nancy Drew), she could not because I did not know how to drive. By the time I learned to drive, however, I had already learned to write fluent essays and to keep Susan Saint and her problems to myself.

I am sometimes reminded that I nearly became a reader rather than a writer in a vivid memory of myself as a young girl slowly picking her way down the stairs of the Quincy Public Library. I know I am leaving the children's library and am en route to the rooms reserved below for adults. The scene is lit from above and behind by a window, through which the sun shines down on the child whose first trip to the adult library saddens me. On mornings when I wake with this memory, I am overcome by sorrow even though I know the actual trip to have been a childish triumph of sorts. I literally read my way out of the children's library in the summer of the fifth grade. Every book, or so I used to think, with the twin exceptions of *Tom Sawyer* and *Huckleberry Finn.* I was averse to neither adventure books nor stories about boys, and read plenty of books about boy athletes, castaways, orphans, princes, presidents, kings, and cowboys, not to mention boy detectives, boy horses and dogs, boy wonders and boy friends. The problem was Mark Twain, a man I held personally responsible for the Tom Sawyer–Huck Finn–Becky Thatcher–Injun Joe diners, motels, and historic houses, along with a detestable cave that plagued my childhood—the Mark Twain roadside attractions in the nearby town of Hannibal, Missouri, a few miles down the Mississippi River from Quincy. When as an adult I finally forced myself to read *Huckleberry Finn,* I came to believe that Twain more than anyone else would have appreciated the enterprising uses the town had made of its native son, perhaps because by then I believed that Huck's desire to "light out for the Territory" was of a piece with other tropes of the West, which could justify anything from genocide to servitude to souvenirs in the name of civilization.

This memory of myself is carefully staged. I can be looking only at the loss of innocence. A young girl. A descent. Away from the light. That I set the scene in a library suggests a loss specific to literacy. Yet here is a child who reads so much that the librarians have declared her an honorary adult and sent her to the adult library where there are even more books than in the children's library, some of them not suitable, she hopes, for children. She should be dancing down that stairway, as I may actually have done, full of herself and in full possession of the tangible proof and token of her recent enfranchisement—a card good for all the books in the adult library. Indeed there were more books there, so many more than the child imagined that she found she could not read her way out, not that summer, not soon, not ever. I can see the girl is on the brink of learning that the books are not hers, that books, even children's books, are copyrighted, someone's property. And, since she already knows that some properties are more valuable than others, before long she will confound their imputed value and her desire, and want only the best books.

I must have suspected even in the children's library that *someone* wrote the books I read, since I had refused even to borrow those written by Mark Twain, and left my own Susan Saint sitting at the curb. Maybe I refused to read his books not simply because I loathed Twain tourist attractions, but also because his books were the only ones advertised as belonging to an author. The others were my stories: I lifted them off the shelves, checked them out, took them home, read them, and returned them a few days later in exchange for more. In the child's economics of literacy, the cycle of exchange depended entirely on *her* reading. It is a childish and even a dangerous view of literacy, for it entirely ignores the labor of producing books (with the possible exception of the material facts of books themselves), and yet it is one that libraries and schools promote when they base children's experience of literacy solely on reading.

Finding out that every book belonged to an author made the adult books different from the children's books I had regarded as public property and treated as I did the equipment on the school playground or neighborhood park. I didn't think I owned the swings, but I believed they were mine while I used them. I read the children's books seriatim—fiction and nonfiction, off the shelves, one after the other, section by section, top to bottom, left to right. There must have been a card catalog, but I remember no one suggesting that I check it. Shelves rather than Dewey guided my reading, aided and limited by my height and what my mother called my "boardinghouse reach," since I was, as they say, tall for my age. What I could reach I read. And at some point, the librarians decided that I had read them all, or more likely that my grasp exceeded my reach, and sent me downstairs. Or more likely still, they probably ran out of prizes, having rewarded me for the most books read by a child in my school, my age, in a week, a month, over a summer, during a year.

Things were not the same in the adult library. Not just the books but the place. It smelled the same (of paste and glue and paper and must), but it neither looked nor felt the same. The books were tightly wedged on shelves, lined up like the aisles of supermarkets. There was just enough room between shelves to make a selection, but not enough to linger, and nothing like enough to stretch out on the floor and read. Truth to tell, I never felt I really belonged in the adult library, and I wonder now if that's because the loss of human space figured the even more important loss of books as stories. I was not ready to give up stories. If I didn't actually read *all* the children's books, I read every one I checked out—from the first word to the last. Today the only books I still read that way are mysteries. I am a proper grown-up about all the books and journals I use in my work. Like a good librarian, I order and maintain them, and even replace those that disappear. They are shelved according to topic in alphabetical order. I can almost always find what I'm looking for. But the mysteries are shelved to replicate the children's library, or at least my memory of it. I am not usually looking for any one in particular, and so I read what catches my eye. And when I want a particular book, I tear the shelves apart looking for it, happier than I care to admit wallowing in the stacks of books surrounding me.

It is only in the occasional glimpses of myself cautiously descending those library stairs that I realize that if I am uneasy about what I will learn in the adult library that may well be because I had yet to learn that *I* could write as well as read books. I am on the brink of believing instead that if I could not read them all, I could at least read the right ones. The right books are literature. Most of Shakespeare's plays and sonnets, some of Donne's lyrics, some of Wordsworth's, *The Canterbury Tales, Paradise Lost, Jane Eyre, David Copperfield,* and *The Scarlet Letter* are literature. I was working from a list. They were on it. It was only later that I learned that it's not that simple, that there is also *the literature*, as in the literature of a field or discipline, the right books *and* the right articles—about history, literature, physics, sociology, law, medicine. And it was much later still that I even thought to ask who made the lists, on which women rarely appear and people of color more rarely, where America is a far-flung replica of an English village, and most of the rest of the world not even that.

The economics of literature is entirely different from that of stories. Frankly, one animal story was as good as the next as far as I was concerned, one biography, one mystery, one romance, one adventure (except *Tom Sawyer* and *Huckleberry Finn*). But the value of stories as measured against literature is very low indeed. Stories are a dime a dozen. Literature is scarce. Almost anyone can tell or write stories (even a child can do it). Not just anyone can write literature (most adults cannot), and not just anyone can read it. Literature is an acquired taste, it seems, and, like a taste for martinis and caviar, it is acquired through associating with the right people, whose discernment guarantees a steady demand for a limited supply of literature. I used my adult card to check out *The House of the Seven Gables*, which I probably chose on the recommendation of my fifth grade teacher but which I read—with some difficulty. I read it not because I liked it, but because I wanted to be someone who liked literature, an experience not unlike that of wondering, while taking the first sip of martini or bite of caviar, if other people actually like the taste of turpentine or cat food, and immediately denying the thought.

Looking back, however, I would not want to have missed a single one of the stories dressed up as literature or, for that matter, all that many of those billed as *the* literature. But I do sometimes wish, on the mornings I wake to watch myself descending those stairs, that I understood why, when I realized I could not read all the books in the adult library, I took smug comfort in believing that only some of them were worth reading. What was my stake in the great books, the ones on the recommended lists distributed to honors students at my school? For years I read exclusively from those mimeographed lists, except for an occasional mistake like *Green Mansions* and some occasional lapses like *Gone with the Wind* and *Peyton Place*, and for many years I was comforted by the list, secure in my choices and certain that I was making progress. No sooner had I knocked off a great book than I had it recorded on a three-by-five card. One per book. Vital statistics—author, title, main characters, and plot—on the front, a short memorable quote on the back.

My devotion to that file bears a suspicious resemblance to my dedication to the *barre*, and I realize now that ballet and literature must be early tokens of my longing to replace the working-class fictions of my childhood with a middle-class fiction in which art transcends class. I see in that file, for instance, the evidence of my desire and struggle to acquire the middle-class habit of privileging authorship. That I remember novels I read in adolescence more readily by title than author is probably evidence that I retained, despite my files, my earlier belief in stories, and possibly even the economic theory in which stories belong to the people who animate them in their reading. In the world of English professors whose ranks I sought to join, however, such mundane matters as the labor of literary production—the work of writing, placing, selecting, editing, printing, marketing, and distributing books—were thought to be distasteful, akin to asking the host how much the caviar cost. Only when I began studying and teaching writing did I finally remember that aesthetics can be as effective a hermetic seal against the economic and political conditions of authorship as are industrial parks and affluent suburbs against the economic privation and desperation of the urban and rural poor.

Sometime during the second year of college I quit recording and filing my reading, probably around the time I began reading books that were banned, or that I believed were: *Tropic of Cancer, Lady Chatterley's Lover, Fanny Hill, The Story of O, The Hundred Dollar Misunderstanding*. But until then no one needed to monitor my reading. I policed myself. Worse, I set out to police my family, whose knowledge of and interest in literature I found sadly lacking. I had to write off my father, who read newspapers, automobile repair manuals, and union materials but who, to my knowledge, never read stories and only rarely told one. I had to write off my older sister as well, since she dismissed nearly everything I did as childish. I managed to impress the importance of literature on my younger sister, since she was accustomed to being bossed around by her older sisters. It was, however, my mother I literally harassed, for she read several books a week and each one provided me an opportunity to improve her taste. So caught up was I in the promise of literature that I chided unconscionably the same mother who first took me to the library and walked me there until I was old enough to go alone, who had the good sense not to tell the first grade teacher I could already read, so she could "teach" me, who read *War and Peace* with me in the eleventh grade, just to keep me company (I only read *Peace*, but she read both), and who never issued any of those dire warnings—about ruining my eyes, turning into a bookworm, or ending up a spinster—that must have kept generations of female and male children alike from reading much at all.

The list that identified some stories as literature also cast its readers as superior to those who like my mother preferred mysteries and romances. I suspect I desperately wanted her to read literature because I believed that if she didn't have her own passport to the middle class I would have to leave her behind when I went away—to college. There are times when I see each great book I filed as also recording an inoculation against the imputed ills of the working-class childhood that infected me and that in turn threatened the middle-class children with whom I studied. I do not think people in the 1950s believed poverty was contagious. They had not yet been taught to see poverty as something people bring on themselves and to spurn the poor as people who didn't get and stay with the program. But I probably did represent a threat to middle-class sensibility that can be ascribed to growing up in a working-class house.

We were a family of five, my parents and three girls, in a four-room house: a kitchen, a living room (known as the front room), two bedrooms, and a bathroom. Attached to the back of the house were an uninsulated and unheated enclosed porch (it would have been a summer kitchen if it had been equipped with a stove) and a storeroom (used as a playroom when the weather was warm). In such small quarters, interior space is social by definition, since to be in a room is to be in either the company or proximity of others. That I knew how to read when I entered school can probably be attributed as much to this social arrangement of space as to any unusual interest or precocity on my part. I would have been there while my mother checked my older sister's homework. My sister may have even taught me to read. But I would not have simply learned to read. I would have learned to read in the social space of the kitchen.

In a middle-class household, a child who insisted on reading in the kitchen during, say, meal preparation would probably be perceived as hostile, and would no doubt either be asked to set the table or shunted off to another room, possibly even her own room. My mother was usually surrounded by her children. So, while I regularly read in the kitchen in the company of my mother and sisters, and was often more attentive to what I was reading than what they were saying or doing, I can recall no one suggesting that the act itself was hostile or that I should read someplace else. It's not just that there was no place to send me. It's that I wasn't held literally responsible for my reading. Some kids sing, some cook, some read. It was a gift, like perfect pitch, not a skill I was honing or my mother was nurturing. What was considered wonderful was my ability to read in the midst of conversation, what my mother called my "remarkable power of concentration." It was not cause for wonder, however, when I focused on grievances, for then my "remarkable power of concentration" became my "one-track mind."

My reading was not cause for wonder or concern at home because my mother believed she could always call me back if she wanted or needed me. But it was cause for concern at school—in fact, according to my mother, a source of considerable consternation for a beloved first grade teacher who, exhibiting none of my mother's admiration for my unbridled reading, went to extraordinary lengths to break me of the habit. She took particular exception to my practice of "reading ahead," to find out what happened to the children and household pets in the Basal Reader. It seems strange to me now that I could have confused a primer for a story, but I took it very hard when the teacher taped the unread portion of the book closed to prevent me from "reading ahead" without her permission. I never untaped the book or directly challenged her right to regulate my reading. But in a rare act of childhood defiance, I remember promptly "reading ahead" when I happened on a copy of the reader in the children's library.

If my "reading ahead" concerned the teacher enough to justify taping the book closed, my habit of interrupting the other children while they were reading must have driven her to distraction, since I can still feel the heat of my humiliation and recall my terror as I stood alone and in tears in the cloakroom, where I had been sent for talking during reading. That happened only once that I can remember. The door that isolated me from the others may have terrified me more than it would have a child accustomed to closed doors. I was not in a dark or windowless room, but I could not hear what was being said in the classroom with the door closed. By some standards the punishment fit the crime. Yet it ignores the conflict that the middle-class practice of reading alone and in silence, only what is assigned when it is assigned, created in a working-class child whose reading had, until then, been part and parcel of the social fabric of home and whose choice of reading matter had been regulated by the holdings of the children's library and her reach.

I was not taught to read in the first grade, but was instead taught to unlearn how I already read by a well-meaning and dedicated teacher authorized by the state to regulate my reading. My father once complained that he never understood me after I went to school. I always thought he was referring to the speech lessons in the second grade that radically altered my dialect from the Southern Midland dialect spoken at home to the Northern Midland spoken by most of my teachers. But now I wonder whether it was a class rather than a regional dialect that stood between us, whether the door that temporarily isolated me from the other children also threatened to closet me permanently from my family. That the ostensible autonomy of middle-class professionals depends on children's internalizing the rules that regulate reading (and writing) seems obvious to me. Less obvious, however, is what part reading and writing practices learned at home, and at variance with those learned at school, continue to play in my intellectual life.

There is no denying that I recreate the cloakroom everywhere I live. It is not uncommon, of course, for academics to furnish their homes with books. It is not even uncommon for academics to read several at a time. But the inordinate pleasure I take from littering all available surfaces with books makes it seem unlikely that in my case books are indexing only my academic enthusiasms. It seems more likely to me, now that I've remembered and reflected on the cloakroom, that the books are there to keep me company, that they are tokens of the absent family and friends whose voices have been muted by time and space. If so, it gives me a measure of satisfaction to believe that this lifelong habit simulates reading as I learned it at home, that even as I read the literature that took me so far from home I have been protecting myself from total class annihilation.

As a young girl, I was not just reading about other people, other places, and other lives. I was reading about people, places, and lives utterly unlike mine. Virtually everything in the fiction I read was fantastic: their houses, their families, their neighborhoods, their neighbors, their clothes, their food, their amusements, their feelings, their romances, their friendships, their conversation, their desires, their problems, their prospects. These things were different not just because literature is not life, but because the drama in the books on the recommended list, at least in the nineteenth-century novels I preferred, either happened in middle-class houses—*Emma* and *Middlemarch*—or, so I now realize, in defense of the middle class and their houses—*Great Expectations* and *War and Peace*. I loved most those novels that held literary open house, the ones that toured prime literary real estate. I doted on the rooms reserved for specific uses, parlors, drawing rooms, sitting rooms, libraries, and only incidentally considered the heroines who retired there to hold conversations, closeted from parents, poor relations, and siblings.

I skimmed descriptions of gardens or grounds, I skipped altogether descriptions of cottages inhabited by tenant farmers, and I seem to have either ignored or forgotten descriptions of servants' quarters and kitchens. The uncertain course of romance and courtship, the tedium of manners, the ceaseless rounds of social obligations also went largely unnoticed. But not interior space, nor threats of losing it. The unheard-of privilege of privacy made palpable by the rooms middle-class heroines occupied made an immediate and lasting impression on me. I have no idea if many other children from working-class homes also acquired from their reading an appetite for privacy. But I am certain that the literature that fascinated me kindled and shaped in me a desire for privacy so acute that only hearing my mother's voice reminds me that not only I but an entire family paid the price of my replacing the sociality of my working-class home with the books that now keep me company at home.

I sometimes wonder what it must have been like to have witnessed rather than experienced my reading. Unlike the heroines in the novels I was reading, the women in my family, in my neighborhood for that matter, lived in rather than visited the kitchen. My sisters and I would sit at the kitchen table talking, reading, studying, drawing, writing, sewing, taunting one another, tattling, boasting, snapping beans, kneading bags of margarine, cutting cookies, cutting out paper dolls and their clothes while our mother talked to us as she fixed meals, baked, mended, cut patterns, sewed, talked on the phone. It now seems to me that all serious conversations were held in the kitchen. My father sometimes quizzed us at supper, gave us words to spell, word problems to solve, multiplication tables to recite. It was easy for me to accommodate him. Since he visited only at mealtimes, however, he never participated in our kitchen conversations, never knew we were picking at and picking up the threads of earlier conversations.

My mother usually let us sit at the table and listen while she and the neighbor women, or female relatives, told the stories that made the kitchen that I remember the hub of our familial and social life. There were stories about pregnancy and childbirth, childhood (theirs and their children's), stories recounting the antics of local doctors, politicians, cops, bosses, nuns, priests, and ministers and their children, and stories encoding the exigent dangers of sex—going too far, getting into trouble, having to get married. Teachers were the only authorities who were never challenged in my presence, though sometimes in my hearing. It seemed to me then that everything of real importance happened in the kitchen, the room where the women talked to each other while their female children listened and learned to be women. But I wonder now if the absence of critique meant the mothers believed the classroom to be an even more important room, though they must at least have suspected they could lose their children, their daughters as well as their sons, to teachers and to the middle class.

My father's familial domain was the living room, where most evenings he would read the local paper and union materials or study car repair manuals and report cards, and where he alone napped, in his chair. The children sometimes also came there to read, perhaps because my mother read there in the daytime, but we were not allowed to talk or play in the living room when my father was there. The family began gathering in the living room only after the television arrived, circa 1955. In what now seems a blink of the eye, the television displaced my father, who finally relinquished his fragile hold on the family to a spate of family programs. I loved those families, perhaps because they confirmed my growing suspicion that even fictive middle-class families were better than real working-class ones, but my father detested the prosaic problems of the television families from whom my mother, my sisters, and I were learning the middle-class scripts that we rehearsed on him.

Working-class houses are not miniatures of middle-class houses, neither of real ones nor of those created by literature or constructed for television. So in one of those remarkable generalizations to which children are prone, I seem to have concluded that since middle-class mores governed the dramatic action in fiction, nothing of real consequence could happen to anyone who does not reside in a middle-class house. Little wonder then that I also fervently believed that my parents had only to acquire such a house to assume consequence and persisted in making plans for moving the family into it, despite my parents' quite reasonable insistence that I well knew that they did not have the money to do so. Like many other working-class children, by the age of ten I knew what things cost, what my father made, and what the money was used for, not to mention the asking price of real estate, along with suitable locations. I wonder now if my terror of working-class inconsequence was not aggravated by two interdependent historical events in the 1950s: the escalating cold war and the end of the postwar recession. The first event radically altered my education, and the second my neighborhood.

By the late 1950s, some of our neighbors had sold or left their rented homes without dining rooms and a bedroom for each child and taken out government-insured low-interest mortgages on the ideal two-story middle-class house, or barring that, the ersatz middle-class tract houses that developers and realtors were selling the unwary. The ideal had a foyer, a free-standing staircase, and hardwood floors throughout, a fireplace in the living room, a formal dining room, a large kitchen with a walk-in pantry on the first floor, three or four bedrooms upstairs, a bathroom up and down, a screened veranda, a full basement and attic, and a detached garage. The house was made of either brick or stone. While the tract houses possessed none of the virtues of the two-story houses I had encountered in my reading and seen advertised on television, save the illusory privacy of bedrooms with doors, that they were known locally as doll houses would have appealed not to my sense of irony, but to my fantasy (apparently shared by the many adults who purchased them) that a new house would reinvent us as a middle-class family. Such houses did not of course even exist in the neighborhood, so those who moved up also moved out.

My family stayed in the neighborhood until after I left for college. But they must have known that I would move out as early as the ninth grade, when the public schools tracked me into college preparatory classes on the basis of my test scores (I forget which tests) and my performance in classes. It seems, though I remember no one saying so at the time, that I was being drafted for the cold war, which precipitated an educational reform, at least in Quincy, that cut across class lines with a flourish that only seems imaginable during periods of extreme nationalism. Nationalism even extended to putting one male and one female Negro on the college track. A fair amount of money was lavished on the education of cold war recruits. Classrooms were well furnished and well maintained, the science and language laboratories (where I studied Russian) were well equipped, the teachers were well educated (most had master's degrees and a few were Ph.D.s), and the student-to-teacher ratio must have been excellent, for I never wanted for attention.

My school day began at 8:00 A.M. and I was rarely back home before 5:00 P.M. There were few electives, and the ones I chose (like journalism) required more, not less, time than required courses. While I continued to study dance until my senior year (when I finally had to admit that diligence is no substitute for talent), I gradually became the school's daughter: National Honor Society, editor of the school newspaper, Student Council, Latin Club, Russian Club, Pep Club, and other societies and clubs that I am grateful to have forgotten. The homework for these cold war classes took from three to five hours most evenings, which I dutifully completed without fail at the kitchen table and checked or completed on the phone. Most of the daily assignments were graded, and the scheduled tests and pop quizzes were buttressed by periodic batteries of standardized achievement and IQ tests. So thoroughly prepared was I for college during my four years of high school that my first two years at the small state university from which I graduated were mostly review, except for writing.

I had not written much besides journalism in high school, and my professors, who did not much admire my mastery of the inverted pyramid, were looking for an essay whose paragraphs elaborated what I now think of as the *generic-corrective-display thesis:* A good many scholars/critics have concluded X, but X ignores Y, which is essential/critical to fully understanding Z (the structure of a poem or the universe, the precipitating causes of the Civil War, the Enlightenment, progress, overpopulation). A student can use this thesis in any class because it both corrects errors in previous scholarship or criticism and displays the student's knowledge of the literature. It took me nearly a year to (re)invent the thesis and three more years to perfect it. It kept my grades high and it probably kept me from learning as much as I might have about writing, even though it gave me plenty of time to perfect my style. Not to put too fine a point on it, this quintessentially modern thesis assumes that reality, which exists entirely separate from and independent of language, is superficially complicated but ultimately governed by simple underlying principles, rules, or verities. It is the thesis of choice among pundits, the thesis that rationalizes what passes for balanced/objective/unbiased reporting by the print and electronic media, the thesis on which most legislation is passed and public policy formulated, and the basis of the recent culture wars in the academy. I no longer believe the thesis, but I believed it then, if only because I desperately wanted to believe in middle-class houses, wherein everything seemed to conspire to protect the inhabitants from any of the complications that beset the people in my house and neighborhood.

I probably visited my first middle-class houses the summer my younger sister and I lay in bed listening to the couple next door read *Gone with the Wind* to each other in their bedroom. They are recorded in my memory as reading voices, one male, one female, quietly enunciating just loud enough for us to hear. We wondered if we should tell them that we could hear them, but we never did because we wanted to hear the story. I never spoke of my affection for the couple next door or of anything that happened at home in the houses of my new classmates or at school. By then I was old enough to know better, old enough to realize that any story I told would incriminate my family and indict my neighborhood. For by then we had been visited by the social worker, whom I remember as a singularly humorless man in a suit, perched on my father's chair asking my mother questions and writing down her answers. She didn't offer food, which put him in the class of official census takers rather than writers. He didn't smile when she described the decor as early Halloween, and she didn't contradict him when he pointed out that there were no bookcases. She didn't tell him that she and her children borrowed books from the library or that the ones we owned were stored under our beds. I had a complete set of Nancy Drew mysteries under my bed, and among us my sisters and I had collected a fair number of the classic girls' books—*Heidi, Little Women, Anne Frank*—along with the adventures of Trixie Belden, Ginny Gordon, and Sue Barton. Although I never asked my mother why she let the social worker think what he would, I must have taken her reticence as a given because I never attempted to explain home to anyone who didn't live there.

Since none of my classmates had gone to my neighborhood elementary school, my parents knew none of their parents or, more precisely, my mother knew none of their mothers. My mother had made it her business to meet and chat with the mothers of my new working-class girlfriends in junior high. But I made no new friends among the other white working-class recruits in my college preparatory classes, and was forbidden, for the usual racist reasons, to do anything more than mention that the Negro girl was also Catholic. All through high school I kept up with working-class girlfriends from the neighborhood school. I even coached my best working-class girlfriend from junior high on her dance routine for the Miss Quincy pageant the summer I went to college. But I kept the old friends separate from the new ones, for the worlds were by then as distinct to me as the children's library and the adult library, as stories and literature. Like reading, tracking radically displaced me, conferring on me honorary middle-class privileges on the order of those afforded by my early admission to the adult library.

Alone, I entered houses made familiar by my reading. I particularly enjoyed living the fiction that food is served rather than prepared, and floors, windows, dishes, and clothes endlessly clean rather than cleaned endlessly. These were phenomena already known to me from my reading. Also familiar were ambitious mothers who took their daughters shopping in St. Louis or Chicago, where they were fitted for gowns that the local newspaper would describe in lavish detail. Familiar though I may have found these customs, my interest in fictional real estate had obscured the importance of manners, no less important in the twentieth-century middle-class houses where my new girlfriends lived than in nineteenth-century novels. The talk was of honors, grade point averages, colleges, sororities, SATs, country clubs, clothes, dances, and dates. In the light of these topics, I could no longer avoid concluding that in this culture, and in the fictional one on which it seemed to rest, the present is a dress rehearsal for a future whose value will ultimately be determined by whether getting into the right sorority at the right school results in marrying the right man.

My own class-based experience of family shielded me from envying any but the material comforts of my middle-class girlfriends. I learned to speak fluent bourgeoisie in those houses. And what I learned there contributed to my college grades and probably even to my academic career. Fluency has not, however, made me a native speaker, for when I am left to my own devices I continue to measure the value of the present in terms of itself rather than the future. The future only interests me when the present becomes intolerable. That I still consider material conditions the sine qua non of my intellectual life is doubtless a legacy of my viewing the middle classes with a literary map of their houses in hand rather than a copy of their conduct book committed to memory. That I never fully assimilated the bourgeois belief that rehearsal predicts the future is without a doubt a working-class legacy. This is not to say that I neither plan nor rehearse. But since neither raises any expectations about my literal ability to control events, I am more inclined to view plans and rehearsals as the moments when I am forcibly reminded of my devotion to contingencies—to the possibility that the essay will be better than the plan and the performance a considerable improvement over the rehearsal, acknowledging all the while the essays that came to naught and the performances that fell flat.

It is probably a measure of their extraordinary faith in education that my parents, who regularly challenged the authority of medicine, the church, and the state, never questioned the authority of the schools over their daughters in our hearing, never resisted the tracking of their middle daughter into college preparatory classes, even though they could ill afford either the new courses or the new friends. The courses radically diminished my chances of fully developing or properly valuing the domestic competencies (cooking, baking, cleaning, ironing, sewing, mending) that other working-class girls acquired at home, or those that the girls in my family learned during summers spent on our aunt and uncle's farm (truck gardening, canning, preserving, tending livestock). To make matters worse, the middle-class houses seeded unspeakable desires having to do with the pleasures of romance, solitude, and economic independence that would naturally follow from the "college education" vaunted at school and taken for granted by my new friends and their parents.

The educational opportunities that thrilled me contradicted most of what was expected of me at home. Yet my parents accepted the economic privations that accompanied my tracking. I paid for my ballet classes by teaching younger children, and the part-time job I held as an honors student required neither that I work the hours nor that I work as hard as my older sister had. My going to college meant not just that my parents would contribute to my support beyond the usual age of eighteen, but also that I would not be contributing to theirs in return for room and board. There is a sense in which my parents reconciled my prolonged economic dependence by turning me into the youngest daughter. They guarded me so carefully that even serious problems and illnesses went unmentioned until I was home on break. Little wonder then that I was younger at twenty than I had been at sixteen or that I began to prefer school to home, the more so since many of my college courses indulged my fantasy of America as a society where I could reinvent myself as a classless, genderless, raceless scholar. I wanted little more during that time than to be free of the town that had held me in thrall, where neighborhoods mapped class and race with a ruthless precision neither acknowledged nor validated by my reading and where the prospects for women at either my house or the houses of my friends had begun to look equally uninviting.

At my house gender was defined in terms of money and work. Among themselves women talked about neither the accumulation of capital nor the consolidation of wealth and privilege through marriage. Women like my mother saw their work as steering adolescent girls through the present-tense dangers of dating and pregnancy rather than the future-tense possibilities of marrying well. Marriage posed financial problems, and its topics were employment, housing, the care and feeding of children, and in my case the loss of financial independence. These working-class marriage narratives did not hold the same promise of untroubled futures that the middle-class ones seemed to hold for my girlfriends. Bearing and raising children are not such attractive propositions for girls who watch and even help their mothers do the work. Nor, for that matter, is keeping house, if the old carpet is not a threadbare heirloom and the provenance of the secondhand furniture is unknown.

Since it was the body of neither a working-class mother nor a middle-class wife but that of the female dancer that had attracted me from childhood through adolescence, I cannot but wonder if on realizing that I would not be a dancer I somehow imagined that as a professor I could turn myself inside out like a reversible garment and cloak my female body in what I believed (via courses and grades) to be my genderless and classless mind. While traces of this desire remain, it nonetheless comes as something of a surprise to realize that I am never more my mother's daughter than when I am writing the essays, papers, lectures, and books that organize my academic life. For it is not when we talk but when I write that I perform uncanny reenactments of my mother sewing, and then that I realize I must have learned to write from watching her sew. What I saw, or now believe I must have seen, was a woman whose pleasure while she was sewing matched mine while I was playing. I suppose what I remember is seeing her thoroughly at ease, for the woman who sewed was entirely different from the one who cooked, cleaned, shopped, talked, and cared for her children. That woman was preoccupied, often weary and worried, and awkward in the presence of strangers. The woman who sewed was none of these. This woman would discuss ideas that animated her long before she ever spread out the newspapers she saved for her patterns, and this woman had discarded all but one by the time she bought the fabric, laid out the pieces on the bias, cut the cloth, hand-basted and machine-stitched the darts and seams of a garment.

Sewing relieved the tyranny of money over my mother's life. She made all her children's clothes, by copying ready-to-wear clothing, except her seams were more generous and her hems deeper, so they could be let out as we grew. My mother never thought of herself as (or allowed anyone to call her) a seamstress. It may have been undue modesty on her part, or she may have preferred her high standing among local amateurs to joining the ranks of anonymous professionals. But I like to think it is because she knew seamstresses do not sew to please themselves. And my mother pleased herself when she sewed. I can remember no time during my childhood when my mother was *not* sewing: our clothes, our doll clothes, our costumes for Halloween and school plays and my dance recitals, not to mention first-communion dresses, confirmation dresses, "outfits" for Easter and Christmas, party dresses, and formals. Dresses, skirts, blouses, and trousers hung perfectly, we were given to understand, only when she found and cut the cloth on the bias. The clothes, the doll clothes, and the costumes were all given equal attention, each piece made as if it were to last forever and to be viewed by an eye as appreciative of detail as my mother's. When I think about this aesthetic as a tribute to her children's acuity, I regret even more the careless indifference each of us assumed during adolescence to these tokens of her esteem. She was literally outclassed by the inexpensive ready-to-wear clothing that devalued and finally supplanted "homemade" clothes, and simultaneously the one domestic practice at which my mother thrived.

In midsummer, my mother would take each of her girls on a day-long shopping trip that she always referred to as buying our back-to-school clothes. It must have been her little joke because she bought nothing at the department stores and children's shops whose stock inspired her copies. Instead, we were directed to try on the school clothes and party dresses we liked—for size. I never saw her make a sketch or take a note. Yet even now I can see my mother examining garments, turning them inside out to scrutinize the mysteries of design, before bustling off to buy fabric. She required us to look at and feel all fabrics she considered suitable and to compare what even now seems to me endless combinations of and variations in texture, hue, and print. Selection of fabrics prefaced even more lengthy discussions of the relative merits of threads, buttons, belts, sashes, laces, piping, decals. These periodic conversations my mother held with each of her girls amidst bolts of cloth exuding the fumes of dye and sizing were supremely pedagogical, for she sought nothing less during these lessons than our full allegiance to the axiology that measures worth in finely wrought distinctions known only to those with intimate knowledge of production. The value of a garment is in its stitchery, which is not solely a measure of competence but also of practice. One slipped stitch spoiled a garment for my mother, and she wanted us to value such details of production. That aesthetic was disappearing even as my mother was teaching it to her children, a fact brought home to her as each of us in turn succumbed to the aesthetic of fashion on entering adolescence.

None of my mother's children would fully appreciate her aesthetic again until we were adults, and my own appreciation has been tempered with varieties of remorse. I lack the skill, the capital, and even the patience to clothe myself with the rigorous attention to detail I learned from my mother. Yet I am never more confident than when I am wearing something I believe she would admire. It is less a particular style of clothing than the certitude that my mother could tell just from the hang of it that I had not forgotten how much depends on the bias. While few garments I own would please my mother, the fact that my best essays are written on the bias would. Even more than what I finally produce, that I do not even attempt to write an essay until I have found a bias would please her, for my practice as a writer is as intricately tied to seeking and following oblique lines that cut across the grain as was my mother's sewing.

A girl can, it seems, learn a great deal about work and its pleasures from watching her mother sew. While I never learned to sew, the fact that I write as my mother sewed probably explains why I take a good deal more obvious pleasure in the intellectual work of being an academic than those of my peers who have difficulty believing writing to be real work. If I enjoy the labor of writing, that can at least in part be explained by my writing as my mother sewed. She made clothes. I make prose. There is a sense in which just as my mother was always sewing, I am always writing. I understood her to be sewing in even her most casual remarks. Once when my son was very young, he asked if we were just talking or if I was also writing. I could have asked my mother that question about her sewing when I was young, and I could ask my son the same question now that he once asked me about his writing. A boy, it seems, can also learn something about these pleasures from watching his mother write. He learned to write from his mother who learned from her mother, and none of us knows when we are talking if we are just talking—or writing—or sewing.

Writing begins for me with something once heard or seen or read that recurs in my mind's eye as a troubling image—myself as a little girl cautiously descending a staircase—which in turn prompts me to seek a narrative explanation for its persistence. My search for a narrative is guided by the bias of the image, in this essay by the inexplicable sorrow the child evoked in me. As I trace lines of inquiry that depend on the bias, I can see there are others besides mine, for there are at least as many biases woven into the fabric of a life as into poplins, wools, and satins. I can see differences in how from one bias I construe the cloakroom as an effort to eradicate traces of working-class sociality from a classroom, and from another I could justify the teacher who sent me there, for I am also a teacher. That I follow my bias does not mean that I cannot see others. It means instead that rather than extol the triumph of the child, I meet my sorrow by sorting the details of her longing to be middle class from those of her struggle against the indiscriminate eradication of the intellectuality of her family at school.

I wish everyone were taught to write on the bias, for finding and following a bias is as critical to writing as it is to sewing. Yet if bias seems even more counterintuitive in writing than in sewing, that is because students are taught that third-person statements are unbiased (objective) and those in the first person are biased (subjective). Little wonder then that by the time they reach college, most students have concluded that to avoid bias they have only to recast their first-person claims into the third person. Delete "I believe" from "racism is on the rise in this country" or "racism has virtually disappeared in this country," and the assertion assumes a reality independent of the writer, who is no longer the author but merely the messenger of news or fact. Students learn what they have been taught, and they have been taught that grammatical person governs the objectivity and subjectivity of actual persons. Step on a crack. Break your mother's back. Hop over it. Save her life.

Most students have learned rules that readers rather than writers believe govern prose. They have not been taught what every writer knows, that one writes on the bias or not at all. A bias may be provided by a theory or an experience or an image or an ideology. Without a bias, however, language is only words as cloth is only threads. To write is to find words that explain what can be seen from an angle of vision, the limitations of which determine a wide or narrow bias, but not the lack of one. Far from guaranteeing objectivity, third-person assertions too often record an unexamined routine in which the writers who follow a bias provided by, say, the "objectivism" of journalism or science confound that worldview/theory/ideology with reality. The bias we should rightly disparage is that which feigns objectivity by dressing up its reasons in seemingly unassailable logic and palming off its interest as disinterest—in order to silence arguments from other quarters.

Writers write on the bias. Writing is about following a bias that cuts against the grain because, like sewing, writing recognizes the third dimension of seemingly two-dimensional material. My mother looked at fabric and imagined clothes she could make from it. I look at language and imagine essays I could write. Just as a piece of cloth can be fashioned into any number of garments, the essay I construct from language is not the only one I could have written. The pleasures in playing out possibilities are matched only by the labor taken to complete the one that eventually stands for them all. It seems to me that middle-class culture and schooling gratuitously and foolishly rob children of the pleasures of the physical and intellectual work of learning generally and writing in particular. Most successful students learn to disown their labor (to claim they have not read the assignment or studied for the test). They disdain their own scholastic achievement as luck or intelligence, and grudgingly accept in its stead the tokens to be exchanged for symbolic opportunities. Take tests for grades, exchange the grades for credentials, use the credentials to launch a career, measure the career by the number of promotions and the size of the paychecks and the amount of stock. Writing is only incidental in this cycle. It is incidental because the cycle deflates the value of the intellectual work of practices like writing in order to artificially inflate the value of ritual performances (achievement tests, reading scores) that can be calculated and minted as cultural currency.

That the present is hostage to the future in any culture that devalues labor seems to me both obvious and tragic. That this country has historically substituted tokens of literacy for literacy practices and then cloaked its anti-intellectualism in alarming statistics about illiteracy and illiterates makes it all the more important that those of us who learned to write teach ourselves to remember how and where that happened, what it was we learned, and especially how the lessons learned from an unofficial curriculum protected us from the proscriptions that have ruthlessly dominated the official curriculum from the outset. The problem is not that writing cannot be learned, for many have learned to write, but that writing cannot be taught as a set of rules or conventions that must be acquired prior to and separate from performance. Leaching all evidence of the labor that produces texts teaches students to see literacy as a spectacle. Writing is not a spectator sport. Learning *how to write* follows from *wanting to write*, for the path a child follows on taking a census seems to lead more directly to writing than the detour that sends children first to reading. Writing is seated in desires as complicated as those that give rise to dancing and sewing, where the rules of play are also subject to the contingencies of performance.

Part II

Publications

Introduction to Part II

Universities are inclined to equate faculty productivity with publication, typically casting quality as quantity, the number of books and articles produced by faculty over a given period—a month, a year, five years, a decade. Publication is the bedrock on which tenure and promotion rest, and producing the right number of things (in the humanities, at most places, a book and a specified number of articles) in the allotted time usually, though not always, results in tenure and promotion from assistant to associate professor, and in some cases from associate to full professor. There probably are professors who also see their own publications solely in terms of quantity, but I suspect that there are also many who, like me, gauge the quality of their productivity on their best work. I consider my best essays to be the ones that expose some of the theoretical complexity required to address even the most mundane practical problems of pedagogy.

Spanning ten years and the continental United States, the seven essays that track my professional journey from Pennsylvania to Texas to California also chronicle my intellectual life as a writer and teacher of writing. "Modernism and the Scene(s) of Writing," "Tropics of Literacy," and "Writing Critical Ethnographic Narratives," were written and published while I was an assistant professor in the Graduate School of Education at the University of Pennsylvania. I wrote "Tropics of Literacy," which was published in 1986, after "Modernism and the Scene(s) of Writing," which was not published until 1987, the same year as "Writing Critical Ethnographic Narratives," which was written last. "On the Subjects of Class and Gender in 'The Literacy Letters,' " published in 1989, was written in 1988, my last year at Penn, and revised during my first summer in Texas. Later that same year, I wrote "Presence of Mind in the Absence of Body" with Michelle Fine, my former colleague at Penn. I also wrote "Telling Experiences" while I was in the English department at the University Texas; it is a short essay that was completed in early 1992 but not published until 1994, two years after I had moved to California. "Writing Permitted in Designated Areas Only" was begun in 1992, shortly after I joined the literature department at the University of California, San Diego, completed in 1993, and published in 1994. I consider it to be not only my first but also a quintessentially California essay.

While writing and publishing obviously occur in time, the noticeable preoccupation with space that characterizes much of my writing also qualifies my publication history. Until recently I presumed that preoccupation to be an effect of rapid changes in my professional zip codes, since I rarely live anywhere long enough to harbor even the illusion of knowing where I am. At the risk of making a virtue of necessity, however, I suspect that space is a cultural as well as a personal preoccupation, and hence human geography is a critical component of social theory and history. Indeed, as Edward Soja argues in *Postmodern Geographies*, a history of space is critical to understanding the simultaneity of postmodernity as opposed to the sequentiality of modernity. I began publishing articles on writing and pedagogy in the second half of the 1980s, during a period Lester Faigley has summarized in *Fragments of Rationality* as "the nation's replacement of the ideal of literacy as a means for achieving social equality with a cynical acknowledgement of education as part of the machinery for sorting people into categories of winners and losers" (1992: 52). In the intervening years, many people in composition studies who do not share that cynicism have tried to make sanctuaries of their classrooms: to remove students from the melee of the compulsory competitions of transnationalism, the recurrent genocides of nationalism, the insistent injustices of racism, sexism, homophobia—in other words, the endless spectacles of the terror of difference that the media increasingly produce as the world "we" live in today. Others like me eventually concluded that the best way to ward off the terror of difference is to make a critical examination of difference the subject of composition.

In the early essays, I tried to replace what I believed to be mistaken understandings of writing with definitions I argued were more commensurate with the pedagogy and politics of universal education. To wit, "Modernism" and "Tropics" now seem to me obvious efforts to persuade readers that widely held definitions of writing and literacy, respectively, hinder rather than support learning and teaching. Though perhaps less obviously, I undertake a similar revision in "Writing Critical Ethnographic Narratives," where I invite anthropologists interested in social change to use their newfound fascination with critical theories to teach themselves how to write and read socially responsible ethnographies. Meanwhile, my own understanding of progressive pedagogy was undergoing radical revision. I entered the academy and the field of composition under the auspices of sociolinguistics, convinced that progressive pedagogy would follow more or less logically from a theory of language that took into consideration the unequal social conditions under which people learn to speak and write. As I expanded my understanding of sociality to include political and historical conditions, however, my own stake in the theoretical preoccupations of modern theoretical linguistics waned. Though I remain interested in the structure of language, I no longer expect linguistics to provide answers to my questions about the language writers use to represent a given reality in their texts.

Whether that representation of reality is called a narrative or an argument—whether it purports to recover a real or imagined event or to lay out a plausible or irrefutable proof—what fascinates me as both a writer and a teacher of writers is the seemingly indefinite and often contradictory articulations of reality in language. In the last three essays in Part II, I frame my questions about writing pedagogy in terms of discursive rather than grammatical practice; this shift from the linguistic to the social structure of language entails a change from structural to poststructural theory. I introduce some terms of this relatively unfamiliar theoretical argument in composition along with an analysis of the social and political frustrations that underlie linguistic breakdowns in "On the Subjects of Class and Gender." Michelle Fine and I explore powerful discursive constraints on storytelling in "Presence of Mind in the Absence of Body," our analysis of sexual harassment narratives written by female respondents to the Penn Harassment Survey. By 1994, when "Telling Experiences" and "Writing Permitted in Designated Areas Only" were published, however, the theory is well known, and in these essays I am primarily concerned with reasserting the human potential of poststructuralism. In "Telling Experiences," I argue that it is a personal boon to think of a narrative as actively constructing rather than merely recalling experience, if only because of the vast possibilities for human agency conferred on storytellers. In "Writing Permitted in Designated Areas Only," poststructuralism underwrites my argument that in classrooms, where writing is tested rather than taught, students are learning *not* to write.

My decidedly poststructural fascination with the *language* of academic discursive practice lacks the kind of direct linkage to contemporary popular culture that I associate with postmodernism. So, while I acknowledge postmodernity as a condition of my life, I remain hesitant and tenuous about postmodern implications in my work. Yet recent postmodern histories of composition by Susan Miller (*Textual Carnivals*) and Lester Faigley, along with Edward Soja's argument for postmodern geography, have certainly encouraged me not only to explore more consciously and systematically the theoretical and practical dimensions of my own use of space in writing, but also to reconsider the importance of space in any effort to account for human experience. One could even argue that space configured as the site of writing will be crucial, as it becomes increasingly more apparent that in composition classes computer networks are redefining writing and writers, that the space of written texts is shifting from the page to the monitor, and that hypertexts in particular shift an authority once exclusively reserved for writers onto readers.

These are undoubtedly new spaces for writers and writing. It remains to be seen, however, whether teachers and students are willing to do more than "upgrade" the technologies of pedagogy that have historically defined composition classrooms. In other words, a computer-linked classroom gives everyone access to more and to more sophisticated methods of surveillance than have ever existed. It is surprisingly easy to eavesdrop, post anonymous messages, and print out transcripts of entire class discussions. Unless teachers invite students to examine ethical issues raised by, say, an untraceable racist, sexist, or homophobic message, however, these new classrooms also provide new spaces to voice old hatreds, and the anonymity that creates a hostile climate in classrooms is also hostile to pedagogy. People in composition have pioneered computer-linked classrooms, which is why some writing teachers are now confronting problems that most teachers in the humanities do not even know exist. The new forms and new forums are not less promising because there are problems. In fact, many are not so much *new* problems as old ones in new wrappings (slurs and poison pen letters preexist bulletin boards). I see the occasional hostile and hateful comments that crop up in transcripts of class discussions as material evidence of the human cost of ignoring the pedagogical issues raised in this section.

Modernism and the Scene(s) of Writing

When I picture writing, I often see a solitary writer alone in a cold garret working into the small hours of the morning by the thin light of a candle. It seems a curious image to conjure, for I am absent from this scene in which the writer is an Author and the writing is Literature. In fact it is not my scene at all. The writer-writes-alone is a familiar icon of art and is perhaps most readily understood as a romantic representation of the production of canonical literature, music, painting, sculpture. And if the icon evokes in me and others an awe out of proportion to its content (it is after all also an image of economic, emotional, and social deprivation), that is probably because we have learned that we are to complete this scene not by projecting ourselves onto the image of the writer, but by assuming the role of reader. Even so, the scene of writing is a text many of us find ourselves reading when we think about writing or, worse, when we are in the very act of writing.

I am struck by how transient are the images of myself as a writer compared to the seemingly immutable picture of the author limned by the scene in the garret. I can catch a fleeting glimpse of myself as I move toward the phone to call a friend about an idea that troubles me, and I can, if pressed, recall that I agreed to give a paper because I hoped it would help me work out an argument for something I was writing at the time. These scenes from my own life, however, are not nearly as convincing in my mind's eye as the scene of writing. Yet very few people I know are positioned as well as I am to recognize the extent to which their lives are organized by writing. I spend most mornings writing; I teach writing; I teach courses on how to teach and do research on writing; and I direct dissertations on writing. It would be absurd for someone whose life is so obviously entailed by writing to deny that writing is woven into the very fabric of her social life.

Despite this overwhelming evidence, however, I am at crucial moments almost fatally attracted to the scene of writing, so much so that in order to send drafts to friends and colleagues I must first exorcise the image of the writer-writes-alone. And if I sometimes long for a garret, even though my own writing experiences invariably contravene the romance (for my prose has been immeasurably improved by these readers), what of all those people who teach composition but study only literature? What defenses do they have against this picture in which the writer is an Author and the writing is Literature? When I advise graduate students who are teaching writing to design a curriculum that rests on principles of revision and response, how do they—many of them have never experienced writing in this way—reconcile such a pedagogy with their own writing practices? Do they feel, as undergraduates often seem to, that I have asked them to collude in an unfair academic practice? If so, do they then subvert their own curriculum? Would thinking there to be something illicit about responding to drafts explain, at least in part, why so many teachers who ask for drafts fail to understand, say, that sarcastic comments in the margins undermine the very pedagogy they seek to enact?

This essay presumes that those who teach as well as those who take composition courses are influenced by the scene of writing, namely, that all of us try to recreate a garret and all that it portends whether we are writing in a study, a library, a classroom, or at a kitchen table, simply because we learned this lesson in writing first. Further, those of us who have since learned no other lessons, who can call to mind no pictures of writing other than the writer-writes-alone, are the most likely to pass that lesson on to a new generation and are the least likely to reconceptualize writing in any of the ways it is being represented by research in composition. Yet if those who teach in colleges and universities were to read research on writing, which is patently not the case (see Burhans 1983; Colvino, Johnson, and Feehan 1980), even there they would find the scene of writing faithfully reproduced in much of the literature on writers' cognitive development and processes. Research on composing that isolates individual writers in laboratories and asks them to interact with a text under the observation of a researcher effectively recreates the scene of writing as a thoroughly modern romance: a scientific narrative in which the garret is now a laboratory, the author a subject, the reader a researcher, and reading an analysis of data.

The purpose of this essay is to examine the scene of writing as an artifact of literary modernism and then to use that examination as a basis for reforming our thinking about writers and writing. Such a restructuring would begin not by ignoring the scene of writing, but by reinserting some of the tensions between readers, writers, and texts that the world represented in the scene of writing so artfully suppresses. Ultimately, I am arguing that the success of curriculum reform movements initiated in the field of composition will depend on disrupting the scene of writing through acts of the imagination that revise the scene to accommodate our students and ourselves—as writers and as readers.

Picturing Solitude in Modernism

The scene of writing places social life on the other side of writing, that which occurs before or after writing, something or someone that must not be allowed to enter the garret. Notice that the image privileges only one event in writing, the moment when the writer is an amanuensis, making transcription a synecdoche of writing. In such a freeze-frame, the writer is a writing machine, as effectively cut off from writing as from society. What we see is a writer writing down words in much the same way the writing machine in Kafka's short story "In the Penal

Colony" did. One implication is that writing costs writers their lives. Likely to terrify writers and would-be writers alike, it is a picture, sometimes the only picture, we conjure when we seek the solitude necessary for writing. In its extreme versions, writers are sentenced to solitary confinement, imprisoned by language and condemned to write without understanding either why they do so or for whom. We know this story well because there are moments when the solitude overwhelms us, when we do not understand the words we are writing, and when we cannot recall our reasons for doing so.

Seen in this way, the picture of the solitary scribbler is taken from the album of modernism, where the metaphor of solitude is reiterated as the themes of alienation in modern art and atomism in modern science. In much of literary modernism, solitude is at once inevitable and consequential, the irremediable human condition from which there is no escape. And whenever writers are pictured there, as they so often are, the writer-writes-alone is a narrative of irreconcilable alienation, a vicarious narrative told by an outsider who observes rather than witnesses life. From James Joyce to Lawrence Durrell, writers (artists) stalk the pages of modern literature alone, much as they do the cities, towns, houses, and rooms they inhabit, their interior lives the landscapes of the novels. Whether they seek solitude, as in Bernard Malamud's *The Tenants,* or ineffectually attempt to emerge from it, as in Doris Lessing's "Children of Violence" novels, these writers cannot escape the loneliness, the alienation, the "fact" of life that modern novels set out to articulate.

An amanuensis merely transcribes language. As a scene of transcription, the scene of writing is one in which the writer is an unwilling captive of language, which writes itself through the writer. And it is this dissociation of writer from both the word and the world that is so flawlessly articulated in great modern novels. Consider John Barth's character Jacob Horner in *The End of the Road.* Jacob's condition is paralysis, and his paralysis is represented as a consequence of a world in which there are only arbitrary reasons for decisions. Told to give just one reason why he should not apply for a job in a local teacher's college, for instance, Jacob recalls:

> Instantly a host of arguments against applying for a job at the Wicomico State Teachers College presented themselves for my use, and as instantly a corresponding number of refutations lined up opposite them, one for one, so that the question of my application was held static like the rope marker in a tug-o'-war where the opposing teams are perfectly matched. (1967: 4-5)

That's the way it always is for Jacob, whose anomie is so complete that he can make neither simple decisions, such as whether to turn right or left, nor difficult ones, such as the extent of his responsibility for his lover's pregnancy, abortion, and consequent death. Throughout the novel, Jacob is represented not as an actor but as the scene of action. So complete is his dissociation that he puts his lover as well as himself in the care of a man he believes to be an insane quack, simply because this man makes decisions. In the same way that Jacob is a place where things happen, rather than someone to whom things happen or someone who makes things happen, the picture of the solitary writer is a scene of action, not an actor and not even the action itself.

In the scene of writing, the writer is merely a clerk, at best an employee of writing, at worst its victim. It is, then, a picture in which the writer bears no responsibility for what is written, since the writer is viewed not as a participant in the act of writing but as a recipient of written language. The writer-writes-alone is an image in which the writer is made to appear a prisoner of both language and society, for the scene resembles nothing so much as a cell. And who has not imagined a cell to be a perfect sanctuary for writing? Do we not refer to Antonio Gramsci's *Prison Notebooks* as if the fact that they were written in prison somehow guarantees their importance? One would not expect to command either the same kind or degree of respect for essays written in a kitchen. It is hard to imagine, in any event, *The Kitchen Journals* as a cultural shorthand for the serious or truthful, whereas the writings of convicted felons, Jack Abbott and Eldridge Cleaver for instance, appear to be all the more significant for having been written in a cell.

The picture that at once immortalizes and immobilizes the solitary writer, arrested in the moment of transcription, is a picture postcard of writing. It is, in other words, an official view of writing and as such exercises the same kind of control over our experience and memory of writing as postcards of national monuments do. Having seen so many postcards of the Grand Canyon, we can hardly look at it, much less remember it, as anything other than glossy three-by-fives. It is likewise difficult to see or remember writing as other than it is portrayed in the scene of writing if that picture frames our experience and governs our memories. To see writing anew, to look at it from yet other vantage points, we must reread an image that we have come to think of as the reality of writing. It is not enough to say that it is only a picture, for such pictures provide us with a vocabulary for thinking about and explaining writing to ourselves and one another.

Modernism is not the way things are, but the way things appear to us, because its metaphors and vocabulary prevail, hence constituting an ideology of experience. In question is not the picture of the writer-writes-alone, for there are undoubtedly such moments in writing. At issue instead is the unexamined assumption that this and only this moment counts as writing. The argument I am making is similar to that of Susan Sontag in *On Photography* and John Berger in *About Looking*. Although they are concerned with how photographs function as what Berger calls "an unexamined part of modern perception itself" (1980: 49), their arguments with respect to photography apply equally well to what I have been calling the scene of writing. Consider the following passage from Sontag's book, which Berger uses to make his point about the extent to which people simply forget that photography *is* a technology:

> Through photographs, the world becomes a series of unrelated, freestanding particles; and history, past and present, a set of anecdotes and faits divers. The camera makes reality atomic, manageable, and opaque. It is a view of the world which denies interconnectedness, continuity, but confers on each moment the character of a mystery. Any photograph has multiple meanings; indeed, to see something in the form of a photograph is to encounter a potential object of fascination. (1973: 22-23)

Their quarrel is not, of course, with photography, but with the commonly held assumption that a photograph is a "particle" of reality, that is, with the virtual identification of photographs with reality. My own quarrel with the scene of writing runs along the same lines. To the extent that the scene of writing encourages the reification of one moment in writing as writing, by excluding all other moments, the image itself is hegemonic, for its authority prevents us from entering or leaving the scene itself.

Pictures do not speak for themselves. They speak to and for the societies that preserve and cherish them. This is as true of photographs, the use of which Sontag and Berger lament, as it is of the image of the solitary writer. Many of the stories that ensue from the scene of writing, for instance, suggest the penalties more often than the privileges of writing. Yet garrets—and their more prosaic counterparts, studies and classrooms and libraries—are obviously signs of the leisure requisite for writing. That same leisure is often wantonly transformed, however, into settings that recall cells: where privilege is transformed into punishment, freedom into incarceration, solitude into isolation. It seems a curious story for a society to tell about itself, a troubling anecdote that recurs whenever we write, talk about writing, and, most important of all, attempt to teach it.

Even today writing is sometimes the penalty exacted for talking out of turn in class. A teacher who assigns such a penalty obviously sees writing as a punishment, and a student who writes such sentences lives for a time in the social isolation of the prisoner. The task itself seems designed to make nonsense out of writing, for the punishment usually consists in writing the same sentence a set number of times. Children, of course, are inclined to enact the punishment in ways that call attention to its absurdity. It is not unusual, for instance, for a child to complete the task vertically rather than horizontally. Thus, the punishment sentence "I will not talk in class" is reproduced in columns: a column for "I," a column for "will," and so on. Is this not a perfect rendition of the picture of a solitary writer who is a writing machine?

Examining Modernist Ideology in the Scene of Writing

The stories of writing readily suggested by the scene of writing form a set of anecdotes, and from this set can be told what Kenneth Burke in *A Grammar of Motives* calls a representative anecdote. Simply put, such an anecdote functions as a proposition that at once organizes and analyzes experience through the processes of reflection, selection, and deflection. For Burke, the telling of such anecdotes is simply what people do. And while some may do it more formally than others, his interest, and ours, concerns their ideological functions. In considering the functions, and dysfunctions, of representative anecdotes, Burke writes:

> Insofar as the vocabulary meets the needs of reflection, we can say that it [a representative anecdote] has the necessary scope. In its selectivity it is a reduction. Its scope and reduction become a deflection when the given terminology, or calculus, is not suited to the subject matter it is designed to calculate. (1969: 59)

In Burke's terms, then, any representative anecdote generates ideology. While it is easy to see that the writer-writes-alone reduces writing to transcription, it is not altogether clear whose interests are being included and excluded by selecting a moment in which writers are represented as dehumanized by the very act of writing. For Burke, of course, the deflections are consequential, so much so that they reduce a representative to an informative anecdote:

> If the originating anecdote is not representative, a vocabulary developed in strict conformity with it will not be representative. This embarrassment is usually avoided in practice by a break in the conformity at some crucial point: this means in effect that the vocabulary ceases to have the basis which is claimed for it. (59)

Hence, even were one to accept the writer-writes-alone as a representative anecdote instructing critics in the reception of literary modernism, it would not follow that the scene of writing also represents the production of those particular works, much less the production of prose essays.

In much the same way that using writing as a punishment teaches the wrong kind of lesson about writers and writing, this representative anecdote of writing as reading or reception can be counterproductive with respect to writing and writing pedagogy insofar as the scene dampens even as it stokes the desire to write. The romance of solitude is usually more attractive than the experience: among contemporary academics, nostalgia for an age of belle lettres often seems a better criticism of what they read than a statement of what they would like to write.

In asking "What's wrong with this picture?" as an explanation of writing, it is instructive to look at how Sontag, a fastidious, not to mention reluctant, modernist, uses the scene in her own writing. The first sentence of the first essay in *Under the Sign of Saturn* is "I am writing this from a tiny room in Paris" (1981: 4). Can there be any doubt that a tiny room in Paris, like a prison cell in Italy, lends a seriousness to writing, when even so chary and trustworthy an observer of modernism as Sontag underwrites her essay on Paul Goodman in that one telling line? Its very appearance at the opening of her book on great modernists suggests that the scene of writing is an irresistible legacy. Yet as Sontag spins out the metaphor in the course of her essay on Goodman, one sees that she has neither unwittingly nor casually begun from a tiny room in Paris. The essay, as it turns out, is about the difficulties she encounters in her attempts to abide such a room.

"On Paul Goodman" is a narrative essay about the requirements of writing, which Sontag depicts as a place in which one can hear one's own voice. A room designed for writing is a room where one's friends do not visit and, most of all, a room where one does not read books. By contrast with much of modernism, in which writing subsumes the writer, Sontag's room is only a respite, a rented room where, despite her efforts "to live for a year without books, a few manage to creep in somehow" (10). So, into the stillness, into the quiet synchrony of the scene of writing seeps the history of her reading, for one of the books she cannot resist reading is Paul Goodman's *New Reformation.* Ironically, in her inability to desist from reading, Sontag resists the most dehumanizing version of the scene of writing. What we see is a provisional independence that is not autonomy from history or society but a solitude that is carefully tended and from which the writer occasionally emerges—to read a few well-loved books written by a select group of writers whose company she keeps by writing this admirable essay.

From Sontag's use of the anecdote, it is easy to see that the scene of writing can be resisted. We might even say that because she controls this metaphor, as she has so many others, she gains the authority it ascribes to those who seek solitude without also making herself into the main character, the prisoner of writing. Thus, while the image of the garret assures us that she is a serious writer, the narrative connects her to yet another serious writer, Paul Goodman, whose written words she hears as she reads his book in that room. So it is that isolation is represented as but a moment in writing, a part of the story she is telling about writing as well as reading.

Stanley Aronowitz, who writes on the hegemony of modernism in *The Crisis in Historical Materialism,* sees in what he calls the "neo-romantic genre" of prose fiction a similar act of resistance, manifest in the fact that most American women writers and minority writers do not write modern fiction:

> The critique might extend to modernism's refusal of continuous narrative, the play of the language game as the prose poem of world, expressionism's

> transformation of the figure into its raw materials, or the spatial rather than temporal referent of modern art. These are the coded forms of non-reconciliation with the given reality, the protest against art's function to recall the coherence of the world in the wake of its splintering. (1981: 278)

As with many statements about forms of resistance, Aronowitz's reminds us that modernism is a philosophy or ideology, a response, if you will, to the frightening "facts" of modern life. It is not, however, the only possible response, and it is certainly not to be confused with the reality it purports to represent. He is protesting, of course, the monism of modernism, the insistence that modernism is a universal experience that, if it is denied by artists, makes their work sentimental or shallow.

The politics of the scene of writing are reproduced in a literary criticism that treats the autonomous text as the homologue of the alienated artist, a literary studies version, one might say, of the ideology Michel Foucault questions in "What Is an Author?" The New Criticism in particular, and literary formalism in general, treats a literary artifact as a discrete object whose origins are as irrelevant as its destination. Seen in this light, the major statements issued about literature by the American New Critics can be read as justifications for an aesthetic that manages the labor of writing in much the same way that Harry Braverman, in *Labor and Monopoly Capital,* argues that Frederick Winslow Taylor rationalized and, thus, degraded the labor of factory workers. Writer and writing alike are subsumed in the production of Literature, just as worker and working are made invisible in, say, the production of Automobiles. Lost in this perspective, of course, is the notion of authorship. Thus, literary critics who say they are writing on Shakespeare or Joyce usually mean particular plays or narratives, for such names refer not to authorship but to products and advertise not writing but canonical texts. It would not be altogether absurd to say that such surnames are brand names in literary studies, for there is a sense in which Joyce is to literary modernism as Ford is to the modern automobile.

In explanation of the extraordinary symbiosis between the modernists and their critics, Fredric Jameson writes in *Marxism and Form:*

> The monographic study of an individual author—no matter how adroitly pursued—imposes an inevitable falsification through its very structure, an optical illusion of totality projected by what is in reality only an artificial isolation. That modern writers have solicited this thoroughgoing "conversion" of the critics to their works as to a kind of "world" is not an excuse for the critical procedure, but rather a phenomenon of interest to be studied in its own right. (1971: 315)

Jameson is speaking in this passage of what he sees as a studied denial of influence, resulting in a critical obduracy to the historical realities to which writers and their critics are necessarily subject. He is not, however, denying the possible worth of studying individual writers. Instead, he is questioning the tendency of the New Critics to represent an author as a technique, and in so doing to reproduce the very conditions of isolation—writer from writing and writer from the world—that modern literature takes as a given.

Like many early opponents of the New Criticism, Jameson locates the problem in a literary criticism that, as he puts it, shares with the modernists "a profound horror of time and fear of change" (320). Jameson, Aronowitz, Sontag, and Berger, however, are far less troubled by the modernists' preoccupation with spatial metaphors than by their conviction that these metaphors accurately reflect a universal, lived experience. They object to the selection of a particular experience qua experience because the part (alienation) that has been selected and reified is too often accepted as the standard against which all other experiences are to be evaluated. Thus, these critics question not the anecdote in which space replaces time, but the hegemony of a modernist ideology that virtually rejects all other moments, all other stories, and, most important, all other experiences except alienation as inaccurate or sentimental.

It is one thing to say that a method or theory of reading is significant, quite another to insist that it is true. The first assertion is within the realm of argumentation and, thereby, that which individuals and society have knowingly fabricated. The second disguises its human origins in the "natural," and insists, essentially and consequentially, that there is nothing to talk about. The problem with treating literature in terms of techniques or formal properties—in short, as objects—is the extent to which such a literary culture comes to bear an uncanny resemblance to the cargo cults that anthropologists, such as Peter Worsley, have documented. Works of literary interest that seem to appear out of thin air are subject to all manner of fetishism. Authorship, production, and marketing are subsumed by the sheer weight of the artifact: poem, novel, play, essay.

Doing Time in the Scene of Writing

In a single gesture, the scene of writing recalls modern criticism's most cherished anecdote about textual autonomy: "The poem is not the critic's own and not the author's (it is detached from the author at birth and goes about the world beyond his power to intend about it or control it). The poem belongs to the public" (Wimsatt and Beardsley 1954: 5). The closed shutters of the garret, the drawn drapes of the study, or the walls of books lining the library all effectively remove the writer from time as well as place. The forcible exclusion of time from the scene of writing is troubling, not least because it reiterates Jameson's claim that time is what the modernists and their critics feared most. Once its absence is noticed, however, time, like Sontag's favorite books, comes creeping in, for shutters, drapes, and even bookshelves defend no one against the ravages of time. The scene of writing is just that, a scene or tableau that represents an event (transcription) as the experience (writing) by removing writer and writing from the influence of both durative and historic time. While the gesture may make a good deal of sense in terms of modernism, it unnecessarily romanticizes writing, which, as everyone who writes knows, takes time.

I can think of no one who has written more convincingly of the menacing presence of durative and historic time in the scene of writing than Albert Memmi. In the prologue to *The Pillar of Salt,* the narrator recounts his own experience as he and other students sit for the exams that will conclude their French university education:

> I look around me at all my comrades. Their heads bent forward, their faces pale, their hair tangled beneath their nervous fingers, they all know what they want. All of them—the old students whose studies have been delayed by the war, and the younger whose luck has not yet run out—all are jealous of time. To gain time, to waste time. But what have I to lose? There is but one final stake for me to risk, and I have perhaps already lost it. (1955: ix)

The narrator tries to circumvent time by mapping space (the windowpanes, the bookshelves, and the aisles between the desks). Marking time by counting objects, the student-narrator performs an act all too familiar to bored students, not to mention prisoners. Yet it is by entering the scene of writing *as the writer* that he finally escapes time:

> To give myself countenance, to escape, I continued writing for seven hours, like all the others. I even made the most of the extra fifteen minutes of grace granted to the stragglers. That is because my whole life was rising in my throat again, because I was writing without thinking, straight from the heart to the pen. (x)

Memmi's narrator enters the scene of writing when he can no longer map time onto space. Hence, the scene of writing supports those modernist narratives in which literary production is a defense against time, for to transcribe "straight from the heart to the pen" is to displace the rational with the romantic.

Overwhelmed by historical, even historic, time—the occupation of France during World War II—the narrator now desires nothing more than to forget. What distinguishes the narrator from the others is his conviction that the past determines the future, for he sees himself as the prisoner of historic events and time as his jailer. In a simple ostensive phrase ("students whose studies have been delayed by the war"), the narrator's political as well as social isolation is intensified, since the others embrace the very oppressor he is trying to resist. His ultimate failure is announced when he accepts "the extra fifteen minutes of grace" as a gift. The writer is granted parole from "doing time" if by writing one means transcribing, that is, converting time into "some fifty pages" (x). Memmi's scene is dramatic because time is experienced by the resisting narrator as it sometimes is in dreams, as a thick substance through which one slowly wends without moving, as a total disjuncture of time and space. So when the narrator finally surrenders to time, his capitulation is both a disappointing denouement and a satisfying release from the moment-to-moment tension of his resistance.

The scene of writing supports many such modern romances. At once justly and unjustly imprisoned, the writer is both hero and antihero, a saint and a sinner whose knowledge promises redemption even as it threatens annihilation. The West can project its most cherished beliefs about writers onto the scene of writing. It is a metaphor for the isolation of "modern man." Certainly one way to interpret Norman Mailer's successful campaign to free convicted felon Jack Abbott is to say that he was able to free Abbott from a real prison on the grounds that the metaphorical prison, writing, is punishment enough. To the extent that the scene of writing is successful as a metaphor, Mailer presumably relied on the parole board's sharing the ideology that writers are already prisoners of society. This being the case, the particular form of Abbott's parole violation (murder) would be consistent, too, since the metaphor also prepares us to believe that writers are a menace to society. The scene of writing is truly a marvelous image. Its stories are hagiographies in which writers are martyrs to Writing. Because their knowledge is at once sacred and profane, their experiences testify to our own fervent desire to write, and to our morbid fear of writers.

When writers are seen as possessed by writing, the immediate consequences to individual writers, celebrity or notoriety, can also be construed as outside the writer's control. Individual writers who are sacrificed on the altars of a profane society, either indifferent to or offended by their work, are at once the victims of society and the burnt offerings of Writing, or Art. If this seems too melodramatic a reading, consider how Thomas Mann's Tonio Kröger explains his life as a writer to his female artist friend, Lisabeta: "It seems to me we artists are all of us something like those unsexed papal singers . . . we sing like angels, but—"(1954: 99). In reply to her protest that his art and hers are a calling, Tonio denies it:

> Don't talk about 'calling,' Lisabeta Ivanovna. Literature is not a calling, it is a curse, believe me. . . . It begins by your feeling yourself set apart, in a curious sort of opposition to the nice regular people; there is a gulf of ironic sensibility, of knowledge, scepticism, disagreement between you and the others; it grows deeper and deeper, you realize that you are alone; and from then on any rapprochement is simply hopeless. (99)

Whether it is the monk's cell of orthodoxy or the prison cell of heterodoxy, the scene of writing valorizes Writing as Sacred and/or Profane Knowledge. The scene denies authorship (writers merely encode messages) by banishing time. Its removal is a deflection, in Burke's terms, and its return, also in Burke's vocabulary, a break in the calculus.

Repopulating the Scene of Writing

Even more alien to the scene of writing than time are women. The prisoner of writing is irrevocably male. Unlike time, this fact cannot be remedied by resorting to deictics. The women referred to by the picture are not women who write. Rather, they are women who support men who write: a muse or a mistress, a doting mother, wife, or sister. So inhospitable is the scene of writing that the room Sontag pictures bears only a superficial resemblance to it. Or consider the room imagined earlier by Virginia Woolf, who, in this passage concluding "Professions for Women," exhorts women to use their newly acquired privilege:

> You have won rooms of your own in the house hither to owned by men. You are able, though not without great labor and effort, to pay the rent. You are earning your five hundred pounds a year. But this freedom is only the beginning; the room is your own, but it is still bare. It has to be furnished; it has to be decorated; it has to be shared. How are you going to furnish it, how are you going to decorate it? With whom are you going to share it, and upon what terms? (1942: 239)

By questioning the terms of occupancy, Woolf connects writing both to writers and to the world. In the simplest of ways, she argues that writing, once a closed shop, is now an occupation open to those few women fortunate enough to learn and practice it.

After a lifetime of writing, indeed, a life largely devoted to literary modernism, Woolf sets down terms for professional women that are much the same as those she articulated years earlier in *A Room of One's Own:* "It takes five hundred a year and a room with a lock on the door if you are to write fiction or poetry" (1929: 109). The room is about having the time and a place in which to write, neither of which can be had without cost to the writer. No one will lock the door for her and, even more important, no one will take responsibility for what she makes of the time she spends there. She takes the room knowing only that she wants to write. In the scene of writing, occupancy is definitive; to see the picture is to know that the male seated there is a writer. Woolf's scene is not definitive. Securing a room is requisite to writing, but not, as it turns out, anything more than the opportunity to exercise the privileges of solitude. Nor does Woolf's room define the writing as Literature, for within a few pages she broadens the scope of the picture:

> For I am by no means confining you to fiction. If you would please me—and there are thousands like me—you would write books of travel and adventure, and research and scholarship, and history and biography, and criticism and philosophy and science. By so doing you will certainly profit the art of fiction. For books have a way of influencing each other. (113)

The room for women writers discussed by Woolf—a serious modernist and a serious woman—is quite literally as pragmatic a proposition as the scene of writing is romantic.

The male who inhabits the scene is both in possession of and possessed by writing. Woolf's unfurnished room is not a purchase but a lease on writing. If her room is also outside history, it is not in deference to the ahistoricism of modernism, but to the fact that women have no history as writers (see "Shakespeare's Sister" in *A Room of One's Own*). Woolf's room is as indeterminate with respect to writing (the genre is unknown) as it is to the writer (whose merit is yet unrealized). The scene of writing, by contrast, determines writing and writer, at least to the extent that the writing is decidedly Literature and the writer is undoubtedly a Genius. The room is an invitation to apprentice oneself to the craft of writing. The scene of writing is bondage to an anonymous master, who is variously known as Art and Literature. Certain about the preconditions of writing, Woolf draws no conclusions about what will happen to the women who try their hand at it. While the scene of writing guarantees the consequences (Literature), it is as much a mystery to the writer as it is to us why he, rather than someone else, is the prisoner of writing. He is elected to write, she elects to write; the scene mystifies writing, the room demystifies it; he is alone, she is in the company of other writers (writing is a house with many rooms); he is product, she is process.

Virginia Woolf is both a modernist and a feminist. She is known as a great modernist because such novels as *To the Lighthouse* and *The Waves* are remarkable literary experiments within the modernist tradition. She is known as a feminist because she examined women's issues in her essays and lectures (*A Room of One's Own* and *Three Guineas*) and in her journals (*A Writer's Diary*). To the extent that these perspectives are incompatible, one might say that modernists mainly read her fiction and feminists her essays to make her their own. So it is as much a matter of reading different Virginia Woolfs as it is of reading Virginia Woolf differently. Yet to the extent that both her essays on women and her novels were literally experiments in writing, Woolf was as concerned with writing processes as with the prose she produced.

In the same way that she returns periodically to the unfurnished room as unfinished business, Woolf repeatedly experiments with language in her novels, as though each one were exploring yet another hypothesis about the possibilities and limitations of language. Of Woolf's experiments with language in *The Waves,* Michael Boyd writes in *The Reflexive Novel:*

> Language is a means of self-creation; therefore, to create a self is to adopt a certain attitude toward language, and this is precisely what each of Woolf's characters does. All the characters, with varying degrees of self-consciousness, speak of language and its relation to reality. By impersonating each character in turn, Woolf is able to present a comprehensive view of possible theories of language. (1983: 107)

Seen in this way, language is both the experience and the arbiter of experience, much as it is in modern language philosophy. While the perspective of each character fastens hope to a different aspect of language—lexicon, tense, meaning—all her characters seek to overcome the arbitrariness of language, that is, try to live with the fact that there are no natural correlates of language in the social world, and long for a language that would reconcile them to, rather than separate them from, the world. And as we might predict, although each perspective on language fails, the experiment of *The Waves* does not. For as Boyd points out, the novel is best understood as an autobiography of Woolf *as a writer in the act of writing.* She sets herself an impossible task in attempting to have her self "catch itself in the act of self-creation but one [a task] that insures, by its very impossibility, the continuance of the effort" (116). Yet the "fact" of alienation does not lead Woolf, as it does many modernists, to its reification. Rather, she resists alienation by writing. It is not a unified self she creates in words, but a self drafted and redrafted as possible verbal repertoires—a self born in language use.

Pragmatic and Romantic Scenes of Writing

One way to think about modernism as it is articulated in the writing of Virginia Woolf and modernism as it is worked out by, say, Thomas Mann or Franz Kafka is to notice that while her response is pragmatic, theirs is romantic. Faced with atomic "reality" and the exclusion of women from writing, Woolf is moved to ask "What do I do about these facts?" while that "reality" (though not the exclusion of women from writing) led Mann and Kafka not to question the facts but to ask "What will these facts do to me?" The same conditions that mobilize Woolf immobilize the others. We might even say that Woolf put the World on trial, in the sense that it is the modern world she interrogates when she examines each character's "theory" of language or limns a room in which women could write. Her "world" is created by speakers who at once create and limit their realities in language. If the world is on trial in Woolf, it is clearly the author who is charged, tried, convicted, and sentenced by the world in the writings of Mann and Kafka. The scapegoats of modernism, from Thomas Mann's Tonio Kröger to John Barth's Jacob Horner, are more victims than victimizers, the randomly selected, self-conscious prisoners of language and society.

The worlds of literary modernists are projections from the rooms in which they are written. Needless to say, the world seen from a garret is not the same as the one seen from Woolf's room. The garret frees writers from the world only to make them prisoners of writing. Thus, they bear very little responsibility for either the world or the word. In effect, the writer is to text as the projectionist is to film: responsible for maintaining the illusion that a novel, poem, or essay is, above all, a freestanding fact, a fait accompli. Just as the projection room absorbs the noise of the technology of film, the garret hides the technology of writing. Author and projectionist are, however, hostages to the ravages of technology so that we, the audience, may enjoy the illusions of art as ongoing events in the world. As Mann's Tonio Kröger sees it, "an artist must be unhuman, extra-human; he must stand in a queer relationship to humanity; only then is he in a position, I ought to say only then is he tempted, to represent it, to present it, to portray it to good effect" (1954: 98). Tonio and the projectionist are the backstage paraphernalia of art and film. The illusions of modern art, like the illusion of film, require that someone stand between the audience and the technology. Their isolation in the projection room or the garret is, then, in the interest of an art whose technology is too painful for the reader or viewer to bear. Hence, the writer in the scene of writing is the victim of both the word and the world, he who mediates the sacred word in a profane world.

The image of the world projected from Woolf's room is a world in the making. To the extent that the room projects a scene of writing, hers is an invitation to experience writing as she has known it: as a process in which we use language to learn about ourselves and others, and inevitably learn most about language. The room is comparable to no other room because it is not yet known what will happen when a writer enters. We know only that writing will not relieve a writer of responsibility for either the world or the word, since a writer enters the room as a speaker might a conversation, in the hope of getting a hearing. Woolf's room is a decision as well as an opportunity to write, but the choice does not guarantee that what happens in that room will satisfy either the writer or the reader. Nonetheless, to write is to resist or subvert alienation with words. Hence, the act of writing is at once a practical and radical demonstration, in which every writer protests the implausibility of language in a world where words might mean anything or everything, but somehow mean neither as much nor as little as we wish.

In Woolf's works, writers are not vanquished by language, or even by writing, as they are in Mann, Kafka, and Barth. Rather, they are constrained by their own desires. Each dreams of a language that says it all, but their dreams are invariably confounded by their own emerging texts, which lead not to reality but to still other stories. While the characters in *The Waves* may impute varying degrees of power to language, and may even represent themselves as its victims, Woolf herself does not separate language from its users or its use. In this respect, she resembles the contemporary American pragmatist Richard Rorty, who also views language as that which can only be fruitfully studied in terms of its use:

> One can use language to criticize and enlarge itself, as one can exercise one's body to develop and strengthen and enlarge it, but one cannot see language-as-a-whole in relation to something else to which it applies, for which it is a means to an end. The arts and the sciences, and philosophy as their self-reflection and integration, constitute such a process of enlargement and strengthening. But Philosophy, the attempt to say "how language relates to the world" by saying what makes certain sentences true, or certain actions or attitudes good or rational, is, on this view, impossible. (1980: xix)

Writing or Philosophy, writ in the large letters of metaphysics or logic, fail to the extent that we expect language to instruct us about the world. So in *The Waves,* when Bernard says, "I begin to long for some little language such as lovers use" (Woolf 1971: 239), his frustration, his desire for language, reminds us that language cannot be possessed, but must be created by the lovers who use it.

Atomism in Classical and Modern Physics

Modernism concerns time in space. And this preoccupation with space and spatial tropes, if not actually generated by physics, is at the very least buttressed by its propositions. To the extent that quantum mechanics and theories of relativity are replacing Newtonian physics during the period of literary modernism and postmodernism, the definition of atoms and, perforce, atomism is changing. One might even argue that Mann, Kafka, and Barth conceptualize alienation in terms consonant with classical physics, whereas Woolf in, say, *The Waves* and Lawrence Durrell in the "Alexandria Quartet" conceptualize alienation in terms more commensurate with modern physics. The differences between classical and modern physics are many. However, it is the potential for total annihilation that makes it inconceivable to argue that modern physics is merely a collection of more accurate axioms about the physical world than classical physics.

Simply put, modern physics necessitates axiology as well as axioms. In modern physics, mathematical precision indubitably leads to more than increasingly accurate descriptions of and predictions about the physical world, for its mathematics could demonstrably and irreparably destroy the very world whose laws of motion it observes. With the advent of nuclear physics, it is manifestly problematic, therefore, to what extent the formulas reflect a physical reality and to what extent they project a reality formulated by the physicist.

Classical physics views the atom as the smallest indivisible unit of matter in space. When many modernists talk about alienation, they mean the notion that the individual is an atomic, self-referring unit. Such a view of the self is consistent with classical physics, where atomism is the scientific correlate of postindustrial anomie. This classical version of atomism is, perhaps, most fully and most frequently articulated in the short stories and novels of Franz Kafka. In *The Castle,* for instance, the protagonist, K, is confronted with the castle as an indisputable fact whose mysteries he cannot penetrate. All attempts to understand are futile because the castle defends a compelling fact, bureaucracy, which like the atom of classical physics can be neither seen nor confronted, only imagined. As K travels from the village to the castle, his journeys are like excursions from the nineteenth to the twentieth century, and the separate spheres of the village and the castle might easily be read as a gloss on Durkheim, so surely do K's repeated journeys to the castle ensure his descent into anomie. His time is mapped as senseless motion, the unmotivated movement of an atom. If one accepts the metaphors of classical physics as metaphors for social as well as physical life, social life might as well be conducted as a silent movie. There can be no point to speech when there is no hope of being heard or understood.

Modern physics not only treats the atom as theoretically divisible, it also can demonstrate its theory. This empirical fact of modern physics, made possible by technology, transforms questions about the extent to which physics is the creation of physicists into urgent practical as well as theoretical concerns. According to John Archibald Wheeler, Niels Bohr and Albert Einstein disagreed not about quantum theory or even about equations, but about the very nature of reality: "To Einstein, the world existed 'out there.' To Bohr, the observer's choice of his observing equipment had inescapable and normally unpredictable consequences for what will be found" (1982: 3). The principle of uncertainty in physics, and in any literature or art based on it, speaks not to cause and effect, but to the "normally unpredictable" effects of observation. In the passage cited here, the observer's problematic contribution to reality is to be understood as a comment on physics, that is, as a critique of the limits of the scientific method to describe an "objective" reality. When this concern is raised first by Woolf and later by Durrell in fiction, the critique is extended to include the uncertain consequences of a narrator's presence in a social as well as physical world. While the issue of perspectivism reaches its apogee for Woolf in *The Waves,* it is in Durrell's "Quartet" that perspectivism is stated as a theory of modern fiction.

A city twice marooned by desert and sea, Durrell's midcentury Alexandria is atomic in the classical sense. Like Kafka's castle, it is a self-referring, provincial, and inscrutable city whose denizens are so remote from Europe that even World War II is repelled by its desert and harbor. Yet unlike Kafka's castle, modern Alexandria is diachronically represented as the most recent archeological layer in the history of the city. Much is made of the ways modernity threatens ancient customs, and fierce tribalism intrudes on the all too civilized pursuits of Alexandria's expatriate inhabitants. Durrell's characters come to Alexandria seeking refuge from modern Europe only to find that they have brought it with them. It is, then, within this more or less classical perspective on atomism that Durrell unleashes the possibilities of modern physics, entering the twentieth-century debate on scientific responsibility armed with both its methods and its metaphors.

The prism and the microscope are coeval in Alexandria, where the ancient and modern world literally coexist, and neither perspective prevails. On the one hand, Durrell's characters reside in Alexandria as if inside a prism, trapped by magic within the apparently smooth, though actually pocked, facades of the city. Each life reflects the refracted lives of the others. This classicism, most evident in the first book, *Justine,* owes more to illusion and enchantment than to science. On the other hand, as the characters move about the city, their movements are observed as if they were particles in a field. In much the way we might read Virginia Woolf's *The Waves* as a Poetics of language in the modern world, we might read the "Alexandria Quartet" as a treatise on modern physics and art. In a note to the second novel, *Balthazar,* Durrell explains his plans for the "Quartet" as follows:

> Modern literature offers us no Unities, so I have turned to science and am trying to complete a four-decker novel whose form is based on the relativity proposition. . . . This is not Proustian or Joycean method—for they illustrate Bergsonian "Duration" in my opinion, not "Space-Time." (1958: preface)

This author's note is reiterated in the notebooks of Pursewarden, the writer whose death reverberates through Alexandria with a far greater force than his life. He, too, imagined writing such a quartet, though it is a project we learn of in the last novel, *Clea,* and one Pursewarden planned not for himself but for Darby, whose writing processes preside over the novels. In his journal entry "My Conversation with Brother Ass," Pursewarden tells Darby, who is "Brother Ass," what he must do if he is to become not a good writer, but a great one:

> You might try a four-card trick in the form of a novel; passing a common axis through four stories, say, and dedicating each to one of the four winds of heaven. A continuum, forsooth, embodying not a *temps retrouvé* but a *temps delivré.* The curvature of space itself would give you a

stereoscopic narrative, while human personality seen across a continuum would perhaps become prismatic? Who can say? I throw the idea out. I can imagine a form which, if satisfied, might raise in human terms the problems of causality or indeterminacy. (1960: 135-36)

Pursewarden's method, like the metaphor in which Durrell conceived the "Quartet," is a curious admixture of classical and modern physics, a literary reenactment of the scientific narrative on space.

As in *The Waves,* in the "Alexandria Quartet" the consequences of atomism are explored as possibilities, rather than announced as facts. These include a refracted personality that exists in virtue of social as well as psychological space and time, and a theory of the novel in which novelists understand words in much the same way scientists would a refracting telescope, as a means by which the final image is wholly the creation of the lens (language) itself. What is explicated in Durrell is what is adumbrated in Woolf, the uncertain effect of the observing writer on human events. Like the modern physicist Niels Bohr, the modern writer Durrell is convinced that knowing where you stand is part of understanding that you are part of the "reality" you attempt to examine—in language. And it is this knowledge that implicates the observer, who must take a measure of responsibility for what is seen from that vantage point: Durrell for the Alexandria he writes and Bohr for the Physics he writes. This perspectival modernism, in which observation is entailed by participation, constructs provisional and partial truths from the fragments of knowledge acquired. While perspectivalism acknowledges the limitations of language, in writing as in physics, the responsibility for words and the world is returned to its users.

Revising the Scene of Writing

If it is romance we require in our pictures of writers and writing, then it will not be an easy charge to revise the scene of writing. Yet there is an urgent intellectual need to reexamine the social and political consequences of the scene, if only because decontextualized research on individual writers' cognitive processes has literally refabricated the scene of writing as a model of corporate activity. Cast as both management and labor, writers are deemed successful by cognitive researchers/readers to the extent that they know and act on principles of efficient management. Hence, in "A Cognitive Process Theory of Writing," Linda Flower and John R. Hayes are able to portray writing as goals (rhetorical problems to be solved) and to describe writers' cognitive processes as interlocking events (planning, translating, and reviewing), the successful completion of which is a satisfactory product (words on a page). Quality control depends on writers' abilities to "monitor their current process and progress," or in the vocabulary and imagery they borrow from Carl Bereiter and Marlene Scardamalia, success or failure in the Flower and Hayes model is determined by the writer's " 'executive routine' " (1981: 374). A theory that conceptualizes the mind as a blueprint and represents its cognitive activity in a flowchart of management techniques not only decontextualizes writing, but quite literally transforms the individual who writes into a writing machine.

What is presented in Kafka as surreal, and thereby as a critique, is offered at this end of the century by Flower and Hayes as a positive and untroubling "metaphor for a process: a way to think about something, such as the composing process, which refuses to sit still for a portrait" (368). If the scene of writing in classical modernism is agoraphobic (writers in garrets are withdrawn from the social world), theirs is a portrait of a writer who is autistic (cognitive processes are profoundly interiorized). The needs and desires of such a writer are, by definition, unavailable to writer and teacher alike, for such a writer is a cognitive cipher whose writing behaviors (pauses, protocols, revisions) are signs that only trained observers can interpret: "people's after-the-fact, *introspective analysis* of what they did while writing is notoriously inaccurate and likely to be influenced by their notions of what they should have done" (368). This cognitivist distrust of the writer's subjective experience is, of course, a social science version of "The Intentional Fallacy," spelled out for literary critics nearly three decades earlier by W. K. Wimsatt and Monroe Beardsley.

The techniques of close reading advocated by New Critics and writing-aloud protocols employed by cognitivists are methodologies designed to protect critics and researchers from the vagaries of authors or subjects as well as from their own subjectivity. Such protection, however, loses its meaning if research presumes that reality is socially constructed and that the goal of research is to describe and understand the worlds in which researchers as well as the writers they study reside. This view of research, which has recently interested those who study academic writing, including Patricia Bizzell, Greg Myers, and me, further presumes that the language in which knowledge is constructed will be more or less authoritative depending on the status of that language as a *discourse* within the community of use. Hence, if cognitive research portrays thinking in the language of scientific management, it is reasonable to conclude that the goals of management, namely, that writers must supervise themselves because writing is a task whose completion depends on the careful use of time, seem appropriate to those who conceptualize and speak from its vantage point. More important still, perhaps, there is a presumption that their readers share this discourse, hence, this ideology—in which the desire to write is converted into the goal of making good, that is, efficient, use of time.

Let me suggest here yet another way of viewing writers in the act of writing that speaks directly to the positive value of lived experience in the study and teaching of writing. What I have in mind requires an act of imaginative resistance. Each of us would need to vacate the garret we have been visiting as readers and occupy a room in a house such as Virginia Woolf inhabited as writers. A descent from the garret will of course be an excursion into the very social, historical, and political circumstances from which garrets have been defending us. Writers who live in such rooms see themselves, perforce, as social activists whose writing can be read and evaluated as a social practice, but cannot be reduced to aesthetic or cultural artifacts, or to cognitive activity. Raymond Williams, who has often considered the issues that arise when we try to relate writing to society, says of his own writing in "The Tenses of the Imagination":

> I am in fact physically alone when I am writing, and I do not believe, taking it all in all, that my work has been less individual, in that defining and valuing sense, than that of others. Yet whenever I write I am aware of a society and of a language which I know are vastly larger than myself: not simply 'out there,' in a world of others, but here, in what I am engaged in doing: composing and relating. (1983: 261)

Williams shares with Woolf the ability to imagine himself in the company of others even as he sits alone writing. And, of course, to return to writing its social as well as its aesthetic and cognitive possibilities is to imagine the materiality of language itself.

Language is what people can and do make of it. If research on student writers has shown us nothing else, it has certainly documented (in Britton et al. 1975, Emig 1971, and L. McCarthy 1985, for example) that most students construe writing solely in terms of their teachers. And apparently students are not wrong in their belief that writing assignments are usually tests, for it has been amply illustrated in the research of Lil Brannon and C. H. Knoblauch, Sarah Freedman, Nancy Sommers, and Francis J. Sullivan, among others, that many teachers do respond in ways that bear out the collective student hypothesis that writing is evaluated in terms of a few selected grammar rules and discourse conventions. If grading practices contradict curriculum, that is, if teachers institute drafts as a component of pedagogy and then treat them as finished essays, it would be foolish to say that students are not learning to write, since they are learning to write what we are teaching them to write. Hence, a question for research and practice alike is not why students write as they do, but why teachers are subverting the very curriculum reforms they introduce—in this instance, undermining the potential value of drafts to their students.

Those who set out to teach writing will not be intellectually persuaded that Woolf's room surpasses the garret as the site of a theory of writing, for one must experience writing as a social practice, must have resided however briefly in the room, even to imagine oneself as a member of a community of writers. Most progressive curricula, such as those of Nan Elsasser and Patricia Irvine, Kyle Fiore and Nan Elsasser, Marge T. Murray, and Ira Shor, are organized from some such experience of community. What these curricula share with one another that they do not share with many decontextualized models of collaborative writing is the belief that collaboration is not itself the goal of curriculum, but a means to an end, namely, a way to acknowledge diverse subjective experience, the individual and collective examination of which is the goal of writing pedagogy as well as research.

The context for research and pedagogy alike is a social, historical, and political construction of the participants whose individual and collective activities inside and outside the classroom determine whether writing is set aside as a school subject or is integrated into their lives. And curriculum or research that denies, out of hand, the value of describing and examining subjective experience and the relevance of that experience to the intellectual activity of writing (not simply how to write, but why people write and under what circumstances) condemns students and their teachers to do the work of writing—exercising the skills and techniques—in isolation from the very conditions that justify writing and learning to write.

To experience, and imagine, writing as a social as well as cognitive act is in itself a form of resistance, in that it allows an individual to learn that the world is not only read, but written, and that the worlds written from the rooms occupied by, say, feminists, women, minorities, students, teachers, or progressive researchers, who do not literally have a purchase on writing, require different ways of reading. Hence, it is imperative that researchers and practitioners who value lived experience begin teaching one another how it can be studied. Teachers in the National Writing Project, for instance, might be invited to examine and critique their experiences, for their contributions have been thus far mostly dismissed as outside the *discourse* of research.

There are certainly lessons to be learned about how these examinations might be undertaken from those urban anthropologists who have begun to practice what George Marcus and Michael Fischer have recently called a *critical anthropology,* whose principles are loosely derived from critical theory, as articulated by Max Horkheimer and eloquently explicated by Martin Jay. Ethnographies grounded in this theory of *negative critique* first recommended by the founding members of the Frankfurt school and later by educational revisionists such as Michael Apple and Lois Weiss and Henry Giroux would set out to identify, describe, and document those cultural practices that prevent or interfere with the teaching of writing in colleges and universities. Roger Simon and Donald Dippo have recently described the work of *critical* ethnography in education as research that goes beyond cultural interpretation to document the politics of cultural practices. Hence, the explicit purpose of all writing research grounded in a theory of social construction is to transform pedagogy by instituting writing as a social and material political practice in which writers endeavor to reconstruct society even as they shape and construct and critique their understanding of what it means to write, learn to write, teach writing, and do research on writing.

I wish to thank the following people for their invaluable contributions to this essay: Michael Boyd, Ric DiFeliciantonio, Michelle Fine, Patricia Johnston, Virginia Kerr, Elizabeth Long, Diane Masar, Marge Murray, Mary Pratt, Janice Radway, Susan Seifert, and Francis J. Sullivan. Whatever problems remain are my own.

Tropics of Literacy

I have come to think of literacy as a social trope and the various definitions of literacy as cultural Rorschachs. By this I mean to draw attention not simply to the fact that every culture and subculture defines what it means by literacy (e.g., Heath 1983; Scribner and Cole 1981), and not even to the equally important fact that the history of the word *literacy* in a single society shows remarkable variation over time (e.g., Ohmann 1985; Resnick and Resnick 1980). Nor am I principally concerned in this article with how researchers have conceptualized literacy in order to study what John Szwed posits may well be "a plurality of literacies" extant at any given moment in a society (1981: 16). Yet, all these works, which explore historical, social, and cultural variation in literate practices, are critical to understanding that a nation can use literacy as a trope to justify or rectify social inequity. In this essay, however, I explore the systematic expression of ideology, the tropics of literacy. Because all definitions of literacy project both a *literate self* and an *illiterate other,* the tropics of literacy stipulate the political as well as cultural terms on which the "literate" wish to live with the "illiterate" by defining what is meant by reading and writing.

Adult Americans, whose literacy has recently undergone intense scrutiny, provide a particularly dramatic example of what I mean by the tropics of literacy. While the sense that "illiterates" are irrevocably different from "literates" is perhaps most apparent in anthropology, where it is customary to use literacy to distinguish between traditional and modern societies (e.g., Goody and Watt 1968), most definitions of literacy in industrialized societies presume that a similar distinction between orality and literacy obtains in the West (e.g., Ong 1982). Moreover, when we move into the area of adult literacy, definitions usually specify which texts adults need to read, hence the widely held notion of conventional literacy as "the ability to read, write, and comprehend texts on familiar subjects and to understand whatever signs, labels, instructions, and directions as are necessary to get along in one's environment" (Hunter and Harman 1979: 7). And, even though in the past decade conventional literacy in the United States has been redefined as functional literacy, Norvell Northcutt's widely cited study (1975) of the Adult Performance Level (APL) also assesses literacy as the ability to perform such literacy tasks as are considered essential to being adult: filling out job application forms correctly, for example, or understanding the check-cashing policies in supermarkets.

The APL study sorted the adult population of the United States into three groups: APL 1 (adults who function in society with difficulty), APL 2 (adults who function in society but are not proficient), and APL 3 (adults who are functional and proficient members of society). Carmen Hunter and David Harman quote an official at the U.S. Office of Education to the effect that 23 million adults are at APL 1, and 34 million are at APL 2 (1979: 26). Needless to say, the literacy crisis referred to in the popular press draws on these large numbers rather than the 5.2 million figure arrived at by a 1979 Census Bureau survey, and it is the higher figures that have been used to petition federal, state, and local government agencies and corporations for the funds necessary to launch and maintain adult literacy programs. The Bureau of the Census, working from data collected in a 1982 survey, amended its earlier figure, and reported in 1986 that between 17 million and 21 million adults are illiterate (U.S. Department of Education 1986; *Education Week* 1986). By either measure, then, a staggering number of adult Americans are now deemed to be illiterate.

Many adult literacy programs prefer functional literacy to conventional literacy, since functional literacy stresses tasks that adults might well believe to be important to their day-to-day lives. In neither case, however, were the adults in question consulted, although the definition of functional literacy that Hunter and Harman stipulate in *Adult Illiteracy in the United States* means to take their interests into account:

> *Functional literacy:* the possession of skills ***perceived as necessary by particular persons and groups*** to fulfill their own self-determined objectives as family and community members, citizens, consumers, job-holders, and members of social, religious, or other associations of their own choosing. (7; emphasis in the original)

Let me emphasize here that my reservations about defining adults as functionally literate or illiterate in no way obviate the responsibility to provide literacy education to the adults who seek programs. Instead, my reservations arise out of a critique of the APL research design, in which Francis Kazemek (1985) points out the remarkable fact that only adults in APL 1 were actually studied. In other words, while the functional literacy of the APL 1 population was tested, the literacy of the other two socioeconomic groups was inferred from the data gathered on the population of APL 1. The implication is that the population designated APL 2 and APL 3 are members of the same social group, separated only by degrees of economic, educational, and professional success, while the individuals identified as APL 1 are a socially distinct group in virtue of their individual and collective inability to decode and comprehend the reading tasks designated by the APL.

As Kazemek's criticism suggests, there are not three but two populations being defined—us and them. Given that any definition of literacy invariably postulates an illiterate "other," at issue here is not so much the validity or reliability of the APL research design, but the alien, illiterate "other" projected by this particular definition of functional illiteracy. It is plausible, at least, to question whether the point of identifying functional illiterates is that there are adults who cannot read and write well enough to function in society, or that there are adults who do not apply for jobs, keep checking accounts, file with the IRS, take out insurance policies, and otherwise participate in the literacy practices that sustain late monopoly capitalism. Were everyone actually required to understand all these forms, I suspect that many of us now considered to be functionally literate would be reassigned to APL 1. For instance, I literally do not understand any of the literature sent to me by the benefits office at my university.

I suspect that one important difference between the members of APL 1 and me is that no one seems to expect me to understand the forms and policies. To wit, my university insures my life and my health, I insure my car with a friend of a friend, and I file my tax forms according to instructions from an accountant. This cadre of institutional and corporate surrogate readers, who are supposedly comprehending these important documents on my behalf, is available to all members of the middle class, many of whom use them more extensively, of course, than I do, and some of whom would also include lawyers and brokers in their reading circle. The point I'm making is really very simple. Functional literacy may be less a matter of decoding and comprehending official documents (since to do so requires specialized knowledge of law and economics as well as written language) and more the fact that I have ready access to the resources I need to use the documents. This is what separates the literate "us" from the illiterate "them."

In *Tristes Tropiques,* Claude Lévi-Strauss tells a story about a tribal chief who, watching Lévi-Strauss make notes while talking with members of the tribe, himself took to pretending to do the same in his interactions with the anthropologist, other chiefs, and members of his tribe. Lévi-Strauss relates this anecdote in an essay called "A Writing Lesson." The lesson he says he learned, and the lesson he says he wants us to learn, is "the fact that the primary function of written communication is to facilitate slavery" (1973: 299). The chief, argues Lévi-Strauss, used writing to consolidate his power over the others. If we take this lesson in local, tribal politics home, he goes on to say, we will find that

> the systematic development of compulsory education in European countries goes hand in hand with the extension of military service and proletarianization. The fight against illiteracy is therefore connected with an increase in governmental authority over the citizens. Everyone must be able to read, so that the government can say: Ignorance of the law is no excuse. (300)

I have encountered similar though decidedly less hyperbolic claims about hegemony and literacy since first reading Lévi-Strauss's essay (e.g., Donald 1983; Olson 1983). Among other things, these essays caution against presuming that adult literacy campaigns, adult literacy programs, and adult literacy students share a common understanding of what literacy may or may not do for adults.

Working with literacy educators and sitting on the boards of adult literacy programs, for instance, has taught me that not many of the people concerned are as circumspect about the putative, absolute value of literacy as Lévi-Strauss. Recently, for instance, the *Philadelphia Inquirer* published an op-ed article, "Literacy Has Many Happy Returns," written by Ted Snowe, an active and informed corporate advocate for adult functional literacy. Snowe makes a compelling, if familiar, economic argument, a plea to the city to "invest" in literacy education and to the citizenry to volunteer as literacy tutors:

> Of course, not all people who can't read and write end up unemployed or on welfare. Nonetheless, hundreds of thousands of Philadelphians are locked out of the new economy [the information economy]. This year more money will be spent treating the symptoms of their unemployment—poverty, crime, drug and alcohol abuse—than will be spent treating one of the root causes—illiteracy. Taxpayers should be outraged at such an economically absurd system. (Snowe 1985)

In the course of his work, which includes tutoring as well as fund-raising and advocacy, Snowe has seen the positive correlations between illiteracy and poverty, crime, and alcohol and drug abuse. He has reached the same statistically unwarranted, though plausible, conclusion that many other literacy advocates have, namely, that *their* illiteracy is a personal misery whose public consequences—unemployment, crime, and so on—cannot be abated without *our* assistance. Therefore, to fund literacy programs and tutor adults is to contribute to the stability of the new economy.

Snowe's is among the most effective arguments for adult literacy education because it identifies literacy as the solution to many of the social and economic problems to which large cities are subject. To the extent that unemployment can be attributed to illiteracy, however, those in APL 2 (adults who are functionally literate but not proficient) would be more likely to benefit from literacy instruction aimed at the new information economy than those in APL 1, for whom illiteracy is only one of many variables correlated with profound poverty. Moreover, the value of literacy is not absolute, but is confounded by race and gender. For example, 15 percent of white male high school dropouts aged 22 to 34 live below the poverty line, compared to 28 percent of white females, 37 percent of black males, and 62 percent of black females (U.S. Department of Labor 1983). Clearly, literacy is neither the only nor the most important variable operating in this social equation. It certainly looks as if some people, and particularly black women, need to be more educated than others just to survive.

The Philadelphia executive and the French anthropologist have both invested literacy with the power to change the lives of illiterates by changing their relationship to society. And, because in both cases literacy is identified as the agent (or agency) of social change, it is a trope in which to construct a variety of possible relationships between a society and its members. No matter that in one version functional literacy would enfranchise the illiterate poor, who are at once a danger to themselves and to us, while in the other, literacy allows a government to surveil its literate population. The tropes invariably tell us who we are by pointing out who we are not. The danger lies not in tropes, but in using the tropics of literacy as the sole explanation of the difference between us and them. As Michelle Fine, speaking about "solutions" aimed at urban dropouts, notes, "Targeting schools as the site for social change and the hope for the next generation deflects attention and resources, critique and anger from insidious and economic inequities" (1986b: 407). Illiteracy does not explain massive unemployment any more than literacy explains bureaucracy.

If, as I have been arguing, literacy tropes invariably project a social relationship between the literate and the illiterate, the resounding failure of literacy campaigns in the industrialized nations of the West may well be a consequence of defining literacy as functional literacy. For, despite Hunter and Harman's generous definition, which focuses on "skills *perceived as necessary by particular individuals and groups* to fulfill their own self-determined objectives," most functional literacy materials define literacy conventionally as a set of reading tasks and reduce reading to lockstep decoding procedures and multiple-choice comprehension questions. Writing, when it is considered at all, is likely to be defined as filling in the blanks and signing on the dotted line (e.g., Colvin and Root 1976). Curricula designed from such materials define the functional illiterate as someone who needs to learn how to follow instructions. While individual teachers and students may well resist the curricula, and many community-based programs explicitly set out to do so (Fingeret 1984: 20-23), in this country literacy progams are funded because of a presumed relationship between illiteracy and unemployment. Hence, adult literacy materials and curricula are written from the perspective of what a literate society *believes* employed adults need to know. Very few programs are designed with the self-determined objectives of adult learners in mind, and fewer still with the goals of political empowerment advocated by Paulo Freire (1970).

Reports on successful literacy campaigns in the Third World usually document Freire's tropic of literacy as social and political empowerment. This trope of liberation, which limns a relationship of social reciprocity between the literate self and the illiterate other, emphasizes writing. In his article on "the Great Campaign of 1961" in Cuba, for instance, Jonathan Kozol (1980) mentions the 700,000 "letters to Fidel" housed in the Museum of Literacy. In their article on a vernacular literacy project at the College of the Virgin Islands in St. Thomas, Nan Elsasser and Patricia Irvine (1985) report that students used Creole to write summaries, essays, and research papers as well as letters to Creole authors and the student newspaper.

Interesting, is it not, that while the Cuban government and teachers and students in St. Thomas can envision a nation of writers, the United States dreams only of a nation of readers?

When literacy means writing as well as reading, the illiterate other is projected as someone who "talks" back, which means that curriculum must provide grounds for a literacy dialogue. Let me illustrate what I mean by these grounds with an example from my own teaching. I recently taught a graduate course called Teaching Basic Writing, in which most of the students had never taught inexperienced adult writers. It happened that one student in the class, who was teaching an adult basic education class (primarily white working-class women), wished to provide her students with an "authentic" reason to write. After a good deal of discussion, the teachers in my class decided to write the students in hers. For two months, the members of the two classes corresponded weekly. By the second week, the teacher reported that while students had earlier tired of writing after five or ten minutes, they now asked to use the first half hour of class (which more often than not was extended to an hour) to write.

The letters her students wrote are intensely personal, a virtual catalog of familial and neighborhood activities. The teachers soon learned to respond in kind so that within weeks they had exchanged a good deal of detailed information about their own lives and concerns. All successful instruction was by indirection. Students learned to format their letters, for instance, by simply reproducing the formats used by the teachers. Spelling was similarly taught and learned. Teachers simply used words that were spelled incorrectly in their responses, and when students wrote back, many of those words were correctly spelled. I mention these aspects of the correspondence because literacy instruction was one reason for corresponding. As it turned out, however, the adult students taught us a great deal that had not been anticipated. Among other things: three out of ten were facing serious health problems; in two cases the primary providers had recently lost their jobs; and one woman had recently moved into a neighborhood where there is no supermarket within walking distance.

These grounds for dialogue are a consequence of interpersonal relationships established in "The Literacy Letters." That these issues were raised and discussed in the course of writing about their lives certainly confirms that adult Americans would be better served by a critical or radical literacy curriculum (Giroux 1983) than by either a conventional or a functional literacy curriculum. Functional literacy requires them to learn to read what we write—our tropes, our worlds, our politics. The letters remind us that in our eagerness to instruct, we forget that "illiterate" others also have tropes for literacy. Dialogic literacy would require us to learn to read the unfamiliar tropes in which they write their lives.

On the Subjects of Class and Gender in "The Literacy Letters"

In "The Discourse on Language," Michel Foucault dramatizes the desire to be "on the other side of discourse, without having to stand outside it, pondering its particular, fearsome, and even devilish features" (1976: 215) in this whimsical colloquy between the individual and the institution:

> Inclination speaks out: "I don't want to have to enter this risky world of discourse: I want nothing to do with it insofar as it is decisive and final; I would like to feel it all around me, calm and transparent, profound, infinitely open, with others responding to my expectations, and truth emerging, one by one. All I want is to allow myself to be borne along, within it, and by it, a happy wreck." Institutions reply: "But you have nothing to fear from launching out; we're here to show you discourse is within the established order of things, that we've waited a long time for its arrival, that a place has been set aside for it—a place that both honours and disarms it; and if it should have a certain power, then it is we, and we alone, who give it that power." (215-16)

What Foucault and other poststructuralists have been arguing for the past fifteen or twenty years is considerably easier to state than act on: we are at once constituted and unified as subjects in language and discourse. The discursive subject is of particular interest to those of us who teach writing because language and discourse are understood to be complicit in the representation of self and others, rather than the neutral or arbitrary tools of thought and expression that they are in other modern theories, not to mention handbooks and rhetorics. Among other things, this means that since writers cannot avoid constructing a social and political reality in their texts, as teachers we need to learn how to "read" the various relationships between writer, reader, and reality that language and discourse supposedly produce.

New theories of textuality are inevitably new theories of reading. And in the field of writing, those who teach basic writers and welcome new ways to read their texts are perhaps the most likely to recognize the possibilities of discursive subjectivity. The poststructural David Bartholomae of "Inventing the University," for example, writes less confidently but more astutely of what student errors may signify than the Bartholomae of "The Study of Error," published some years earlier at the height of the field's enthusiasm for empirical research and error analysis. For the startling power of a discourse to confer authority, name errors, and rank order student texts speaks more readily to the experience of reading basic writing than promises of improved reliability or validity in the empirical study of errors. While empiricality is far from moot, it makes little difference if one is right if one is not talking about that which most concerns writing and the teaching of writing. Or, as Sharon Crowley has put it, "the quality of the power that is associated with writing varies with the degree of authority granted by a culture to its texts" (1985: 96). In this society the authority that teachers are empowered to grant to or withhold from student texts derives from the theory of textuality governing their reading.

The question then is how to read what students write. And at issue is the unquestioned power of a pedagogical authority that insists that teachers concentrate on form at the expense of content.

> I'm siting at home now when I have more time to write to you I enjoyed rending your letters. I under stand reading them one word I had a little trouble with the word virginia but know about me well that is hard but I will try.

The errors in spelling and punctuation in this passage are serious, but not nearly as egregious, I suspect, as the tradition that warrants reducing a text to its errors. Remember the anger you feel when someone corrects your pronunciation or grammar while you are in the throes of an argument and you can recover the traces of the betrayal students must experience when a writing assignment promises them seemingly unlimited possibilities for expression and the response or evaluation notes only their limitations. The errors are there, and the passage is hard to read. Yet to see only the errors strikes me as an unwarranted refusal to cede even the possibility of discursive subjectivity and authority to the woman who wrote this passage, barring of course that of basic writer, which an error analysis would without question grant her.

Changing the Subject

This is an essay about the ways discourses construct our teaching. In postmodern theories of subjectivity:

1) all subjects are the joint creations of language and discourse;
2) all subjects produced are ideological; and
3) all subject positions are vulnerable to the extent that individuals do not or will not identify themselves as the subjects (i.e., the effects) of a discourse.

Those who occupy the best subject positions a discourse has to offer would have a vested interest in maintaining the illusion of speaking rather than being spoken by discourse. Postmodern rhetoric would begin by assuming that all discourses warrant variable subject positions ranging from mostly satisfying to mostly unsatisfying for those individuals named by them. Each institutionalized discourse privileges some people and not others by generating uneven and unequal subject positions as various as stereotypes and agents. Hence, it is at least plausible to expect most, though not all, of those individuals whose subjectivity is the most positively produced by a discourse to defend its discursive practices against change. And it is equally plausible to expect some, though again not all, of those individuals whose subjectivity is the most negatively produced to resist its discursive practices. Feminists, for example, regularly resist discursive practices that represent female subjectivity solely in terms of reproductive biology. Of course, neither verbal resistance nor other material forms of protest against such reduced subject positions are universal among women.

Discursive resistance requires opportunities for resistance. Altering an institutionalized discourse probably requires an unremitting negative critique of its ideology, a critique that is most often carried out in the academy by attempting to replace a particular theory (of science or art or education or law, for example) with another. Recently, theoretical battles have proliferated to such an extent that a cover term, *critical theory,* has come to refer to a variety of ideological critiques of theory, research, and practice across the academy: critical legal studies, critical practice, critical anthropology, critical pedagogy, and so on.

Discursive resistance, however, need not be conducted in such abstract terms as we have recently witnessed in the academy. The more usual practice would be for those individuals who are ambivalent or threatened by their subject positions in a given discourse to interrupt the very notion of the unified self—the traditional Cartesian notion that the self is a transcendent and absolute entity rather than a creation of language and ideology—in their spoken and written texts. Such interruptions are likely to take one of two forms: reversing the negative and positive subject positions in a given discourse—as Carol Gilligan does in her feminist revision of the research on the development of moral reasoning among adolescent girls; or re-presenting a stereotype as an agent in a discourse the least committed to the preservation of the stereotype—as Toni Morrison does in representing African-American women and men as the agents rather than the victims of events in her novels.

Studies of these and other interruptive practices, rhetorics of resistance in which individuals shift subject positions from one discourse to another or within a discourse in their speaking and writing, would constitute empirical inquiry into the postmodern speculation that language and discourse are material to the construction of reality, not simply by-products reflecting or reproducing a set of nondiscursive, material social structures and political formations. Knowledge of multiple subject positions makes possible both the practical and the theoretical critiques that interrupt the assumption of unchanging, irreversible, and asymmetrical social and political relations between the privileged and unprivileged subjects represented in a particular discourse (see Williams 1977, especially 75-141).

What is needed is research that addresses what Stuart Hall has called "a theory of articulation," which he describes as "a way of understanding how ideological elements come, under certain conditions, to cohere together within a discourse, and a way of asking how they do or do not become articulated, at specific junctures, to certain political subjects" (1986: 53). Since articulation separates intentions from effects, or production from reception, Hall has reinserted the possibility of human agency into poststructural theory. More specifically, articulation distinguishes between the desire to be unified in a discourse and what happens in practice, namely, what individuals do in and with the unified subject positions offered them by such recognizable institutional discourses as, say, science, art, education, law, and religion or ethics.

"The Literacy Letters"

What I mean by research on the rhetorics of discursive practice and attendant practices of resistance is amply illustrated in a curriculum project I have referred to elsewhere as "The Literacy Letters" (see Brodkey 1986a). The letters were generated in the discourse of education, since they were initiated by six white middle-class teachers (four women and two men) taking my graduate course on teaching basic writing and sustained by six white working-class women enrolled in an adult basic education (ABE) class. The woman who was teaching the ABE class and taking my course hoped that corresponding would provide the students in her class with what she called an authentic reason to write—on the order of a pen-pal experience for adults. The experienced English teachers from my class, most of whom had not taught basic writing, set out to learn more about the reading and writing concerns of their adult correspondents. As for me, I welcomed the chance to study correspondence itself, which seemed to me a remarkable opportunity to examine both the production and reception of self and other in the writing and reading of personal letters.

Permission to photocopy the letters as data for research was granted by all correspondents before the first exchange. For the two months that they wrote, the correspondents agreed not to meet or talk on the phone. The data, then, are the letters written by the six pairs who wrote regularly: one pair exchanged letters eight times; one pair seven times; two pairs six times; and two pairs five times.

When the teachers first reported that they found writing the letters stressful, I attributed their anxiety to the fact that I would be reading and evaluating their letters as well as those written by the students in the ABE class. But their uneasiness persisted despite repeated assurances that I wouldn't look at or read the letters until the semester's end, a standard procedure meant to protect the educational rights of those who agree to participate in classroom research. After reading and thinking about the letters, however, I am no longer so inclined to assume that my presence as such was as threatening or intrusive as I first thought, though doubtless it contributed some to their anxiety.

Learning to Read "The Literacy Letters"

Research on basic writers (e.g., Bartholomae 1980, 1985; Perl 1979; Shaughnessy 1977) as well as my own teaching experience amply prepared me for the ungainly prose produced by the women in the ABE class. But nothing I had read or remembered from my own teaching prepared me for occasional moments of linguistic as well as discursive awkwardness from the teachers. I am not referring to the necessary clumsiness with which the teachers sought their footing before they knew anything about their correspondents, but to intermittent improprieties that occurred once several letters had been exchanged. In fact, I found these occasional lapses so perplexing that it's fair to say that the teachers' unexpected errors, rather than the students' expected ones, led me to think about the letters in terms of the poststructural discursive practices of reproduction and resistance. Only discourse, more specifically the power of a discourse over even its fluent writers, I decided, could begin to explain the errors of these otherwise literate individuals.

That educational discourse grants teachers authority over the organization of language in the classroom, which includes such commonplace privileges as allocating turns, setting topics, and asking questions, is clear from sociolinguistic studies of classroom language interaction (e.g., Stubbs 1976). Many teachers, including those in this study, attempt to relinquish their control by staging opportunities for students to take the privileged subject position of teacher in, say, group discussions or collaborative assignments that grant them, at least temporarily, a measure of control over educational discursive practice. Attempts to transform classroom discussions into conversations between peers are thwarted to the extent that teachers fail to realize that their interpersonal relationships with students, as well as their institutional ones, are constituted by educational discourse. While the power of a discourse is not absolute, neither is it vulnerable to change by individuals who ignore its power, only by those who interrupt or resist or challenge the seemingly immutable reality of unified subjectivity. In much the same way that you don't resist racism by denying that racism exists, but by confronting it in yourself and others, teachers cannot divest themselves of those vestiges of authority that strike them as unproductive by ignoring the institutional arrangements that unequally empower teachers and students.

At the outset, the teachers in this study attempted to mitigate the power of educational discourse over themselves and their correspondents by "playing" student. Their letters are replete with the desire to represent themselves as students of writing pedagogy and their correspondents as their teachers. The longest-running correspondence, for instance, was initiated by a teacher who wrote: "I think that some of the things you could tell me might help me to understand what I can do better when I try to help my students learn to improve thier [*sic*] writing." Since none of the students made suggestions about either curriculum or instruction, roles were not reversed. But making the requests seems to have mooted the possibility of the teachers practicing the most authoritarian "dialect" of educational discourse in their correspondence. To wit, no teacher reduced personal correspondence to spelling or grammar lessons; nor, for that matter, did any of the students from the ABE class ask to be taught or corrected.

Bear in mind that the writers of the letters are not held by the usual arrangements between teachers and students. To be sure, the teachers are teachers and the students are students. But theirs is what might be called an extracurricular relationship, arranged by the authorized teacher. While the teachers assiduously avoided lessons and hence avoided even the possibility of displacing the classroom teacher's authority, there are nevertheless times in the letters when it certainly looks as if by ignoring rather than contesting the authority of educational discourse, they retained control over such discursive privileges as determining what is and what is not an appropriate topic. The teachers exercise their authority infrequently but decisively, whenever one of their correspondents interrupts, however incidentally, the educational discursive practice that treats class as irrelevant to the subjectivity of teachers and students. Telegraphed by linguistic and discursive lapses, the refusal that signals the teachers' unspoken commitment to a classless discourse provokes additional and more pronounced discursive resistance from the ABE writers.

Personal Narratives in "The Literacy Letters"

Discursive hegemony on the part of the teachers is most obvious and discursive resistance on the part of the students is most dramatic during storytelling episodes. Personal correspondence evokes personal narratives. The teachers tell a variety of stories in which they represent themselves as busy professionals trying to resolve conflicts among work, family, and school. Social research on storytelling suggests that in exchange for being granted the time it takes to tell a story, the teller is expected to make it worth the listener's while by raising for evaluation or contemplation that which is problematic or unusual about the narrative conflict and its resolution (see Labov 1972; Pratt 1977). That the teachers tell stories representing themselves as guilty about their inability to find enough time is not surprising, since their busy lives have been made all the more complicated by recently adding course work to schedules already overburdened by responsibilities at work and home. Nor are the responses to their stress stories unexpected, for the women from the adult basic education class console and commiserate with the teachers in much the way that research suggests interlocutors ordinarily do. The teachers, however, occasionally respond in extraordinary ways when their correspondents reciprocate with stories about their lives.

The ABE students do not tell narratives about not having the time to fulfill their obligations to the three spheres of work, school, and family. Nor are their stories about internal conflicts like guilt. Instead, they write most frequently about external threats to their well-being and that of their families and their neighbors. While work and education often figure in their stories, they are important only insofar as they materially affect their lives: a family is besieged by the threat of layoffs; lack of educational credentials means the low paychecks and the moonlighting that rob families of time with the overworked wage earner.

Clearly teachers and students alike told class-based narratives. Yet the teachers' markedly inept responses to their correspondents' narratives suggest that the hegemony of educational discourse warrants teachers not only to represent themselves as subjects unified by the internal conflicts like guilt that preoccupy professionals, but also to disclaim narratives that represent a subject alternatively unified in its conflicts with an external material reality. This refusal to acknowledge the content of their correspondents' narratives, most explicable as a professional class narcissism that sees itself everywhere it looks, alienates the ABE writers from educational discourse and, more importantly, from the teachers it ostensibly authorizes.

Don and Dora

The seven-letter exchange between the teacher and student I'll call Don and Dora is disarming. Frequency alone suggests that both teacher and student found corresponding satisfying. For some weeks they wrote about movies, food, and their families, all topics introduced by Don, who represented himself in his initial letter as a complex subject, specifically, as a young man beset by personal failings his correspondent would find amusing:

> I won't tell you how long I like to stay in bed in the morning—though I do stay up very late at night (watching old movies)—but let's just say that it's past 11 AM. Oh well, we all have to have at least one vice. Unfortunately, I have more than one. One of my others is Chinese food. There's a Chinese food cart parked right outside the window of the library where I work, so every afternoon I dash out when the line slacks

off. . . . I usually try to get some vegetable dishes, even though I almost always end up getting the most highly caloric item on the menu.

His comedic self-presentation is amplified by this final request: "Please let me know what you're doing: do you like Chinese food (and if so, what kind?), do you like old movies (and if so, which ones?), do you think I'm too weird to write back to? I'll look forward to your responses, comments, complaints, etc." In her response, Dora picks up the topics of movies and food. "I to enjoy the old movies and (love Chinese food)," she writes, but then goes on to conclude about them both, "so [I] guess that make two of us that are (weird)." Notice that while she responds to his question—"Do you think I'm too weird to write back to?"—writing back is itself material evidence that Dora doesn't find Don's tastes *too* weird. Dora is, as she puts it, "looking forward to writing back this is my first letter I ever wrote."

Over the next few weeks, their letters follow this pattern. Don writes extended and humorous anecdotes that portray him as a man at odds with himself at work, school, and home, and Dora offers consolation by letting him know how amusing she and the other women in her class find his stories: "Rachel [her teacher] ask me to read your letter to the class we all though that your grandmother and father was funning about the candy." After dutifully playing audience for some weeks, however, Dora dramatically reverses the pattern when she asserts herself not only as a narrator, but as the narrator of tragic rather than comedic events, in a letter that in its entirety reads as follows:

> I don't have must to siad this week a good frineds husband was kill satday at 3:1 5 the man who kill him is a good man he would give you the shirt off of his back it is really self-defense but anyway I see police academy three it was funny but not is good as the first two

Dora's narrative limns as stark a reality as any represented in "The Literacy Letters." However, her abrupt shift from a narrator who reflects on the aftermath of violence to a student who answers a teacher's questions—"but anyway I see police academy three it was funny but not is good as the first two"—is, for me, one of those moments when the power of discourse seems the most absolute.

It's not implausible to imagine that in telling a narrative Dora is trying out the more positive subject position afforded narrators by the discourse of art, which Don has held throughout their correspondence. But art is only a respite, it seems, for Dora shifts quickly from narrator back to student. Yet in that brief moment when she inserts herself as the narrator, Dora takes on the more complex subjectivity afforded by the discourse of art to narrators. Though short, the story she tells is one in which the narrator's sympathies are clearly divided between the survivors—the friend and the murderer—a narrative position that Dora grounds in the extenuating circumstances of moral character (a good man "would give you the shirt off of his back") and law ("it is really self-defense"). Her narrative point of view considers not the grisly fact of murder and not even what motivated the murder, but the notion that murder is a consequence of circumstances rather than character.

Narrative strikes me as a potentially effective mode of resistance, for the rules governing storytelling more or less require Don to respond to the content of Dora's narrative. Since Dora attenuated the full interruptive force of the discourse of art on educational discourse by interjecting the comment about the movie, however, she effectively lost her hold on the rhetorical practice in which the narrative critiques a teacher's exclusive right to initiate topics. The abrupt shift from narrator back to audience returns, or offers to return, teacher and student alike to the already established subject positions of teacher/narrator and student/audience.

Even if Dora's interjection is understood as hesitation, Don might have assisted her by simply responding to the content of her story. He might have asked about motive or even asked why she says nothing about the victim. But Don's response suggests only that he is nonplussed:

> I'm sorry to hear about the problem that you wrote about last week. It's always hard to know what to say when the situation is as unusual as that one. I hope that everything's getting a little better, at least for you trying to know what to say and do in that situation.

Several issues about the fragility of the unity that even the most privileged subjects are able to achieve in language and discourse come immediately to mind. Most obvious, perhaps, is the syntactic lapse in the final sentence ("I hope that everything is getting a little better, at least for *you* trying to know what to say and do in that situation"). Less obvious, though equally to the point, is the way that Don's linguistic facility, under the circumstances, only amplifies the discursive inadequacy of this passage as a response to the content of her narrative.

Bearing in mind that she has just told a story in which the "problem" is the aftermath of murder—her friend's husband is dead and the good man who killed him presumably faces prison—the assertion that this is a matter of manners ("It's always hard to know what to say when the situation is as unusual as that one") is not simply inappropriate. It constitutes a discursive retreat that threatens to reconstitute Don and Dora in the most profoundly alienated subject relationship of all—self and other—and to give over their more or less satisfying discursive relationship as narrator and audience. Even the demonstrative adjective, *that*, underscores the distance Don places between himself and the world in which he resides and the other and the world in which she resides. The contrast between this awkward first paragraph and the plans to visit his grandmother on Mother's Day that complete his letter effectively reiterates the terms of their continued correspondence.

In her next letter, Dora again responds to the content of Don's letter, "I am glad to hear that you are going to see your grandmother." And though she makes no further mention in this or any future letter of the murder, she writes "I hope you get more energy about work," which is followed by "I wouldn't want to see you living in Kensington with the rest of us bums. ha ha." It certainly looks as if she has acknowledged the threat of othering by noting that his self-proclaimed and amply documented laziness throughout their correspondence would, in the eyes of many, make him one of the others—"the rest of us bums"—whose subjectivity he's denying. That her class antagonism increases after the next letter, in which he narrates in the usual humorous detail his visit with his grandmother, is evident in the fact that for the first time she makes no reference to his anecdote and ends a brief account of her own Mother's Day with "I got call back to work today. I am very nervous about it. it like started a new job." In his next letter, in which he makes no mention of her job, Don follows yet another extended narrative about a day at the beach with "Keep cool and write soon!" But this time Dora ignores both the narrative and the imperatives and does not write again.

Don's response is characteristic of the kind of discursive uneasiness that arises whenever one of the students interrupts the educational practice that deems such working-class concerns as neighborhood violence irrelevant. And while this is admittedly one of the more dramatic examples, it suggests the extent to which unacknowledged tension over the control of subject positions contributes to rather than alleviates class antagonism, for we see that the teacher's desire to be preserved as the unified subject of an educational discursive practice that transcends class overrides the student's desire to narrate herself as a subject unified in relation to the violence that visited her working-class neighborhood.

Rita and Esther

The second example comes from the six-letter exchange between an experienced secondary English teacher I'll call Rita and the most fluent and prolific writer from the ABE class, a student I'll call Esther. The set itself is unusual, since these are the only correspondents whose letters are often of similar length. From the outset, it's easy to see that Esther is not only actively resisting playing "student" but sometimes even tries to play "teacher." In response to Rita's initial letter, for instance, Esther first compliments her—"My classmates and I read your wonderful letter"—but then faults her for what she neglected to mention: "You never stated your age or your country in the letter. And also where your Grandmother's home was." And unlike the other ABE writers, in her first and subsequent letters Esther asks for information that Rita has neither offered nor alluded to:

> What is it like where you live and what are the shopping areas like. How is the transportation and the Climate there. What kind of food do you like to eat. You didn't say if you were married, or if you have children. Please write back and let me know.

Though this is admittedly an insight considerably improved by hindsight, the class antagonism that erupts later can probably be traced to Rita's ambivalance about their relationship, for she seems unable either to accept Esther's assumption that they are peers or to assert herself as a teacher. Rita's reluctance to declare herself as either a teacher or a peer may explain her refusal to do more than name the suburb she lives in or the nearby mall in answer to Esther's questions. In short, Rita replies but does not answer Esther's questions.

In a letter near the end of their correspondence, following yet one more futile effort to establish what Rita's life is like—"Do you live near a beach or the shore? Are you going anywhere special this Summer?"—Esther writes this explanation in response to Rita's comment that she sounded "a little discouraged" in her last letter:

> I'm going to have to look for another house because, the Restate is Selling the house unless somebody invests in it and wants me to stay his or her tennant. That is why I was a little discourage because I didn't have a chance to save any money. I'll still answer your letters. Thank you for writing back.

This is a remarkable passage if only because it is one of the few times in the letters when anyone mentions money by name. There are plenty of coded references to money: vacations taken or not taken, the buying of gifts, the cost of public transportation and food. But this particular statement is about money, about the simple economic fact that changing housing requires capital. And given what Esther has written, Rita's response strikes me as a perverse misreading:

> It is difficult to save money. Do you have any idea where you will move? What kind of home are you planning to buy? Interest rates are low now.

The peculiarity arises in the increasing unconnectedness of Rita's sentences to Esther's assertions. The first sentence is a response to Esther's assertion that she hasn't "had a chance to save any money." And the second sentence relates to Esther's claim that she will probably have to move. But in light of what Esther wrote, the assumption that Esther is planning to buy a house or that interest rates are of any consequence to her is, to say the least, surprising. That the question confounds Esther is evident in her next letter, which begins with a passing reference to Rita's sister, whose illness Rita mentioned in her last letter, followed by a brief but pointed attempt to correct the misunderstanding:

> I'm very sorry to hear about your sister. I hope she gets better. About the house. The only way I could buy a house is by hitting a number in the Lotto.

As lessons in elementary economics go, this is about as clear as any I know. Yet Rita's response to this assertion is, on the face of it, even more bizarre than her statement about interest rates. To wit, she ignores Esther's topic, which is housing, and reintroduces gambling, lotto, as a topic they might discuss:

> Do you play Lotto frequently? I never think that I can ever win one of those lotteries. Did you ever know anyone who won? Some people play faithfully.

This is a near-perfect example of cross talk, for two conversations are now in play—one about housing and another about gambling. And were this a conversation between peers, Rita would be charged with illicitly changing the topic, since it is she who introduced the conversational gambit in which Esther's instructive hyperbole—"the only way I could buy a house is if I win the Lotto"—is taken at its face value, and lotto, which is not the topic but the comment, is transformed into the topic, now in the form of questions about gambling. It's a familiar teacher's gambit for controlling what does and does not count as knowledge, a remnant, perhaps, of the institutionalized silencing that Michelle Fine suggests "more intimately informs low-income, public schooling than relatively privileged situations" (1987: 158).

The salient fact here is that educational discourse empowers teachers to determine what is worthwhile in a student's contributions, presumably even if that judgment has little or no linguistic basis and even if a teacher-student relationship is not entirely warranted. Remember that Esther has been representing herself as an adult whose financial status is precarious and that she has gone to some pains not to occupy the student position that Rita has finally assigned her. It is in Esther's final letter, in which she makes one last attempt to establish subjective parity between herself and Rita, that we see the devastating pedagogical consequences of preserving this particular privilege of educational discursive practice:

> I don't play the Lotto everyday except on my birthday when it July 11 (7/11). I'm really messing up this letter. I'm going to an award dinner on May 30th at 7 p.m. And when I get a lucky number. I don't know anyone that ever won. Thank you for your nice letter. Bye for now.

Esther wrote better letters at the beginning than at the end of the semester. The disintegration of syntax ("when it" for "which is") in this, her last letter, augurs the disappearance of the working-class adult subject she has been representing and the articulation of the adult basic writer, a subject unified by its errors, its sentence fragments ("And when I get a lucky number") and its rhetorical disjunctures (the sentences and phrases whose meanings are recoverable only by association). That Esther sees the failure as her own ("I'm really messing up this letter") echoes Foucault's assertion that it is the power of discourse to create the illusion that "it is we, and we alone, who give it that power." Finally overwhelmed by educational discourse, the adult subject retreats into silence.

Ellen and Pat

The eight-letter exchange between the student and teacher I will call Pat and Ellen is by many standards, including my own, the most successful not simply because they wrote the most often, but because Pat's letters grew longer and her errors fewer over the two months she corresponded with Ellen. While she shares the other teachers' aversion to class, Ellen differs considerably from them in her initial and repeated representation of herself as unified in relation to family: "I have been married for 21 years," "[I am] the mother of two teenagers," "I'm a very family-centered person." Ellen's representation of her familial self is often completed or articulated by Pat, when, for example, she writes, "I'm all so marry for 22 1/2 year. I have 4 kids." The self unified in relation to family is reminiscent of that represented in many of the working-class narratives, except that the self articulated in their letters is decidedly female.

That gender is a crucial dimension of their subjectivity first becomes apparent when Ellen responds to Pat's physical description of herself with this measured assertion of identification: "It sounds as though you and I look somewhat alike." In this instance, it is Ellen who articulates or completes a representation of self initiated by Pat and hence Ellen who identifies herself as the embodied female subject represented in Pat's physical description. This particular articulation stands out because it is the only corporeal representation of self in the letters and because it is also the only self-representation offered by one of the students that a teacher articulates. To be sure, Ellen's articulation is tenuous, qualified immediately by "somewhat," and later by assertions such as "I'm trying to lose some weight before the summer season comes so I won't be so embarrassed in my bathing suit" that suggest the middle-class woman's all-too-familiar uneasy relationship to her body.

In the course of their reciprocal articulation, and the co-construction of themselves as gendered subjects, Pat and Ellen tell and respond to stories that narrate their shared concerns as mothers. And it is as mother-women that they ignore the class differences that overwhelm the correspondents in the other two examples. Their mutual concern for their children's education, for instance, overrides material differences between their children's actual access to education. Ellen writes that she and her husband will be traveling to Williamsburg to bring their daughter home from college for the summer: "So far, each year that we've gone we've had to move her in the rain. It would be nice to be able to keep dry for once during all of the trips back and forth to the car." Pat advises Ellen to "think positive," responding not to the fact that Ellen's daughter attends a private college while her son goes to a local community college, but to the prediction that it will probably rain. In what appears to be yet another attempt to lift Ellen's spirits, Pat then recalls that she, her husband, and three children took a trip to Williamsburg eight years earlier, about which she has only this to say: "Williamsburg is a beautiful place."

Toward the end of their correspondence, Ellen and Pat recount their experiences of Mother's Day. Ellen's story is short:

> I hope you had an enjoyable Mother's Day. Did your family treat you to dinner? B [Ellen's daughter] cooked the meal and we had a combination Mother's Day and birthday celebration. My husband was one of those Mother's Day presents when he was born so every eighth year his birthday and Mother's Day fall on the same weekend so it was quite a festive time with lots going on.

Pat responds with an elaborate narrative, at least four times longer than any letter she has written, in the course of which she introduces class concerns that unify her identity as the mother and hence differentiate her experience as a mother from Ellen's. In other words, Pat's narrative interrupts their mutually constructed gender identity with a representation of herself as a subject unified in relation to Mother's Day that differs considerably from the self represented in Ellen's narrative.

In the first of five episodes, Pat establishes mood, explaining that on the Thursday evening before Mother's Day, after finally succeeding in bathing and putting the younger children to bed, she found herself "down hartit" and worrying about how hard her husband works at his two jobs and how his not being at home much means that she feels "like a mom and a dad." She follows this orientation to her state of mind with a second episode in which her two older children ask what she wants for Mother's Day. She reports telling her son that "a card will do" but confiding to her daughter that "what I want you can't affordit." Pressed by the daughter to tell, she admits to wanting "a ciling fane for my dinning room." Pat indicates that a ceiling fan is out of the question by writing "she laugh and so did I laugh." The third episode, which opens with an account of the complicated child-care arrangements made in order for her son to take her window shopping for ceiling fans that Friday evening, includes a brief description of the shopping spree ("There are lots of fanes to look at but I like this one fane a lots"); a scene in which the son surprises her by giving her the money to buy the fan; and an account of what happens when they return home where the children are waiting ("They all where happy for mom but not as thrill as I was inside of me"). On Saturday, the fourth episode begins with a gift of flowers from her son and his "girl friend" and concludes with dinner with the younger children at McDonald's, where a young woman at the counter tells Pat that her son "is an inspiration to the young people here" who "miss he but there is hope for the future." (In a previous letter Pat has explained that her son worked at McDonald's for a year and a half while attending a local community college, but had since taken a job at a hospital, where, after three promotions, he was making 10 percent more than he had as manager of the night shift at McDonald's.) She concludes the fourth episode with "I was so proud of him. Went I was told this." The fifth and final episode begins on Mother's Day morning with her husband making breakfast, after which she receives a box of candy from the smaller children, a card containing ten dollars from all the children, two "shorts sets" from her grandson, and yet another box of candy from the son's "girl friend." Reflecting on events in the conclusion of her letter, Pat writes: "I was surprize it was a beautiful motherday weekend. I feel like I writing a book so I am lifeing now."

The demonstrations of familial affection in Pat's narrative apparently resolve her internal conflict (discouragement). In a family where money is scarce—the husband works two jobs, the son holds a full-time job while attending community college, and the daughter is employed—the members shower the mother with cash and commodities. Rather than confine their celebration of the mother to service (cooking for her or dining out) the family extends it to include both the material tokens (the flowers, the fan, the clothes, and the candy) and the thrill of consumption (the material event of shopping and paying for the fan). The ritual acts of consumption and service that dramatize the mother's value in this working-class family temporarily align all its members with the economy. In other words, the economic realities that are continually threatening its unity are replaced by a four-day fantasy in which the family compensates the mother for her emotional and physical labor.

Middle-class families do not ordinarily celebrate motherhood with consumption rituals. What Ellen has described is the familiar middle-class service ritual in which the mother is released from the specific task of cooking, a symbol of the domestic responsibilities that threaten to alienate mothers who also work outside the home. In response to Pat's narrative, Ellen writes, "I enjoyed hearing about all your very nice Mother's Day surprises. It sounds as though you have a very loving and considerate family. They must really appreciate how hard you work and all of the many things you do for them." Ellen's is a gracious comment that fully acknowledges their shared understanding of mothers' work and once again articulates their mutual identity as gendered subjects. But Ellen's response fails to articulate Pat's representation of her own and, by extension, Ellen's subjectivity as contingent on class. It is not just that their families understand the mother differently. I suspect that the working-class celebration of the mother would strike Ellen as too much and that the middle-class celebration would strike Pat as too little.

Differences in their material circumstances separate them as mothers (neither Ellen nor her middle-class family needs ritual relief from economic hardships), and Ellen's comment fails to acknowledge that Pat's class-based narrative places them in distinct rather than the same subject positions as women.

Ellen concludes her letter with a suggestion that draws Pat's attention to what is not said: "Since this is the last week of your classes you can wrtie [*sic*] me at my home address if you think that you will have the time and would like to continue writing. I know that I would enjoy hearing from you." Pat understands the absence of any expressed desire to write as well as read her letters to mean that Ellen has lost the enthusiasm for writing she expressed in earlier correspondence: "At first I was nervous about writing to someone I didn't know, but now I enjoy writing them and look forward to your letter each week." By invoking the institutional auspices under which they have been corresponding—"this is the last week of your classes"—Ellen effectively shifts from the discourse of art in which they have both been representing and articulating their subjectivity as mothers in personal narratives to the educational discourse in which Pat would presumably be a student writing for a teacher.

Pat interrupts the shift in discourse and subject positions that Ellen has suggested when she writes, "I would like to know, if you would still wiriting me, or not if not it has been nice writing to you. I don't know if it help you are not, I know it has help me a lot. Thank you very must." Pat offers yet another version of their educational relationship in which she and Ellen would continue to learn from one another by corresponding, but she makes it clear, I think, that the decision to write as well as read is Ellen's. And Ellen chooses not to write back.

Conclusion

Since the late 1970s, that is, since the publication of Pierre Bourdieu and Jean-Claude Passeron's *Reproduction in Education, Society and Culture,* many teachers and parents, and some administrators and social theorists and social scientists, have been concerned about the extent to which schools not only tolerate but legitimate the very forms of classism, racism, and sexism that American education is publicly charged with eliminating. I mention this by way of pointing out that law provides educational opportunity for those it designates as the subjects of social and economic discrimination. Indeed, it is the state that provides a good deal of the funding for the adult basic education program that the working-class students in the study were attending. Yet the data remind us that law does not protect these students from the dialect of educational discourse in which a teacher's control over discursive practice is contingent on the ideology that classroom language transcends class, race, and gender.

The teachers in this study are not ogres—far from it. They are energetic and inventive practitioners committed to universal education. In their writing, however, that commitment manifests itself in an approach to teaching and learning that many educators share in this country, a view that insists that the classroom is a separate world of its own, in which teachers and students relate to one another undistracted by the classism, racism, and sexism that rage outside the classroom. Discursive hegemony of teachers over students is usually posed and justified in developmental terms—as cognitive deficits, emotional or intellectual immaturity, ignorance, and, most recently, cultural literacy—any one of which would legitimate asymmetrical relationships between its knowing subjects, teachers, and its unknowing subjects, students. To the credit of the teachers who participated in this study, none took the usual recourse of justifying their discursive control by focusing on errors in spelling, grammar, and mechanics that are indubitably there and that make reading the letters as difficult as reading Lacan, Derrida, Foucault, or Althusser. Yet the teachers frenetically protected educational discourse from class, and in their respective refusals to admit class concerns into the letters, they first distanced and then alienated themselves from their correspondents.

While educational discourse defends its privileged subjects against resistance, against the violence that Dora narrates, against Esther's lesson in economics, and even against Pat's much celebrated Mother's Day, the linguistic and rhetorical uneasiness with which these attempts to articulate working-class subjectivity were met suggests that the class-free discourse that seems immutable in theory is, in practice, a source of some ambivalence for the teachers in this study. What is immediately challenged by the narratives is the rhetorical practice in which the privileges of one subject—to tell stories or decide what the topic is—materially diminish the rights of other subjects. What is ultimately challenged is the ideology that class and, by extension, race and gender differences are present in American society but absent from American classrooms. If that's true, it is only true because the representation by students of those concerns inside educational discourse goes unarticulated by teachers.

To teach is to authorize the subjects of educational discourse. We have all been faced with the choice that Pat gave Ellen. To say no to writing is to say no to differences that matter to those students who live on the margins of an educational discourse that insists that they articulate themselves as the subjects teachers represent, or not at all. To say yes to writing is to say yes to those alternative subjectivities that Dora, Esther, and Pat represent in their writing and that are left unchallenged when they are not articulated by Don, Rita, and Ellen. In this instance, teachers and students alike lose the opportunity to question the extent to which class figures in any individual's rendering of a unified self. Resistance inside educational discourse is then a practice in cooperative articulation on the part of students and teachers who actively seek to construct and understand the differences as well as the similarities between their respective subject positions.

The author wishes to thank the students in her class and Rachel Martin and the students in her adult basic education class for generously contributing their letters to this study. She also gratefully acknowledges those whose advice she sought during the drafting of this essay: Mark Clark, Michelle Fine, Ellen Garvey, Henry Giroux, Diane Masar, Ellen Pollak, and Jan Radway.

WRITING CRITICAL ETHNOGRAPHIC NARRATIVES

This article assumes that educational anthropologists are interested in critical theory, or what Marcus and Fischer called "a renewal of the critical function of anthropology as it is pursued in ethnographic projects at home" (1986: 112), because critical theory argues that social institutions, such as schools, are sites of cultural hegemony. In other words, I am presuming that educational anthropologists, like many other academics, are interested in grounding their research in a theory of social construction because they wish not only to describe and analyze social practices but also to interrupt those social practices they believe oppress certain designated classes inside educational institutions, namely, students, teachers, minorities, and women. Hence, whether one's interest in cultural criticism derives from the work of the founding members of the Frankfurt school or from that of educational revisionists, such as Friere's Pedagogy of the Oppressed *(1970), Bowles and Gintis's* Schooling in Capitalist America *(1976), Bourdieu and Passeron's* Reproduction in Education, Society and Culture *(1977), Apple and Weiss's* Ideology and Practice in Schooling *(1983), and Giroux's* Theory and Resistance in Education *(1983), to name only a few, the goal of critical ethnography is always the same: to help create the possibility of transforming such institutions as schools—through a process of negative critique.*

As I am using the term here, a *negative critique* is any systematic, verbal protest against cultural hegemony. It might be spoken or written, addressed to any number of audiences, and delivered in any of a variety of forms, not the least important of which is our own curriculum and pedagogy. In this article I focus on some issues that researchers who wish to advocate for change by writing *critical* ethnographic narratives are likely to encounter, and I confine my remarks to the formulation of narratives written expressly for academic readers. For most if not all scholars, academic publication determines whether or not we will be asked to address any of the other audiences that constitute what Simon and Dippo have called the "public sphere" (1986). It is worth remembering that academics are invited or allowed to speak on such public matters as education not simply because they are well informed, but because they are affiliated with some respected academic institution or school of thought. Thus, before entering any other public dialogue on education, academics demonstrate the possible worth of their contributions by first getting a hearing within the academy.

In the case of ethnographers who first formulate a public narrative for academic readers, it seems likely that this narrative, which is told to other academics, will become the text to which all other tellings will refer. In other words, once the *academic* narrative has been formulated and published, that narrative is likely to function as the authoritative text to which all subsequent retellings and problems in interpretation will refer. In any event, storytelling ordinarily works this way, or at least that's the way it seems to work when storytellers have reason to believe that some listeners or readers already may have heard or read the story. The worst-case scenario for storytellers, of course, is cross-examination, a legally sanctioned form of public talk in which inconsistencies between a signed statement—the official narrative—and a verbal retelling of events under oath in court can have extraordinary consequences. I mention it here because I believe that the narrative that is first told to and for academics probably functions as the official narrative and thus exercises a similar kind of control over the content and the expression of content in subsequent tellings in the public sphere.

Negative Critique

If this is the case, then the critical ethnographic project—negative critique—is made all the more difficult, though I believe not impossible, if researchers must satisfy the expectation of systematic protest against cultural hegemony in a narrative written to meet the conventional expectation that scholarship is, by definition, an unbiased account of events told by a disinterested researcher. A narrator who explicitly sets out to perform a negative critique is an undeniably interested researcher, for there is an a priori assumption that hegemonic practices occur in all institutions in which power is unequally distributed. So, an ethnographer who enters the scene on the presumption that the social arrangements in a particular school or classroom will favor the interests of a dominant group is undeniably looking for hegemonic practices. It is, however, arguable whether or not the topic of hegemony is any different from the more familiar ones in anthropology—kinship or metaphor or structure. To presume hegemony is to be guided by the theory and previous research; to identify, describe, and analyze its particular forms in a particular setting is well within the tradition of scholarship.

The topic is academic as long as researchers bear in mind that hegemony is not a fact but a construct that derives its meaning and value within a theory that argues that social arrangements are not immutable because hegemonic practices are produced in and sustained by a system that is socially constructed. To work within the theory is to presume, however, that the point of research is both to identify hegemonic practices and to articulate contradictions in the social system that would make those practices vulnerable. And it is, of course, the explicit use of research to advocate for change that makes critical research academically suspect, for it is widely believed that scholarship and advocacy either are or should be kept distinct, if only to protect academics from undue influence from powerful constituencies outside the academy.

Elsewhere I have argued that epistemological upheavals in the humanities and social sciences, and particularly in anthropology, make it difficult to maintain the position that most academic arguments are all that different from what is sometimes called everyday logic or mundane reasoning (Brodkey 1987d). Let me be more specific. Negative critique is at once a story of cultural hegemony and an argument for social change. Therefore, an ideologically candid narrator is running the risk that far too many readers will reject the narrative out of hand as an academic tall tale, unless some provision is made for calling into question the belief that while scholarship persuades readers by appealing to the universal and immutable laws of logic and reason, advocacy persuades by appealing to the contingent and mutable emotions and sentiments of readers (Toulmin 1957; Perelman and Olbrechts-Tyteca 1969). To make the argument that all research is contingent on a discursive practice, that its very coherence as research depends on the viability of a discourse or ideology that supports it, is not enough. Not all academics are persuaded by the arguments in the works of, say, Michel Foucault. Fortunately, it is not necessary that all readers be persuaded by critical ethnographies, only that they accept them as a viable form of scholarship. Hence, there is a sense in which negative critique is a pedagogical undertaking, insofar as it is necessary to teach readers how to understand and evaluate a critical ethnographic narrative.

As I see it, the problem confronting critical ethnographers is much the same as the one Samuel Beckett and Bertolt Brecht met when they first produced such non-Aristotelian plays as *Waiting for Godot* and *The Mother* for middle-class audiences. Their audiences had grown accustomed to viewing plays formulated according to the *Poetics,* and hence applied such Aristotelian categories as temporal unity to evaluate these new, non-Aristotelian dramas. Likewise, those who have grown accustomed to writing and reading ethnographic narratives in which the narrator's political interest is implied rather than stated will need to be shown how explicit cultural critique is possible inside academic discourse.

The point I'm trying to make is that whenever one wishes to tell stories in ways that contradict the way stories are usually told, one needs to make it worth the reader's time to learn how to read, interpret, and evaluate a new narrative form *and* make it possible for readers to do so. I think that the increased interest in critical everything (critical teaching, critical legal studies, critical medical anthropology) suggests that the first condition is being met, for there seems to be a growing academic readership, judging by academic conferences, journals, and presses, prepared to see if critical social science research is worthwhile. Presuming this to be the case, it remains to be seen how ethnographers might go about teaching themselves to write narratives that are consistent with critical theory, and to teach others to read and evaluate them *as critical ethnographic narratives.*

I am arguing that critical narratives be written and read as yet another kind of academic discourse, as narratives that can be understood and evaluated in terms of critical theory. But, in order to be understood within the context of critical theory, to have this research judged first in terms of its own theoretical propositions—as one might first evaluate ethnographies of language in the classroom with respect to the linguistics used to analyze classroom language interactions—we will need to ask what makes a critical narrative *critical.*

Toward a Theory of Critical Narrative

I suggest that we broach the problem of writing and reading critical ethnographic narratives from the vantage point of narratology, a branch of literary theory that studies systematic variation in narratives. And, in the interests of clarity, I confine my remarks about narrative to the work of Seymour Chatman (1978), in whose theory a narrative consists of story and discourse. So, one of the first things critical ethnographers will need to do is to be more circumspect about using *story* when they mean *narrative.* By *story,* Chatman means the events, and by *discourse,* the expression of events in a narrative; or, if you like, story is the what and discourse is the how of narrative. Story and discourse is a simple and useful distinction, insofar as when narrators focus on the story, readers tend to forget that someone is telling it, and when the focus is on the telling, the discourse, readers are unable to forget that someone is telling the story.

Since critical theory invariably generates stories about cultural hegemony, the specific narrative problem for ethnographers is how to tell the story in ways consistent with both scholarship and negative critique. In principle, attention to discourse as an ideology, that is, presuming that a way of telling is also a way of knowing, is perfectly consistent with both scholarship and advocacy that derives from critical theory. Critical theory presumes that cultural hegemony is materially produced in language. In addition, there has been a fair amount of research in support of the presumption that in the course of privileging those ways of knowing and telling (the ideologies) that serve dominant interests such as capitalism, schools ignore other ways of knowing and telling that might speak more directly or fruitfully to the interests of nondominant groups. I have in mind work such as Anyon's study (1983) of the high school history textbooks used in urban working-class schools, in which she shows that very little space is given to the history of labor unions, and that very little of what is included concerns successful strikes. This and other studies like it are very good at revealing how these histories serve corporate ideology, but they also remind us that the goal of critical research is not to replace one ideology with another (that is, to replace corporate histories with labor histories), but to point out the ideological warranting of history as it is told in these corporate texts.

Critical narrators, then, are narrators whose self-consciousness about ideology makes it necessary for them to point out that all stories, including their own, are told from a vantage point, and to call attention to the voice in which the story is being told. In critical narratives, it is from the narrative stance or conceptual vantage point of critical theory that a story of cultural hegemony is generated. That means that the events related have been *conceptualized* by a narrator who sees, organizes, interprets, and narrates social events in terms of critical theory. Where another ethnographer might "see" a particular social event as worth relating because it illustrates how conflict was resolved or provides an interesting case for a discourse analysis of language interaction in a classroom, the critical ethnographer will consider an event worth recording and reporting because it exemplifies a hegemonic practice.

There are problems involved in sustaining a conceptual narrative stance, particularly because ethnographers, having once launched a narrative, are inclined to present material from what Chatman calls the narrative stance of perception, in which a narrator is presumed to be an eyewitness to a story that happens independent of both ideology and narrator. In other words, once they have explained their presence on the scene, which is often done in an introductory personal narrative (Pratt 1986), ethnographers tend not to draw the reader's attention to the fact that a story is being told. Needless to say, experience and story are often confounded when a story is told as if it were the event witnessed.

I am arguing, then, that uninterrupted third-person ethnographic narratives effectively revert to perceptual rather than conceptual narrative stances. The assumption of perceptual narrative stance is so common in book-length ethnographies that even narrators like Shirley Brice Heath in *Ways with Words* (1983) who have already identified their narrative stances in introductory personal narratives are seemingly absent. Consider this passage, in which perception and conception are confounded by the use of the third-person historical present:

> On Friday afternoon . . . as soon as the children get home from school, the pace in Trackton begins to change. The yards are swept, and riding toys are put on the front porches, as all wait for the paychecks to come home. More often than not, the paycheck has been cashed, and the father or mother will bring the goodies to be distributed. Potato chips, light bread (store-bought loaves of white bread), apples or oranges, small plastic toys, and tiny bags of candy or gum are the usual favorites. (70-71)

The use of what is commonly called the *ethnographic present,* the historical present, which gives this passage its immediacy, also confounds story and experience by the very fact that the reader cannot locate the narrator. Are we to understand "Friday afternoon" as an unchanging sequence of events that constitutes a virtually uninterruptible reality? If so, from this perceptual narrative stance is told a story so profoundly determinist that the historically present set of events appears to me to be unchangeable.

There is, moreover, an unmistakable and awkward similarity between the customary use of the ethnographic present (in which ethnographers represent data as at once immediate and irremediable) and the use of the historical present in colonial travel narratives (in which explorers reported their experiences of exotic peoples). Consider, for example, John Barrow's description of the Bushman cited in Pratt's "Scratches on the Face of the Country; or, What Mr. Barrow Saw in the Land of the Bushmen" (1985):

> Confined generally to their hovels by day, for fear of being surprised and taken by the farmers, they sometimes dance on moonlight nights from the setting to the rising of the sun. . . . His cheerfulness is the more extraordinary, as the morsel he produces to support existence is earned with danger and fatigue. . . . The bulbs of the iris, and a few gramineous roots of a bitter herb and pungent taste, are all that the vegetable kingdom affords him. By the search of these the whole surface of the plain near the horde was scratched. (119-20)

The perceptual narrative stance in this passage also represents the eyewitness narrator as the instrument rather than the agent of the narrative. And here, too, the use of the third-person historical present lends the scene an immediacy that seems immutable. In this case, it is clearly a narrative stance that presents the indigenous population as incorrigibly cheerful despite the constant threat of annihilation from war and famine. Given that these very people were subsequently colonized, one begins to wonder to what extent a seemingly innocent aesthetic device such as a perceptual narrative stance in the historical present may have contributed to a belief that opposition would be negligible. I am not arguing that Heath intends readers to see the residents of Trackton as wholly determined by history, but I am suggesting that the effect of the uninterrupted historical present makes it possible to conclude that "Friday afternoon" obviates the possibility of change by confounding story and experience.

Having made such a strong and admittedly hyperbolic imputation against adopting a perceptual narrative stance, as I see it manifested in the practice of writing in the ethnographic present, let me caution against assuming that the solution is simply to tell critical ethnographies from a conceptual narrative stance. While I think it to be both theoretically sound and honest to draw attention to one's ideological position as narrator, the conceptual stance explains only that the story generated from critical theory will concern cultural hegemony. It is in discourse, in the telling of the story, that critical ethnographers are most able to enact negative critique. In Chatman's account of narrative discourse, some narrative voices are more audible than others, and a narrative voice is made most audible by interrupting the flow of the story and calling attention to the fact of narration. In other words, instead of a reader doing what I did with Heath's narrative, critical ethnographic narrators would interrupt their own stories.

The best example of marking narrative voice in an ethnography that I know about comes in Magda Lewis and Roger Simon's "A Discourse Not Intended for Her: Learning and Teaching within Patriarchy," which tells the story of how Simon's graduate seminar, Discourse, Text, and Subjectivity, favored the discursive practice of Simon and those male students who also used it by silencing the women. It's an old story that many of us have told and heard any number of times. What distinguishes their narrative and makes it a negative critique, rather than just another story about cultural hegemony, is a very simple and salient, interruptive technique that might be called scripted turn-taking. Simply put, Lewis and Simon take turns commenting on the story, and we know and believe that because their commentary is labeled "Magda Lewis" and "Roger Simon."

It soon becomes clear that although her story and his story are about the silencing of the women (that critical theory is generating the story), her voice and his voice speak of different experiences of hegemony. The dramatic moment in their narrative concerns the class discussions of Janice Radway's *Reading the Romance* (1984). At the end of a paragraph summarizing the study and explaining its place in the course, Simon recalls its unexpected additional importance this way: "What provoked me to rethink my pedagogy was not our examination of women reading romance but the experience of the women students' reading Radway's text under the determinant conditions of our graduate seminar" (Lewis and Simon 1986: 463). Lewis's explanation of her own and other women students' thoughts is not so brief, though the following seems to summarize her position: "In part the reason the text of the book enraged us was the context within which we read it and the realization that what was going on with the women in Radway's study was precisely what was going on with us in the classroom" (463). The turn-taking draws attention to their respective narrative voices, insofar as readers are able to hear that Lewis and Simon did not have the same or even a common experience, even though they agree that the story is about silencing. In this passage, it might even be said that while each is voicing an experience of an interested participant-observer, the effect is to clarify that Lewis's urgent interest and resistance is the catalyst for Simon's reevaluation of his material contribution to the silencing of women students in the classroom.

The narrative lesson one learns, however, is that in voicing their differences narrators can refer to some of the complexity of experience that any story necessarily reduces. My argument is that a critical voice can do this by pointing out disparities between the story and the experience, in this instance by calling attention to the fact that the consequences of silence are unevenly felt by these two participants. In turn, their attempt to document the unevenness of their respective experience seems to me an effective demonstration of why theory, including critical theory, without research on practice is dangerously abstract.

Critical Narrative as Negative Critique

New ways of writing require new ways of reading. What Lewis and Simon have done in their text is make it possible for readers to join them in struggling with the difficult and necessary process of voicing two experiences of silencing, by showing us that the story of cultural hegemony is experienced differently by different people. Voicing these differences *is* the negative critique, out of which arises the possibility for transforming that classroom into a place where women's voices as well as men's can be heard. In much the same way that the women are represented as resisting what Lewis and Simon call "male discourse" by questioning the easy authority with which Simon encouraged students to distance themselves from the women in Radway's study—by keeping the talk theoretical—the marked narrative voices in which Lewis and Simon comment on the story interrupt the authority of an academic tradition that tells stories from the vantage point of theories but disregards the possibility that practice critiques theory, that the story generated by theory can be evaluated in the discourse that recalls experience.

Those of us who look to critical theory for a way to transform educational practices will need to teach ourselves how to narrate stories of cultural hegemony that make it clear that a negative critique is the process by which each of us confronts our respective inability to comprehend the experience of others even as we recognize the absolute necessity of continuing the effort to do so. We can begin to do this by writing critical ethnographic narratives instead of continuing to tell stories that confound narrative and experience. We can only hope to transform a hegemonic practice with a narrative that insists on interrupting a story told in a classroom or in the academy that has acquired the status of lived experience, reality, logic, science, or any of the other seemingly unassailable stories that have acquired the status of authoritative discourse. The only way to fight a hegemonic discourse is to teach ourselves and others alternative ways of seeing the world and discussing what it is we have come to understand as theory, research, and practice. While such an approach will not persuade those who are committed to other understandings of the meaning and value of scholarship, it should be possible to enter critical ethnographic narratives into the academic record and thereby sustain the conversation on hegemonic practices.

This article is based on a paper presented at the eighty-fifth annual meeting of the American Anthropological Association, at the invited session "Critical Theory in Education: Advocacy, Methodology, and Pedagogy," in Philadelphia on December 4, 1986. I would like to thank Michelle Fine, Marge Murray, and Frank Sullivan for their invaluable advice during the writing and rewriting of this essay.

Linda Brodkey and Michelle Fine

Presence of Mind in the Absence of Body

We commonly tell stories about what happens to us and what we make of our experience. In a sense, then, the stories documenting our lives tell what we find worth remembering and contemplating and sharing with others. It is of course the "others" who complicate the telling of stories, for stories are not usually told to ourselves alone, but to those we hope will understand our construction of events. The stories included in this essay concern the sexual harassment of students by professors. We have tried to reconstruct the historical and institutional circumstances of the telling along with the stories told because the transformative potential of the narratives cannot be understood apart from the context in which they were written and read.

The sexual harassment narratives were written by undergraduate and graduate women at the University of Pennsylvania in response to an open-ended question on the 1985 Penn Harassment Survey (de Cani et al. 1985). For many women students of this generation, as Annette Kolodny put it, "feminism is either outdated—because of the naive belief that 'there aren't any problems any more'—or is a distorted melange of media images and Reagan-era backlash" (1988: 461). For some of them, Kolodny adds, "feminism is both personal and problematic" because their mothers "tried to reject traditional family roles in a society that offered their offspring no compensating structures and amid a movement too new to prepare us all for the consequences of such radical change" (461). Yet the women who wrote these narratives know what sexual harassment is. Their narratives confirm the findings of survey research on college and university campuses: women students are routinely harassed; postsecondary institutions have been egregiously hesitant to address harassment (much less write, publish, and enforce sexual harassment policies); and remedies for reporting and grieving sexual harassment favor, if not harassers, their institutions (Robertson, Dwyer, and Campbell 1988). After reading and reflecting on these narratives, we have come to believe that the future of academic feminism is activism, and that activism begins in pedagogy.

The Penn Harassment Survey was sent to students, faculty, and staff in March 1985. The committee reported that 1,065 of the 2,251 usable questionnaires included answers to open-ended questions. In reply to the open-ended question asking them to describe an experience of harassment, thirty-seven of the sixty-six undergraduate women respondents reported harassment by either professors or teaching assistants; forty-four of the sixty-eight graduate responses concerned professors. While we did not include their narratives in this essay, readers will be interested to learn that of the thirty-six untenured women faculty at Penn who wrote about harassment, seventeen reported being harassed by fellow faculty members (thirteen of them senior faculty) and one by her dean; that twelve of twenty responses from tenured women faculty concerned another faculty member (including two department chairs); and that eighteen of the thirty-two women staff who responded reported being harassed by either their supervisors or by faculty members (ix-x). That any woman at Penn is potentially subject to harassment, regardless of status, reminds us that some men violate women's civil rights as a matter of course and that they do so with relative impunity inside the academy.

The narratives clarify the findings of the Penn survey, namely, that women are reluctant to report sexual harassment and reticent when they do because they suspect that institutional indifference will lead to reprisals of one sort or another. We think their fears are justified and in turn warrant feminist curriculum intervention. What we have learned from women's narratives of their experiences of harassment, however, suggests that we will need to encourage all students, and women in particular, to explore not so much the fact but the complexities of harassment. After all, harassment sits at the nexus of gender, power, and sexuality in the academy—as it does in all institutions. Exploring it will take the students and us far outside the boundaries of legal definitions and institutional remedies, and it will even take us outside current feminist analyses of gender and sexuality, for most women students judge sexual harassment to be beyond the reach of law and feminism.

To teach this new generation is to try to understand that they encounter sexual harassment as women whose civil rights have been guaranteed since birth, and hence as women who have believed themselves to be protected by those laws—and have only recently found that they are not. And to work with them is also to realize that even as their narratives reveal the partiality of their visions of gender and sexuality, they critique the partiality of our more seasoned feminist analyses of gender inequity and sexual violence. We are arguing for feminist pedagogies to accompany what Donna Haraway calls "situated and embodied knowledges," the partiality and plurality of which contest "various forms of unlocatable, and so irresponsible, knowledge claims" (1988: 583). Partial perspectives exert a sobering influence on feminist pedagogies, privileging self-conscious acts of critical vision and imagination that are openly hostile to the already established vantage points of either relativism or totalization, which Haraway sees as "promising vision from everywhere and nowhere" (584). Yet she is also suspicious of all "innocent" positions, including what can be seen from the vantage points of subjugation, and offers positioning as a responsible political and epistemological feminist practice for continuing the conversation on gender already in progress in the academy. The pedagogical and political project then is to interrogate the ways in which the sexual harassment narratives undermine the transformative potential of narration by effectively withdrawing their narrators from the conversation we had hoped they would enter.

Telling It Like It Is/Was and Like It Isn't/Wasn't

Given that the Penn Harassment Survey focused primarily on sexual harassment, and given the demographics of students at Penn, the narratives written by undergraduate and graduate women raise almost exclusively the concerns of white women from the middle and upper social classes. Yet their narratives confirm the findings of other campus surveys and hence frustrate any hopes we may have had that knowledge of civil rights defends women against their harassers. Of particular concern here are the narratives written in response to question 21:

> It would be helpful to us if you would describe this experience in detail. Please do so omitting any incriminating information (e.g., names, courses, etc.). You may include a separate piece of paper if necessary.

Ignoring for the moment the likelihood that the proviso to omit incriminating information may have also discouraged many women students from including details of any kind and the fact that the quarter inch allotted for response was inadequate, we offer the narrative below as typical, inasmuch as the woman provides a markedly attenuated description of the event itself relative to the elaborate explanation of both her professor's behavior and her decision not to report him.

> When the incident happened, his attention lasted about one month. It did not occur to me that it was sexual harassment per se because I don't tend to think in terms of deviant behavior. I perceived a troubled man experiencing a mid-life crisis, and more important, a colleague with whom I genuinely shared intellectual commitments and interests. Unfortunately, he saw a young, bright cutsie who could help him with his work and who could potentially serve as an escape route from his unsatisfactory marriage. Basically, all I had to do was make my "No" repetitive and very clear, but the situation was so muddled and in many ways, not so cut and dried as sexual harassment. Things occurred on a very subtle level and are not reported for this reason. All professors have to say is "She's unstable, paranoid, imagining things or lying, etc." Graduate women don't have a leg to stand on. (File 403-31)

Many statements in this account warrant commentary. She refers to "the incident" but never describes what her professor actually did. We are not certain if she considers the "attention [that] lasted about one month" sexual harassment and hence "deviant behavior" or if, as she later asserts, "the situation was so muddled and in many ways, not so cut and dried as sexual harassment." She contrasts her complex view of him ("I perceived a troubled man experiencing a mid-life crisis, and more important, a colleague with whom I genuinely shared intellectual commitments and interests") with his simple view of her ("Unfortunately, he saw a young, bright cutsie who could help him with his work"). Here lies her conflict. And it matters because she has located the danger in his gendering of her, that is, in her being turned into a woman. For she goes on to explain that his professional abuse is but a preface to an attempt to transform her into a woman whose body "could potentially serve as an escape route from his unsatisfactory marriage." She tells us that she dealt with her harasser as one might an unruly child ("Basically, all I had to do was make my 'No' repetitive and very clear") and then explains that she and all the others have no other recourse, since "all professors have to say is 'She's unstable, paranoid, imagining things or lying, etc.' " And her last words, "Graduate women don't have a leg to stand on," summarize both her own situation and her position on the gendering of women by their male professors.

Leaving Your Body to Science

We have a good deal of sympathy for this graduate woman's rendering of the academic world she inhabits, where her experience of gender has been reduced to a choice between slut and madwoman. While we delight in her refusal to take her professor's extracurricular forced-choice exam, we are, nonetheless, troubled by the argument that she and other women students use to represent their strategies for resisting harassers, for it certainly looks as if their practice is to transcend their bodies and deny that women students are women. We say this because of the stunning regularity with which women students position themselves in their narratives as disinterested bystanders who have been asked not to describe what happened to them, but to explain why professors harass their women students:

> This behavior increases when his wife leaves town, if we are in a situation involving liquor or if we are in the presence of other individuals who find this behavior entertaining. (File 947-31)
>
> Male faculty in a department in which I conduct research make suggestive comments, joke and tease most of the time. There are no female faculty members of the department and my assumption has always been that they were simply ignorant of how their behavior was affecting the females who are associated in this department. (File 431-61)
>
> He was drunk which I'm sure contributed to the problem. (File 344-51)

What troubles us about the women's explanations of the extenuating circumstances surrounding acts of harassment is the extent to which each has positioned herself as a narrator who, because she has personally transcended the experience, is "free" to evaluate her harasser's behavior from the vantage point of an expert witness. She does this by assuming a clinical posture with respect to sexual harassment, treating the event as a mere symptom of a disease she must diagnose. Instead of a personal narrative recounting her own anger, sorrow, pain, or even pleasure, she impersonally catalogs his motives: he drinks; his wife is out of town; his colleagues egg him on; he's socially maladroit; he's old; he doesn't know any better. She's taking good care of him. That wouldn't concern us much except that the narrative positions women assign themselves suggest that they understand their own survival to depend on the ability to cleave their minds from their bodies. This mind-body split reproduces in each of them the very cultural ideology that has historically been used to distinguish men from women and justify gender oppression. By severing mind from body and then privileging the "mind's" dispassionate, even clinical, explanation of events, each woman materially reproduces in her narrative the very discursive dichotomies that have historically been used to define a seemingly endless string of culturally positive terms (male/mind/reason/culture) in contrast to a negative string (female/body/intuition/nature) (see Caplan 1986).

We take such representations of self as mind by women students as pleas to be seen by professors as not women. In poststructural terms, the women attempt to achieve unity and coherence as writers in an academic discourse, often called science, that has in recent history offered a few privileged white males the comforting belief that they and they alone legislate reality. These men reside in a world in which "mind over matter" means that what counts is what each individual man can know, understand, and represent as empirical. While poststructural theories argue convincingly that the unity afforded our divided sense of ourselves as discursive subjects is an illusion (Belsey 1980; Brodkey 1989a), we are presumably most attracted to discourses that promise to represent us to ourselves and others as empowered subjects—as the agents who speak the discourse rather than the objectified subjects of which it speaks. For many faculty and students, scientific discourse regulates academic speech and writing. And we think the women students are trying to reproduce a version of scientific discourse by positioning themselves as narrators who, having transcended their bodies, are then entitled to use their dispassionate observations as the bases of their clinical explanations of men's motives and cynical speculations on institutional reprisals. What happened to their bodies (sexual harassment) is not problematic and hence plays little part in the narratives; why it happened (his motives) and what might happen (reprisals), however, remain problematic long after the event, and hence the narratives tell the story of a torturous struggle to represent themselves as genderless.

We see each woman student as offering to pay an exorbitant, not to mention impossible, price for the coherent self represented in her narrative. In exchange for her "mind," she leaves her body to science. Such a strategy for resisting harassment, however, uncritically accepts the illusory coherence of scientific discourse and presumes that human subjectivity is essentially rather than multiply determined (overdetermined) in democratic societies. Yet there is overwhelming evidence in theory, research, and practice that mind, body, gender, and sexuality are not facts we must live with but social constructions we have learned to live by.

Learning to Stand Together

Our goal in this essay is to discern the potential for a liberatory pedagogy of political analysis in the sexual harassment narratives. We understand such inquiry to be transformative, that is, intellectual work in which students and teachers think in terms of both epistemology (ways of knowing the world) and activism (ways of acting in the world). To this end, we have found it useful to review the narratives first in light of feminist standpoint theory (Hartsock 1985), and then in light of critical pedagogy (Giroux 1988) for educational projects of possibility that pose teachers and students as intellectual and political agents.

In *Money, Sex, and Power* Nancy Hartsock argues that because women experience themselves as continuous with the world and men experience themselves as discontinuous with the world, they stand in materially different relationships with themselves, other people, and the world of objects. Thus, women and men view the world from entirely different and indeed opposing standpoints. Hartsock traces the construction of these opposing and gendered epistemologies to early childhood experiences of body and boundary as described in the work of Nancy Chodorow (1978), reasoning that girls, "because of female parenting, are less differentiated from others than boys, more continuous with and related to the external object world" (238). Such a division of labor in parenting, argues Hartsock, means that "girls can identify with a concrete example present in daily life" while "boys must identify with an abstract set of maxims only occasionally present in the form of the father" (238). Relationality is particularly useful in explaining how women reason from experience. And it is plausible to conclude, as Hartsock has, that designating women as the primary caretakers of children might result in gender-differentiated epistemologies, in which even harassed women would tend to see, create, and value relationality.

While Hartsock's notions inform us about what the Penn women might have been trying to do in their narratives, the idea that a single feminist standpoint could account for all women is not plausible. It obscures the complexity and diminishes the importance of differences such as race and class in women's lives. Further, the theory does not address the extent to which personal development through "object relations" is confounded by the cultural hegemony that affects the way women think about, talk about, and organize against harassment in the academy. In other words, the struggle toward standpoint cannot be abstracted from the struggle against the distractions and attractions of dominant ideology (Gramsci 1971). It is, after all, inside an academic hierarchy of asymmetrical relations between students and teachers that women students answered question 21 like "good" students, representing their personal experience of sexual harassment in the same disinterested terminology used in the survey.

Saturating standpoint theory with the understanding that cultural hegemony is also determining, we are better able to understand how women students might have independently arrived at similar political stances in their narratives of sexual harassment. Instead of *describing* what happened, their narratives try to *explain* what happened by imagining what might have motivated their harassers and what might have happened had they reported the harassment. A standpoint of relationality may account for the formal structure of the narratives, but the contents spell hegemony. The transcendent narrator is a standpoint from which a writer can relate the concerns of harasser and harassed alike. But the motives and reprisals women name come out of that dreary stockpile of conclusions, premises, and arguments that individualism and proceduralism commonly use to explain why "you can't fight city hall" and why men cannot be held accountable for harassment.

The political potential of the standpoint of relationality as an activist epistemology is severely tested by the content of the sexual harassment narratives inasmuch as it becomes clear that when women link the incident to men's motives and institutional reprisals, they are left standing alone and wishing they were not women. Their analysis of motives and reprisals leads them to believe that since men harass women for untold reasons, women who report harassment will be subjected to more of the same arbitrary treatment from the institution. The dispassionate language in which graduate women speculate on institutional reprisals is academic, and this strikes us as all the more eerie not only because it reproduces the mind-body split, but also because their fears are far from academic. Consider, for instance, the way in which this student juxtaposes form and content in the following passage:

> *I* think female graduate students *probably* bear the brunt of sexual harassment at the University. Most of the guys who harass you or *just make life difficult* are your teachers and dissertation committee members. Graduate students here have no power. We're dependent on our departments for financial aid, and are afraid that these professors could blackball us in our future careers. (File 344-51; emphasis added)

Because sexual harassment is woven into the very fabric of faculty-student relations, women do not as a matter of course appeal to legal remedies; institutional procedures only further jeopardize their professional lives. Student complaints about sexual harassment are not likely to be taken as seriously by the institution as allegations of capricious grading or irregular office hours. While the modulated phrasing may mean that women students are confronting irrational behavior from their professors by responding rationally, and relationally, the very act of using their heads effectively preempts their taking an activist stance.

Hartsock understands the epistemology of standpoint as liberatory:

> Because of its achieved character and its liberatory potential, I use the term "feminist" rather than "women's standpoint." Like the experiences of the proletariat, women's experience and activity as a dominated group contains both negative and positive aspects. A feminist standpoint picks out and amplifies the liberatory possibilities contained in that experience. (1985: 232)

We do not see relationality in the sexual harassment narratives as liberatory or even potentially so, and think it could only become so if feminist educators were willing to work with students to imagine liberatory possibilities not raised when analysis fetishizes individual men's motives and institutional reprisals. In other words, we see relationality as an epistemology that helps to explain the reasoning of women students who experience inequity, bypass their outrage, and rationalize that the way it is, is all there is.

A subjugated standpoint does not necessarily facilitate collective activism on behalf of women who, in the absence of support, have individually devised ad hoc strategies for deflecting harassment. With such strategies, a particular woman may be able to prevent or protect herself against individual acts of harassment. Such strategies, however, neither interrupt nor disrupt the material and ideological gender asymmetries that organize the academy. They do not call public attention to sexual harassment as simply the most overt and explicit of those practices that remind women that we are not card-carrying members (pun intended) of the academic club (and again).

What we've learned from reading these narratives is that if the women appear not to have said "what really happened," that was because we were only listening for the legal categories that count as sexual harassment: that is, evidence of social transgressions that are specified by the equal opportunity guidelines and that can be documented empirically in terms that courts understand. The voices of women students in the sexual harassment narratives speak of a pervasive, routinized, and institutionalized sexual intimidation calling for a far more radical institutional project than heretofore suggested by either adversarial law or positioned feminism.

The violent behaviors that feminism and law bracket as sexual harassment and that institutions then treat as exceptional practices do not begin to capture the sense of danger lurking in the women's narratives. The unspoken oppression strikes us as all the more brutal when, as in the following example, difficulties with language suggest that the author may also be a foreign student:

> I went to private office to visit this person. He greeted me at the door, closed the door and locked it. He leaned over me, standing very close and started unbuttoning my overcoat. I fumbled with coat buttons trying to make light of/ignore his behavior, and trying to dissipate his sexual attention. He helped me remove my hat, coat, scarf and hang them up. He took my hand and led me over to couch in office. We had often sat in that part of the office before to chat, with him on couch (often lounging) and me on chair facing him. He sit down on couch and pulled me by my hand to sit next to him. I pulled to try to sit in chair as per usual; he would not let go. He lay down on couch and pulled me down to sit next to him on edge of couch, near his hip level. He released my hand and I moved back to far end of couch. There were no chairs nearby. I could not move to sit elsewhere without drawing tremendous attention to my action: 1) I would be overtly rejecting him if he was seriously pursuing me sexually; 2) I would be quite rude if he then decided to pretend he had no sexual intentions. My first thought was not to provoke him since the door was locked and the office quite soundproof. He kept urging me to sit closer to him and I declined. He finally took my hand and pulled me, I resisted but moved closer as a last resort before an outright struggle and possible scream. He kept holding my hand. He then tried to pull me down on top of him, coaxing me verbally. I refused. I stayed upright and using as much strength as necessary and shook my head no, looking him straight in the eye. Luckily, he wanted to seduce me, not assault me violently. (File 1974-31)

Her narrative reminds us that even though legal categories account for his behavior, she appeals not to law but to popular psychology to explain her professor's motives: "I felt that this incident was due more to an ego-attack of older man (mid-sixties) rather than the machinations of a sexual psychopath." If a stranger had attacked her on the street, no doubt she would have seen it as an assault. But she casts her professor's "strange" behavior in the most benign light possible—by contrasting him to a psychopath—presumably so that she can imagine completing her studies:

> We have resumed our usual interactions. In this case, there was enough of a personal friendship to use as a basis to deal with the incident on a person-to-person way. Had that not been the case, however, I would have risked losing the support of an internationally renowned scholar with

> impressive professional contacts and influence. That's quite a bit of leverage to have over someone, isn't it? (File 1974-31)

This narrative is unusual because its extensive analysis is grounded in a description of the event itself. To be sure, she offers the usual explanations of motives, but she elaborates the harassing incident in tandem with her many modes of resistance before stating her ambivalence about the institutional vulnerability of women graduate students.

When oppression is normalized, privatized, and rooted in a powerful and pervasive institutional ambivalence toward the oppressed, a woman student is more likely to pose and resolve the conflict in her narrative by glossing the incident and concentrating on explanations:

> A mutual sexual attraction grew between myself and a professor. It was in part physical—in many settings and to people at large, the professor projects his sexuality—but was also based upon the discovery of shared values. This bond struck a chord with me, as I felt very lonely and isolated, for the usual—and institutionalized—reasons that graduate students feel this way. (File 1851-31)

Her seeming calm is soon belied, however, by a catalog of fears iterated in many of the narratives:

> I shortly grew alarmed both at the power of my own feelings and the increasing power of the professor's feelings.
>
> Although I did not feel physically threatened—that seemed unlikely—I became afraid that he would begin to manipulate me by using the power of my own feelings and my need for him.
>
> This fear arose as I learned how he was irrationally competitive with us [graduate students].
>
> I felt that I had lost both his respect and his important professional support.
>
> I knew if needed he would not "go to bat" for me in the personally influential ways that professors have to work for their students. (File 1851-31)

In a later, more sustained, passage she explains why the fears that simmer internally are not to be expressed formally:

> It seemed impossible to resolve the situation by talking it over with him—the relationship always had an unspoken nature about it, and he very likely would have stonewalled me, making me feel totally responsible

> for what had happened. I did not feel that it would be helpful to speak to any other faculty members given my own involvement and the provocative and controversial nature of a sexual and political relationship which is not even supposed to exist. I also feared discrediting myself and I felt that the faculty's personal loyalties rested with this professor. (File 1851-31)

The women know they've been treated unfairly by their professors. And while they do not blame themselves, their reluctance to insist that professors are responsible leaves women students recognizing harassment but transfixed rather than transformed by their knowledge of oppression (see Fine 1986a). The fact that personal knowledge does not necessarily become grounds for political action is clear not only from the narratives but also from the survey. Even though 45 percent of graduate and professional women students reported some sexual harassment over the previous five years, more than 80 percent handled it "by ignoring or going along with it or by avoiding contact with the offender." And, indeed, only between 0 percent and 6 percent of graduate students (depending on the type of harassment) report filing a formal grievance in response to an incident of harassment (de Cani et al. 1985: vii).

Feminist interpretation means reading these stories as true but partial accounts of sexual harassment. But feminist pedagogy strives to recover the intellectual and creative energy dispersed when women try to transcend their bodies and find themselves standing alone against their harassers. This is a pedagogy that would transform that wasted individual energy into a collective desire to identify and examine the institutional practices that succor sexual harassment and begin to institute counterpractices that do not. The possibilities for pedagogy examined in the next section arise out of our analysis of the narratives and pose a feminist project in terms of transforming the scene of institutional harassment so that women in the academy are free to study and teach—with our bodies and minds intact.

Learning How to Speak in the Academy

In this section we set out to amplify in pedagogy some political projects that we now think may have been attenuated in the sexual harassment narratives. We do this realizing that the survey itself may have encouraged harassed women to resolve prematurely the tensions and complexities their narratives posed. The designers of the survey had hoped that open-ended questions would offer women students an opportunity for both critique and empowerment. Instead, women respondents commonly took this opportunity to consolidate experiences about which they were seemingly quite ambivalent and effectively returned all responsibility for advocacy to the committee. At least this is how we have come to understand the lengths some women went to in thanking the committee:

> Thanks for your concern over this issue. I realize that I was less than responsible to my fellow students for not pursuing a formal complaint but I'm glad to help with the survey. (File 1799-11)
>
> I do appreciate being able to tell someone about this who will take this information seriously. (File 1851-31)
>
> I thank you for conducting this questionnaire. I hope you publish the results and information on the procedure for reporting situations. (File 1486-11)
>
> Thanks for listening! (File 1418-31)

We take seriously Henry Giroux's reminder that "oppositional political projects . . . should be the object of constant debate and analysis" (1988: 69). We recommend basing the curriculum on a *negative critique* of futile individualistic attempts to interrogate or interrupt forms of institutional oppression organized around gender, race, and social class. Central to this project is the demystification of institutional policies and practices that cloak social inequities. We need to engage young women and men in exploring how our analyses of the causes and consequences of social inequities construct not only our understanding of the present but also our images of what is possible in the near or far future. Unable to imagine institutional change, the women who wrote the sexual harassment narratives default to reworking relationships with faculty or, even more consequentially, to reworking or denying their bodies.

Feminist pedagogy begins by animating the policies and procedures that contribute to harassment. The faceless image of authority sustains the illusion that institutions are immutable and hence oppression is inevitable. This is the illusion feminists must first seek to dispel if we hope to enable young women and men to see oppression as mutable through critical and collective reflection and action. A pedagogy intentionally remote from political activism incidentally fosters the very alienation, individualism, and cynicism we confronted in these narratives. We were heartened to find young women who grew up in the wake of civil rights legislation and witnessed the victories and losses of feminism in the courts and state legislatures struggling against harassment. Their collective narrative, however, is a story of despair, for each woman encounters the lechery of professors alone, with little hope that law can, or that the institution will, intercede on her behalf. And so she tries to rise above the scene of harassment in narratives reminding us that the halls of academe are littered with the bodies women students leave hostage in their flight from professorial treachery.

We could set an intellectual and political process in motion by asking students to imagine how a series of university representatives might respond to the narratives. What would the university counsel, the lawyer whose job it is to subvert grievances and suits against the institution, make of a narrative about the institutional threat of violence rather than an actual act of violence? How might the director of the women's center respond? Or a feminist professor? A nonfeminist professor? A faculty member who has been or thinks he may be named in a sexual harassment suit? The editor of the student newspaper or the alumni magazine? And what about the dean of the school? The man or woman chairing the department? The president of the university? The president of student government or the faculty senate? The counseling staff? What changes if we know that the narrator is white, black, straight, gay? While the list is far from complete, it points out that since institutions speak not one but several "languages," students need to apprise themselves of the range of "dialects" representing their university.

At any given moment in a university's history, its representatives will be unevenly committed to preserving the status quo, which means that the possibilities for political change are always contingent on revealing heterogeneity within what only appears to outsiders to be a single voice. While it is nearly always the case that the university lawyer will not hear such a narrative, the other representatives are not as predictable. Having imagined what university representatives might do with the narrative as written, how might a particular narrative be rewritten to secure a hearing from each of them? We are not suggesting an "exercise" in writing for audiences, but recommending that students do this kind of imaginative work before they meet and interview representatives concerning their jobs and their positions on harassment of women or minority constituencies on campus. This collaborative work requires students to take careful notes, report back to peers and faculty, and compare findings and impressions; they should do this before making any decisions about who and what to write, and before making plans for more sustained collective action. We see what can be learned from representatives of the institution as a first lesson in understanding how power is or is not dispersed locally and as a first step toward interrupting the illusion that institutional authority is literally anonymous.

What happens next is of course contingent on what students and teachers are willing to deem appropriate under the circumstances. Students might go on to write a white paper on the status of women students on their campus, a series of articles for the student or a city newspaper, a pamphlet for entering students and their parents, a broadside for students, faculty, and staff. Or they might decide that their preliminary research warrants additional studies of the institution and its relations with students on a number of issues that include but are not bounded by sexual harassment. The point is that it would be pedagogically irresponsible to set up an intellectual exploration such as we are suggesting and assume that students will have succeeded only if they reproduce familiar feminist analyses, that is, execute what we have already conceptualized. There is no feminist standpoint they must find. There is instead a feminist project, struggling to find the crevices in the institutional facade that glosses over oppression of students, staff, and faculty across lines of race, class, and gender.

The unevenness of commitment to the status quo does not mean that any particular strategy meant to engage university representatives in a conversation will result in desired or desirable political change. We have only to review the political successes of the New Right in the academy and elsewhere to realize that heterogeneity is itself no guarantee that discussions will move administrations to more progressive policies. While speaking is certainly a form of action, institutional representatives often understand talk as a way of appeasing and defusing student, faculty, and staff activists. Students as well as educators need to bear in mind that talking and writing to representatives may not be enough unless they are also willing to enlist support from institutions that are (or have representatives who are) interested in their university. Included among the possibilities are the press, professional organizations, legislators, community activists committed to gender and race equity, alumni, well-known political "radicals" who are willing to visit campus and speak out for students, and parents who thought that education would support, not undermine, their children. While political networking is as difficult to learn as to maintain, a network is critical both as a lever for starting conversations inside the institution and as an alternative if or when a conversation breaks down. Outside the boundaries arbitrarily set by the academy, moreover, young women and men are sometimes better positioned to notice and interrupt the institution's version of reality and protectionism, and so better positioned to represent themselves as informed and critical agents of change.

Learning What to Do When Talk Is Just Talk

Women have been known to contemplate and even commit outrageous acts when conversation fails. The most dramatic example we know of happened at the University of Pennsylvania in the early 1980s. Once a week, with great regularity, the campus was secretly decorated with photographs of prominent male faculty members whose pictures were captioned WANTED FOR CRIMES AGAINST WOMEN and signed by the Women's Army. Along with others, we presumed this to be the work of a small group of undergraduate women who, distressed that conversations with the provost, university government, and individual faculty failed to draw sufficient attention to sexual harassment, resorted to extraordinary methods for naming the problem.

University officials and many faculty members were alarmed that the Women's Army was irresponsibly accusing men—which it was. Yet we also read these actions as evidence of the women's despair over adamant institutional refusal to listen and act. At the time Penn had an elaborate set of mechanisms for voicing student dissent, but "listening" was revealed as a way to appropriate dissent, that is, to appease "angry young women." We have heard that at some other institutions, young women on campus welcome parents on Parents Day with the gruesome statistics of the likelihood that their daughter will be harassed or raped—or both—during her four years at college.

We are not recommending these strategies. They are not attempts to alter the conditions of women's lives. They are the voices of despair that institutional indifference provokes. People have been known, however, to throw caution to the wind when institutions refuse to talk, or when they intentionally set out to confound by offering talk in lieu of policy. Women are particularly vulnerable once they are engaged in conversation, since the willingness to talk is considered the most important evidence of growing trust and cooperation. And most of us, needless to say, find it excruciatingly difficult to break frame and go public, even when it becomes evident that the official conversation is fruitless.

While the Penn Women's Army and its sisters elsewhere do not provide models of political projects aimed at transformation, the outrageous is nonetheless of untold pedagogical value. Worst-case scenarios stretch the sense of possibility even as they terrorize the imagination. Images of the irrational strategies we may want to avoid help us to imagine how to insist that institutions take seriously their conversations with women.

Feminist Archives for Intellectual Activism

An archive of feminist intellectual activism is needed to chronicle the varied ways of identifying, analyzing, interrupting, and, under exceptionally perverse circumstances, disrupting gender-based power asymmetries in the academy. Feminist activism must reposition itself inside a larger politics of solidarity with "other self-conscious political projects" (Harding 1988: 163), which at the very least would also include struggles based on race, ethnicity, class, disability, and sexual orientation. Such an archive could already be stocked with reports of the reemergence of women's consciousness-raising groups on campus; core curricula that mainstream feminist, African-American, and Third World scholarship (and organized efforts to marginalize or eliminate them); charters for establishing women's centers; arguments for developing gay men's and lesbian women's studies programs; policies of professional organizations that monitor the use of sexist language in presentations and publications (Conference on College Composition and Communication); and the presence of African-American studies and women's studies courses within accredited programs (American Psychological Association).

As impressive as we find this list, the narratives caution us that far more is needed. This new generation of women is equipped with a striking sense of entitlement and yet beset by fears that their female bodies are liabilities, their minds are male, their professors are likely to corrupt their intellectual relationships, and their legal rights are hollow. We cannot anticipate what they will contribute either to the archive or to the struggle, but social history assures us that it will not be precisely what we added. After all, they inherited rather than advocated for the gains of the 1970s, yet they share the threat of stunning disappointments in the future.

Perhaps the lesson we most need to learn is that it is as important for students as it is for teachers to become researchers; students as well as teachers are intellectuals and need to see themselves as informed political agents. We have learned that teachers and students need to collaborate critically across generations, histories, life circumstances, and politics to create curricula and pedagogies that seek to transform institutions not by reproducing or resisting the practices of oppression, but by confronting the institution on intellectual grounds. Only thus can we imagine a context in which every woman's story realizes its full liberatory potential and no woman declines to tell her story because "any information would be incriminating" (File 2174 C3 1).

We take this opportunity to thank the Quad Women's Group, the undergraduate women at Penn who in the four years we met with them weekly surprised and delighted us with stories of their lives as students, daughters, lovers, and friends. This essay is infused with dreams, desires, and fears that materialized in those sessions and emerge here in our own academic dream of a story in which women stand together in their struggle to reclaim the bodies that accompany their minds.

Writing Permitted in Designated Areas Only

The international sign that bans smoking in public places can also be read as a sign of cultural hegemony, a frequent and forcible reminder that in democratic societies civic regulations commonly inscribe the will of the dominant culture. That there are two versions of the sign suggests that the dominant culture is of at least two minds when it comes to smoking in public places. One version of the sign prohibits smoking altogether, and the other regulates smoking by appending a note that may be more familiar to smokers than to nonsmokers: "Smoking Permitted in Designated Areas Only." This second sign, signaling the temporary segregation of smokers from nonsmokers, is part of the same expansionist public policy as the first, which seems likely to succeed eventually given the rapidly diminishing number and size of public spaces where smokers are still allowed to smoke. In the meantime, however—so long as they remove themselves to those designated areas—smokers constitute a literal and figurative body of evidence that a desire to smoke remains strong enough in some people to withstand the ever increasing pressure of social hostility and medical injunctions. That smokers commonly honor the signs, either by not smoking or by smoking only in designated areas, provides smokers and nonsmokers alike with continual public enactments of civil power, namely, the power of the professional-managerial middle class to enforce the public suppression of a desire it has recently identified and articulated via science as endangering its well being—as a class.

I am using "middle class" as it is defined by Barbara Ehrenreich in *Fear of Falling*. "This class can be defined," she writes, "somewhat abstractly, as all those people whose economic and social status is based on education, rather than on the ownership of capital or property" (1989: 12). The middle class, which includes professionals and managers but excludes entrepreneurs, accounts for only about 20 percent of the population but "plays an overweening role in defining 'America': its moods, political directions, and moral tone" (6). As the middle class has become conscious of itself as a distinct and privileged class based not on capital but on cultural capital over the past thirty years, she argues, its class anxieties have been expressed increasingly in cultural and political conservativism. Although the middle class and its anxieties are the subject of Ehrenreich's book, I think it's fair to conclude that the ubiquity of middle-class values as American values relies in large measure on middle-class definitions of the working class as inimical to the middle class and to America.

The nonsmoking sign has radically and no doubt permanently altered the public behavior of smokers and nonsmokers in many regions of the country. At issue, however, is whether these or possibly other even more punitive legal and economic sanctions will ultimately not only regulate smoking but also extinguish the desire to smoke. While I doubt that I would much care if people lost the desire to smoke (and as a smoker I could probably live with the loss of that desire), I care a good deal that more than a century of publicly regulating the desire to write in North American schools seems to have eradicated it in many people. I am couching my case for the "deregulation" of writing and writing pedagogy in terms of the seemingly more reasonable campaign to ban smoking in public areas because, just as smokers are arguably surrogate targets for the tobacco industry, I consider composition to hold students hostages to a peculiarly American version of meritocracy.

There is no doubt in my mind that this society prohibits and regulates smoking in public areas because the tobacco industry has thwarted efforts to outlaw the sale of cigarettes by submitting itself instead to ever more stringent government regulation. The industry's success has, of course, shifted the burden of responsibility onto consumers, smokers whose desire to smoke could, before public concern about secondary smoke, be defended as a constitutionally protected individual right. In the current cultural climate, however, any defense of smokers' civil liberties can be, and sooner rather than later probably will be, met with a rarely voiced but easily inferred *subtext* from scientific studies of secondary smoke: "Cigarettes don't kill. Smokers do." Unlike "Guns don't kill. People do," the *text* produced and circulated by the National Rifle Association in defense of what it claims to be an absolute constitutional right to bear arms, a subtext on the order of "Cigarettes don't kill. Smokers do" is not in the public domain, and therefore not readily available to public scrutiny. A subtext that asserts *not* smoking to be an act of moral as well as civic virtue is a nonetheless influential and powerful text precisely because as a subterranean text it insinuates rather than argues its claims. In much the same way that white supremacists code racism by claiming they are not racists, just proud of being white, the subtext permits the antismoking campaign to continue publicly condemning smoking while silently indicting smokers. It goes without saying, or should, that the tobacco industry is hardly likely to point out that smokers are the designated culprits in a subtext that protects its economic interests, for such a subtext would effectively insure companies that sell cigarettes against liability in suits brought against them by smokers. Nor does it seem likely to me that tomorrow, or even the next day, the signs that now target a smoking cigarette will be replaced by signs that target a cigarette smoker.

At least as long as the sale and use of tobacco remain legal, the signs are likely to continue to issue civil directives to, rather than moral indictments of, smokers. Increasingly, however, there is evidence that a subtext indicting smokers is emerging as a *text* in the public service announcements aired by local television stations, and evidence, too, that the spots that identify the culprits and assess their culpability trot out the usual suspects, working-class women of all colors and working-class men of color. During the fall of 1992, the commercial stations in San Diego, where I live, regularly aired two such public service announcements. The first depicts a woman in the delivery room whose joy in giving birth is dramatically and abruptly reversed when a white male doctor orders the newborn to intensive care. An explanation of sorts is provided by a flashback of the woman smoking and drinking at a party. She and her *irresponsible* social behavior are blamed for the infant's peril; the doctor and his *responsible* professional behavior represent its hope for survival. The other public service announcement focuses on a young Latino seated on a sofa beside a Latina child. As they sit staring at a television in a poorly lit and poorly furnished room, he is oblivious to the girl, who coughs every time he takes a drag on the cigarette. Like the pregnant woman, the Latino is indicted and his irresponsible social behavior identified as imperiling the child. The adults in both spots are held morally responsible. The indictments of smokers are furiously confounded, however, by some familiar middle-class anxieties about white women and about women and men of color.

Set in the public space of a hospital, the delivery-room trauma at the very least suggests that a medical intervention is both possible and justified when a woman (she is marked for pregnancy, not race or ethnicity) behaves in ways believed to jeopardize a fetus. The medical intervention, warranted in this instance by the flashback, is represented as a beneficent act on the part of the doctor and the hospital. This is not the only example of medical charity toward fetuses that is known to us, however, and feminist analyses of reproductive technology do a great deal more than suggest that women may themselves be in need of protection from medical-legal traditions and practices in which their interests are represented as conflicting with and subordinate to those of fetuses (see, for instance, Hartouni 1991; Martin 1987). Any interpretation of the spot depends on deciding in whose flashback the woman is smoking and drinking. It could be that the woman is remembering the party, or that the doctor or even one of the nurses is imagining the scene. Since the camera focuses on the woman's horrified expression immediately before the flashback, however, it is most likely her memory, which at the very least suggests that the woman has assumed, or is at least capable of assuming, moral responsibility for her past behavior (including responsibility for getting pregnant), and may also suggest that she plans not to behave similarly in the future.

In my reading, the birth trauma teaches the woman to see herself as the doctor does, or, more precisely, to look on her pregnant body as he does, as a uterus. His medical gaze is in this case a middle-class gaze, which views not smoking as not only reducing the risks to which fetuses are prone but also enacting a public commitment to the middle class, which advertises smoking as endangering its well-being as a class and not smoking as one of its many virtues as a class. Hence medical agonism between the female and the fetus is projected onto working-class rather than middle-class women and attributed to "differences" in class behavior. Such an advertisement invites working-class women of all colors to resolve the narrative conflict between fetuses and themselves and, in the course of aesthetically resolving that narrative, to close the material gap between middle-class women and themselves by not acting on their desire—to smoke? to drink? to have sex?

The synoptic recoding of material conditions—including access to and availability of prenatal care—as matters of individual choice and merit is a familiar middle-class belief, amplified by a rhetorical appeal to ethos, which in this instance focuses exclusively on the *character* of smokers rather than, say, the cost and quality of health care or the political influence of the tobacco industry. The campaign to privatize schooling by way of vouchers created a similar illusion that all *good* parents would be able to choose the schools their children attend, when in fact such a tax credit would have enabled only a fraction of middle-class taxpayers to exercise their "right" to choose. Representing smoking (and drinking) as vices of working-class women circumscribes middle-class civic responsibility, for, in singling out these women, the narrative valorizes their behaviors at the expense of systemic practices that impinge on the health of poor women and children. I am not arguing that smoking is moot. Rather, I am arguing that the narrative told by the public service announcement does considerably more than warn pregnant women against smoking, and I am suggesting that advertising the suppression of desire as a virtue of middle-class women exonerates the entire class from its responsibility for inequitable health care, even as it holds poor working-class women entirely responsible for their own health *and* that of their children.

The spot featuring the Latino narrates no such belief that he holds or ever will hold himself accountable to either the child or the middle class. The Latino is outside law, at home, the private space where the state, despite a fair amount of evidence to the contrary, represents itself as helpless to intervene without due cause. My sense that he is an outlaw has to do with his being portrayed as oblivious to the child's peril. Since Latinos are commonly depicted in the media as familial, I cannot but wonder whether this man is even a blood relative. And if he is just a "friend," perhaps that would explain why he is being caricatured as unlikely to assume even a measure of responsibility for the well-being of a child not his own. For unlike the woman, whose possible guilty knowledge at least makes her a candidate for remediation, the Latino is projected as incorrigible, the smoker whose absolute difference from middle-class nonsmokers is irremediable. That the culprit who is not just ignorant but stupid is a Latino, and that he had only to notice the child and put out the cigarette to transform what I see as a gratuitously reactive message into a proactive one, is reason enough to suspect that the ostensible purpose is not the only and perhaps not even the primary purpose of this particular public service announcement.

Rather than contributing to the campaign against smoking, this spot seems to target not Latinos who smoke so much as middle-class people who have been taught that immigrants generally and Latino immigrants in particular threaten what the English Language Political Action Committee, in a letter to California voters in the 1992 election, called "the language of unity and opportunity," in the absence of which "we'll [English speaking voters] be faced with *years of unrelenting pressure* for a costly multilingual, multicultural society" (ELPAC 1992, emphasis in the original). No one speaks in this spot. But that this particular man and child do not speak implies that if they cannot speak English, they do not have a right to speak for themselves. The English Only movement commonly represents not speaking English as evidence of immigrant indifference or hostility to American values (see, for instance, Baron 1991; Crawford 1992). Presumably, then, a Latino smoker who does not speak English, may not be family, and may not even be a U.S. citizen represents a threat not just to the Latino family, not just to the middle class, but to the nation. This none too subtle identity of language, class, and nation as one and the same is disturbing for any number of reasons, not least among them that language education is invariably the site at which many of the vested political interests of the middle class and the state are reencoded as identical subtexts in putatively apolitical curricula. As the dismissal of Joseph Fernandez, chancellor of the New York City public schools, in February 1993 so dramatically illustrates, efforts to raise political subtexts to the level of texts (the Rainbow Curriculum) and make them available to public scrutiny are likely not only to raise the ire but also to provoke the enmity of those who believe their political interests are better served in subtexts than in texts (see Kohl 1993).

Let me reiterate that I am not arguing for or against smoking. What I find disturbing in the public service announcements is the strategic targeting of female ignorance and male stupidity as endemic in specific classes or other groups of people. Such a spin is uncannily reminiscent of policies that have historically singled out the individuals most likely to benefit from literacy education as those who accept not only the middle class's version of itself as an inherently virtuous and hence meritorious class, but also its caricatures of the working class, the working poor, and the just plain poor as criminally illiterate, promiscuous, violent, seditious. Public policies that represent only to write off these constituencies constitute and also regulate the middle class by depicting conduct becoming to its members. Nowhere is this more evident than in policies regulating public education. Conservative and liberal policies alike produce curricula that justify disciplining all the children, regardless of class, according to some widely received middle-class definition of learning and teaching (cognitive development, cultural literacy, critical thinking), and every policy implicitly or explicitly also justifies punishing students, parents, teachers, and administrators who challenge its exclusive authority by threatening them and the children with expulsion from the middle class (tracking, ranking, flunking, detention, suspension, expulsion). My point is that the curriculum, like the Constitution, commonly represents society itself as classless, and hence class membership as entirely within the control of individuals or families.

Composition classrooms are the designated areas of American colleges and universities. Composition courses are middle-class holding pens populated by students from all classes who for one reason or another do not produce fluent, thesis-driven essays of around five hundred words in response to either prompts designed for standardized tests or assignments developed by classroom teachers. Since most prompts and assignments are so many variations on the notorious "Write an essay about what you did on your summer vacation," the form and contents of successful student essays are likely to display knowledge of and fealty to middle-class values. If you are middle class, you must convince the teacher (reader) that someone you met or something you did on vacation made you appreciate your family or your country. And if you are working class, you must convince the teacher (reader) that by working hard or reading the right books you acquired a taste for things middle-class and American. Middle-class and working-class children alike are expected to exemplify rather than question such venerable notions as the undisputed "educational" value of travel, literacy, and work in their essays, even though some working-class children may have to betray their families in the process, and some middle-class children collude in happy family fictions. The fiction that the family and the nation are united solely on behalf of children lends credence to the notion that literature, history, physics, psychology, and so on are unified on behalf of the middle class. Like summer vacations, it seems, great books are coherent from a middle-class perspective, and students who fail to see or appreciate and represent a principle that unifies a work of literature and distinguishes it *as* literature in the form and contents of their essays are sent off to composition to learn how to see the obvious and to write about it—in five hundred words or less.

It has always seemed to me gratuitous to regulate writing and writers via the contents of prompts and assignments, since a policy of coherence is already being "objectively" executed by assessing student writing on the basis of form and format: the grammar, spelling, diction, and punctuation along with the thesis sentence, body paragraphs, and conclusion. Perhaps both are necessary, however, because while form identifies class interlopers (working-class ethnic and black students), content singles out class malcontents. While it seems to take longer in some cases than in others, composition instruction appears to have succeeded best at establishing in most people a lifelong aversion to writing. They have learned to associate a desire to write with a set of punishing exercises called writing in school: printing, penmanship, spelling, punctuation, and vocabulary in nearly all cases; grammar lessons, thesis sentences, paragraphs, themes, book reports, and library research papers in college preparatory and advanced placement courses. It is probably worth wondering whether the most successful students are not those who learn early on that writing assignments are occasions for students to display and teachers to correct errors, and not, as one might think, invitations for students to write about and teachers to respond to ideas.

Like smokers who enter public areas designated for smoking, students in required composition classes publicly enact the power of the middle class to enforce the suppression of writing and writers, a desire it has long identified as inimical to its best interests as a class in literacy campaigns calling for a nation not of writers but of readers (Brodkey 1986a). Writing is also a desire that has been historically albeit ambiguously articulated as dangerous to the nation, via curriculum and pedagogy in which authors are depicted as martyrs to Literature, condemned to live in splendid isolation from the rest of us in garrets or penthouses (Brodkey 1987b). Writing and writers may be represented as well beyond the reach of middle-class rules of conduct, but good student writing has repeatedly been defined, taught, and evaluated in American schools as good manners. That much seems apparent in any handbook or style manual. It is well known in the field of composition that this version of good writing and, by extension, good writing pedagogy, as a matter of training students to produce well-formed essays on demand, was firmly in place at Harvard (where composition was invented as a college subject) by the late nineteenth century (see Douglass 1976; Halloran 1990). And it is also known by some in the field that not all that much has changed at Harvard, or elsewhere, in the past hundred-some years (see Berlin 1987; Crowley 1990; Faigley 1992; Miller 1991).

It is fair to say that, despite what may appear to be radical shifts since the 1960s in how writing is taught—despite, that is, a twin focus on the so-called writing process and personal experience of students—in a good many public and private schools, colleges, and universities, composition continues to do what it was established to do: guard the gates of the professions by offering what, in *Textual Carnivals,* Susan Miller calls "a consciously established menu to test students' knowledge of graphic conventions, to certify their propriety, and to socialize them into good academic manners" (1991: 66). In other words, the *text* explicitly used at Harvard and similar private and public institutions in the nineteenth century to justify the regulation of students and their writing is an implicit *subtext* in even seemingly liberal textbooks to this day (Faigley 1992: 132-62). Students may now be invited to write personal essays, and students may even be encouraged to revise them, on the advice of teachers and peers, but the persistent subtext guarantees that teachers will revert to verbal fluency in their comments and thus that teachers will continue to test, certify, and socialize students according to the dictates of an unacknowledged middle-class constituency. While what counts as fluency varies over time and place and population, that is, it may be more or less generous in one era than another, or may mean subject-verb agreement for students with low placement scores and diction for advanced placement students, the policy of isolating and then reifying selected formal features of student texts as markers of verbal fluency does not.

It is this deflection that concerns me, not only because it fecklessly begs the issue of content, which is undoubtedly crucial to writers and writing, not to mention readers and reading, but because fluency surreptitiously calibrates all writing to middle-class notions of literacy, and then installs a middle-class version of fluency as the *exclusive* standard by which to measure the value of any and all written texts. For by that standard, not only most student texts but most academic texts and many of the canonical as well as noncanonical texts academics study would probably fare poorly, since they usually are narratively and rhetorically and even syntactically more complex than the forms vaunted by style manuals. That the rules of scholarly writing are not synchronized to the taste of the middle class is most evident when a pundit accuses scientists or social scientists of using jargon to disguise the fact that a study "proves" the obvious or when pundits lambaste professors of literature *not* for using jargon or for studying the obvious, but for raising topics like masturbation or homosexuality or canonicity or colonization or any other notion these media-sponsored, self-appointed guardians of the people (also known as *the public*) see as challenging their authority to dictate what and how professors and students *should* be reading and writing.

Measured primarily by its fealty to rules prescribed by handbooks and style manuals, a fluent but invalid theory of physics would be a better text than a less fluent but valid one. Since creationism theories often are more fluent than most Darwinian theories, in some composition programs (as in some quarters of society) the fluency of the one, which makes it the better *text*, would effectively also make it the better theory. Invoked as a single or even supra criterion, fluency is dangerous because it assumes there to be a necessary and positive correlation between clear *writing* and clear *thinking*, which any honest student can tell you is patently not the case. The fluency trick, and it is seen as a trick by many students, is to write a thesis statement simple enough that it can *appear* to be adequately elaborated and naturally resolved in the requisite number of words. My son, who once explained this to me in some detail, in high school went so far as to make it a policy never to read literature about which he would be asked to write, on the grounds that reading would unnecessarily complicate his understanding of the assignment and increase the difficulty of producing the kind of essay his teachers wanted. In other words, this white, middle-class boy (and no doubt countless other middle-class children) possessed of verbal fluency had learned that a good composition ignores rather than addresses the complexity of topics and treats the reader instead to a display of verbal fluency.

The will of the middle class to regulate whatever it sees as threatening to its interests as a class cannot be overestimated. One need only call to mind Richard Bernstein's sly condemnation of the new *Random House College Dictionary* in the *New York Times* a few years back to see how furious some middle-class pundits can become when linguistic descriptions refuse to confirm linguistic prescriptions that are used to justify the middle-class hegemony over good English. After asserting that some will no doubt welcome the attempt to eliminate sexist language and to identify potentially disparaging usages, Bernstein produces the agonism for which journalists are justifiably notorious: "But Random House lexicographers *acknowledge* that the dictionary is likely to arouse opposition, particularly from those who feel it has bent to political fashions, dropping its role as an arbiter of *correct usage* in favor of a kind of anything-goes descriptivism" (1991, emphasis added). Prescriptive linguistics is a discredited theory to the extent that the rules it imposes ignore language structure and usage, and the explanations it provides are incorrect or suspiciously incomplete. Strictly speaking, prescriptivism is not a candid theory. It is precisely this lack of candor in prescriptivism, and in many other commonsense theories about language, society, culture, history, literature, economics, biology, physics, and so on, that frustrates academics, whose work is grounded in candid theories, but whose "public" credibility the media increasingly measure against the standards of commonsense theories. Surely middle-class common sense contributes to, if it has not actually created, the chilling effects at the National Science Foundation, which of late seems unusually intent on funding (or at least appearing to fund) only science of practical value, that is, of immediate, marketable value.

What we are more likely to see than linguistic analysis in prescriptive accounts of language, and in arguments based on them, is an unfettered will to control social and political reality by stemming the inexorable tides of linguistic variation and change and, barring that, an utterly self-righteous and self-serving devaluation of new usages. Since English handbooks prescribe usage (albeit in the guise of description), their continued, nearly universal use in composition courses and programs as the *exclusive* arbiters of fluency and the invocation of fluency as the *exclusive* measure of writing ability bespeaks a commonsense influence in the field out of all proportion to its influence in any of the other academic fields and disciplines. In other words, while the middle class grudgingly concedes the necessity for counterintuitive theories in the sciences, and to a lesser extent even in the social sciences, however infuriatingly daunting and inaccessible it may find them, many pundits and even some professors assume that the language theory on which writing pedagogy is (or should be) based must be the same one they believe should prescribe usage for not only the middle class but all Americans. Hence any pundit can claim with relative impunity that the purpose of composition is to police the grammar, spelling, punctuation, usage, and so on of students and be seen by many people as only making common sense. I should add that these same commonsense pundits and professors can and do, with equal impunity, assign literature professors to the same beat, for the language they seek to protect is thought to *live* in the literary canon. Middle-class literacy is a form of cultural capital that once seemed to rest on the gold standard of prescribed books and language, but turns out to be a volatile form of cultural currency whose seemingly stable value is alarmingly easy to destabilize in practice. A neologism here, a split infinitive there; a novel by Toni Morrison, Sandra Cisneros, Leslie Silko, or Amy Tan here, a work by Americo Paredes, Ishmael Reed, or Rigoberta Menchú there. Adding any or all would apparently wreak havoc on the exchange value of English as a world language and Western literature as the exclusive depository of universal and timeless truths.

It is this widely held and largely unexamined middle-class belief in its absolute right to prescribe virtually everything, from what fork to use to what music to record and words to publish, that vexes me as a theorist, researcher, teacher, and program administrator. It is as a program administrator, rather than as a theorist, researcher, or teacher, however, that I finally realized the devastating and pernicious consequences of rampant prescriptivism on the field of composition. For the pundits and professors who—without ever so much as looking at the syllabus—rallied and railed against the decision to reform the required one-semester first-year undergraduate writing course at the University of Texas at Austin seemed able to stoke anxiety over a syllabus entitled "Writing about Difference" in large part because prescriptivism is after all *just* common sense.

After a hundred-some years, any fool apparently can see, because it is after all only common sense, that students can't write because they can't spell, punctuate a sentence, or tell an adjective from an adverb, a phrase from a clause, a restrictive from a nonrestrictive clause, and so on. That many students do not attend to these matters in their writing does not mean they do not know the rules. To conclude that knowledge of the rules is the problem is very like presuming that middle-class adolescents whose rooms are a mess don't know *how* to clean them. The critics knew better, no matter how many times I explained that common sense is not always good sense in writing pedagogy, that attending to form while writing inhibits some writers to the point of distraction, that matters of form are commonly dealt with not as rules, independent of the texts produced, but when writers have a stake in what they are saying. Prescriptivists always know better, because like the commonsense theory that supports them, they confuse symptoms for causes, and so do not ask, as people in my field have, why after years of learning rules, students still act as if they have never heard of them. Composition teachers are not doctors, and do not prescribe for what *ails* students and offends the sensibilities of those who would prescribe even more of the same medicine that many of us have good reason to believe may account for the widespread amnesia among students (see Shaughnessy 1977; Bartholomae 1980; Hartwell 1985). It's not that students do not know rules. If anything, they know too many of them: never use *I*, never start a sentence with *and*, always state the thesis in the first paragraph, always conclude by paraphrasing the thesis. They know the rules of composition. They just don't know what composition has to do with anything save the fluency trick.

If you want students to learn to write, students who for years have been learning *not* to write, it is probably a good idea to recreate the circumstances under which others have turned to writing. While it is not the only reason, a good many literate people write when speech fails, that is, when something they have decided is worth reflecting on and asking others to contemplate is sufficiently complex that writing about it seems more promising than just talking it over with someone. This is at least a reason that a good many students would understand, for they live in the same troubling world as their teachers, a world where speech is just as likely to have sometimes failed them as it has us, and thus a world where writing is just as likely to hold the same promise for them as for us, unless teachers use it as bait for yet another fluency test. Everyone who worked on "Writing about Difference" saw the syllabus as inviting students to use writing to develop informed opinions on complex issues raised in the aftermath of civil rights law. While nearly everyone has an opinion on discrimination, I have learned, it seems that hardly anyone offers what could be called an informed opinion, one based on an understanding of law, its application by the courts in particular cases, and the implications of legal decisions for classes who are named in antidiscrimination legislation and for those who are not. Such ignorance and confusion seems made for writing, since the arguments that are at once the hardest and the most worthwhile to make in writing are those that readily acknowledge that the complexity of a situation allows not for one, not for two, but for an indefinite number of *arguable* positions.

As the director of lower-division English at Texas, in the spring of 1990 I recommended that the Lower Division English Policy Committee require all the graduate-student instructors of English 306: Rhetoric and Composition (known as English 101 or Freshman English in most places) to teach from a common syllabus, to be known as "Writing about Difference," for one year rather than continue the practice of providing new teachers textbooks the week before classes and requiring them, as well as experienced graduate-student teachers, to design their own courses. In large measure, my decision to use a common syllabus was an effort to offset what I believed to be the worst consequences of a long and bitter history of conflict between composition and literary studies in the English department at Texas. When the university fired most of the lecturers in English at the request of the department in the mid-1980s, several years before I agreed to come and direct the program, the department lost nearly all the instructors whose practical knowledge of composition justified pedagogical autonomy. By the time I assumed the directorship of lower-division English courses in 1989, only a handful of graduate students were enrolled in the Ph.D. program in rhetoric and composition, and a good many graduate students in literature resented being asked to design writing courses that, as one student put it, were conceived in ignorance, since he had never taken such a course himself (having tested out of it), and were therefore destined to fail. He and many others, in other words, saw the practice that some faculty later construed as protecting the academic freedom of the graduate-student instructors as protecting faculty who, because they are not required to teach composition at Texas, preferred to dismiss the problems of writing pedagogy in convenient rationalizations.

The English department dealt with the newly created shortage of staff to teach lower-division courses by voting, nearly unanimously, to reduce the two-semester sequence of composition courses for incoming students to one, in return for which the department agreed to forgo teaching writing about literature, and to teach writing from expository prose in the remaining course. That decision created problems for the graduate-student instructors and the program director alike, since graduate students in literary studies typically know a good deal less about expository prose than about literature. Little wonder, then, that student evaluations of the courses and the teachers often reflected these facts, and that often the same teachers who fared poorly as teachers of composition received considerably better course evaluations when they taught sophomore literature surveys (see Brodkey and Fowler 1991).

Writing program directors are commonly held responsible not only for their own course evaluations but also for those of courses taught by graduate students they direct or supervise. And in addition to being held responsible for all the lower-division courses in both literature and composition taught by graduate students, at Texas, as at most places, the director approves transfer credits and adjudicates grade complaints, appears on behalf of graduate-student teachers at formal grievances, and stands in as the defendant for any graduate-student instructor named in a suit against the university. These mundane duties not only define the usual institutional arrangements under which I and a good many others direct composition or lower-division programs, they radically distinguish us from most of the professoriat, inasmuch as we are held legally as well as ethically accountable for courses taught by graduate students in our departments. The department at Texas offers more than fifty sections of English 306 to approximately fifteen hundred students every semester, nearly all of them staffed by graduate students. Given the odds, my concern that most graduate students in literature are probably not particularly good teachers of writing convinced me that sooner or later I would be asked to explain to a court why I had not better prepared them to teach a course required of all entering students who do not pass a proficiency exam or take an equivalent course elsewhere. And even though many graduate students are more eager to learn about writing pedagogy than they once were, their ignorance of writing as a field of study only heightened my concern that many students could rightfully claim that they had not done much writing in English 306, let alone learn much of anything they had not already learned all too well in high school.

The decision to teach one semester of composition provided a rationale for an administrative reorganization of lower-division courses in which the same person would direct the programs in both composition and literature. While that may sound feasible, the institutional and intellectual history of the fields is such that literary studies largely depends on theories of reception, and composition on theories of production. Simply put, reading is not writing, nor is writing reading. A little less simply, a reception theory accounts only incidentally for the production of written texts. And, while some theories of reading seem more friendly to production than others, none suffices because none is meant to account for writing. For some years now, I have argued that poststructuralism is the friendliest of the language theories to writing and writing pedagogy, if only because it deals with the part language plays in constructions and representations of self and other, along with everything else we call reality (see Brodkey 1992a, 1989a). Anyone who teaches writing as more than a set of rules that students should learn and follow is likely to find such a theory attractive, at least initially, for collapsing the distinction between form and content also suggests that an adequate theory of writing would account for the contingencies of *what* is said as well as *how* it is said, and from that it follows that an adequate theory of writing pedagogy would teach students how to deal with the theoretical inseparability of form and content in practice. While the nearly two hundred graduate students at Texas do not all subscribe to a single theory, I suspect the current interest in writing and pedagogy among graduate students at Texas and elsewhere positively correlates with their widespread interest in and facility with critical theory, specifically with theories of language that at least suggest an account of the production as well as the reception of written texts.

Although the committee of faculty and graduate students that wrote the "Writing about Difference" syllabus made what might be called a courtesy gesture toward prescriptivism by requiring a handbook written by two local opponents as part of the course, the syllabus cobbles together the two language theories, structuralism and poststructuralism, that have supported virtually all scholarship on composition and literature for the past forty-some years. At least, I am not aware of any *scholarship* that is explicitly warranted by the commonsense precepts of linguistic prescriptivism, although it is arguable that many of us implicitly acknowledge the power of prescriptions in our own writing and in our literary preferences. As the title suggests, "Writing about Difference" derives from poststructuralism, for the counterintuitive and theoretical notion of *difference* concerns the part language plays in fabricating realities that use received definitions of difference to explain inequitable social, political, and economic treatment of particular groups or classes of people as arising out of or justified by inherent differences among people. What is not apparent in the title, but made explicit in the syllabus, is that all the writing assignments focus on the *structure* of arguments, by far the most important of which are opinions in discrimination suits, some of which are from the Civil Rights Act of 1964, the Education Amendments of 1972, and the Bill of Rights; others are commentaries on legal opinions and issues raised by legal theory.

In asking students to identify and summarize and evaluate the claims and grounds in the arguments they read and wrote, in light of warrants, we risked teaching them (or at least convincing them that we believe) that texts can be adequately analyzed and evaluated in relative isolation from other texts, and also that good reasons *alone* explain which laws are passed and legal opinions handed down. I suppose some students might have reached these or perhaps similar conclusions, but to have done so would have meant missing the point of the course, namely, that argument means precisely that, that every assertion is arguable (including those made by laws and by the courts, and those published in scholarly journals and handbooks, not to mention those expressed by their teachers and classmates). Thus, a chapter from legal scholar Martha Minow's decidedly poststructuralist *Making All the Difference: Inclusion, Exclusion, and American Law,* with which notions of difference were introduced, in turn became the material to be summarized, analyzed, and evaluated.

In my own defense, and on behalf of the others who worked on the syllabus, I would like to say that we took the position (which, along with claims and grounds, we borrowed from the philosopher of ordinary language Stephen Toulmin) that warrants bear visible traces of discourses—not in the sense that linguists are apt to mean discourse (as stretches of text above the level of the sentence) but as discourses are defined by poststructuralists, as the ideologies or vantage points from which everyone views reality. By way of example, in a case we planned to use in the course, *Chambers v. Omaha Girls Club, Inc.,* Crystal Chambers, a single black woman, argued that the club violated her civil rights by firing her when she became pregnant. The majority opinion in favor of the defendant turns on the club's requirement that all employees sign an agreement to be role models, but the minority opinion argues that since the club offered no empirical evidence that such a thing as a role model exists, the plaintiff cannot be fired on the grounds that she was not a *good* role model. The club argued (and the court agreed) that violating Chambers's civil rights was a justifiable "business necessity," since an unmarried pregnant employee is a poor role model in an organization dedicated to preventing pregnancy among its largely adolescent, black, female population. The majority opinion in *Chambers* is arguably based on common wisdom, the minority opinion on science. If you accept that distinction, then it is also arguable that received opinion and science are warranted by two distinct discourses, and that in *this* court and in *this* case a precept warranted by common sense prevailed over science. Without either invoking the recent history of privileging the testimony of expert (scientific) witnesses over the accounts of ordinary people or resorting to what is called students' personal experience (what they have heard at home, at school, and in churches or synagogues), relatively inexperienced undergraduate writers could identify, analyze, and evaluate even these seemingly unassailable legal arguments by focusing on claims, grounds, and warrants. In other words, it is possible to argue that a single black mother would be the best role model, that she would be the worst one, that black women have a greater responsibility to be role models than white women, that it is unjust to require poor black women to be good role models when rich white women are not also expected to perform this function, that an anecdote is superior (or inferior) to experimental research as testimony—for these claims and more are implicitly or explicitly either raised in or implied by *Chambers*, not to mention the other cases selected for the course. The point is not to agree or disagree with an opinion, but to locate an unquestioned assumption and explore (argue) its possible ramifications.

Learning argument alone is a demanding task, though we admittedly made it more daunting still by asking students to construct arguments in the context of antidiscrimination law and legal opinions. That was a deliberate decision on my part, not to introduce multiculturalism (the courts are rarely accused of harboring multiculturalists) but to offer students what I consider the quintessential academic experience, the often exhilarating and at times even liberating experience of making a sustained analysis and critique of unexamined assumptions; it is an intellectual privilege tantamount to an academic right, founded on the willingness to lay out a *candid* argument in support of a position. While most students are willing, even eager, to acknowledge that "everyone has a right to their own opinion," few are willing to acknowledge that invoking this seemingly democratic principle in lieu of an argument is likely to be seen as an admission that an opinion is based on either no reasons at all or on reasons that will not withstand scrutiny. The syllabus takes their inexperience with and anxiety about public disagreement into account, yet invites all students to argue with texts of unmistakable importance, to plaintiffs and defendants in the first instance, but also ultimately to the citizenry. (See Penticoff and Brodkey 1992 for a full description of the intellectual considerations raised by our approach to argumentation.)

I make no apologies for asking students to read law or legal cases or essays and to base their writing on what they have read. Nor do I see any reason to apologize for asking them to read and write about difference simply because the topic makes people uneasy. Eighteen-year-olds are not very large children. They are young adults. They can legally vote, marry, drive, and enter into contracts; the men among them can be drafted into the military, any among them can enlist, and all among them are subject to the full penalty of law if convicted of a crime. They may be young, but they are not children in anyone's eyes but their parents' and, when it suits them, their own. And even though they may not know much about antidiscrimination law, surveys of entering classes suggest that college students increasingly believe discrimination to be a problem: about 20 percent of the class of 1991 agreed with the statement "Racial discrimination is no longer a major problem in America" (*Almanac*, 13), compared to 15 percent of the class of 1992 (Collison 1993, A31). While student attitudes are not in themselves sufficient grounds for a course, they suggest topics of interest and, in their turn, topics amenable to writing.

We professors do students and ourselves a disservice when we collude with institutions that insist on representing the first two years of college as the thirteenth and fourteenth grades, in order, I presume, to justify herding them into large lecture halls and keeping them on ice until the survivors amass enough credits to reemerge as juniors. In composition, the infantilization of students is most evident in courses that prescribe rules for what ails them, but probably the most pernicious in those that condemn them to writing from personal experience. Students may be young, but they are not stupid. Many probably resist writing from personal experience because even in this area, where they are supposedly undisputed authorities, teachers invariably invoke form and assess their lives along with their grammar, spelling, and so on. Probably the safest and smartest way to handle such assignments is to lie. And telling lies then makes it all the easier for students to resist the exhortations of process pedagogy, since drafting and revising an essay in which you have little or no stake is foolish.

The pedagogies of process and personal experience are valiant efforts to circumvent the institutional power and authority of teachers over students. These seemingly progressive approaches fail to the extent that both deny that composition teachers *are* the designated institutional representatives of the power and authority of language. Would that the power and the authority of language were confined to classrooms or even to forms, that discourses were as easily shucked off as handbooks and Richard Bernstein seem to believe. But then, trade presses and pundits with an economic stake in dispensing prescriptions, and in denying that they are themselves empowered not by their prescriptions but emboldened by a middle-class will to prescribe, are not in business to teach writing. But schools are, or should be, and if they are not, and we who work in them are not, then they and we are the unwitting accomplices to the most recent commonsense attack on all the uncommon, counterintuitive theories that generate scholarship, and without which there would be far fewer discourses in which to challenge common sense. What distinguishes the most recent attack on the professoriat is that the professors who have joined forces with the pundits also invoke common sense in excoriating colleagues with whom they disagree. They do not, however, just make commonsense arguments in faculty meetings and before the faculty senate, or even in open letters to their colleagues—in forums where common sense can be checked against the kinds of intellectual contingencies that have traditionally exposed some of the limitations of received wisdom. Instead, they make common sense in newspapers and on talk shows, where familiar theories comfort and unfamiliar ones discomfort the middle class. At the University of Texas, the unchecked forces of common sense were permitted to silence those of good sense when the administration capitulated to the din of negative publicity and rescinded the authorized departmental committee's right to make and institute policy to meet the curricular goals of its course offerings (see Brodkey and Fowler 1991; Brodkey 1994a).

Public criticism of the committee's decision came from several quarters in the university: two professors of composition, two in literary studies, and a handful in other departments and schools. The collective position is probably best represented by an advertisement that appeared in the student newspaper under the title "A Statement of Academic Concern." It was later learned that the advertisement, signed by fifty-six professors (there are more than twenty-two hundred on the Austin campus), was paid for by a check drawn on the account of the Texas Association of Scholars, an affiliate of the National Association of Scholars (Henson and Philpott 1990a, 1990b). While many people might argue that members of the NAS are conservative or even reactionary, NAS recruitment advertisements and essays published in its journal, *Academic Questions*, suggest an academic group bonded by an uncharacteristic devotion to common sense, or at least to using commonsense arguments against colleagues with whom they disagree. In addition to taking the egregious liberty of renaming the syllabus—calling it "Difference—Racism and Sexism" rather than "Writing about Difference"—the advertisement states as its primary concern "that the new curriculum for Freshman English distorts the fundamental purpose of a composition class—to enhance a student's ability to write—by subordinating instruction in writing to the discussion of social issues and, potentially, to the advancement of specific political positions" (*Daily Texan* 1990). It apparently just takes a bit of common sense to know that form cannot be taught in tandem with content, or that all graduate-student instructors are of one mind about what positions students must take on "social issues."

The collective position taken in the advertisement, however, is a considerably more restrained commonsense criticism of colleagues than the one written some weeks earlier by the most persistent and vocal of its signers, Alan Gribben, then a professor of American literature at Texas. In a letter to the editor of the local newspaper, Gribben claimed that students "will begin having their social attitudes as well as their essays graded by English Department instructors in what has to be the most massive effort at thought control ever attempted on the campus" and then used his assertion to justify this rather startling recommendation:

> I hope that alumni and taxpaying Texas citizens will remind Standish Meacham, liberal arts dean, Joseph Kruppa, English Department chairman, and Linda Brodkey, director of lower-division English, that if so fundamental a course as English 306 can be blatantly politicized, then the state Legislature and the UT faculty, administration and board of regents

> have a right to consider abolishing required English courses. (Gribben 1990b)

This, too, is apparently just common sense, for while I never heard from either of these quarters directly (I have no way of knowing if unnamed callers who in the days following this letter threatened to cut off or otherwise mutilate selected parts of my body represented any of the constituencies identified), the university effectively canceled the plan when it postponed implementation of the syllabus, without providing the policy committee or the department any formal procedure for reversing the postponement. No terms were given in the first instance, nor later, because the president of the university refused even to meet and discuss the syllabus with the committee.

Common sense prevailed at Texas. Alan Gribben was later quoted in the *Chronicle of Higher Education:* " 'If you really care about women and minorities making it in society, it doesn't make sense to divert their attention to oppression when they should be learning basic writing skills' " (Mangan 1990). This strikes me as being of a piece with the opponents of sex education, who seem to think that adolescents would not even know about sex if their teachers would only refrain from mentioning it. Another professor of American literature circulated his own countersyllabus, based on principles of copyediting and bearing some unfortunate reminders that even full professors of English can and do make errors in punctuation and spelling (Duban 1990). A professor who writes handbooks, and a coauthor of the one required for "Writing about Difference," published an editorial in the student newspaper identifying rhetoric as "the subject matter to be taught and learned" and defining an introduction to rhetoric as focusing "on the logic and validity of arguments, the development and enrichment of ideas, the appropriate arrangement of subject matter, and the power and correctness of language" (Ruszkiewicz 1990). Rhetoric as techniques devoid of content is just common sense. The other coauthor of the handbook made the argument in the popular press and a professional journal that since student texts should be the focus of instruction, teachers should assign no readings, so students can write about their own ideas (Hairston 1991: B1; 1992: 186). There is just no arguing with common sense.

The common sense that characterizes the arguments of professors who took exception to the syllabus is amply reiterated by pundits. Richard Bernstein, who would later take lexicographers to task for not sharing his devotion to grammatical correctness, introduced a *New York Times* feature article on "political correctness" with the mistaken but fluent claims that the course was being taught, and that it had replaced the "literary classics" with what he described, without asking to see the syllabus, as materials some people said gave the course "more relevance" but others said made it "a stifling example of academic orthodoxy" (1990: 1). Such ill-informed hyperbole seems to me a classic example of journalism's commonsense precept that news is newsworthy only if there are two (and only two) diametrically opposed sides to a story. Never mind that his sources are reacting to the idea of the syllabus, not responding to it. Never mind that, in claims ostensibly about writing, the reporter and his sources are concerned only about what students will read. George F. Will used his syndicated column to lambaste the course, about which he knew so little that he described one at another university, and then took the occasion of his outrage to remind his readers that teachers are supposed to teach grammatical correctness, not political correctness. Judging by what I have read, the most wonderful thing about possessing common sense must be the satisfaction of saying in so many words that it goes without saying that you are right, that there would be nothing to talk about if people would just see "reason"—end of conversation.

The end of conversation is also the end of language. My most abiding fear is that, just as the signs regulating smoking do not satisfy the desire to ban smoking, even the most stringent regulation of writing by prescription would not satisfy professors and pundits whose faith in the doctrine of meritocracy is so fragile as to justify silencing any challenge to the triple identification of language, class, and nation as one and the same. Women, Latinos, and Illiterates are paraded before us as fetishes in a spectacle of patriotism and caricatured in narratives on national defense because a vocal and persistent minority of the middle class projects its fears onto their bodies. The results of what amounts to a cultural Rorschach are passed off as common sense, and common sense is in turn used to warrant state regulation. Thus the nation's fetuses must be protected from feminists and their dupes; its citizens must be defended from the south by fences; its language must be policed. In this scenario, medicine, the Immigration and Naturalization Service, and the schools are the sites where doctors, border patrols, and teachers are installed as the gatekeepers of the nation, and any reluctance on their part—to prevent abortions, turn back undocumented workers, identify illiterates—becomes a reason for regulating them as well their charges. If I must be a gatekeeper, and if all teachers are by definition, I at least insist on my right to imagine a more inclusive America than the America projected by the most recent purveyors of common sense.

To my mind, the charges of political correctness mask my even more heterodox offenses against the orthodoxy that grammatical correctness is the sine qua non of both writing pedagogy and middle-class privilege. Yet had professors and pundits who reacted to the very *idea* of difference bothered to look at the syllabus for "Writing about Difference," they might have noticed that antidiscrimination law reproduces the nearly canonical middle-class presumption that America is (or at least is meant to be) a classless society. For only when a society guarantees the civil rights of all its citizens can it even hope to convince any but the already privileged that the privileges of, say, professors and pundits are entirely owing to individual merit. While you or I might like to believe that *our* privileges are wholly or even mostly merited, all campaigns to persuade the citizenry that individual merit rests on the writing of fluent English, or on any other ability we might name, are and will remain suspect in the face of discrimination.

If composition can be said to abet middle-class illusions of meritocracy, then the deregulation of writing is about replacing that empty promise with pedagogy that honors the First Amendment by teaching students that freedom of speech is meaningful only if the citizenry is literate. Not just functionally literate. Literate. Not just fluent. Literate. Literacy is not just skills, nor is it abilities. Literacy is attitude, entitlement, the entitlement that middle-class privilege masks in prescriptions but that writing lays bare in the sheer force of the desire to see and to get readers to see what can be seen from where the writer stands. Virtually everything depends on the desire for a hearing, for it is that desire that makes the learning of rules or anything else that might also clarify a position welcome to the writer. Writers take stands. In standing for writing pedagogy, I have also taken a stand against what I see as gratuitous and cynical representations of composition students as unruly children who lack discipline. In part that means standing with others in the field who have also expressed reservations about the institutional arrangements under which writing is taught as composition. I see those conditions as justifying everyone from poison pens to professors to pundits to prescribe—without benefit of theory, research, and practice—what students and their teachers should be doing in composition courses—in the name of common sense. In standing for writing, I have taken a stand against others in the field, in the academy, and in the media who refuse to consider even the possibility that prescriptions that seem to regulate only the "correct" use of language threaten to extinguish altogether the desire to write—in middle-class and working-class students alike. Unless regulating that desire *is* the point, I suggest that we begin again and try to teach writing—for a change.

I would like to acknowledge the following people for their generous intellectual contributions to the argument I lay out in this essay: Lester Faigley, Michelle Fine, George Mariscal, Robert McDonell, Susan Miller, Roddey Reid, and Barbara Tomlinson.

The members of what came to be known as the Ad Hoc Syllabus-Writing Group were Margaret Downs-Gamble, David Ericson, Shelli Fowler, Dana Harrington, Susan Sage Heinzelman, Sara Kimball, Allison Mosshart, Stuart Moulthrop, Richard Penticoff, John Slatin, Maria Villalobos, and me. The syllabus is copyrighted in my name.

TELLING EXPERIENCES

I began thinking of experience as stories we tell about ourselves the day I overheard my four-year-old son talking to himself about his life as he played alone in his room. That's when it occurred to me for the first time that if children say aloud what adults have learned to keep to themselves, then at that very moment I could be unwittingly composing an autobiography to myself not unlike the one I could hear my son declaiming. I have since forgotten that specific installment from Jesse's life story, but not the scene in my mind's eye of the child interrupting his own play with odd bits of narration. Yet when I look on this scene, I am not only reminded that the past intrudes itself on the present. I am convinced that the child, now a young adult, is more likely to recall episodes from his autobiography than any part he played in transforming events into his experience.

So much conspires against Jesse's remembering that he is the narrator of his life. Everyone knows that people have experiences, which they then recall in speaking and writing. "You'll never guess what happened to me" announces an intent to recount something that is over and done with. It flies in the face of common sense to suggest that our anecdotes do not so much reconstitute as constitute experiences. We are taught to tell stories as if narration were incidental to experience. Yet if Jesse teaches himself to remember, as I and others have, that he is the narrator of his experience, there is a chance that what he learns about composing himself in the course of drafting his autobiography will challenge cultural practices that insist that experience is independent of self and that both are separate from their expression in language.

I learned about telling and listening to personal experience narratives from the women who gathered at my mother's kitchen table. That's where I was taught to find something interesting in even the most artless accounts, to side with the teller, and to accept events at face value. But it is also where I learned that a story about personal experience invites listeners to join the teller in reflecting on troubling events—a child's behavior, a parent's or in-law's criticism, infidelity, pregnancy, unemployment, low wages, high prices, ill health. As I remember it, personal experience narratives posed rather than solved problems, which were explored and extended in either commentary or more narratives.

In more fanciful moments, I see my mother's kitchen as a parliament of narratives, the place where mothers met to legislate family life in the neighborhood. But that image came later, after consciousness-raising groups had replaced the kitchen parliament, the women's movement had begun to publicize stories of women's domestic lives, and the personal had become political—for me and a good many other women. Yet to this day I savor moments of identity learned in my mother's kitchen and practiced in women's groups, moments when being taken at my word and taking another woman at hers affirm my membership in a community of women. There is a sense in which identity with other women empowers those who recognize themselves in stories of women's experiences. As important as identity is to women, including me, there is, however, a sense in which identity can be as dangerous to women as sexism, sex-based discrimination, and sexual harassment.

Just as representing experience as independent of teller and telling collapses distinctions between event and narration, political solidarity based on identity exchanges narratives of self for fetishes of the self, a bad bargain for any number of reasons, not least that ready-made selves fit most women about as well as ready-to-wear clothes. A fetishized self is a dangerously idealized woman, a standard that finds actual women lacking and that justifies excluding some women as *not* something: not feminine, not feminist. Identity fetishes of the self devalue the complex selves that emerge in narratives of personal experience by offering to relieve us of the burden of composing ourselves in exchange for the illusion that we will always be the same, never different, as long as we identify ourselves as a kind of woman. Little wonder then that ready-to-wear identities make us even more anxious to deny everything about ourselves that differs from the fetish and encourage us to project that anxiety about the differences in ourselves onto others.

Some of the stories told in my mother's kitchen did little more than make a virtue of the whiteness of the working-class women gathered there. I recall the women talking about not allowing their white children to swim in the town's public pool with black children (melanin was believed not to be indelible). I remember others reporting rumors of black families planning to buy or rent in what had been a poor but white neighborhood. And then there were the stories about unknown white girls whose reputations were ruined because they had been seen with a black boy (I remember there being many girls but only one boy), and there were rumors about white girls being sold into white slavery and black women cruising white neighborhoods in search of white men and boys. Unlike the personal experience narratives that the women told about their own lives, the no-name children, adolescents, and adults fetishized in these accounts are black and white caricatures. Rather than pose problems for the women to discuss, these miscegenation stories terrorized and silenced the members of the kitchen parliament.

Stories about the terrible sexuality of black people represent white women not as the rightful legislators of domestic life but as the hapless victims of desegregation: they stand to lose their white children, white neighborhoods, good names, freedom, and husbands, sisters, and brothers to miscegenation. The prefabricated stories that excluded black people from my mother's kitchen in fetishes of whiteness and blackness recycled white supremacist propaganda, wherein political soli-

[illegible]ts solely on white identity, on convincing white people that whiteness is [illegible]lesirable that all black people wish to be white.

[illegible]se identity fetishes make a virtue of a single dimension of self (race, color, [illegible]class, sexual orientation, ethnicity, nationality, age, religious affiliation), [illegible]value storytelling, which involves everyone in a process of composing themselves as the more or less multidimensional characters of their experiences. Identity fetishes cynically exclude those people on whom we project our differences even as they deny us a chance to explore differences within ourselves in narratives of experience. For it is difference, not identity, that links us to those who are not ourselves, those possible selves that are acknowledged and cherished only by people who can recall composing themselves when they narrate their experience.

PART III

Presentations

Introduction to Part III

Academics are usually encouraged rather than required to present papers at scholarly conferences and deliver lectures at other institutions. There is a widely held belief, however, that in addition to offering a chance to meet scholars in your field, a conference is a good place to rehearse before an audience of your peers arguments you plan to use in essays. I have found this to be true and not true. While I often discern a fair number of limitations in an argument in the course of writing a fifteen- to twenty-minute conference paper, there is rarely enough time for questions. The few that get hurriedly asked are often related to the topic but tangential to the argument: "Why didn't you talk about what I would have talked about if I had given a paper on that topic?" On those occasions when I am invited to lecture, that is, to talk for forty to fifty minutes and answer questions for fifteen to thirty minutes, however, people invariably ask questions and make comments that substantially affect my thinking. The extra time may be even more crucial for the audience than for the lecturer, since it seems that in the additional minutes more people begin to wonder how arguments intersect, and so want to know where the case at hand fits and what the consequences may be of accepting, rejecting, or modifying the stated or implied conclusions of a speaker's argument.

Much as I value what is learned from discussions that follow lectures I have given and attended, however, I am also mindful of Erving Goffman's assertion in "The Lecture" that "a public lecture contains a text that could just as well be imparted through print or informal talk. This being the case, the content of a lecture is not to be understood as something distinctive to and characteristic of lecturing" (1981: 172). Goffman makes this assertion in the context of his argument that the delivery of the text is only one and not necessarily the most important event on such occasions. As I understand it, since the publicized lecture (or conference) advertises its sponsors and audience along with the lecturer, the occasion is distinguished by the power of institutions to produce *lecturers* as well as lectures. In the course of this characteristically Goffmanesque analysis, a caustic demystification of a familiar and even banal social performance, readers are forcefully reminded, therefore, that since *everybody* is a corporeal being, ultimately *no body* transcends the institutional space it inhabits.

After the lecture, this "functionary of the cognitive establishment," the lecturer that Goffman concludes is hired "to protect us from the wind, to stand up and seriously project the assumption that through lecturing, a meaningful picture of some part of the world can be conveyed," returns along with everyone in the audience "to the flickering, cross-purposed, messy irresolution of their unknowable circumstances" (194-95). I remembered this essay when I was selecting papers and lectures for this section because many of my texts bear the diacritics of my stage fright, a tremolo that sometimes besets me when I stand at a podium to speak before a large audience. After rereading Goffman, however, I wonder if the vibrato in my voice is also a recognition that more than my performance is at stake. I dealt with the stage fright by scanning my own texts as I would poems, and for several years relied on these markings to approximate English phrasing when I was reading aloud. I am still dealing, as is everyone else, however, with the impossible desire to make the world fully comprehensible in language.

My stage fright has receded enough over the years for me to treat the diacritics as mementos of a time when I believed, or at least I want to believe I believed, the success or failure of the unspoken contract that Goffman invokes to rest solely on my *delivery* of a text. In any event, I like to think the texts selected for this section were written and delivered to honor an agreement on the order of the one Goffman argues warrants such gatherings, and that even if I do not imagine myself to be able or even willing to stave off the wind, my weather reports are of at least as much use as other such bulletins. Yet unlike Goffman, I believe the content of these texts to be distinct, for while I borrow notions and phrases and sometimes even whole paragraphs from papers and lectures for some of my essays, I have learned that the arguments do not travel well.

That the texts of my papers and lectures are not the texts of essays seems most apparent to me in "Transvaluing Difference," which was written for the 1989 Conference on College Composition and Communication (CCCC). It is the only one that has been published, and the editor of *College English* published it not as an essay, but as an "Opinion." I do not mean that an opinion is not an argument, but that in my work, at least, an opinion tends to be a preliminary argument, an argument that there is sufficient evidence to warrant making an argument. In "Transvaluing Difference," for example, the case for the pedagogical value of difference depends largely on a story about my experience as a Peace Corps volunteer in Senegal. It is not the status of anecdotes that concerns me here, for I am not alone in noticing the presence and value of narrative in argumentation. It is, instead, the verbal exploration that I most value in my preliminary arguments. I think of them as leaves in a verbal sketchbook, preliminary and figurative studies limned from specific vantage points. Senegal represents a vantage point from which to see difference. It is not the only, the best, or even a real or necessary prospect, but it seemed to me at the time one that might persuade some people that there were sound practical reasons for the emerging theoretical interest in difference. I look at difference from other vantage points in subsequent papers and lectures, as well as in essays, for I remain fascinated with the pedagogical possibilities that difference holds for writing.

The four unpublished papers presented at CCCC and the two lectures that complete this section were written after the University of Texas summarily scuttled the syllabus entitled "Writing about Difference." For a couple of years, no matter what the topic of my paper, most of the questions at the annual conference were about what happened at Texas. So, while I do not even broach the issue of local politics in "On the Intersection of Feminism and Cultural Studies" (1991) or "Hard Cases for Cultural Studies" (1992), the papers were written in the heat of negative publicity about the syllabus and delivered at the conference in the chilly aftermath of administrative censure. When I presented "Critical Ethnography" at the 1993 preconference workshop on research, however, the questions that were asked concerned problems people were encountering in the course of writing ethnographic accounts based on their own data. While the final paper, "At the Site of Writing," delivered at the same conference in 1995, also prompted no questions about Texas, its content arises out of the same specter of injustice that preoccupied me during the writing of "Transvaluing Difference," and its argument is based on the same poststructural theory of language and discourse.

Also included in this section are two lectures, one about the sorry fate of difference at Texas and the other about the effect on pedagogy when difference is used as the intellectual warrant for what many people call multiculturalism. "The Troubles at Texas" was written in 1991, while I was still at Texas, and delivered the same year at the Penn State Conference on Rhetoric and Composition. There is not, however, so much as a passing reference to Texas in "Difference and a Pedagogy of Difference." I wrote the lecture for the Institute for Teaching and Learning at the University of Chicago in 1993 and have presented versions of it at several places since because it lays out practical grounds for theoretical arguments about difference that concern teachers of writing. The discussions that follow are invariably lively and usually provocative, for difference entails a good many intellectual upheavals, not least among them a shift in language theory.

I have not forgotten lessons learned at Texas, for the virulent strain of anti-intellectualism that surfaced there in the early 1990s has since been eroding the quality of intellectual life for many students and teachers across the country. It is an anti-intellectualism that regularly calls on the forces of common sense to discredit intellectual dissent. Their First Amendment right is one of the few legitimate recourses U.S. citizens have to protect themselves against the absolute power of common sense. The academy has historically opposed common sense, not good sense but the received wisdom that makes it seem reasonable to many people to teach writing as skills or grammar and unreasonable to teach it in any of the seemingly counterintuitive ways it is taught by people who look closely at what else producing an essay requires. Common sense is not always good sense. Because it is not, scholars in my field continue to examine and reflect on the practice of writing, which remains considerably more complicated than any theory generated to account for it, and, happily, considerably more exciting in practice than in theory.

Transvaluing Difference

American scholars have more than a passing interest in academic freedom because historically the relationship between the academy and the state has been uneasy. And a good deal of this uneasiness has to do with the long academic tradition of questioning received wisdom, common knowledge, the very doxa by which society lives. Yet we have only to recall the reports of the November 1988 meeting of the National Association of Scholars (NAS)—in the *Chronicle of Higher Education,* the *Nation,* and the *New York Times*—to realize that when "minority," feminist, or progressive scholars examine and challenge academic doxa, the right-wing membership of the NAS proposes to meet that challenge with charges of heterodoxy, charges that we have come to associate with, say, Accuracy in Academia. Like Accuracy in Academia, the NAS recalls a time when consensus reigned in the academy, and it seeks in its journal, *Academic Questions,* and an unspecified number of NAS fellowships to "recall higher education to its classic function of imparting the heritage of our civilization" (NAS materials).

There are reports that an NAS audience cheered when Alan Kors, a professor of history from the University of Pennsylvania, identified women's centers, lesbians, and gays as the "academic totalitarians" behind "antiharassment policies, racial awareness programs and the enshrinement of 'diversity' as a value for the university" (Weiner 1988: 644). I'm prefacing my remarks on transvaluing difference with this extraordinary academic transmogrification of difference, and indeed academic opposition to academic freedom, because I stand before you as one of the feminists and progressives the right-wing members of the NAS find unconscionably different and characterize as totalitarian. By the standard articulated in Kors's diatribe, a great deal of what I care about and work on is objectionable, for I do not think my scholarship is unaffected by either my feminism or my progressivism, nor do I think his scholarship exists independent of his politics. And while I hope that not all NAS members literally believe Kors's other widely quoted remark—"The barbarians are in our midst" (Joseph Berger 1988)—I'm worried that the ad hominem strategy effectively obscures the new theories of language and reality, which have generated a fair amount of feminist, progressive, African-American, and Third World scholarship, but apparently have also challenged the doxa that the NAS is so eager to defend that some of its members have resorted to what amounts to academic terrorism.

I'm speaking of course about poststructural theories, theories challenging the notion that language and reality are independent of one another and arguing instead that language and reality are dependent, that words constitute worldviews, and hence that any attempts to describe reality are necessarily partial accounts, that is, they are limited by what can be seen and understood from a particular vantage point and provisional, by definition, because any theory is an incomplete and interested account of whatever it sets out to explain.

As a language theorist, I have found social construction theory, and in particular the notion that we construct and constitute a world in our words, fruitful, if only because I so regularly encounter students and colleagues who presume that, with the notable exceptions of advertising and propaganda, a spoken or written text refers to a universal reality independent of language. By this logic, speakers or writers can argue that they bear no responsibility for the consequences of racist, sexist, and homophobic language, since "nigger," "bitch," and "queer" simply refer to an already given reality that language only reflects. I've chosen the most objectionable terms I can think of to point out that the theory that language constructs reality, that what we know of reality is dependent on language, argues that the language used to register the most violent objections to difference thrives in part because of our desire to ignore difference and hence our own complicity in the very political inequities that African-Americans, feminists, lesbians, gays, and progressives on the University of Pennsylvania campus have been attempting to rectify with a harassment survey and antiharassment policies that Alan Kors characterized as the dangers of "tolerance and diversity" (Weiner 1988: 644).

It's not tolerance or diversity that feminist, African-American, Third World, and progressive scholars are talking about. We're talking about the limits of universality, about the need to recognize that the negative valuing of difference—*not* white, *not* male, *not* heterosexual, *not* middle class—is socially constructed and can therefore be socially reconstructed and positively revalued. To focus on difference rather than tolerance or diversity is especially hard for those of us who were taught that racism, classism, and even nationalism could be overcome if people would only recognize that the similarities among people far outweigh the differences. And perhaps for some of you, as well as for me, the lesson that differences are superficial was unmistakably brought home in Edward Steichen's photographic essay *The Family of Man;* in the prologue Carl Sandburg wrote:

> There is only one man in the world
> and his name is All Men.
> There is only one woman in the world
> and her name is All Women.
> There is only one child in the world
> And the child's name is All Children.

I learned that lesson in the fifth grade. And, even though my teacher had to point out to me that the pictures weren't showing that it's better to have a baby in a hospital than in a field, I learned to believe in the universal human condition. And it wasn't until the Peace Corps that I began to see the limits of the lesson, began to realize along with others that where you are born, when, to whom, and under what circumstances makes a difference and began to wonder whether focusing on similarities wasn't distracting me from noticing the consequences of difference, namely, inequity.

Not everyone needed to travel as far as I did to learn that difference matters, for the kinds of differences, and the negative consequences of those differences, that I was seeing as a volunteer in West Africa others were able to observe at home. Some of us only witnessed the political and economic consequences of difference and some of us felt them personally, but many of us learned, I think, that language plays its part. Babies in Senegal starved not because the bureaucrats were talking, but because they were talking about who among them was the most powerful and hence could take the most credit for "saving" the first victims of the Sahara shift and that round of victims of the Biafran war, rather than talking about the equitable distribution of milk and food.

And I'm worried that what Alan Kors is reported to have said at the 1988 NAS meeting is likely to be as consequential to our lives as teachers as were those meetings to starving and now dead children. For indeed, just as the bureaucrats squandered the precious time needed to save human lives determining who among them was the most powerful, Kors would have us spend our precious time defending our right to be in the academy rather than considering how to begin teaching students that language is neither a poor tool for translating thought nor a mirror in which reality is dimly reflected, but part of reality, and in writing classrooms a substantial part at that.

Many and perhaps even most of the students I teach are unprepared to take responsibility for the content and implications of the claims they make about the world. They have learned, though one wonders if this is what they were actually taught, that any and all claims made in the third person are potentially objective, and that objectivity is more or less guaranteed if the writer can provide three or more examples in support of the claim. This seems to be true irrespective of their politics, since I hear versions of "everybody has a right to their own opinion" from across the political spectrum, and it seems that most also believe that teachers cannot assail third-person claims buttressed with examples from printed texts. This procedural version of writing defines not only their rights and responsibilities as students, but also mine as a teacher. Among the students we teach, then, the theory that language and reality are independent of one another means that our rights and responsibilities as their teachers extend only to the formal expression of their claims, and that our job is to teach them how to modify third-person claims, but not to interrogate the contents or consequences of their claims, or of any claims, for that matter, that satisfy these formal conditions.

The world I live in is not as simple or syntactic or procedural as the world the students come from. The theory of language out of which they and some of my colleagues operate presumes that specificity, definition, and expansion more or less guarantee that students will self-correct as they adjust their claims to match the empirical reality to which they presumably refer. Well, I don't think there is a literal empirical reality to which they refer—and that I can make available to them because I know about it and they don't. And since I understand my work neither as teaching them how to say what they already believe in more acceptable ways nor as teaching them to think what I think, I am obligated to extend to them the same rights, and the same responsibilities, I enjoy as an academic. I am obligated to instruct and support them in a critique of received wisdom, which in their case, as in mine, means a sustained interrogation of the doxa out of which claims about reality arise and to which their claims and mine contribute. In other words, they need to learn that objectivity isn't guaranteed by syntax and three or more sources; they need to learn to ask, as a matter of course, what you have to believe to say that "women's place is in the home" or "women should receive equal pay for equal work"; and they need to ask whose interests are served with claims like "desegregation destroyed the public schools" or "desegregation is the only way to overcome racism."

If nothing else, we want students to learn that just as facts do not speak for themselves, an interpretation is partial. We want them to begin to realize that when you speak or write you are doing something, other than following procedures, and that in the same way that cabinetmakers make furniture and musicians make music, writers animate words, and these words are as much a part of the material world as tables and records and concerts.

I don't think what I'm suggesting is barbarous or totalitarian. But then I can't think of any reason why I would be nostalgic for either an America or an academy in which the special interests of some are passed off as in the national interest or in the best interests of scholarship. I'm as suspicious about the consensus that the NAS insists used to exist in the academy as I am about any claim that presumes to certainty. But I'm as certain about my right to be in the academy (despite my difference) and my responsibility to students (despite our differences) as I am about Alan Kors's right to be worried and the NAS's responsibility in misrepresenting poststructural theories as unjustifiable intellectual dissent.

—Conference on College Composition and Communication, 1989

On the Intersection of Feminism and Cultural Studies

It's no secret among feminists that white, professional women are more likely than women of color or working-class women to privilege gender over race, ethnicity, and class, or that many of these women attribute the success of the feminist political and academic projects over the last twenty-some years to essentializing gender. It's not just that white feminists forget that most women are of color, or that most women are working class, but that they believe gender discrimination overrides their race and class privileges. For feminists who can distinguish between the absolute and relative privileges of being white and middle class, the work of women of color is critical to understanding that feminists simply cannot justify essentializing gender in theory, research, and practice.

I want to make a case for what critical legal studies scholar Kimberle Crenshaw calls intersectionality, by which she means that "the intersectional experience is greater than the sum of race and gender" (1989: 140), to which we might add ethnicity and class and a string of differences like sexual orientation, ability, and age. Crenshaw confines herself to race and gender not out of indifference to ethnicity or class, but out of respect for her data, which concern Title VII discrimination suits brought by black women against their employers. When the district court rejected the suit of the five black women plaintiffs in *DeGraffenreid v. General Motors Assembly Division, St. Louis*, it reasoned as follows:

> Plaintiffs have failed to cite any decisions which have stated that Black women are a special class to be protected from discrimination. . . . Thus, this lawsuit must be examined to see if it states a cause of action for race discrimination, sex discrimination, or alternatively either, but not a combination of both. (141)

In other words, the plaintiffs are told that, under the law, they can be black or they can be female, but not both. In *Moore v. Hughes Helicopters, Inc.*, a suit alleging that the employer discriminated against black women in promotions, Crenshaw reports that the court concluded that

> Moore had never claimed before the EEOC [Equal Employment Opportunity Commission] that she was discriminated against as a female, but only as a black female. . . . This raised serious doubts as to Moore's ability to adequately represent white female employees. (144)

In this case, the black female plaintiff is told that she cannot represent white females because she is a black female. In a third case, *Payne v. Travenol Laboratories, Inc.*, the court found that the black female plaintiffs were discriminated against on the basis of race, but did not then extend the remedy to black male employees "for fear," writes Crenshaw, "that their conflicting interests would not be adequately addressed" (147). To summarize, the courts issue uncanny echoes of the words Gloria T. Hull used to argue against the tendency to treat race and gender as discrete categories of experience and analysis: *All the Women Are White, All the Blacks Are Men, but Some of Us Are Brave.*

I think feminism must defer to Crenshaw's argument, not simply because it's embarrassing to find out that white feminists think like white male judges, but because multiply-disadvantaged classes like black women challenge not only antidiscrimination law, which recognizes only those classes designated under Title VII, but any form of feminism that privileges gender by refusing to see that race or race and class and gender are geometric, not arithmetic, combinations and that a "failure," as Crenshaw puts it, "to embrace the complexities of compoundedness is not simply a matter of political will but is also due to the influence of a way of thinking about discrimination which structures politics so that struggles are categorized as single issues" (166-67). Intersectionality is an attempt to rewrite feminist theory—from the bottom up—a relentless critique by a black feminist legal scholar who insists that theory account first for what law calls "hard cases," the culturally contingent legal practices that ground the title of Hull's book in the experiences of black women and no doubt in classrooms as well as courtrooms.

I see a precedent for theorizing from the complexities of teaching practice in the work of Mina Shaughnessy, who insisted that the errors of basic writers—our hard cases—could teach us more about writing and writing pedagogy than the "flat competence," as she put it, "of students who learned to get by but who seemed to have found no fun or challenge in academic tasks" (1977: 2). We need to guard against teaching flat competence, which means restructuring writing theory from the ground up so as to take into account the very compoundedness that eludes theory and excludes those marginalized groups—including those who find no fun or challenge in academic tasks and their teachers who find very little of either when they are forced to teach intellectually barren courses. I can think of no better way to begin than to teach ourselves how to teach writing about social and political issues—cultural studies—in college writing courses. All of which presumes, of course, that people who are old enough to vote are old enough to deal with the discomfort of trying to make democracy work—for all of us.

—Conference on College Composition and Communication, 1991

Hard Cases for Writing Pedagogy

When I was a child, my family lived a few doors away from the neighborhood witch, an elderly spinster whose house, obscured from view by weeds and overgrown shrubs, was set off from the street and curious children by a tangled bank of moss. In the summer of my fifth year, some of the other children and I took to snatching pieces of moss from the bank, in some long forgotten childhood ritual of bravura. Late one afternoon, the witch, no doubt exhausted from standing sentry against these inexplicable assaults on her property, let us know in clarion tones that she had called the cops and they were on their way. All the children ran and hid. When the policeman knocked on my mother's door, I was secreted in my usual hiding place under the stairs to the front porch and so perfectly positioned to overhear their conversation, which I have since forgotten. But I remember that neither he nor my mother said anything during that visit to disabuse me of my conviction that kids could be jailed for picking a neighbor's moss.

For a time, I believed that I wasn't languishing in some cell because the policeman failed to find me, and that my mother, having found me soon after he left, preferred meting out her own punishment to turning me over to the law. In my working-class childhood cosmology, the police *were* the law and elderly spinsters with moss banks were the witches, two of the hazards I learned to avoid, along with the insurance salesmen, child molesters, and social workers who threatened me and my family. Neither the civil rights movement nor the student protests changed my mind about the wisdom of avoiding the police; the women's movement, however, radically changed my mind about spinsters, even those with moss on their banks. But sometime during the sixties I also learned that the police are not the law, that the law is more complicated than any of its representatives—cops, lawyers, judges, juries, legislators, citizens. And somewhere in all this complexity that is law, I began to see myself as a citizen whose civil liberties and civil rights are guaranteed by constitutional law. And, more importantly, over the years I have realized, along with a good many other people, that the laws enacted by legislation and administered by the courts are subject to change and interpretations that may or may not be in my best interests.

If the little girl hiding under the stairs is ignorant of the law, then what of the woman who reads and thinks about law, who is not a lawyer or a law professor, but a white, middle-class English professor who studies and teaches writing? What warrants her interest in law? For the fact is that while it is not a crime for citizens to read and discuss law, not even for composition teachers, law, like medicine, is represented to the citizenry as beyond the comprehension of ordinary people, even those who have read a ton of critical theory and several more of student essays, who have signed their names to countless binding contracts, and who, to their sorrow, read, write, and act on bureacratic-legalistic prose most of their working days. Given the extent to which law permeates not only our lives but the lives of all citizens, I do not think it's inappropriate for teachers and students to read law, to think about law, to write about law. In fact, I think it's a good idea, if only because far too many students I teach have about as complicated an understanding of the law as that little girl hiding from her mother and the cop under the stairs.

For me, then, the question is not whether law could or even should be a topic in composition courses. It is rather a question of how law enters a composition course—by way of rhetoric or critical theory. Both are viable, and either route offers interesting and seemingly indefinite possibilities for writing pedagogy. Rhetoric has historically provided citizens the means to defend themselves before the law, and many of us could easily design any number of productive composition courses based on rhetorical analyses of the Bill of Rights, the Civil Rights Act of 1964, the Clarence Thomas–Anita Hill hearings, the policies governing student life on our respective campuses. My own interest in critical theory led me not to rhetoric but to critical legal studies, the set of essays and books produced over the past decade by a group of scholars who have, in one way or another, made the vulnerability of legal reasoning the basis of their scholarship. Their motives are candidly political, despite differences among them, inasmuch as all argue that the exclusion of such so-called extralegal contingencies as lived experience, depth psychology and cognitive psychology, social and political theories, and literary theories justifies strict doctrinal reasoning at the expense of those people whose rights are systematically denied them by unjust laws or discriminatory practices.

I was taught, as were many people in this country, that all are equal under the law. And, if I have since also learned that the principle of due process is far too often contradicted in practice, I do not see widespread practices of inequity as good reasons to settle for anything less than the kind of democracy we were promised in ninth-grade civics. In fact, I see those inequities as, more than anything else, the reason I was attracted to critical legal studies, for critical legal scholars are not ashamed of their desire for a just world. It's a simple enough desire, complicated—as one might expect—by differences among scholars about how best to achieve equity in a society whose laws only obliquely acknowledge the differences that justify taking into account the extrinsic "evidence" that strict legal reasoning disallows, the very circumstances that make some cases "hard" cases.

The court opinions that most interest me are those that many in law would, I think, call hard cases, by which I believe is meant that while the conflict between plaintiff and defendant needs to be adjudicated, the legal issues raised by the suit are seen as too particular to be of general use to law. I take this to mean that law is about as excited by that which is not covered by precedent as most social science researchers are by what are called outliers, the phenomena, incidents, and data that defy ready explanation and whose existence challenges the rules, principles, hypotheses, and theories governing the interpretation of events. Yet these hard cases are precisely the ones I find the best suited to writing pedagogy. In fact, I think them to be appropriate for the very reason law finds them unsuitable. They are visibly arguable. With hard cases, it is relatively easy to see that things are not as simple as one might wish, easy to see that law does not cover the case, easy to see that an argument has to be made. In other words, hard cases are those in which the argument one lays out is of even more concern to the writer and reader than the opinion held.

What I would call critical writing pedagogy begins when students redefine and assess arguments in terms of the cases they make rather than the positions they take, when students realize that "legal interpretation," as legal scholar Robert Cover so succinctly and eloquently argues, "takes place in a field of pain and death" (1986: 1601). While civil law may not seem at first to be as consequential as criminal law, where defendants can and do lose their lives and liberty, I take Cover to mean that legal interpretations, unlike, say, literary interpretations, violently change people's lives. Before *Roe v. Wade* women were not legally guaranteed the right to safe abortions. Afterwards, they were. When the consequences of interpretation are visible, as they are in law, argumentation ceases to be an exercise in formal reasoning, at least for me, which shift from form to consequences raises questions about what needs to be taken into account if legal equity as well as legal resolution is at stake.

Among the contingencies considered by critical legal scholars, none strikes me as more productive to writing pedagogy than Kimberle Crenshaw's account of the failure of nearly all social theories to account for intersectionality, the multidimensionality of experience. Crenshaw is specifically concerned with the consequences to black women of treating race and gender as mutually exclusive categories, which negative effects she illustrates by citing from court opinions on employment discrimination suits brought by black women. In *DeGraffenreid v. General Motors Assembly Division, St. Louis*, for instance, the court that found against the five black women who brought suit, alleging that the seniority system perpetuated discrimination against black women, wrote:

> Plaintiffs have failed to cite any decisions which have stated that Black women are a special class to be protected from discrimination. The Court's own research has failed to disclose such a decision. The plaintiffs are clearly entitled to a remedy if they have been discriminated against. However, they should not be allowed to combine statutory remedies to create a new "super remedy" which would give them relief beyond what

> the drafters of the relevant statutes intended. Thus, this lawsuit must be examined to see if it states a cause for action for race discrimination, sex discrimination, or alternatively either, but not a combination of both. (*DeGraffenreid* 1976: 143)

Crenshaw points out that in the court's view there is no sex discrimination that the company's seniority system could perpetuate because even though General Motors only began hiring black women after the Civil Rights Act of 1964, it had hired women (white women) for a number of years before 1964. Thus, not all women would be negatively affected by the last-hired first-fired rule. According to Crenshaw, the court is unmoved by the plaintiff's refusal to consolidate the case of race *and* sex discrimination with another alleging only race discrimination against General Motors because in the court's opinion, "the legislative history surrounding Title VII does not indicate that the goal of the statute was to create a new classification of 'black women' who would have greater standing than, for example, a black male" (*DeGraffenreid* 1976: 144).

Crenshaw's interest in the intersection of race and gender in the lives of the five black women who brought suit against General Motors is fueled by the injustice she attributes to the court's insistence that race and gender are mutually exclusive. Such thinking, she argues, apparently leads the court to conclude that "Congress either did not contemplate that Black women could be discriminated against as 'Black women' or did not mean to protect them when such discrimination occurred" (1989: 142). Intersectionality makes easy cases hard, complicates them and our reasoning by insisting that one man's dependent variable may well be a black woman's life.

As I understand it, intersectionality is about getting down to cases. It means that not only the courts but also the rest of us must refuse to play by the rules that are reified in either theory or practice if our strict adherence to them justifies rather than remedies inequities. Abandoning those rules does not, however, mean abandoning reason, but redefining argumentation to include vantage points that are ignored when, as in this case, a legal opinion does a better job of defending a particular school of legal reasoning than of protecting the rights of citizens. You will recall that the court wrote that a class called black women exceeds "what the drafters of the relevant statutes intended" (143). The court is confident that it knows what the original intentions were and that those intentions supersede any claims five black women might make on behalf of black women. It seems in this instance that the court's commitment to intentionality as the principle for interpreting legal claims exceeds its interest in the employment practices that provoked the suit against General Motors. By invoking a theory of original intentions, the court obviated the legitimacy of any claims the five black women might have made on Title VII statutes for legal remedy, and at the same time the court also delegitimated the class of black women of which these women are members. Such thinking effectively denies them their rights and their reality in a single stroke.

DeGraffenreid and other cases cited by Crenshaw clarify as little else in my experience has the devastating effects of binary, single-dimensional reasoning, the judicial havoc of intentionality, the violence that the desire to reduce complexity visits on five black women by the simple expedient of insisting that they represent themselves as either black or female, but not as black women. Binary thinking is hardly confined to the courts, nor do all courts reason by intention, but court opinions are among the few arguments in the public domain where one can see for oneself the human hazards of binary thinking. Neither the judiciary nor its claimants are served when a desire for simplicity overtakes the desire for justice. A similar desire for simplicity serves neither the field of composition nor its students and teachers.

The most disturbing simplicity concerns the convenient fiction that form exists independent of content. It's a fiction sold in most handbooks and rhetorics designed for students, and a fiction that many students have been forced to buy since the first grade, whether or not they believed it. So thorough a fiction is it that the students who enter college are as appalled when a history teacher corrects their grammar as they are when a writing teacher questions their content. History is content, and English is form. It's a fiction supported by a linguistic theory in which language is treated as independent of thought and reality, and in which language is viewed as a reflection of rather than constitutive of thought and reality. In linguistics it's a theory. Elsewhere the theory is a fiction. It's a dangerous fiction for writing students and teachers, if only because it presumes that the theory that enables linguists to ignore content in order to concentrate on form is an appropriate theory for language users. I can think of little that would be more terrifying in practice than speakers and writers who cared only about grammar. Yet most of the students I teach have learned to write, and have learned that I expect them to write, as if only form mattered, as if the contents of their essays were moot, except insofar as the words in the sentences of their paragraphs must demonstrate their knowledge of forms.

Formalism plagues composition pedagogy in much the same way that intentionality does legal reasoning, inasmuch as institutional valorization of a particular binary opposition creates and sustains the illusion that most students and judges couldn't think their way out of a paper bag. That both do not so much think as enact a routine no matter what the situation calls for, no matter what the consequences to actual people might be of mechanically going through the motions, so to speak, suggests to me that we have created the very monsters sociolinguist Dell Hymes once claimed children would be if they only learned and acted on grammatical rules and ignored the social conventions of language use in their homes and neighborhoods.

I can't speak for judges, but I believe most students can and do think through any number of complex social issues, and that many would do so in their writing classes were they convinced that composition teachers valued the difficulties that attend complicated reasoning practices as highly as they clearly do writing a well-turned phrase. The pedagogical principle here is simple: never ask students to write anything you think is simple because you already have an answer in mind. The pedagogical practice is of course more complex. One of the reasons hard cases are attractive as well as hard is that they remind us that life is complex, not simple. When I think about *DeGraffenreid,* I realize that while I believe General Motors discriminated against the five black women, my immediate desire is to interrupt the complacent simplicity with which the court presumes to represent the original intentions of the Title VII statute. Here's the passage on which the court bases its conclusion:

> It shall be an unlawful employment practice for an employer to fail or refuse to hire or to discharge any individual, or otherwise discriminate against any individual with respect to his compensation, terms, conditions, or privileges of employment, because of such individual's race, color, religion, sex, or national origin. (Article 703)

I'm too well trained a literary critic to assume out of hand that any writer's intentions are literally in a text for any reader to see. As far as I can tell, the court hangs its opinion that race, color, religion, sex, and national origin are discrete categories on the assumption that the "or" before national origin signals the last item in a series of mutually exclusive items. And no doubt many people read a series that way. But it is not the only possible reading. Since the credibility of the court and the lives of the plaintiffs hang in the balance, moreover, it seems reasonable to consider other readings, perhaps even one that would not presume that an implied "either" is governing the series, but presumes instead that the "or" marks the last term in an inclusive set of classes in all or any of which people may be members. An inclusive "or" would make it possible to combine the classes for purposes of litigation, but perhaps even more importantly, intersectionality complicates the easy application of a simple rule of either/or, which warrants intentionality, much as it might complicate the simple fiction that says English teachers don't care what you say as long as you say it right.

—Conference on College Composition and Communication, 1992

CRITICAL ETHNOGRAPHY

When I teach graduate seminars on ethnography, I always begin by telling students that ethnography is the "science of hanging out." I do that not only because I have a penchant for paradox—which of course I do—but also because I want to remind students that *two* traditions, science and art, inform ethnography, and that one of the reasons ethnography often promises more than it delivers has to do with the tendency to resolve the paradox in the text by suppressing the tradition of hanging out. Everybody hangs out, of course, but not everybody makes a living hanging out—in the field. Fieldwork is being there, being on site, being observant, being interested, but the data collected in the field are not so entirely unlike those you might gather when you're off duty, so to speak, as to justify ignoring what virtually every child learns about how to keep listeners interested once you have the floor. Anyone who has ever suffered through a scene by scene by scene by scene account of a movie—as told by a child—knows what I mean, and knows that young children lose the force of the narrative as they amass the details of description.

Most ethnographies do that, overwhelm readers with description at the expense of narrative, though ethnographers do so *not* out of ignorance of the conventions of storytelling, but out of the mistaken conviction that a thick description will somehow satisfy the tradition of science and that a narrative will expose the account as *not* science, *not* research, *not* worth reading. To deny the narrative dimension of research is part of the scientific tradition, in the sciences as well as the social sciences, but as recent work on the narratives governing science so amply illustrates, you can run but you cannot hide. You cannot hide from the narratologists (e.g., Landau, Myers), who will uncover the narratives buried under the pile of "facts," and you cannot hide from the feminists (e.g., Martin), who will elicit the "sperm sagas" told to generations of medical students, and you cannot hide from other composition teachers, who are also there, also struggling to make it work, also confronting the conflicts that beset virtually everyone who tries to teach writing under the carnivalesque institutional arrangements Susan Miller talks about in *Textual Carnivals*. And in light of Miller's book, and Sharon Crowley's recent essay in *PRE/TEXT* on the continuing use of untenured and untenurable part-time and adjunct faculty in composition programs, we need to ask ourselves why composition research would want to bury an institutional history in which writing programs seem to exist only to legitimate high culture, and in which student texts are valued only insofar as they inflate the value of literary texts.

My point is that thick descriptions alone cannot interrupt the kinds of institutional arrangements that make it appear that if only teachers were good teachers and students were good students, everything would be fine. As important as I believe teaching to be, I think it is foolish to pretend that the institutional conditions under which students study and teachers teach are incidental to writing theory, research, and practice. Writing program administrators know better, part-time faculty know better, faculty in the two-year schools know better, and graduate-student teachers know better. The value of narratives, as I see it, is that narratives tap cultural practices and rewrite cultural subtexts as cultural *texts*. In other words, I see narratives doing the same intellectual work in everyday life as the formal theories scholars use, that is, making explicit that which is implicit and making it available to public scrutiny. But I believe narratives are in large measure more successful not because they are inherently better but because theoretical discussions exclude those who lack the leisure to become fluent in theory.

I speak fluent theory, but long before I learned theory I had learned how to tell and listen to stories, and it's probably fair to say that the theories I like the best are the ones that either tell good stories or allow me to tell a good story. From where I stand, the good stories articulate poststructural language theory, since that is the theory that has given me the most to think about over the past few years. Poststructural narratives try to account for the part language plays in the fabrication of social reality, and the theoretical notions that make such narratives potentially critical in my work are the redefinitions of *discourse* and *human subjectivity*. In structuralism, you may recall, discourse is a stretch of text above the level of the sentence. But in poststructuralism, discourse is not literally a text. It is an ideology that leaves traces of itself in texts and in textual practices. Simply, if you have ever tried to get a doctor to admit that what the medical profession calls discomfort is what you call pain, and failed, you have a pretty good idea of how a discourse called medicine can insinuate itself into the most mundane conversational practices of its speakers. I think that's what Foucault means when he says that discourses speak us. It's pretty easy to see if you're not a doctor, and a bit harder (though not impossible) if you are, that part of what's going on in such talk is a hierarchical definition of self (doctor) and other (patient) in the course of which the relationship is defined as one in which medicine has the right to define not just pain, but also whose knowledge counts as knowledge. What the doctor knows, or at least knows about, is research that discriminates pain by degrees so that what is called discomfort rules out any need for medical attention. That is cold comfort, of course, for someone who is in pain, for your being defined as a medically uninteresting patient also means that a doctor can effectively dismiss you, by definition.

Examples like this one suggest a need for *critical* ethnographies in which the descriptions support narrative accounts of discursive practice. Of late, one of the practical things poststructural theory has caused me to wonder about is how anyone learns to write, let alone comes to like writing, given what passes for writing instruction in American schools. In my experience, most students have learned that they don't like to write: don't like learning the rules, don't like drafting and revising, don't like writing groups, don't like keeping journals, and don't like writing personal experience essays. In short, they don't like what they've learned as writing in school. And believing this, I have this sense that when they do what I ask, they're playing along with me, even though they believe, say, a revision to be a charade, out of pity for a teacher who means well. So strong has this belief grown over the years that I am more than a little suspicious when a student professes to like to write. I'm surprised even though I was one of those people who liked to write and wrote extensively outside school, and even though my own son is one of those people. I don't think his interest in writing is genetic. I think it's cultural. I think he learned to write and to like writing as surely as the others learned not to write and to hate writing. All this goes on in the same country, the same schools, and the same classrooms, but most of the children learn a terrible lesson about not writing while a very few others are learning the one that we would like to think we are teaching.

What I want is an ethnographic narrative that would account for my sense that the children who learn to like writing form a subgroup wherein they engage in a set of discursive practices that are culturally distinct from those that are learned at school. It's not that I believe the children who write literally know one another, just that they would vary from their peers who do not like writing in culturally recognizable ways. I have some ideas about what might distinguish them, but ideas that are suggested by theory, research, and practice are just that, possibilities that are likely but not necessarily those that would characterize children who like to write. I am trying to reconstruct in this didactic narrative things I put together without nearly this level of self-consciousness in an effort to explain how I went about exploring an ethnographic possibility that I may or may not pursue in earnest. This is by way of arguing that in my case, theory, research, and practice are always in such proximity that even when I focus on one I see the others in my periphery. In other words, any assertion I eventually argue from data I gather will have to satisfy my understanding of poststructuralism, ethnography, and writing and teaching practices. That means I will try to construct a critical ethnographic narrative, that is, one that challenges not just what others believe but also what I believe about children who like to write.

In an effort to keep myself honest, I have been conducting studies on two child writers. The first is an autoethnography of myself as a child writer, an autoethnographic narrative, which I am revising, and the second study would eventually be an ethnographic narrative based on fieldwork I am conducting with a thirteen-year-old girl who wrote a novel last summer, which *she* is revising. I am using *autoethnography* as Mary Louise Pratt defines it, as those instances when "colonized subjects undertake to represent themselves in ways that *engage with* the colonizer's own terms" (1992: 7). I see myself as perfectly situtated to do that because I am a classic example of a working-class kid whose professional success is commonly attributed to middle-class schooling, but who has reason to believe she owes her success as much or more to intellectual practices she learned at home—in her working-class family and neighborhood. One of the many things I've learned about myself as a writer in the course of conducting these interviews with myself is that I wrote before I could read and before I entered school. As impossible as that may seem at first glance, I remembered conducting a census (in the wake of the 1950s census, no doubt) some time in my fourth year. I remember not the census but a family narrative, in which I ask all the neighbors who are home when they are going to die and "record" their answers in my Big Chief tablet.

This is a family story about my success in school, but in my autoethnography I also see it as story about a working-class family and neighborhood in a small town in Illinois in the 1950s. My mother believes children worry about things like death, as did the neighbors, apparently, since no one told me not to ask the question, and no one suggested therapy. At least in the story, everyone played along with the child, and so it is not all that difficult to imagine that such resounding success at writing (these home interviews entailed food) in my early years might have offset years of wildly unpredictable grades on school essays. Though I do not often admit this, I was not able to predict grades on my written work with any degree of accuracy until I was a Ph.D. student. That I continued to write, despite my uncertainty about reception, at the very least suggests that the census may have sustained me when my superior knowledge of the rules of literary explication did not always pay off.

Like Amelia, the young girl I've been hanging out with, I also tried my hand at novels as a child, but my stories always got bogged down in my firmly held conviction that if I didn't know how to do something, I couldn't let my heroine do it either. Need I mention that I grew up Catholic? Perhaps not. When I wanted my heroine, Susan Saint, to jump in her car and drive off in hot pursuit of the villain, she and I were left standing at the curb, since neither of us could drive. So I decided to wait until I grew up to write novels, to wait until I had learned all that the grown-ups knew. Need I mention that I haven't written any novels? I would guess that I learned that deference to things grown up at school, since that deference to the privilege of authorship, which seems literally to have prevented me from writing when I was eleven, apparently didn't exist in my home or neighborhood when I took the census—before I went to school and learned what? Not to write? Not to take what I wrote seriously?

One of the reasons I love talking to Amelia about her writing is that she talks like a writer, not a student. About four months after she finished the sixty-page, single-spaced manuscript of the novel, called *Academy Days*, and right around the time we began working together, Amelia decided to revise it. Set in the far future, *Academy*

Days is the story of Robin Lefler, a young white woman a few years older than Amelia, during her first year at the Star Fleet Academy. In the course of the narrative Robin falls in love with another cadet, Wesley Crusher, and staunchly defends her friends (Tasha Yar, Geordi, Deanna, and Data) from vicious and wholly unprovoked remarks made by members of a small but vigorous clique of arrogant and insensitive cadets (male and female) who provide the conflict in this first-person narrative. If you are a Trekker, you probably recognize the characters from *Star Trek: The Next Generation* who appear in Amelia's novel, and you may also know that it is not all that uncommon for *Star Trek* fans to write novels, that there is a commercial market for mainstream novels and a lively market in what the fanzines call "slash lit," stories that work out sexual relationships between, for instance, Captain Kirk and Mr. Spock (Penley 1992). Amelia's story takes up none of these erotic possibilities because she's not that interested in the original *Star Trek*, or in any of the adult characters in either series, for that matter. She is only interested in adolescents, and her story deals with the kinds of issues that a middle-class white girl who has not yet dated might be interested in and with the kinds of issues that a middle-class white girl who is concerned about bigotry might be interested in. She writes about falling in love, which she doesn't know a good deal about but is thinking about, and she writes about racism, sexism, and cyborgism, which she knows a good deal about and thinks about enough that it is central to the action in her novel.

I like *Academy Days*, but Amelia is not satisfied with it at all. The first time I interviewed Amelia, she interrupted my nice orderly inventory of her writing history and announced that she was thinking about how to revise the manuscript, which I had just finished reading that morning. When I asked why, she said:

> It just didn't work, the idea, the concept did work (click), but you know it didn't come out the way you had in mind. I had a picture in mind. The novel doesn't work. A couple of the characters are dead. Some are 20 years older [in the series]. (Brodkey 1992b: 5)

Not two weeks later, by the second interview, she had begun the revision. She reread the version I had read, and two days later abandoned the draft altogether and opened a new file on the computer. She decided to scrap all but the two main characters, Robin and Wesley, and possibly a villainous male adolescent character, and she decided to dispense with adults by the simple expedient of making Robin an orphan. When I asked what she hoped to get by not using characters from the series, Amelia said, "A better story. Makes more sense. Everything will work together. When you have your own characters, you can't mess them up (you made them up)" (Brodkey 1993: 2). It would still be a girl-meets-boy at the academy story and would still be about defending your friends from the bigotry of the clique, but the secondary characters would be her own. And the third time we met, Amelia announced she was thinking about creating new characters and names for the roles of Robin and Wesley, but keeping the setting and the plot. But when I finally got around to asking about the revison she had decided she didn't really want to talk about it—yet.

I'd like to tell you that Amelia didn't want to talk about the revision because she's already acquired that writerly superstition about not talking about a work in progress. And there might be some of that in her refusal, but I suspect it's something I did. I think that by the third interview I had begun to act like a researcher or a teacher, that I was more interested in my questions than hers. I began the third session by asking Amelia what she thought about the comments her teacher wrote on an autobiography she had written, and I was fishing because I didn't like most of the comments. I didn't like that the first one in the right-hand margin was "Amelia. Is this double-spaced" and that the first one in the left-hand margin was "nice entry into a biography." Like the doctor with the patient, I tried to make her see herself as I saw her, a victim of prescriptive formalism who would say what I wanted to hear—in her own words, of course. And, in a sense, she told me part of what I wanted to hear, that the comments were OK but she wished the teacher had said what she thought of the essay.

I think Amelia is saying she wants both, not one or the other, and I also think that her polite but firm resistance in this third session is a warning that Amelia does not define herself as either her teacher's student or *my* research subject. Amelia is a writer. Part of what she does in her writing is articulate her complex human subjectivity. And that complexity is evident, I now see, in her revisions—in her decision to scrap the first version and begin anew, in her decision to replace the secondary characters, and then the main characters, but not the plot. Amelia is a young girl writing a novel about being a young girl. She's interested in the formal problems her teacher mentions in the margins, but that's not all she's concerned about as a writer. She's interested in some of my questions about her reading and writing practices, but that's not all. She's more interested in *what* she's writing. Amelia does not so much reject these adult versions of herself as refuse to be a willing student or research subject all the time. Sometimes Amelia gets fed up with the grown-ups and creates herself as an orphan—in her writing. And when she got fed up with me, she let me know she really did not want to talk about the *Star Trek* universe by politely refusing to answer questions with "I don't know. I'd have to think about that." By the fifth refusal I finally caught on, and Amelia and I agreed to forget my questions and just hang out. Which was great because I found out where punkers buy their hair dye. But that's another story, or so I hope.

—Conference on College Composition and Communication, 1993

At the Site of Writing

As a schoolchild I was preoccupied by Africa. While there are probably many reasons why that is so, one of them has to do with the way geography was taught. Year after year, Africa was scheduled for May, and year after year school was out before my teachers got around to Africa. I now see the absence of Africa as a lesson in the politics of schooling, for while *I* may have been preoccupied by Africa, my teachers seem to have been preoccupied by England and the Soviet Union. As I remember it, England was a place inhabited by little girls just like me (confirmed by my pen pal), and the Soviet Union was a space populated by stern parents who forced their children to eat beets (which I abhorred) and black bread (which I imagined to be stale and dirty). Needless to say, I longed to visit England and worried that I would starve to death if "our side" lost the cold war. While I worry that I learned pretty much what I was supposed to have learned about England (our ally) and the Soviet Union (our enemy) in geography, I worry more about what I may have learned from the tantalizing annual erasure of Africa from the curriculum and the planet.

What saddens and chills me is that the Africa I "wrote" in the absence of instruction bears an uncanny resemblance to the Africa in the nineteenth-century travel narratives that Mary Louise Pratt discusses in "Scratches on the Face of the Country: or, What Mr. Barrow Saw in the Land of the Bushmen." What Mr. Barrow and countless other travelers apparently saw were places whose peoples they could literally and figuratively overlook. She is not arguing that these are consciously self-serving, conspiratorial, capitalist, or imperialist accounts, but instead that the popular examples of the genre form a large set and that the set does the ideological work of producing and representing Africa as a place that can be colonized, and that can be restored to prelapsarian splendor by the *presence* of white people. The Africa I imagined, my Africa, was "inspired" by that set of discursively produced representations that were disseminated for at least a hundred years before a young white girl projected herself onto an apparently uninhabited and unexplored landscape—as Sheena, Queen of the Jungle. That Africa needed me, needed Sheenas and Tarzans, Boers, U.S. and Soviet economic aid, U.S. and Soviet technology, and U.S. Peace Corps volunteers.

It wasn't until I joined the Peace Corps that I ever gave a moment's thought to my childhood preoccupation with Africa or dealt with any of the discrepancies between the landscape of my imagination and Dakar, Senegal, the physical place whose geography I was learning and whose mundane streets had constantly to compete against the altogether more delightful jungle terrain of the romance in which I had long starred. I hope it's clear by now that this is an anecdote about discursive representations of space that need to be challenged because they make the world comprehensible to the members of one group of people at the expense of people in other groups. I chose Africa because the discursive production of Africa *preceded* the material inequities that proliferated and followed from the literal and figurative maps of the traveler-explorers, who wittingly or unwittingly created that space to accommodate successive groups of *white* people: traders, settlers, missionaries, bureaucrats, anthropologists, soldiers, Peace Corps volunteers. In other words, space is as crucial a component of critical theory as time because cartography, like history, is the prerogative of the powerful and the representation of space a discursive means of naturalizing and rationalizing the inequities of the present.

Specifically, cartography designates certain spaces as sites. As I am using it here, a site is a space whose definition is critical to maintaining hegemony *and* to countering it. The interlocking sites of modern state hegemony in the United States—the nation, city, community, work, home, church, school—produce meritocracy by proclaiming each to be a place where deserving individuals *used* to live untroubled lives from cradle to grave. In the most recent version of the nationalist narrative, America used to be first among nations; its cities were monuments to its greatness and its respect for community evident in every neighborhood and small town. Men worked hard and married for love, in well-attended church weddings; couples waited until *after* marriage to have babies and buy the home of their dreams, where children were raised by tireless mothers who cleaned and cooked during the day while their children went off to school to learn the three Rs from equally devoted teachers who maintained strict discipline. On Sunday mornings, families went to church and in the afternoons read the classics. These deserving Americans died peacefully with dignity at home of old age in their sleep, and their funerals were well attended.

This is the America invoked by the Contract with America, where everyone used to know who everyone was—who the good Americans were, who the good providers, the good mothers, and the good children were, the good teachers—and everyone knew what was what, knew what a good home was, a good education, a good book. American children worked hard in American schools because schools were the proving grounds of both individual and national merit. The way it never was is the way we wish it were because we long to be, *and to be among*, the blameless subjects of meritocracy, for merit is the secular equivalent of innocence. Men who do not make enough money to support their families, women who work outside the home, children who do not live up to their potential, and teachers who do not teach the basics are sent off to the uncharted and overpopulated territories of the *other* Americas, the unseemly and overpopulated sites reserved for those whose differences, real or imagined, threaten the unity of the nation and the coherent narrative on meritocracy.

There is no place for nonbelievers in this America, for the contract to defend America from the disenfranchised extends to disenfranchising anyone who criticizes the relentless demonization of pregnant teenage girls, anyone who opposes legislative efforts to criminalize abortion and homosexuality, or anyone who rejects the specious claims of reverse discrimination that are driving anti–affirmative action initiatives. The contract is only with believers, its provisions expressed publicly by Lynn Cheney, whose argument against funding the National Endowment for the Humanities and the National Endowment for the Arts in her *New York Times* opinion-editorial entitled "Mocking America at U.S. Expense" represents the endowments as funding the sites of subversion, where radical academics and artists stage assaults on the indisputably objective principles of enlightenment at the expense of innocent taxpayers. The equation of criticism and critical theory with mockery and subversion is a necessary part of the Contract with America, inasmuch as the contract disciplines believers along with disbelievers, by drawing lines in the sand that so contract the borders that even some Republicans are threatened with exile. Now that the moratorium on antiabortion legislation will soon be over, for instance, there are already signs that Republicans who support abortion rights will find themselves on the wrong side of the line, and those signs are warnings that the most vocal of them may also find the strategists who misrepresented the arguments of, say, Lani Guinier just as eager to misrepresent their arguments for abortion (Toner 1995).

It is tempting to believe that in an America based on merit and innocence there would be plenty of room for composition. After all, from its inception at Harvard in the mid–nineteenth century the composition classroom has been a site of merit, one of the guarantors that a college degree would, as Wallace Douglas puts it in "Rhetoric for Meritocracy," "be a certificate of merit, of demonstrated potentiality for participation, at significant levels, in the affairs of the nation" (1976: 130). But at this end of the twentieth century, despite the continued popularity and innocence of current-traditional rhetoric, still taught in half of college courses, by Sharon Crowley's estimate (1990: 139), and despite an unbroken history of testing, that is, nearly one hundred and fifty years of sentry duty defending the gates of higher learning across America against successive waves of would-be meritocrats, virtually everyone outside the field of composition and a surprising number of people inside the field see all composition classrooms as sites of remediation. Remediation is not a provision of the Contract with America, where three-strike laws show a decided preference for lifelong imprisonment over lifelong learning.

I said earlier that the definition of space as a site is critical to maintaining hegemony *and* to countering it. The irony in the case of composition is that while not opposing the representation of composition as the site of remediation probably contributed to the growth of the field in the 1970s, when the dominant liberal ideology supported open admissions, in the 1990s the dominant ideology is conservative. In an episode of the 1995 conservative narrative on schooling, for instance, the New York state legislature demanded that the City University of New York (CUNY) eliminate remedial classes. It is probably an index of how far right liberals have drifted that *New York Times* columnist A. M. Rosenthal, who agreed with no other part of the legislative assault on CUNY, agreed that remedial classes do not belong in colleges, even though he says aloud what the legislature does not, that he believes the classes are probably taken by "minority" students. I don't know *who* takes the classes, but the legislative intolerance of remediaton appears to be an intolerace of people of color, whose inclusion on American maps has always entailed legal struggle (*Brown* and affirmative action) and whose exclusion has always entailed legal chicanery (separate but equal, Proposition 187, defunding CUNY).

To the extent that we persist in insisting on our own innocence and that of our students, composition not only misrepresents itself but also seriously misapprehends the contemporary map of meritocracy, where the site of innocence is now the exclusive preserve of the putative victims of affirmative action. On the same day and in the same article that the *New York Times* reported that Senator Bob Dole "said he would seek to end preference programs for women and minorities" is included the finding of a federal commission reporting "that despite the growing complaints from white men who say they have been harmed by affirmative action programs . . . 95% of the senior management jobs" are held by white men, even though "white males are only 43% of the workforce" (Holmes 1995). Perhaps the aggrieved white males are innocent enough to believe that the remaining 5 percent would be theirs were it not for the preferences shown this generous quota of women and minorities.

I doubt it. But what I do not doubt is that the desire to be innocent is learned in the interlocking sites (of nation, city, community, church, home, school) and that in classrooms where, as Susan Miller puts it, "the student is imagined to be (and in participating in the course is generally *required* to be) a presexual, preeconomic, prepolitical person" (1991: 87), the pedagogical price exacted for innocence of the students and teachers is writing. Put another way, the current-traditional rhetoric, which Sharon Crowley has argued "is quite literally cut free from its obligation to be persuasive and is reduced to technique, play, or display" (1990: 169), offers students and teachers innocence in exchange for "the obligation to be persuasive," for while writers are constantly cognizant of the obligation to be persuasive, students are kept blissfully ignorant of any but the obligation to follow the instructions and turn in their assignments on time, and teachers ignorant of their obligation to engage with the claims students make in their writing.

Evidence that teachers as well as students learn innocence at great cost comes from a remarkable example that Barbara Kamler uses to explain the limitations of genre pedagogy in Australian elementary schools. Genres, which are derived from systemic linguistic analyses, are roughly comparable to modes, inasmuch as both are distinguished by characteristic conventions. The assignment given to the third grader whose text follows is to write a set of instructions. Here's what a little boy wrote under the title "Girls into Concreate":

This potion will turn girls into concreate
Ingrediance
1 kg. concreate
2 girls
1 eye from a bat
Method
1) tip 1 kg of concreate into tub
2) drop eye into conreate in tub
3) put girls into concreate, make sure girls are sitting up right
Note
This potion will not work if add to much concreate

The child's teacher was a student of Kamler's, and "Girls into Concreate" was submitted to her as evidence of the success of genre pedagogy with the children in her class. According to the requirements of the pedagogy, the teacher's evaluation of success is based on the child's use of the conventions required by the genre (actions, imperatives, sequence) and includes only a suggestion on completing the procedure. "It would have been even better with a concluding step after step 3 of the method," the teacher writes: "When concrete girls have set can be used as ornaments in home or garden" (Kamler forthcoming: 4-5).

It is difficult to read "Girls into Concreate" as anything other than an example of a pedagogy that preserves this little boy's innocence (of the violence such a procedure enacts) at the expense of little girls, and that not incidentally preserves the teacher's innocence as well, for she extends the violence along an adult trajectory by suggesting domestic uses for dead girls. Pedagogy is about these local matters, about the site where time and place and text converge, the site at which a teacher is authorized to interrupt and counter such assertions. Anything less at this site would be complicitous with discourses that write the instructions for "Girls into Concreate" that little boys copy, much as those discourses once wrote Africa for me.

—Conference on College Composition and Communication, 1995

THE TROUBLES AT TEXAS

There are what I think of as *the troubles* at The University of Texas. In April of 1990 the English department policy committee I chaired voted to revamp the ailing composition course, known locally as English 306, by requiring the graduate students who staff the fifty-some sections of the one-semester first-year writing course to teach argumenation from a common syllabus, "Writing about Difference," for one year. From mid-May to mid-July 1990, I met with a number of graduate students and faculty members, known locally as the Ad Hoc Syllabus-Writing Group, to develop a syllabus (see "Writing about Difference: The Syllabus for English 306" in this volume). In late July 1990, a month before the start of the new school year, the dean of liberal arts sent the department a memorandum explaining that he had decided to postpone implementation of the syllabus for one year. That left us without a syllabus for a course that approximately three thousand students (about half of every entering class) are required to take and that the English department is required to staff and teach.

I began by saying there are troubles at Texas because, as far as I can tell, the decision to scuttle "Writing about Difference" had nothing whatever to do with the syllabus we wrote, for to my knowledge no one in central administration ever asked about it, much less read it, and no one outside the syllabus-writing group saw or asked to see it until after after the postponement. If the troubles cannot be traced to the syllabus, and I don't see how they possibly could be, I cannot but wonder whether there were extraordinary, perhaps even extracurricular, reasons for the dean's unexpected announcement and unprecedented decision. Yet in his memorandum to the department, the dean said only that he had decided to postpone what he mistakenly calls not the syllabus but "the new curriculum for English 306"—"because *we* need to address concerns and misunderstandings about the course, expressed within the university community and because *I* believe that additional time for planning and consultation will ensure the best course possible" (Meacham 1990, emphasis added). In his memo, the dean aligns himself with neither the administration nor those of us who developed the syllabus, but stands alone, thus disclaiming any responsibility *he* might have to defend the committee and the department from the "concerns and misunderstandings about the course, expressed within the university community." That ambiguous "we" condemned the dean, the chair, and me to a relentless and fruitless round of fall meetings —with department chairs, deans, and wealthy alumni and donors, many of whom seemed impressed by our plans; some of whom wished we would teach grammar, spelling, and punctuation instead; some of whom seemed surprised and disappointed to learn that we never had taught literature in English 306 (and indeed could not without changing the catalog description); and none of whom seemed much interested in hearing about the syllabus.

It's not just that the dean is rhetorically naive, which I think may well be the case, for he seemed to believe that if I had persuaded him I could persuade everyone, including those who have other ideas about what ought to be taught in composition courses. It's that he seemed to be incredibly, even perversely, naive about his responsibility as dean, so naive that when he resigned without warning in January of 1991, leaving the department and the committee to fend for themselves, he still seemed not only bewildered by my failure to win universal support for "Writing about Difference" but also more interested in that unsurprising fact than in my insistence that his institutionally sanctioned postponement had effectively forced me and other members of the committee and department to lobby endlessly ("planning and consultation") what he so loosely identified as "the university community" (donors, deans, and department chairs) for the right to implement policies we were already authorized as a duly constituted departmental committee to make.

I can look back at the dean's memo and see in it a none too subtle piece of authoritarian politesse. Not to put too fine a point on it, the memo specifies the price of ransoming the syllabus. The syllabus held hostage by an unnamed group, in what the dean calls "the university community," would be released only in the unlikely event that its proponents could in an unspecified period of time with an unspecified amount of "planning and consultation" persuade opponents to cease publicizing their opposition in state and local newspapers, opposition that the dean euphemistically calls "concerns and misunderstandings expressed within the university community" in his memo. The sad fact is that the dean, who wrote and delivered the ransom note under the threat of continuing negative publicity, considered himself a proponent of the syllabus and in the same memo reassured the English department that not only would he "continue to support strongly . . . the concept of a writing and rhetoric class centered on the themes of diversity and difference," he also had the "assurance of the administration that they support this concept as well" (Meacham 1990).

By January the dean who had pledged strong support in July had resigned. And by January the administration—in the person of William Cunningham, the president of the university—had steadfastly refused repeated requests to meet with members of the policy committee or to permit us to field-test the syllabus in a few sections, while fecklessly linking our syllabus to what he pejoratively dismissed publicly as "multiculturalism." That President Cunningham refused even to meet with members of the policy committee while alluding to our work to parents and alumni and donors in phrases reminiscent of the sentiments, if not always the language, used in advertisements for the conservative National Association of Scholars strikes me as egregiously partisan political favoritism.

According to notes student reporter Jenny Huang made on a copy of the official transcript of President Cunningham's speech to parents in October 1990, he added this unscripted, seemingly impromptu remark immediately after mentioning that multiculturalism was "a topic of rising concern these days on campuses across the nation":

> Multiculturalism has become a code term for some people, signalling efforts to politicize the curriculum by promoting a particular ideology. We must not, and we will not permit such developments. (Cunningham 1990: 5)

It is a sentiment the president seemed to have liked so much that he expanded on it in a speech delivered a few months later to a group of donors:

> "Multiculturalism" is, as you know, a much-discussed topic on virtually every campus in the nation. You may have read something about the debate at the University. Unfortunately, "multiculturalism" has become a code word for some people, a signal of efforts—real or imagined—to use the curriculum to promote "politically correct" ideologies or viewpoints. We must not, and we will not, permit such a development at the University. (Cunningham 1991a: 8)

Apparently, it took until February of 1991 for the president to adopt the media-invented lexicon for his anxieties about multiculturalism, even though Richard Bernstein was warning readers of the *New York Times* as early as late October 1990 of "the rising hegemony of the politically correct" (Bernstein 1990). Perhaps the president learned his vocabulary lesson from reading the many subsequent editorials and feature articles on political correctness in *Newsweek, New York Magazine,* and the *New Republic*. Or, instead of reading the syllabus, perhaps he was reading the *Houston Chronicle,* which in early February announced the resignation of the entire policy committee under the "nonpartisan" five-column banner "Effort to Include Bias in UT Class Aborted," followed the next day by an "official" editorial titled "Good Riddance."

While the president's fears may have been consolidated by national media attention in the months following the postponement, he was repeatedly counseled against multiculturalism in the local press during the spring and summer of 1990. Weeks before the troubles over the syllabus for English 306 erupted, for instance, the *Texas Monthly* published Gregory Curtis's "Behind the Lines: The Bring-Something-Texan-That-You-Want-to-Burn Party," whose indictment of the dean of liberal arts and the chair of the English department for their commitment to multicultural education seems to rest on his conviction that "it is by now an unfortunate *fact* that substantial numbers of English professors think of themselves not as teaching literature but as teaching politics" (1990: 5, emphasis added). In light of that "fact," it is little wonder that many of the letters protesting our plans that were published in the student newspaper in June expressed suspicions about the politics of professors in the department. Nor, in the light of that "fact," is it surprising that Alan Gribben, the professor in the English department whose fears were published locally by the *Austin American-Statesman* ("Politicizing English 306") and nationally by the *New York Times* ("A Civil Rights Theme for a Writing Course") in late June, could simply assert with impunity that the course "has now fallen prey to the current mania for converting every academic subject into a politicized study of race, class and gender" and go on to say that the revision "has to be the most massive effort at thought-control ever attempted on the campus" (Gribben 1990b: 5).

Local frenzy over the syllabus seemed to come to a head three weeks later, however, when fifty-six faculty members from the university publicized their opposition in an advertisement in the student newspaper ("A Statement of Academic Concern"). The language in the local advertisement is reminiscent of that in a national advertisement that used to run regularly in the National Association of Scholars (NAS) journal, *Academic Questions*, and occasionally in campus newspapers and popular magazines ("Is the Curriculum Biased? A Statement of the National Association of Scholars"). There are alarming allegations in the text of "Is the Curriculum Biased?" foremost among them the association's unsupported claim that its "examination of many women's studies and minority studies programs discloses little study of other cultures and much excoriation of our society for its alleged oppression of women, blacks, and others," which "facts" lead the association to conclude that "the banner of 'cultural diversity' is apparently being raised by some whose paramount interest actually lies in attacking the West and its institutions."

As near as I can tell, the national association's advertisement is meant to articulate the heretofore unexpressed anxieties of members and would-be members (disaffected faculty members and administrators) and to urge them to keep these insidious intentions in mind when they are faced with curricular proposals on their respective campuses. The last—and italicized—paragraph mobilizes these anxieties as the warrant for going public:

> *We urge our colleagues to demand clear explanations and cogent arguments in support of the proposals being so rapidly brought before them, and to reject any that cannot be justified. The curriculum is and should be open to change, but we must rebut the false charges being made against existing disciplines. We must reject the allegations of "racism" and "sexism" that are frequently leveled against honest critics of the new proposals, and which only have the effect of stifling much needed debate.* ("Is the Curriculum Biased?")

Those friendly to the NAS are colleagues. Those whose ideas run counter to its own are represented without benefit of personal pronouns altogether. They are instead a mere collection of passive-voice accusations: "false charges being made against existing disciplines" and "allegations of 'racism' and 'sexism' that are frequently leveled against honest critics." In the tradition of cold war think tanks, the association states the threats to Western civilization, which in turn warrant taking whatever measures members deem necessary to defend themselves, their disciplines, and the West against an amorphous enemy with ideas so unthinkable, it seems, that no existing personal pronouns in English can adequately articulate the distance "honest critics" must keep between themselves and the aliens—who are threatening to topple *their* institutions, *their* disciplines, *their* nation.

Plenty of my colleagues practice and teach what is being called traditional criticism. Some of them publish essays grounded in the principles of practical criticism. Some are indifferent to theory. Some are curious about it but not interested in reading it. And some are hostile to theory. But few of them could be fooled by such an ad, for only a handful are solipsistic enough to imagine that theorists are their enemies, or to believe that colleagues with whom they may disagree hope to destroy them, the literary canon, and literary criticism, much less the West and its institutions. I only wish I could believe that the president of the University of Texas were as well defended as most of my colleagues against the unsupported allegations and hyperboles in the NAS ad. That he has no recent practical experience of departmental life may explain, though it does not justify, his eagerness to ignore decisions voted on by the committee authorized to make and implement policy; to ignore departmental votes of confidence in the actions taken by that committee; to ignore requests to meet with the committee and requests to field-test materials developed for "Writing about Difference"; to ignore letters from other writing program directors, other academics, and concerned citizens; and to ignore the Modern Language Association statement questioning the distortions of the syllabus by its academic opponents (Frances Smith Foster 1991).

That President Cunningham is not a scholar but an administrator does not, however, justify his yielding to local or national special interest groups as ex cathedra arbiters of faculty decisions at the University of Texas. The president is fond of reminding those who inquire that not he but the dean postponed the syllabus. In a response sent to Ellen Pollak and all fifty-seven of her colleagues in English and American studies at Michigan State University who signed a letter arguing against the postponement, President Cunningham wrote:

> English 306 is a Freshman-level composition course, and its purpose is to serve the instructional needs of freshmen students in all of The University's colleges and schools. The course revisions proposed by several members of the English Department appeared to be quite controversial and were not embraced by large sections of the University

faculty. It is also important to point out that the decision not to implement the revised syllabus in the 1990-91 academic year was made by the Dean of the College of Liberal Arts and announced in August of 1990 in order that campus debate could take place. (Cunningham 1991b)

While it is nominally true that the dean, not the president, sent the memo, the president is responsible for the actions deans take and is authorized to rescind those that are not in the best interests of the university. Perhaps the president would be willing, however, to take responsibility for the prose he has signed. In that one paragraph, he reduces a syllabus to "revisions proposed"; misrepresents a duly constituted departmental committee as "several" faculty members; aggrandizes the several faculty members who opposed the decision as "large sections of the University faculty"; and transmogrifies "planning and consultation" into "campus debate."

I find it difficult to imagine, moreover, what resolutions the campus would have debated. "Resolved: Extremism in the defense of academic privilege is no vice"? What would have been the point of these debates? To confirm that professors who know nothing about the theory, research, and practice of teaching composition are entitled to "their opinions"? To educate voters? Alumni? Donors? Students? To stage forensic spectacles, on the order of televised presidential debates, for the amusement of journalists? Politicians debate. Faculty argue—in committees and meetings and in their publications. I cannot imagine what the president of the University of Texas was thinking of when he singled out *one* of what must be dozens of duly constituted departmental policy committees to meet opponents in such a forum. I seriously doubt that he would have required the physics department to put off teaching chaos theory had some ill-informed folks objected to the word *chaos*. Instead of worrying about whether the campus had an opportunity to debate decisions made by one committee, the president ought to have been concerned that postponement abrogated the academic freedom along with the authority of the faculty members responsible for lower-division courses in the English department.

There is trouble at Texas. And trouble is not a problem. Problems are what the policy committee described and analyzed and resolved during the course of its deliberations about English 306. Problems are what members of the syllabus-writing group were locating and describing and analyzing and trying to solve during the two months we worked on the syllabus for "Writing about Difference." Paula Rothenberg's *Racism and Sexism* was a problem for us; we couldn't figure out how to use enough of it to justify asking students to buy the book. We reasoned that we would have to drop either the book or the court opinions. We decided to drop the book because we believed the legal opinions to be more critical to learning how to analyze, evaluate, and write arguments. It was a hard decision to make. There are quarters heard from in Rothenberg's reader that are not expressed in court opinions. And not using a reader meant locating appropriate readings for the court opinions and securing permission to use them in a multiple-section course, a loathsome task at any time, but particularly in the summer when academics are hard to reach. I was reluctant to use readings we had selected in lieu of ones that had been published by a press and hence undergone a cycle of review that at least said that someone other than Linda Brodkey thought them worth using in an undergraduate course. It was a problem that we had not yet located a full and accessible essay on role models, for instance, to accompany the decision in *Chambers v. Omaha Girls Club, Inc.* (The majority opinion and the dissenting opinion turn on the club's requirement that instructors be role models.)

We agonized over the number of writing and reading assignments, the kinds of assignments, the phrasing of them—whether to include a task analysis in all writing assignments or only in the long ones. The sequence of writing and reading assignments was a problem—as was the relationship between them—for we wanted students to examine the *structure* of the arguments they read and wrote, to identify the claims, grounds, and warrants used, and to evaluate them in light of the exigencies of antidiscrimination law and the contingencies of actual cases. Some opinions, such as the *Chambers* decision, argue that what is called a business necessity justifies discrimination. In other words, while the court agreed that the Omaha Girls Club had discriminated against Crystal Chambers, a single black woman, when they fired her because she was pregnant, it went on to argue that discrimination was justified in this instance because "the Girls Club established that it honestly believed that to permit single pregnant staff members to work with the girls would convey the impression that the Girls Club condoned pregnancy for the girls in the age group it serves" (*Chambers* 1987: 701-2). We wanted as many so-called hard cases as we could find because we wanted students to learn for themselves to mediate the exigencies of rules and the contingencies of circumstances in their writing (see "Writing about Difference: 'Hard Cases' for Cultural Studies" in this volume).

On the very day that the dean was meeting with the president and provost about postponing the syllabus, graduate students and faculty members were at a workshop on the problem of making tokens of the few students of color enrolled in writing classes by expecting them to represent an entire race or ethnic group. How to teach teachers not to make tokens of students was a problem. How to teach every student to judge each case on its merits *as an argument* was a problem. How to teach argumentation as largely a matter of exploration rather than demonstration was a problem. How to teach, not preach, difference was a problem. Problems can be stated, discussed, and solved, if only provisionally, to the satisfaction of those working on them. There is information to be taken into account, goals to be stated and restated, and ample occasion for criticism and persuasion. All of which is to say that most of us believe problems can be solved because we believe solutions to be largely a matter of clearly stating a goal or a set of goals, identifying problems, and then laying out and "testing" possible solutions. And all of this means that we believe in argumentation itself.

We haven't had any problems at Texas since the dean solved *his* problem by "postponing" our decision to implement the common syllabus and instantaneously and irrevocably transformed our problems into what the Irish call the troubles. Unlike problems, the troubles are not solved by talking things over or sitting down at bargaining tables. Compromises are unthinkable because opponents see their interests as mutually exclusive. The troubles seem only to be exacerbated by the pretense that they can be resolved rationally, as many of us who attended the Conference on College Composition and Communication (CCCC) session "Freshman English and Social Issues: The Debate at Texas" saw for ourselves in March 1991 when Maxine Hairston, John Ruszkiewicz, James Kinneavy, and John Slatin debated the syllabus. They spoke in anger, pain, fear, and sorrow, and in those idioms also spoke of their desire to restore reason to their respective worlds. Collateral damage is to be expected, of course, when people who see their day-to-day intellectual problems as troubles abandon the civil pretense, perhaps, but a civil contract nonetheless, that their disagreements can be amicably resolved. The troubles are the insurmountable problems that result when local problems are appropriated by a group that is not interested in resolving local problems but is interested, instead, in exploiting local problems for its own purposes. Cynical escalation of local problems into troubles is one of the strategies routinely employed by colonizers, who need to obscure self-interested actions that would otherwise be immediately recognized as the unwarrantable denial of human rights they are. No matter the venue, the consequences to all who are colonized, including the collaborators, are devastating.

At the moment, however, I am more interested in the strategic practices of the colonizers, specifically in the representation of the group to be colonized as incapable of self-governance. Grounds for colonizing the English department are spelled out to the locals by Gregory Curtis in the *Texas Monthly:* "For about the last five years, the English department at UT has been, as a professor might say, rent in two" (1990: 5). There are the "generally older and more established professors who believe in traditional literature and traditional teaching" and the "younger professors who see literature as a 'tool of opposition,' as a typical phrase goes, and teaching as a way of proselytizing for their gender, their race, or their radical—most often specifically Marxist—political beliefs" (1990: 5). In stark cold war terms: the enemy is within. The gentleman scholars in the department are beset not by radical students (as in the 1960s) but by radical colleagues "who have nothing but contempt for the society they are supposed to help educate and hatred for the state that pays their salaries" (1990: 5).

The president of the University of Texas effectively underwrote the warrant for colonization by not publicly defending faculty members against this or subsequent representations of disagreements about policy in the department as insurmountable troubles. His silence in the face of repeated assaults on faculty integrity, more than anything that was printed, gave credence to the take-it-to-the-public strategy practiced by opponents of the syllabus. It is arguably his presidential silence, for instance, that is responsible for the report in the fall 1990 National Association of Scholars *Newsletter* that praised the leadership and members of the Texas chapter of the NAS for going public with their complaints. In addition to singling out Alan Gribben and his allies for praise, the *Newsletter* mentions that the postponement followed " 'A Statement of Academic Concern,' signed by fifty-six faculty members—including seventeen NAS/TAS [Texas Association of Scholars] members—[which] appeared in the *Daily Texan* [the campus paper] urging that the course be withdrawn" ("NAS Impact, Texas": 5). From where I stand, the NAS credits it members with a victory that was technically a no-show. The advertisement appeared in the student newspaper on July 18, 1990, and on July 23, 1990, the dean announced that he was postponing the syllabus for a year. In the five-day interim, the president and the provost of the university met privately with the dean and the department chair.

For the record, the NAS *Newsletter* fails to mention that some of the fifty-six faculty members (there are more than twenty-two hundred on the Austin campus) who signed "A Statement of Academic Concern" later claimed not to know that the advertisement was paid for with a check drawn on the Texas affiliate's account (see Henson and Philpott 1990a and 1990b). Nor does the newsletter mention the letter Professor Gribben wrote to a wealthy donor in which he spells out his three-stage plan for salvaging the department along with his career, which plan resembles one he published a year earlier in *Academic Questions* for salvaging what remains of English departments. The Gribben Plan for Texas is as follows: (1) "the English department should be placed in receivership indefinitely . . . and then governed by a new English chairman appointed directly by the . . . Provost"; (2) "the department's faculty should be divided into a Department of Critical Theory and Cultural Studies and a Department of English Literature and Language"; and (3) "barring the accomplishment of these steps, the two university-wide required English courses (E 306 and E 316K) should be abolished, thus ending the necessity of hiring additional English professors at the rate they have been recruited for the past decade from the most radicalized (but prestigious graduate programs across the nations [*sic*])" (Gribben 1990a).

There is trouble at Texas. Whenever an administration gratuitously contravenes departmental decisions, it colonizes a department's intellectual life along with its administrative autonomy. I used to consider English department meetings to be the best evidence that we had entered a period of self-censorship. For there are obvious differences between the department meetings held in the spring before and the fall after the postponement. In the spring meeting, while three faculty members argued vociferously against the committee's decision to implement a common syllabus and to adopt the Rothenberg reader, they argued against the decisions without accusing the committee of bad faith. Discussion among the more than one hundred faculty members and graduate students who attended the meeting covered a broad terrain of concerns ranging from possible readings to requests for clarification, from practical problems about the difficulty of reading court opinions to the intellectual possibilities of teaching arguments by working in one of the few remaining venues where arguments have consequences. By the end of the discussion, some faculty members were even excited enough by the plan to teach writing from court opinions on discrimination suits that some 10 percent volunteered to teach a section, even though the policy did not apply to faculty members, and even though volunteering also meant attending a presemester orientation to the course and meeting regularly during the semester with a group of graduate teachers, who would also be teaching the syllabus. This was a happy turn of events for the composition program, since the department had voted as recently as 1985 to require but not teach the very course some faculty were now volunteering to teach. That vote only makes sense if you read it as a claim that composition is by definition remedial and hence should not be taught at the University of Texas.

No such intellectual enthusiasm for writing pedagogy was expressed by any faculty member or graduate student, however, in the September meeting following the postponement. The other members of the policy committee and I sought and won a vote of confidence for the committee. We neither sought nor desired a vote on the syllabus itself, since the committee was fully authorized, as were all the previous ones for at least the past twenty-five years, to do precisely what we had done. Questions were few and answers short in a meeting dominated by Robert's Rules of Order. I doubt that anyone in the room believed we were talking about a syllabus, writing, or anything other than political solidarity in the face of unwarranted administrative intervention. In a secret ballot taken at the meeting, the department affirmed its confidence in the committee by a vote of forty-six to eleven, with three abstentions, and shortly thereafter the Associated Graduate Students of English followed suit in a mail ballot, fifty-two to two, no abstentions. These are votes expressing commitment to academic freedom, which includes the right of faculty to develop a syllabus to meet curricular goals, and these are votes, needless to say, that the president ignored whenever he gave speeches to donors or responded to faculty from other institutions.

The troubles have made a mockery of public meetings at Texas. At a department meeting in the spring of 1991, for instance, all thirty-six faculty members present voted unanimously—with virtually no discussion—for an English 306 syllabus designed by the committee chaired by James Kinneavy. No one voted against it, no one abstained, and no one volunteered to teach it. That is not to say there was anything wrong with the syllabus, but that the syllabus was not the issue. The issue was that a department committee believed it needed to protect its members and its work from an onslaught of negative publicity. Events justify the committee's seeking departmental backing for the course. But bear in mind that these events, which led to and followed on the postponement, and which in their turn created such remarkable political solidarity within the department, have silenced all but the political register of public speech. We registered our political solidarity and political dissent, but the politics of publicity and postponement effectively colonized the intellectual life along with the administrative autonomy of the department.

I have reached the point in the narrative when any reasonably experienced storyteller would insert an epilogue or coda. In fact, while I knew I could not match "Reader, I married him," I had hoped the Kinneavy syllabus would be the denouement. But it seems the vote resolved nothing more than an installment in an ongoing saga, which may turn out to be as long as Texas is large. In June of 1991, the acting dean posted what I think of as the first call for rehearsals for *306, The Sequel*. In a letter to the chair, Dean Robert King (whose surname is itself proof, I suppose, that we are not dealing with literary realism here) announced that he was returning the department to a form of governance known as a Budget Council, which "will by definition consist of all and only the Full Professors in the Department" (King 1991). Dean King's decision is based, he goes on to say, on the fact that "twice during my earlier deanship I suspended hiring through lack of confidence in the recommendations being made by the small number of faculty serving at any one time on the Executive Committee" (King 1991). He does not mention that most members of the Executive Committee were elected by the entire faculty, or that it included elected representives from all ranks, or that the chair could appoint two more members, say, women or minority representatives if none were elected from their meager number in the department. Nor does Dean King mention that when he suspended hiring two years ago, he wrote the chair that his decision was based on "complaints from a number of your colleagues . . . in the Department of English about a lack of balance in hiring new faculty" and "talk of 'polarization'; ideological and political considerations—non-academic considerations," which "were said to play an increasing and unacceptable role in the recruitment of new faculty" (King 1989). Nor does Dean King mention that he seems to be following the Gribben plan for salvaging the English department. [In 1992, the year after I left Texas and the year before he retired, Dean King removed the Rhetoric and Composition program from the English department.]

Since I cannot provide a coda, the least I can do is leave you the cold comfort of this anecdote recounted by Patricia Williams in her book *The Alchemy of Race and Rights*. She says that many law students find this and others of her stories confusing. I do not. And I trust you will not.

> Walking down Fifth Avenue in New York not long ago, I came up behind a couple and their young son. The child, about four or five years old, had evidently been complaining about big dogs. The mother was saying, "But why are you afraid of big dogs?" "Because they're big," he responded with eminent good sense. "But what's the difference between a big dog and a little dog?" the father persisted. "They're *big,*" said the child. "But there's really no difference," said the mother, pointing to a large slathering wolfhound with narrow eyes and the calculated amble of a gangster, and then to a beribboned Pekinese the size of a roller skate, who was flouncing along just ahead of us all, in that little fox-trotty step that keeps Pekinese from ever being taken seriously. "See?" said the father. "If you look really closely you'll see there's no difference at all. They're all just dogs."
>
> And I thought: Talk about your iron-clad canon. Talk about a static, unyielding, totally uncompromising point of reference. These people must be lawyers. . . . How else do people learn to capitulate so uncritically to a norm that refuses to allow for difference? How else do grown-ups sink so deeply into the authoritarianism of their own world view that they can universalize their relative bigness so completely that they obliterate the subject position of their child's relative smallness? (To say nothing of the position of the slathering wolfhound, from whose own narrow perspective I dare say the little boy must have looked exactly like a lamb chop.) (1991: 12-13)

I'm with that little boy. And from where we stand, differences matter.

—Penn State Conference on Rhetoric and Composition, July 1991

Difference and a Pedagogy of Difference

I understand multiculturalism to be largely a *curricular* rather than a pedagogical reform. While I share the principles of inclusion that motivate faculty around the country to add multicultural materials to their reading lists or multicultural courses to their curriculum, and would like to believe that these principles motivate my work as well, I hesitate to think of what I do as multiculturalism in part because I work in composition, a field where pedagogy has historically taken precedence over curriculum—in theory and in research—but where curriculum commonly overrides pedagogy in practice, not least in the view of those who insist that my only job is to police language. In other words, the visible disciplinary content of most college composition classes—the handbooks, rhetorics, readers, topics, and even the writing assignments—often obscures and sometimes obviates the invisible *pedagogical* content of composition courses—student writing. Since writing pedagogy sets out to animate a desire to write, my interest in curricular changes, including multicultural reforms, depends on what I imagine that material contributes to a pedagogical representation of students to themselves *as writers*, as members of a privileged group who see themselves as entitled to articulate worlds in words.

The content of the visible curriculum represents writing as knowledge of the conventions of written language, which are encoded in handbooks, rhetorics, and readers and often reencoded in our evaluations of student essays. Little wonder that most students see writing as a matter of learning and following rules, and that many take a dim view of pedagogies that do not enforce the curriculum and instead represent writing in extracurricular terms. For extracurricular versions of writing require students to take responsibility for their assertions, which means taking into account the part language plays in representing a reality in which the writer has a *vested* interest. In the invisible curriculum, writing cannot be reduced *to* or separated *from* syntax and rhetoric, as it so often is in the visible curriculum, because what is said is not considered apart from how it is said. It is in pedagogy that teachers articulate a nexus of language, thought, and reality that is often ignored (as not the content of composition) or deferred (until students have learned the rules) in the visible curriculum.

My pedagogical bias concerns what I see as a tendency to conflate curriculum and pedagogy in higher education and hence a tendency to forget that a syllabus, even one that includes voices from other quarters, is probably a better index of curricular than of pedagogical goals, a better index, that is, of what we wish students knew than of our desire to hear from them. While the presence of multicultural voices is of potential pedagogical value, that a syllabus includes the novels of Toni Morrison or Sandra Cisneros does not necessarily mean that students are being taught to read them. Nor do multicultural *essays* read themselves, certainly not the ones by bell hooks on whiteness, Earl Shorris on the heterogeneity of identities among Latinos, Hyo-Jung Kim on growing up Korean female in the United States, and Vito Russo or Walter Rico Burrell on living with AIDS, which are included in the writing program I direct. A curricular reform of the magnitude suggested by multiculturalism requires a pedagogical reform of equal magnitude. By that I mean that before adding multicultural materials to our courses, we need to ask ourselves what we expect students to *do* with these texts: texts that many Anglo students read as accusing them of genocide, slavery, and discrimination or treat as excursions to the sideshows of real culture; texts that many students of color see as the same old same old, more gestures of white liberal guilt or futile reminders of what might have been had not this or this or this happened.

If students read the new texts as they were taught to read the old ones, their conclusions are understandable. For judged in the light of the old texts, few of which specify their vested interest in topics, the arguments made in the new texts are excessive and their writers easily dismissed as too vehement, too angry, too personal, too biased, too political. Those of us in what is called English studies need to give some real thought to whether what the *Chronicle of Higher Education* proclaimed the age of "post-theory" should be taken as evidence of the success of critical theory, which is what the theorists cited—Jacques Derrida, Stephen Greenblatt, Jane Gallup—are reported to believe (Winkler 1993). While many, if not all, of my colleagues seem to have accommodated critical theory, most of the undergraduates I encounter would be surprised to learn that the culture wars in the academy were over theory and were not, as the pundits argued for the benefit of a considerably larger audience, valiant efforts on the part of a small group of concerned faculty to rout the insidious forces of "political correctness" that threaten to erode such venerable "American" traditions as the uncontested and uncontestable universal truths of Western art and science. If the popular view prevails over that of the theorists, if students cannot hear the voices that have been added to our courses, it will be because they are distracted by the white noise that makes it nearly impossible to hear lyrics spoken in unfamiliar cadences. While there is nothing much I can do for those students who refuse outright even to listen to unfamiliar voices, there is a good deal I can do pedagogically to reduce the volume of white noise for those who cannot hear for the din of common sense.

The white noise that most consistently impairs hearing is the commonsense belief that cynically denies that difference matters by dismissing it as superficial or maligning it as divisive. By this reasoning, the distinctions among the terms *physically challenged, disabled,* and *handicapped,* among *Negroes, blacks, African-Ameri-*

cans, and *people of color* are said to be trivial. No matter that the point of view shifts from one where something calling itself tradition or science reserves the sole right to define difference to one where people defined as different redefine difference for themselves. Difference, concludes sociologist Todd Gitlin, is essentialism, the basis of identity politics, and identity politics is antithetical to what he calls the "commonality politics" of the left, which he claims "acknowledges 'difference' but sees it against the background of what is not different, what is shared among groups" (1993: 18). No matter that Gitlin uses a spin on difference popularized by pundits the likes of George Will rather than a recognizable theoretical definition. The work of pedagogical reform begins here, in learning and teaching a theoretically recognizable and responsible version of difference.

In contradistinction to commonsense versions of difference, I offer a Foucauldian, poststructural version, which defines difference not as an attribute of someone or something, but as a negative quality that is *imputed* to someone or something as an essential and defining feature that rationalizes the surveillance and regulation of an entire population in search of the often trivial but consequential "differences" that justify systematically isolating groups of people for special and inequitable treatment. It is not difference but systematic denials of these regimes of surveillance and regulation that divide us. It is these regimes that authorize the commonsense epistemologies that consistently represent difference as negation or lack or abnormality that most students know. It is these versions that those who insist on redefining their differences in positive rather than negative terms seek to subvert. And it is varieties of commonsense epistemology that pedagogy must transvalue, for if multiculturalism is to be seen as part of the regeneration of a society rather than held up as the fetish of its decline, difference must be posed as a condition of community.

The language theory that tolerates and arguably even warrants some of the most outlandish commonsense definitions of difference is structuralism, and so it is this quintessentially modern theory of language that must be broached first, if we plan to *teach* the texts that modernism either dismisses or maligns on principle. Whether we are talking about the early-twentieth-century argument for the linguistic structuralism of Ferdinand de Saussure or later versions such as that laid out by Noam Chomsky, the distinction between *langue* and *parole,* or competence and performance, the overwhelming intellectual contribution of linguistic structuralism to other forms of structuralism, including modernism, is a wholesale suspicion of practice. Those who would not be deceived seek the invariant patterns, rules, principles, universals, and laws that variation in local practice obscures: the unconscious of psychoanalysis, the base of classical Marxism, the deep structure of linguistics.

Like many poststructuralists of my generation, I began as a structuralist and continue to respect many of its projects and even to employ some of its principles of analysis. In particular, I value the work of linguists who document indigenous languages and that of sociolinguists who argue for the viability of what is known as Black English Vernacular as a dialect of English governed by underlying rules as linguistically logical and complex as those of the other dialects (Labov 1972). And were the world a place where difference meant only, or even usually meant, variation in a set rather than variance from a norm, where difference did not ordinarily mean *not* white, *not* male, *not* middle class, *not* heterosexual, I might well have remained a structuralist. My quarrel is not with a theory that recognizes that language generates distinctions, but with one that out of fealty to a theory that dismisses local practice as *theoretically* uninteresting ignores the practical consequences of imputing differences to actual people.

The myopia of linguistic structuralism to powerful political practices is irresponsible to the extent that it ignores the human misery perpetrated in the name of difference out of a desire to establish itself as a nomothetic theory, one that issues the laws governing a specified field of knowledge. Nomothetic theories can be seductive, particularly if you imagine yourself to be on the right side of the law. In an article ostensibly reassessing the value of linguistics to composition, for instance, Frank Parker and Kim Sydow Campbell conclude that "linguistics and composition can be seen as symbiotic; linguistics provides part of the theoretical foundation for composition, and composition provides a practical application and testing ground for linguistic theory" (1993: 310). The relationship between theory (linguistics) and practice (composition) is not of course symbiotic, not if linguistics retains the right to define both theory *and* practice. In their model, linguistics is a discipline because linguistics is a freestanding theory with no inherent practice, and composition is an interdiscipline because composition has an inherent practice (teaching techniques) but no theory. As a testing ground for linguistics, the field of composition and its inhabitants effectively stand in the same relationship to linguistics as the residents of deserts and reservations do to those who deem their lands suitable sites for such practical scientific applications as the testing of bombs and the storage of nuclear waste. A theory that transcends practice on principle excuses its own collusion in those practices of human diminution, exclusion, and extinction that directly or indirectly follow from that theory.

Let me clarify the kind of problem I see arising from the decision to sever theory from practice. The structuralist separation of language from thought and reality is a theoretical convenience on the order of the separation of form and content in, say, some theories of literature, rhetoric, and philosophy. The separation is not meant as an empirical distinction, but as a way to organize, regulate, and evaluate the linguistic study of language, and to distinguish linguistic structuralism from other theories of language. The structuralist argument concerning the arbitrary or neutral relationship between language, thought, and reality is an explanation of linguistic variation, which explanation does not intend to account for the aesthetic, social, political, and historical dimensions of language or the circumstances under which people speak and write. When these matters are sometimes undertaken at the discretion of individual linguists, they are understood as the extralinguistic concerns of *applied* or *hyphenated* linguistics.

Structural linguistics is an attempt to explain neither language nor the contingencies of its acquisition and use, but only those "aspects" of language that theory deems linguistically interesting: for instance, that phonological and morphological variation in, say, the word for cat, across languages where such a word appears, is not linguistically meaningful, and thus the linguistic relationship between sound and sense is arbitrary. While it may be true that the order of linguistic pairs like white/black, Anglo/Latino, American/Asian-American, American/Native American, heterosexual/homosexual, self/other, and man/woman is arbitrary in the narrowly defined linguistic sense that views local practice as deceiving, few people live in a world where the nomothetic logic of linguistic structuralism is more compelling than the local logic of racism or sexism or ethnocentrism or homophobia. A particularly pernicious version of commonsense epistemology that seems to derive support, however perversely, from linguistic arbitrariness is the belief that such pairs are natural sets whose ordering cannot therefore be altered without disturbing the natural order of things, or what students are more likely to call human nature. These natural pairs are understood as a given, inviolable reality independent of language and thought. It is an epistemology that supports the student who insists that generic "he" is natural, that "he or she"—or worse, "she or he"—sounds unnatural, and that interrupting the natural flow of language transmogrifies perfectly innocent and natural usage into the unnatural, "politically correct" language of feminists and feminist sympathizers.

The commonsense belief that language ordinarily plays no part in politics, no substantative role in the construction of reality, except of course for its "unnatural" use in propaganda and advertising, creates a fair amount of white noise in the day-to-day teaching of writing. Unless we make it worth their while, students experience the poststructural critique of this commonsense epistemology as one more attempt to silence their true feelings and stifle their natural creativity with yet another set of rules, as alien as many of the others in handbooks, and even more unsettling. The loss of generic "he" is the more likely to be felt as a loss of self if students have not been introduced to the counterintuitive notion that human subjects are formed *in* social relations, not outside them, and that the language in which we represent ourselves as selves matters, as does the language in which we are represented.

It matters foremost whether representations are simple or complex, if only because complexity provides grounds for resisting the received identities, the stereotypes, that are used to rationalize inequitable social treatment. It matters a good deal, for instance, that characters in Toni Morrison's novels are complex rather than simple representations of African-Americans because their complexity challenges not only centuries of simple aesthetic representations, but also the more recent ones that social science has constructed and that politicians use to caricature black families as unnatural matriarchies run at the taxpayers' expense. It's not just that such representational simplicity confounds race, class, and gender, but that it denies the complicity of language in the construction of so-called crises in the black family—from welfare mothers to pregnant teens to school dropouts to gang violence—whose imputed differences distract us from scrutinizing the related discursive practices that sustain the systemic, institutional inequities in health care, education, law, and employment among the poor and the working poor.

If reality is posed as exterior to language, it is also anterior to language, which would mean that writers are literally not responsible for what they say they see or think. Like the writers portrayed in modern fiction, writers are amanuenses, technology, writing machines, as in Kafka's "In the Penal Colony." They are not implicated in the production of reality because these purveyors of modern reality—of the simple truths, the hard facts—are also its victims, innocent bystanders of history. In modernism as in structuralism, the separation of language from thought and reality is the ultlimate alibi that guarantees the innocence of writers and readers alike, since language is not only separate from but a poor reflection of real thought and real reality, the material realities that ostensibly exist independent of language. Words are not deeds, speech is not action, form is not content. "Sticks and stones may break my bones, but words will never hurt me." I wanted to but didn't believe that as a child, and I neither believe nor wish to believe it now. That's because I am persuaded that a theory based in practice knows that language is material rather than immaterial, knows that words are deeds, and recognizes the adage as a child's incantation against the pain and violence of words that wound.

At this juncture, I consider poststructuralism as articulated in the work of Michel Foucault to be the only theory of language based on practice sufficiently complex to explain at least some of the concerns of writing pedagogy. While I realize that some practitioners who are daunted by Foucault's prose dismiss him as needlessly abstract, infuriatingly abstruse, and generally unintelligible, I can remember many of these same complaints being leveled at Noam Chomsky and the graduate students who eventually reinvented linguistic structuralism from a Cartesian perspective. It's not that the then unfamiliar theory was impossible to understand, but that the theory undermined the empiricism that provided the disciplinary authority of linguistics. Foucauldian poststructural theory challenges the empirical and Cartesian scientific hegemony that privileges both early- and late-twentieth-century linguistic accounts of language universals and hence whatever claims to authority structural linguistic theory exercises over composition. While I am more concerned about our desire to be colonized by structural theory than by structural theory or theorists, I am suspicious of any theory that reserves the right to govern from abroad, so to speak, on the grounds that its theoretical interest in universals is by definition more important than my theoretical interest in practices.

My interest requires a theory of practice, which begins, as I see it, by defining discourse as a worldview, ideology, theory, or epistemology, a way of knowing that selects and organizes and represents as worth taking into account what is seen from a particular vantage point. That means that I privilege discursive realities above what others call empirical or material reality because I am theoretically persuaded that it is likely that discourses theorize all realities and hence what individuals see and represent as reality in practice. In other words, I cannot imagine writing, thinking, or seeing outside of discourse, and I increasingly distrust people who insist that they do, particularly people who claim to speak the simple truth, who claim to be objective, who claim to be neutral. For those are people who all too often protect their own epistemological biases from scrutiny by passing them off as reality or truth, while imputing the dangerousness of theory, ideology, bias, and difference to me and anyone else who admits the complications and limits of their own positions.

The feminist historian of science Donna Haraway argues that only nonscientists seem actually to believe in what she calls the "doctrines of disembodied scientific objectivity—enshrined in elementary textbooks and technoscience booster literature" (1988: 376). While she is probably right, believers far outnumber nonbelievers in the population that concerns me, including the one I teach, nearly all of whom have learned that objectivity is good and subjectivity is bad, and few of whom have ever asked whether that naive version of objectivity is even desirable, let alone possible. Haraway, who argues that knowledge is partial because it is, by definition, limited to what can be seen from a particular vantage point, concludes that the received version of objectivity is neither possible nor desirable. It is not possible because human vision is literally and figuratively partial. Just as the human eye can see only what it is capable of seeing, a theory is partial, that is, an incomplete and interested account. Nor, as I understand her argument, is it desirable to define objectivity in science as unsituated knowledge, since a freestanding theory would be what she calls a "god trick," what can be seen from everywhere and nowhere, which would excuse scientists from dealing with the ethical considerations that scientific practice needs to take into account.

The caveat in Haraway's argument for the partial vision of situated knowledge that most concerns writing pedagogy is the refusal to privilege, ad hoc, what can be seen from any one vantage point, which is also a refusal to assume, a priori, that a view from below is necessarily better than one from above. A comprehensive understanding requires a full hearing from all quarters. College classrooms are if not ideal at least among the best possible places to hold such hearings, since the academy is one of the few places where common sense does not reign supreme and where there is sufficient leisure to lay out arguments in the kind of detail that such hearings require. As I see it, Haraway provides pedagogy an epistemological basis for distinguishing responsible from irresponsible public argumentation. For if we refuse to privilege the vantage point, then it is not the position writers take but the cases they make from particular vantage points that concern pedagogy. Media representations of the culture wars give the impression that theoretical battles are either of no real consequence, just academic, or so consequential as to constitute a clear and present danger to students, the academy, and civilization. From where I stand, the wars are the result of enlisting the forces of common sense to quell *academic* challenges to *academic* theories that support commonsense epistemologies that have a vested interest in separating language from thought and reality, and that not incidentally define *writing* as an intransitive verb. In composition that amounts to agreeing that form is the content of both the visible and the invisible curriculum, which means that a writing assignment is a lure, not an invitation to write but a prompt sufficiently attractive to make students write enough for us to surveil and correct their grammar, spelling, punctuation, and organization.

The commonsense view of language and composition makes any pedagogical practice that exceeds policing student language suspicious because it challenges a hierarchy wherein others claim the right to discipline student thought. By this logic, if law is the exclusive academic property of the law school, sociality of the sociology department, and history of historians, then grammar, punctuation, spelling, and organization belong to composition. And by this logic, composition bears very little relationship to writing, where knowledge and application of the rules are not considered apart from the project at hand. A poststructural pedagogy of difference articulates the uncommonsense epistemology of situatedness that deliberately reconnects language to thought and reality. Such a pedagogy presumes that a writer must stand somewhere in order to write at all, and that the issue is not whether a writer is biased, for all writing is biased by definition, but whether the bias can withstand *academic* scrutiny, that is, whether the bias produces simple representations that effectively say there is nothing to talk about or complex representations that invite argumentation.

In my experience, students have learned to close down arguments at precisely the point where I think productive argumentation begins. They do this in moves that either undermine their right to engage in argument (of course that's only my opinion) or discredit argumentation (everybody has a right to their own opinion). While there are probably any number of reasons from inexperience to ignorance that might account for students' desire to avoid argumentation, that they do so at precisely those moments that call for laying out a case in support of their opinions suggests either that students do not have any support or that they fear that in specifying the grounds for their differences of opinion they will violate a social principle that enjoins against disagreeing with anyone in public—for whatever reasons: politeness, futility, violence. And were I defining argumentation as they are likely to have known it, as forensic spectacles in which the only positions are pro and con or the purpose of which is to air political spins, I would support their refusal to engage strangers in public argumentation. For teachers often forget that students are not just strangers to us but also to one another, and yet on campus must live in a proximity that among the middle class at least is usually reserved for intimates. If we want students to engage in public hearings, then we must teach a version of argumentation that is productive rather than reductive.

In the time that remains I'll discuss argumentation as we have begun asking graduate-student instructors to teach and practice it in the program I direct, which is one of five undergraduate writing programs on the campus of the University of California, San Diego. The internal structure of the university is unusual, inasmuch as the five colleges are organized by themes rather than disciplines. The college whose writing program I direct is Warren College, and its *theme* is the individual and society. The writing sequence is two quarters, followed by a third course called Ethics and Society, and the three courses make up the general education requirement for the college. Historically, half the students who enter Warren College identify themselves as engineering or computer science majors, though it is not also the case that half the class graduates in those majors. In sum, the entering population is perhaps a little more visibly committed to the received versions of science and objectivity described in Haraway than some of the students I have worked with at other universities, and so may have a greater stake in defending the separation of language, thought, and reality. By that I mean that a good many students are likely to reject, without so much as a hearing, arguments that directly or indirectly challenge commonsense versions of objectivity.

Frankly, I do not much care whether students believe the arguments that writers lay out against the absolute objectivity of objectivity, but I do care whether they give these arguments as well as those written from other unfamiliar perspectives a full hearing. I care for a number of reasons, foremost among them that I understand the critique of received wisdom to be if not the only at least one of the most important purposes of scholarship. In order to ensure that students at least hear what those who argue that *their* vested interests are not served by commonsense versions of objectivity or difference have to say, we have privileged what I see as an academically responsible version of argumentation over other forms of argumentation and other forms of writing. While I make no special plea for the philosophical viability of Stephen Toulmin's description and analysis of argumentation, we describe and require students to describe arguments with some of the terms that Toulmin uses to describe the layout of arguments—claims and grounds invariably, and warrants and qualifiers when appropriate. The lexicon allows teachers and students to discuss the *intellectual* contents of arguments, which is nearly impossible when discussions are conducted in the more familiar vocabulary of thesis sentence, body paragraphs, and conclusions, terms that students understand as limited to the formal expression of claims.

In the Warren College Writing Program, students examine in some detail both the arguments they write and those they read as a preliminary to the privilege of either agreement or disagreement. In other words, descriptive summary precedes analysis and critique in order to ensure that public discussion is based on some recognizable reading of the material at hand. It is not that all the students have to agree that a particular argument is either the only one or even the most important one in an essay, but that they can recognize the essay from the summary. Students are required to describe arguments by identifying claims that are supported by grounds and deciding which among them is primary in a particular essay. Every essay contains multiple claims, only some of which are argued, that is, supported with examples or illustrations or data whose use is warranted by some principle or procedure of evidence.

For the most part, we do not focus on warrants or encourage students to call for warrants, since warrants are rarely explicit and their pedagogical value is arguably limited to pointing out when a student has invoked an inappropriate warrant for academic argumentation. The divine authority of the Bible is not an appropriate warrant for academic cases, though it may well serve as a cultural or historical or aesthetic warrant. Few academics accept personal experience as a warrant for a statement of fact, unless it is marked as a *narrative* of experience, that is, presented as analysis rather than fact. Many forms of common knowledge that warrant a good many arguments outside the academy are considered illicit warrants inside the academy, particularly if they fly in the face of some warrant that has achieved the status of common knowledge in a particular field. The happy endings that a good part of the reading public uses to define good novels, for instance, would be a risky warrant to use to evaluate novels in a literature course warranted by modernist principles of fiction.

There are limitations to requiring students to summarize arguments before evaluating them. Some students who are offended by certain positions have complained about being required to summarize arguments with which they disagree. Some who recognize that description and evaluation are artificial distinctions want to foreground evaluation in their summaries. While I do not consider agreement a prerequisite of reading, I recognize that the elision of description and evaluation in summaries can be vexing. And were our reasons primarily to test their reading, I would abandon summaries. But the summaries are meant to warrant their *writing*, by grounding their evaluations of arguments in the texts rather than in reactions to notions that for one reason or another either confirm or disconfirm some commonsense belief they hold dear. All the essays students read in the first quarter argue or assume that reality is constructed via discursive representations. Students are assigned to one of three topics by group, and each group is responsible for a written report and an oral presentation of its topic—the representation of race and ethnicity, gender and sexuality, or AIDS. Readings either articulate or complicate a representation. In sum, the readings are about how to do things with words, about, that is, the conjunction of language, thought, and reality, words as deeds, so that students are fully apprised that writers who take upon themselves the privilege of representing a world in words are responsible for their representations. In the reading and writing assignments, we are attempting to represent students to themselves as writers formed in social relations, that is, as writers who have a vested interest in particular discursive representations and who recognize that in the context of the course, at least, the highest value is placed on complicated rather than simplifed representations of human subjectivity.

In encouraging students to see themselves as writers, we are attempting to discourage them from identifying with infantilized representations of students as the entirely innocent victims of the circumstances of class, race, ethnicity, religion, nationality, gender, sexual orientation. Seeing students as writers requires us as teachers to resist what Susan Miller calls "a perduring sentimentality" in composition to insist that a student be "a presexual, preeconomic, prepolitical person" (1991: 87). I see the pedagogical measures we have taken as our effort to resist, and encourage students to resist, *all* reductive representations of human subjectivity and thereby clear a space for what, in an essay defending Michel Foucault's hermeneutics of resistance, the philosopher John Caputo calls "the right to be different" (1993: 253). As I understand his argument, to be different is to refuse identities that predefine us and to take up instead the possibilities that are contained in not knowing who we are. I see writing as imminently well suited to difference and resistance, if writing pedagogy legitimates exploring the residual possibilities of situated individuality that modern technologies of individualization attempt to nullify. It is in transvaluing and articulating the possibilities of difference that we are likely to welcome the complexities of multicultural representations as part of a human project to resist identities that are not in our own best interests.

—Twenty-fourth National Institute on Issues in Teaching and Learning,
University of Chicago, 1992

PART IV

Teaching

Introduction to Part IV

Teaching is commonly evaluated on the circumstantial evidence of course descriptions and syllabi, course evaluations, teacher observations, teaching awards, and word of mouth. I usually fare well by these measures, probably because I plan courses carefully enough that the syllabus presents a fairly accurate week-by-week schedule of the work required of students. Students know what they will read and write and when assignments are due in the courses I offer. I even include descriptions of all the writing assignments, often accompanied by instructions on how to complete them. As much as may be learned about a teacher's instructional goals from a syllabus, however, such documents are not accounts of pedagogy. Pedagogy is what happens. All who were "there" have stories to tell, stories to tell themselves or someone else about the experience of being there. Like all human experiences that people take the trouble to narrate, stories about pedagogy are invariably invitations to reflect on the conflicts and resolutions that interest and trouble the narrator.

In the literature on composition, the narrators are usually teachers. So the problems posed are usually the kinds of things that teachers worry about: what to teach students about writing and what to do with the writing students produce. These seemingly basic concerns continue to vex even the most experienced teachers because they are not as simple as one might think, at least not to anyone who has taught long enough to have learned that few students enter college confident that anything they learn about writing from writing assignments or from anything a teacher or another student says about their writing will be of much value to them. There are any number of explanations of how so many students might have independently learned such terrible lessons about writing and themselves, despite the best efforts of, in many instances, informed and dedicated teachers. In addition to my own work, much of which suggests a good deal outside as well as inside the classroom that conspires against learning to write, several recent histories of composition identify social and institutional arrangements that are radically opposed to the best pedagogical efforts of individual teachers (Berlin 1987; Crowley 1990; Faigley 1992; Miller 1991).

That the odds on writing pedagogy are not favorable means that courses must be planned with additional care. The two essays on teaching undergraduates in this section, for instance, acknowledge institutional arrangements that exist not only at the University of Texas, but in many universities with large undergraduate populations. These arrangements usually entail offering and staffing multiple-section required courses known at most places as Freshman English. These courses are usually housed in English departments, taught by graduate students and lecturers, and taken by entering students as part of their general education requirements. Some faculty member, increasingly someone in the field of composition, is usually assigned to oversee classes, prepare instructors to teach the courses described in the college catalog, and supervise instruction during the academic year. The first essay, "Writing about Difference: The Syllabus for English 306," includes an account of how decisions about writing and reading assignments were reached by the committee formed to develop the syllabus, the table of contents for the course reader, a semester-long writing and reading schedule, and the writing assignments. The second essay, "Writing about Difference: 'Hard Cases' for Cultural Studies," which I wrote with Richard Penticoff while he was still a graduate student in rhetoric and composition at Texas, situates the course in terms of local history and the field of composition.

The last five essays in the section were written by graduate students who have taken a course I regularly teach called Ethnographies of Literacy. The course description, which has varied some over the years, is designed to introduce graduate students to issues ethnographers face *as* writers. Because most students who take this course have not conducted fieldwork, and so are not familiar with the harrowing processes of transforming data into information, they are inclined to consider ethnographic texts entirely in terms of reception and to ignore the problems of production altogether. In other words, while their expectations of texts varied considerably, they read as readers, not writers, of ethnographies. My decision to assign an autoethnography as the seminar paper is based, then, on my conviction that the problems of representation in ethnography cannot be understood apart from the problems of collecting and transforming data collected in the field. Since there is not also time to conduct fieldwork in a class that surveys the literature on ethnographic representation, students were asked to treat themselves as informants and to ground their autoethnographies in data collected from self-interviews.

I developed two interim assignments to assist students: a literacy inventory and a literacy anecdote. In "The Ethnography of Literacy," John Szwed argues for a variable literacy that would document not only school-based literacy but also the vast array of reading and writing practices that are implied by a term like *literacy*. For the literacy inventory, students record their reading and writing activities for two full days, noting the time, place, and genre. In addition to establishing that even graduate students in English studies who write regularly spend considerably more time reading than writing, the inventories reveal the disproportionate amount of time given to unacknowledged reading and writing: they read hundreds of signs, logos, labels, directions, and cereal boxes, for instance, even though they already know the content; they read and fill in forms with numbing regularity; they make and revise lists with a precision worthy of poetry. These are not the reading and writing practices ordinarily invoked to justify literacy campaigns.

The literacy anecdote is the result of memory work of the kind I undertook to write "Writing on the Bias." Simply, the assignment advises students to work back from the most recent to the earliest literacy experience, to remember when and where writing and reading took place, and then to isolate sets of memories by themes. Perhaps the stories seem obviously related to present writing and reading practices, or the stories seem suspiciously unrelated; perhaps the writer is inexplicably drawn to a memory. Memories are treated as data, and "calculating" their status as cultural material is meant to approximate how data gathered in the field are transformed into information. While every student contributes a literacy anecdote to class discussion, the discussion seems to have greater influence on the autoethnography than the anecdote, which is usually radically transformed or sometimes not used at all in the final version. My own sense is that in the course of discussions students realize that their personal histories are also cultural histories, and that a good many people besides themselves did their "best" writing outside school, read under the covers with a flashlight, hated using those fat pencils to draw letters, kept diaries that were read, received diaries they did not use, did not write their own first book report. These experiences are common to the successful literates who enter graduate programs in English studies, and probably other fields as well, and hearing them seems to clarify for many students that literacy is invariably a cultural as well as an individual performance. To wit, anecdotes are given their ethnographic torque, or an additional one, during discussions.

I ask students to photocopy their drafts for all the members of the class to read at least three weeks before the final version is due. The class meets for a peer review session, during which each student in turn leads the discusssion (thirty to forty minutes) of another's draft. Everyone also receives written responses from the discussion leader and me, including answers to the list of questions writers append to their texts and unsolicited commentary readers also think may be useful. I scheduled the workshops because my own encounters with the unfamiliar idiom I was asking students to produce suggested that writers and writing would benefit by making the work of writing cultural analysis and criticism more visible. I like to think that since students unanimously recommend the workshop on course evaluations, discussion and commentary clarify the cultural material that distinguishes autoethnography from autobiography. Yet it may simply be the sociality that recommends workshops to graduate students, many of whom labor under the illusion that they are alone in finding writing to be hard work.

When I started working on "Writing on the Bias," I had already read a good many ethnographies and a fair amount of the literature, done fieldwork, published an ethnographic case study and articles on ethnographic narratives and literacy, given papers on these topics at national conferences, and taught graduate and undergraduate courses on both ethnography and literacy. The assignment that I gave myself and that eventually took me two years to write, after a decade of preparation, the four graduate students at the University of California, San Diego, were asked to complete in a ten-week quarter, and the graduate student at the University of Texas in a five-week summer session. When they entered the seminar, moreover, most of them were unfamiliar with the literature on ethnography and literacy as well as autoethnography, which is a staple of neither anthropology nor literary studies. All of them, however, had more than a passing acquaintance with literary narratives, and many of them were also familiar with the use of personal narratives in autobiography, not to mention undergraduate courses.

On the face of it, the autoethnography, which requires writers to cast their personal experience in a cultural frame, is less familiar than similar assignments that instruct writers to present themselves as interesting individuals/characters to, say, college admissions committees or composition teachers. Yet these culturally situated narratives seem to me more, not less, personal than most essays in which writers deliberately set out to distinguish themselves as unique individuals. If, however, individuality is seen as a quality of narration rather than experience, then it would be the presence of writers *as* narrators that recommends these autoethnographies as personal narratives. In other words, the demands of cultural analysis and criticism seem to have alerted writers to the narrative possibilities of their experience, for while they treat themselves as characters in their life stories, they *present* themselves as narrators of their lives. Writers who are narrators remind us that if what we call personal experience is a narrative production, then there is a good deal to be learned from narration not only about stories but also about experience.

Writing about Difference: The Syllabus for English 306

English 101 is called English 306: Rhetoric and Composition at the University of Texas. While I was there (1988-92), three thousand students (approximately half of every entering class) were required to take the one-semester introduction to college writing. There has been nothing comparable to English 102 taught at Texas since 1985, the year the English department fired its lecturers and dropped the second-semester class, English 307: Introduction to Literature and Composition, from its course offerings. When I was appointed director of lower-division English in 1989, I was given to understand by both the college catalog and the department chair that graduate-student instructors were not to use literature in English 306, only expository essays. I mention these institutional peculiarities at the outset of this discussion of "Writing about Difference," the syllabus developed for English 306, because nearly all the sections (more than fifty a semester) offered during the academic year were staffed by Ph.D. students in literary studies. My request that all graduate-student instructors teach English 306 from a common syllabus for at least one year was an attempt to teach the teachers how to teach writing while teaching writing to the students enrolled in their classes.

I like to think that "Writing about Difference" would have gone some way toward simultaneously instructing teachers and students, for the syllabus was designed to do that. Elsewhere, Richard Penticoff and I have discussed the intellectual rationale for concentrating on argument, difference, and court opinions in a writing course taught by graduate students in literary studies (see "Writing about Difference: 'Hard Cases' for Cultural Studies" in this volume). In this discussion of the syllabus for "Writing about Difference," however, I concentrate on the work of students and faculty who developed the course. Indeed, it is impossible for me to contemplate "Writing about Difference" apart from writing the syllabus—the writing and reading schedule, the writing assignments, and the reading material—in what became known as the Ad Hoc Syllabus-Writing Group.

Following the Lower Division Policy Committee decision to use a common syllabus in English 306 for the 1990-91 academic year, I circulated a memorandum inviting interested graduate students to join the five faculty members from the policy committee who had agreed to consult during the summer. Since "Writing about Difference" was to be taught by graduate-student instructors, it seemed reasonable to include them while decisions were being made, even though there were no monies available for either faculty or student consultants. The following people met weekly at first and later biweekly from mid-May through mid-July 1990: Margaret Downs-Gamble, David Ericson, Shelli Fowler, Dana Harrington, Susan Sage Heinzelman, Sara Kimball, Allison Mosshart, Stuart Moulthrop, John Slatin, Maria Villalobos, and me. Richard Penticoff, the graduate student who was unanimously elected to chair the group, set and kept us to a rigorous work schedule.

Penticoff's schedule meant that we had already begun to revise the penultimate draft of the syllabus for a course that was to begin at the end of August by July 23, 1990, the day the dean of liberal arts announced his decision to "postpone" the course for a year (see Brodkey 1994a and "The Troubles at Texas" in this volume for narrative accounts of the postponement). For the two months before the postponement, however, one of two graduate-student assistant directors of lower-division English, Shelli Fowler, and I wrote and submitted more writing and reading schedules and writing assignments than I care to remember to the scrutiny of the Ad Hoc Group. As the group grew more accustomed to examining and questioning our work, criticism became more pointed and fruitful, and so within weeks Fowler and I were generating more-acceptable schedules and assignments, though none was accepted on sight. By mid-June we were blocking out new schedules weekly, writing new prompts and revising old ones, which were circulated in advance and discussed in detail during our meetings. I probably learned more in those two months about how to sequence and phrase writing assignments than I had in the previous fifteen years. My own experience of that collaboration was so positive that I would no longer even consider designing a course for others to teach without benefit of such counsel.

The policy committee decision authorized me as the director of lower-division English to develop a syllabus to be called "Writing about Difference" and to use court opinions in antidiscrimination cases in education and employment to teach argumentation in English 306. At the time of the postponement, I had not finished writing instructional material on argumentation, which we planned to teach along lines suggested first in Stephen Toulmin's *The Uses of Argument* and later adumbrated in *An Introduction to Reasoning*, the textbook he wrote with Richard Ricke and Allan Janik (see "Writing about Difference: 'Hard Cases' for Cultural Studies" in this volume for a discussion of teaching argumentation). On my recommendation, the committee voted to supplement court opinions with Paula Rothenberg's social issues reader, *Racism and Sexism: An Integrated Study*, in all sections of the course taught by graduate-student instructors. Also on my recommendation, the committee voted to adopt Maxine Hairston and John Ruszkiewicz's *Scott, Foresman Handbook for Writers* for the academic year. The selection of court opinions was left to my discretion, along with all other decisions about developing, sequencing, and integrating writing and reading assignments for the course.

Fowler and I began by trying to coordinate the court opinions with sections of the reader and the handbook. We soon realized, however, that neither of us could find enough relevant material in *Racism and Sexism* to justify asking students to buy it. I explained the problem to the department chair, for in the absence of a quorum on the Policy Committee, some of whose members were out of town, I needed his permission (which he granted) to cancel the order for the reader. When Fowler and I encountered similar problems with the handbook, I rationalized the expense on the usual grounds that it could be used as a reference book in other courses.

While I would rather learn that a textbook is not suitable before than after requiring three thousand students to buy it, neither Fowler nor I was eager to develop writing assignments based only on court opinions and an English handbook. After all, it was not legal argumentation as such we planned to teach in English 306. Instead, we hoped to engage students in a discussion of difference by providing them legal decisions in which arguments about discriminatory practices in employment and education are worth examining because it matters not only whether the court rules in favor of the plaintiff or the defendant but also what the argument made to justify a decision does and does not take into account. In other words, we wanted students to treat cases heard by the court as arguable and not to accept decisions with which they agreed or dismiss those with which they disagreed without examining the evidence. Since we chose opinions that argue social rather than legal issues on the advice of legal scholars, we used the same principle to select supplementary essays.

The decision to accompany each opinion with an essay, however, opened up so many possibilities that it is highly unlikely that all our final selections would have withstood the rigors of practice. The best that can be said of them is that they elaborated topics discussed in the opinions. Part I of the Appendix lists the court opinions and essays we planned to use. Legal opinions are in the public domain and do not require permission. We noted the titles but did not reproduce essays we had not received permission to reproduce without cost by the date of the postponement. Also included in the Appendix are the writing assignments (Part II) and a day-by-day syllabus (Part III). In one instance, teachers were asked to choose between two opinions, a case on the right of a male student to bring a male escort to a high school prom (*Fricke v. Lynch*) and one on the right of a female student to play on an all-male high school football team (*Lanz by Lanz v. Ambach*). While both cases deal with issues with which recent high school graduates are likely to be familiar, some teachers doubted they could keep students focused on free speech in a case where the right to political protest is affirmed on behalf of homosexuals.

The decision to divide each class into five writing groups was determined by enrollment, which was capped at twenty-five, with most sections running near or at full enrollment. The syllabus we developed assigned students to groups by the second week, required students to work regularly in their groups, and required each group to present its case to the rest of the class. We established the groups to focus students and teachers alike on student writing, and we increased the amount of formal and informal writing required of students by reducing the amount of reading. The plan required the entire class to read three essays and one legal opinion in addition to the opinion and essay assigned to each group. Harvard law professor Martha Minow was kind enough to grant us permission to use two proof chapters (edited to make one reading) from *Making All the Difference,* scheduled to be released later, in the fall of 1990. Peggy McIntosh gave us permission to use the working paper "White Privilege and Male Privilege." Richard Kluger, author of *Simple Justice*, allowed us to reproduce "The Spurs of Texas Are upon You," a discussion of *Sweatt v. Painter*, the 1950 Supreme Court decision that ended legal segregation at the University of Texas. While students were required to read only two opinions (*Sweatt v. Painter* and the opinion assigned to their group) and four essays (the three mentioned here and the one assigned to their group), their packets were to have contained all the opinions and essays used in the course.

The plan called for considerably more student writing, as well as discussion of student work in progress, than in previous years. In addition to the usual entering and exiting in-class writing assignments (prompts not decided on by the date of postponement), every student was to have written ten brief responses to reading assignments, which we called scripts and created to teach students to locate and summarize arguments, define terms, and acquire a language in which to discuss arguments as arguments. Not incidentally, the scripts were also designed to provide students with "scripts" for in-class discussions of readings. Each student was also to have written six full-length essays, not counting revisions, designed to integrate material from scripts, writing groups, and class discussions into their essays, and to culminate in an opinion (the case had not been decided on at the time of postponement). This final assignment was to have been photocopied and distributed to the rest of the class. The prompts for "Writing about Difference" were written to assist teachers as well as students. The prompts for the ten scripts are characteristically brief. Script Assignment 6 was "Summarize (in about 50 words) a principal claim and its grounds in the plaintiff's argument in *Sweatt v. Painter*." The prompts for the six formal writing assignments, however, include task analyses, instructions on the kinds of intellectual work the assignment requires. These analyses are the result of submitting assignments to the Ad Hoc Syllabus-Writing Group, whose graduate-student members were quick to ask what students would need to know and do in order to write a successful essay in response to a prompt.

In addition to the informal and formal writing assignments, group members also were to have written four peer critiques and to have presented the case assigned to their group in a format decided on by the group. Writing prompts for peer critiques were to have been developed in workshops at the presemester orientation (in late August) for teachers of English 306, where we also planned to discuss how to facilitate student presentations of cases. The writing and reading schedule appended to this essay notes where peer critiques and group presentations (a day was set aside for each group) were to have occurred in the schedule, as well as the assignments and due dates for the scripts and essays. The day-by-day writing and reading schedule is for Monday-Wednesday-Friday classes. We planned to write the Tuesday-Thursday version after perfecting the three-day schedule.

I copyrighted all the material developed in the Ad Hoc Syllabus-Writing Group for "Writing about Difference" under my name to ensure that all inquiries about the course would be directed to my office. Publicity about the course generated incessant curiosity and speculation about the readings, but it was a rare journalist who even asked about, much less requested a copy of, the writing assignments or the writing and reading schedule. I discuss the consequences to composition and writing pedagogy of unrestrained, unverified, impoverished, ill-informed, and ill-willed media accounts of the course in "Making a Federal Case out of Difference: The Politics of Pedagogy, Publicity, and Postponement" (1994) and in "Political Suspects?" (1991) which Shelli Fowler and I wrote for the *Village Voice*. Readers interested in deciding for themselves the relative merits of the syllabus we were developing for "Writing about Difference" are invited to examine it for themselves.

Appendix

The table of contents for the reader (Part I), the prompts for the scripts and writing assignments (Part II), and the day-by-day schedule (Part III) have been adapted for this essay from the course packet under preparation for "Writing about Difference," the syllabus for English 306: Rhetoric and Composition, at the University of Texas at Austin.

Part I: Readings for Writing about Difference

Martha Minow, "Making a Difference" and "Sources of Difference"

Peggy McIntosh, "White Privilege and Male Privilege: A Personal Account of Coming to See Correspondences through Work in Women's Studies"

Sweatt v. Painter

Richard Kluger, "The Spurs of Texas Are upon You"

Group 1

Chambers v. Omaha Girls Club, Inc.

Group 2

Gutierrez v. Municipal Court of S.E. Judicial District, County of Los Angeles

Bill Piatt, "Toward Domestic Recognition of a Human Right to Language"

Group 3
Nelson v. Thornburgh
Richard K. Scotch, "Disability as the Basis for a Social Movement: Advocacy and the Politics of Definition"

Group 4
University of Pennsylvania v. EEOC

Group 5
Fricke v. Lynch
Donna J. Dennis and Ruth E. Harlow, "Gay Youth and the Right to Education"
Lanz by Lanz v. Ambach
Deborah Rhode, "Association and Assimilation"

Part II: Writing Assignments for Writing about Difference

Script Assignment 1: Cite a passage from Martha Minow's essay (give the page number) and explain (in about 50 words) why you think it is worth thinking about.

Script Assignment 2: Explain (in about 50 words) which of Minow's arguments against the five assumptions about difference you find the most or least convincing.

Script Assignment 3: Make a list of five privileges (similar to the ones generated by Peggy McIntosh) that people who either see or hear do not have to think about or explain.

Script Assignment 4: Define (in about 25 words) the legal terms assigned to you by checking the recommended sources in the Undergraduate Library. Since your definition is part of the lexicon for the class (which your instructor will duplicate), you need to define each term on a separate page and cite the sources used to compose the definition.

Script Assignment 5: Summarize (in about 50 words) one claim and its grounds from Richard Kluger's "The Spurs of Texas Are upon You" and explain (in about 50 words) why you think it is worth thinking about.

Script Assignment 6: Summarize (in about 50 words) a principal claim and its grounds in the plaintiff's argument in *Sweatt v. Painter.*

Script Assignment 7: Summarize (in about 50 words) a principal claim and its grounds in the defendant's argument in *Sweatt v. Painter.*

Script Assignment 8: Summarize (in about 50 words) a principal claim and its grounds in the argument made by the Supreme Court reversing the decision made by the lower court in *Sweatt v. Painter.*

Script Assignment 9: Summarize and assess (in about 100 words) one of the primary claims and its grounds in either the plaintiff's or the defendant's argument in the case assigned to your group.

Script Assignment 10: Summarize and assess (in about 100 words) one of the primary claims and its grounds in the deciding opinion, minority opinion, or dissenting opinion in the case assigned to your group.

Writing Assignment 1: Martha Minow challenges what she identifies as "five closely related assumptions that underlie difference dilemmas" (p. 106). Summarize the argument that Minow makes against the assumption assigned to your group. This assignment requires you to (1) identify the claim Minow makes concerning the (un)stated assumption underlying "difference" and (2) identify the grounds (or evidence) she uses to support her claim that the assumption is problematic, that is, open to doubt. Once you have identified the claim Minow asserts and the grounds she uses in support of her assertion, you will be able to write a 200- to 300-word summary of her argument against the assumption.

Group 1—Assumption #1: Difference Is Intrinsic

Group 2—Assumption #2: The Unstated Norm

Group 3—Assumption #3: The Observer Can See without a Perspective

Group 4—Assumption #4: The Irrelevance of Other Perspectives

Group 5—Assumption #5: The Status Quo Is Natural, Uncoerced, and Good

Writing Assignment 2 (Group Assignment): Working with the summaries each of you has already written, your writing group will develop a collective summary that best represents Minow's argument against the assumption assigned to your group. The group summary you turn in will be distributed to the other members of the class. This assignment requires each of you to:

1. Read the five summaries written by the group members.
2. Rank the summaries. Assign each summary a score. Give a 1 to the summary you think is best, a 2 to the second best, and so on. Assign each summary a different score even if you feel that two or more are comparable.
3. Name the criterion (or criteria) that you think is (are) governing your ranking.

Once the summaries have been individually ranked, members of the group need to compare their rankings and discuss the criteria governing their selections. At least one member of the group needs to take notes. As a group, you will then need to decide which criterion or criteria to use in constructing the group summary.

The summary you turn in as a group may well include passages from one or all of your individual summaries, or you may decide to write a new summary based on your rankings and discussions. The final version should be about 200 to 300 words. Append a brief statement (about 50 words) explaining the criterion or criteria used to create the group summary along with the notes taken during your group discussions.

Writing Assignment 3: Write a documented essay of about 700 words defining, examining, analyzing, and critiquing one of the stereotypes (an oversimplified belief or opinion about a person or group of people) assigned to your group. Apply what you have learned concerning unexamined assumptions about difference to explore problems raised by the stereotype. This assignment requires each of the you to:

1. Choose one of the stereotypes assigned to your group (see below).
2. Generate a list of characteristics associated with the stereotype.
3. Research the stereotype by (a) locating books and periodicals that complicate the "stereotype"; (b) keeping a bibliographic record of your sources (see *The Scott, Foresman Handbook for Writers* [*HB*] 593-601 if you need help); and (c) copying materials from sources you think you might want to cite in your essay (see *HB* 602-5, if you need help).
4. Discuss your list and research with the other members of your group.

The draft of this essay needs to include (1) a definition of the stereotype, (2) an analysis of insights and limitations of that commonly accepted definition, incorporating information from your library sources, and (3) a critique of unstated assumption(s) not dealt with by the stereotype, incorporating information from Minow's essay.

Group 1: Unwed mother/philanthropist/pregnant teen/role model

Group 2: Blind man/blind woman/handicapped individual/activist

Group 3: Foreigner/English speaker/Hispanic/employee

Group 4: Asian woman/professor/M.B.A./bureaucrat

Group 5: Homosexual/heterosexual/the perfect date/good student or female athlete/male athlete/good sport/jock

Writing Assignment 4: Reviews of academic books and essays are a specialized genre. For this assignment, each of you will write a 500- to 700-word review essay of the article assigned to your group. Because scholarly writing concentrates on convincing readers that the evidence used to ground claims is warranted, the purpose of a review is to evaluate how well a particular book or essay has accomplished this goal.

This assignment requires you to (1) reread the article, (2) select what you think are the principal claims, (3) identify the grounds used to support the principal claims, and (4) assess how well the grounds warrant the claims made.

Write a title for your review and begin your essay with a full citation of the article. See *HB* (647-68): citing articles and chapters from books. In the review itself, construct an argument evaluating the effectiveness of the entire article. Support your position by assessing how well the grounds supporting the principal claims are warranted.

Writing Assignment 5: A court opinion summarizes and evaluates the arguments made by the plaintiff and the defendant and provides a rationale for affirming or denying the case made by the plaintiff. An opinion may consist of one or more of the following: (1) the argument that supports the court's decision (majority opinion); (2) an argument that dissents from the argument in the majority opinion but supports the court's decision (minority opinion); (3) an argument that dissents from both the opinion and the decision of the court (dissenting opinion). If your group has been assigned a case in which there is a majority opinion, a minority opinion, and a dissenting opinion, focus on one in your essay.

Building from the work you have already done in scripts 9 and 10, this assignment requires you to (1) reread the case assigned to your group, (2) choose an opinion (if there is more than one), (3) reread the relevant law(s), (4) identify the principal claims and grounds in the opinion, and (5) assess how well the grounds warrant the principal claims in the opinion.

Write an essay of about 700 words summarizing and evaluating an opinion in the case assigned to your group. Summarize the opinion before assessing the grounds used to warrant the argument.

Writing Assignment 6: A legal opinion is an argument explaining the court's reasons for finding in favor of the plaintiff or the defendant. In its argument the court applies principles of law to specific cases. Forming an opinion is first a matter of deciding to what extent the complaint against the defendant is justified by law(s) *and* then deciding to what extent the circumstances of a particular case mitigate law(s). Arguments for both the relevance of legal principles and mitigating circumstances concern warranting the grounds used to support the claim(s) made to justify the decision.

This assignment requires you to (1) read the materials (the brief and possible laws), (2) summarize the plaintiff's case, (3) summarize the defendant's case, (4) evaluate the plaintiff's case with respect to law, (5) evaluate the defendant's case with respect to law, (6) evaluate the plaintiff's case with respect to circumstances, (7) evaluate the defendant's case with respect to circumstances, (8) decide in favor of the plaintiff or defendant, and (9) formulate an argument supporting your opinion

Write an opinion (500 to 700 words) in which you give your reasons for finding in favor of the plaintiff or defendant. Your opinion needs to take into account both a legal principle and the circumstances of the case. You may, if you wish, use additional materials for establishing circumstances. You are, however, restricted to either the laws cited in the case or the others in your course packet. [These materials were not yet in the course packet when implementation of the syllabus was postponed.]

Part III: Monday-Wednesday-Friday Schedule for Writing about Difference

Required Texts:

The Scott, Foresman Handbook for Writers (*HB*)
English 306: Course Packet

Note: Syllabus indicates the number of copies of each assignment needed *in addition to the original.*

Week 1

Wednesday 8/29

Class activity
Course overview
Syllabus
Policy statement
Scholastic honesty statement

Friday 8/31

Reading Assignment
Martha Minow, introduction to *Making All the Difference* (due Wednesday 9/5)
HB, Planning, 34-44; Summarizing, 602-5; Sexist Language, 402-9; Denotation/Connotation, 158-62 (due Friday 9/7)
Script Assignment 1
Issue raised in Minow (50 words, one cc due Wednesday 9/5)
Library Assignment
Undergraduate Library tour (due Wednesday 9/5)
Class Activity
In-class writing assignment 1 (35-40 minutes)

Week 2

Monday 9/3 **Labor Day (no class)**

Wednesday 9/5

Class Activity
Turn in one copy of script 1

Summarizing re claims and grounds

Demonstrate using Minow essay assigned on 8/31

Assign students to writing groups

Writing Assignment 1

Summary of assumption in Minow essay (one copy to instructor, four copies for writing group, due Monday 9/10)

Friday 9/7

Writing groups

Plan summaries of Minow section

Week 3

Monday 9/10

Class Activity

Turn in five copies of writing assignment 1

Discussion: Sorting and ranking summaries of Minow

Writing Group

Sorting and ranking summaries of Minow

Writing Assignment 2 (Group Assignment)

Group summary of assumption in Minow essay (one copy, due Friday 9/14)

Wednesday 9/12

Reading Assignment

McIntosh, "White Privilege and Male Privilege" (due Monday 9/17)

Script Assignment 2

Working definition of difference re Minow (about 100 words, one cc due Wednesday 9/14)

Writing Group

Sorting and ranking summaries of Minow

Friday 9/14

Class Activity

Turn in one copy of writing assignment 2

Turn in one copy of script 2

Discussion of Minow essay

Part I (group summaries)

Part II (defining difference)

Script Assignment 3

Working definition of privilege re McIntosh (about 100 words, one cc due Monday 9/17)

Reading Assignment

HB, Bibliography, 593-601; 602-5 (due Wednesday 9/19)

Writing Assignment 3

Documented essay analyzing a stereotype (two cc due Monday 9/24)

Week 4

Monday 9/17

Class Activity

Turn in one copy of script 3

Discussion of "White Privilege and Male Privilege" (re claims and grounds for definitions)

Reading Assignment

HB: MLA Documentation (23 C) 638-71 (due Wednesday 9/19)

Wednesday 9/19

Class Activity

Discussion: Documenting sources

Writing Groups

Explore arguments for writing assignment 3

Script Assignment 4

Compiling a documented lexicon of legal terms (one cc due Monday 10/1)

Friday 9/21

Class Activity

Discussion: Exploring arguments for writing assignment 3

Writing Group

Explore arguments for writing assignment 3

Reading Assignment

"The Spurs of Texas Are upon You" (due Wednesday 9/26)

Fourteenth Amendment (due Wednesday 9/26)

Sweatt v. Painter (due Friday 9/28)

Script Assignment 5

Claim and ground from "The Spurs" (50 words, one cc due Wednesday 9/26)

Week 5

Monday 9/24

Class Activity

Turn in two copies of writing assignment 3 (complete draft; revision due Monday 10/8)

Discussion: Critiques

Critique Assignment 1

Critique of writing assignment 3 (two cc due Friday 9/28)

Writing Groups

Exchange copies of writing assignment 3 (draft essays)

Begin critiques of writing assignment 3 (draft essays) (two cc of critiques due Friday 9/28)

Wednesday 9/26

Class Activity

Turn in one copy of script 5

Discussion: Claims and grounds in "The Spurs of Texas"

Friday 9/28

Class Activity

Turn in two copies of critique 1

Discussion: *Sweatt v. Painter*

Reading Assignment

Group case (due Wednesday 10/10)

Essay related to the case (due Wednesday 10/10)

First Amendment, Title VII, Title IX, Rehabilitation Act, Pregnancy Discrimination Act (due Monday 10/8)

Script Assignment 6

Summary of claims and grounds of plaintiff's argument in *Sweatt* (one cc due Monday 10/1)

Week 6

Monday 10/1

Class Activity

Turn in one copy of script 6

Turn in one copy of script 4 (legal lexicon)

Discussion: The plaintiff's argument in *Sweatt*

Reading Assignment

HB: "How to Write a Review," 762-67 (due Wednesday 10/3)

Script Assignment 7

Summarize the claims and grounds of the defendant's argument in *Sweatt* (one cc due Wednesday 10/3)

Wednesday 10/3

Class Activity

Turn in one copy of script 7

Questions: Reviewing

Discussion: The defendant's argument in *Sweatt*

Writing Assignment 4

Review the essay assigned to the group (two cc of draft due Monday 10/15)

Script Assignment 8

Summarize the claims and grounds of the court's opinion in *Sweatt* (one cc due Friday 10/5)

Friday 10/5

Class Activity

Turn in one copy of script 8

Discussion: The court's opinion in *Sweatt*

Week 7

Monday 10/8

Class Activity

Turn in two copies of revised writing assignment 3

Discussion: Antidiscrimination law

Wednesday 10/10

Class Activity

Questions: Antidiscrimination law

Exploring arguments for review essay

Friday 10/12

Class Activity

Questions: Review essay

Writing Group

Exploring arguments for review essay

Week 8

Monday 10/15

Class Activity

Turn in two draft copies of writing assignment 4

Critique Assignment 2

Critique of writing assignment 4 (two cc due Friday 10/19)

Writing Group

Work on critiques

Wednesday 10/17

Writing Group

Continue working on critiques

Friday 10/19

Class Activity

Turn in two copies of critique 2

Writing Assignment 5

Summarize and assess the arguments of the plaintiff, the defendant, and the court in the case assigned to your group (one cc due Monday 10/29)

Writing Group

Work on writing assignment 5

Week 9

Monday 10/22

Class Activity

Analyzing arguments

Script Assignment 9

Summary and assessment of plaintiff's or defendant's argument in the group case (about 100 words, one cc due Wednesday 10/24)

Wednesday 10/24

Class Activity

Turn in one copy of script 9

Discussion: Plaintiff's or defendant's argument

Script Assignment 10

Brief summary and assessment of argument in the court opinion or dissenting opinion (about 100 words, one cc due Friday 10/26)

Writing Group

Discussion: Summarizing and assessing the court opinion(s)

Friday 10/26

Class Activity

Turn in one copy of script 10

Discussion: Arguments in the court opinion(s)

Group Presentation Assignment

Presentations are to include summaries of arguments, assessments of arguments, relevant essays, positions of all group members, and arguments not considered by the court (one cc due 11/12-21)

Week 10

Monday 10/29

Class Activity

Turn in one copy of writing assignment 5

Writing Assignment 6

Write an opinion based on the transcript (one draft cc due Monday 11/9)

Writing Group

Plans for writing assignment 6

Wednesday 10/31
Class Activity
Discussion: Formulating an opinion
Writing Group
Discussion of opinions

Friday 11/2
Class Activity
Discussion: Formulating an opinion

Week 11

Monday 11/5
Class Activity
Library/group conferences with instructor

Wednesday 11/7
Class Activity
Library/group conferences with instructor

Friday 11/9
Class Activity
Turn in one copy of writing assignment 6 to writing group
Critique Assignment 3 (two cc due Wednesday 11/14)
Writing Group
Exchange drafts
Begin critiques

Week 12

Monday 11/12
Writing Group 1
Present case

Wednesday 11/14
Class Activity
Turn in two copies of critique 3
Writing Group 2
Present case

Friday 11/16
Writing Group 3
Present case

Week 13

Monday 11/19

Writing Group 4

Present case

Wednesday 11/21

Writing Group 5

Present case

Friday 11/23 **Thanksgiving**

Week 14

Monday 11/26

Class Activity

Turn in two copies of writing assignment 6 (groups exchange)

Critique Assignment 4 (two cc due Friday 11/30)

Wednesday 11/28

Writing Group

Work on critique 4

Friday 11/30

Class Activity

Turn in two copies of critique 4

Week 15

Monday 12/3

Class Activity

Discussion: Opinions

Wednesday 12/5

Class Activity

Turn in writing assignment 6 (copies for everyone)

Course evaluation

Friday 12/7

Class Activity

In-class writing assignment 2 (35-40 minutes)

Writing about Difference: "Hard Cases" for Cultural Studies

Some twenty years ago, James Kinneavy introduced A *Theory of Discourse* with a formidable catalog of the institutional barriers facing composition:

> Composition is so clearly the stepchild of the English department that it is not a legitimate area of graduate study, is not even recognized as a subdivision of the discipline of English in a recent manifesto put out by the major professional association (MLA) of college English teachers, in some universities is not a valid area of scholarship for advancement in rank, and is generally the teaching province of graduate students or fringe members of the department. (1971: 1)

That composition dismantled many of these institutional defenses in a remarkably short time is a testament of sorts to the virtues of scholarship. Composition is now a legitimate area of graduate study at many state universities; recent Modern Language Association "manifestos" declare composition to be a field; and at many state universities, at least, scholarship on writing counts for tenure and promotion. That improved conditions for scholars do not necessarily extend to teachers is nowhere more evident than in the Wyoming Resolution, the critique of the continued institutional misuse of graduate students and part-time faculty to staff most college writing courses made at the annual Wyoming Conference (see "Statement of Principles and Standards" 1989).

Far too many composition teachers still work under appalling conditions, even in institutions where there are graduate programs in writing and where research on writing is grounds for tenure and promotion. They teach too many courses and too many students each term, and they are neither paid well enough nor prepared well enough to teach writing. Most of the professoriat can justify treating writing teachers as guest workers in the academy, for most probably imagine writing pedagogy to be much as Ian Watt once represented it—simply a matter of doing "all the hard and often unpleasant work of reading and correcting a lot of student papers week after week"—even if they do not also share his conviction that composition research and English handbooks alike "spy upon the obvious" (1978: 14). Composition *is* pedagogy. But pedagogy can be reduced to correcting student papers only if you imagine yourself to be the writing police, for those who make a fetish of grammar or style also imagine themselves to be protecting the literate from the illiterate who threaten the powerful homology of one nation/one language/one culture, without which such prescriptions would be revealed as the self-interested protection of privilege that they are.

"Students' Right to Their Own Language," a resolution adopted by the 1974 Conference on College Composition and Communication and reaffirmed several times since, publicly denounces ill-informed and self-serving language policies as "false advice for speakers and writers, and immoral advice for humans" (see preface to "Students' Right to Their Own Language" 1974). The syllabus drafted for "Writing about Difference" at the University of Texas may not address precisely the same issues as the 1974 resolution, but opposition to the syllabus is curiously reminiscent of the political climate in which the resolution on language was drafted and ultimately adopted. Whether the controversy is about dialect or difference, it seems, opponents just say no, perhaps because difference and dialect alike challenge "many long-held and passionately cherished notions about language" ("Students' Right" 1974: 1).

As it has come down to us from poststructural language theories, difference tries to account for the practice of defining by negation, of accentuating the positive, so to speak, by distancing the positive from the negative term in a pair or set and hence affirming the positivity of the preferred term at the expense of that from which it "differs." That we can make these distinctions in language is a tribute to the human intellect, except when we forget that we must then take responsibility for the consequences of defining real human beings as different. Unlike *diversity*, a word that recognizes variety without attempting to analyze the part language plays in making distinctions among people, *difference* challenges the culturally and socially sanctioned practice of imputing extraordinary human value to some people by diminishing the worth of others. In other words, "ability" and "disability" may be an arbitrary linguistic pair, but the legal and educational consequences of being defined as "disabled" or "abled" are not arbitrary. It matters a great deal whether you are the unmarked (normative) or marked (deviant) term in such pairs as white or black, Anglo or Hispanic, American or Asian-American, male or female, straight or gay, young or old, monolingual or bilingual. Such binary oppositions are more than theoretically interesting examples of human cognition, for the processes of defining by negation are sometimes used to justify the political and economic practices of exclusion.

Among other things, difference falsifies the analytical and pedagogical fiction that form is literally separable from content. To our minds, it is a fiction that serves the interests of neither students nor teachers, if only because most students believe that teachers talk form but mean content, and good teachers worry that students may be right. Yet when writing teachers assume the right to assess the content of student writing, they disturb the order of things, notably, the commonsense belief that grammar, style, and rhetoric are independent of the production and reception of knowledge, that language conveys ideas or reality or even truth, but plays no critical part in constructing them. Writing progams that attempt to institutionalize the rights of teachers and students to assess the content of writing risk being deemed presumptuous, the more so if that right is claimed on behalf of graduate students and lecturers. For what amounts to a right in "content areas" is likely to be seen as unwarranted privilege—a license to indoctrinate students or an open invitation for instructors to impose a particular political bias—in a first-year writing class. No matter how unjustified the charges, they are believed because many believe pedagogy to be a matter of transmitting culture by precept, and correctness to be the reigning precept in writing pedagogy. According to this logic, composition teachers, themselves a marginalized cohort whose intellectual work with students remains marginal to the institution, may legitimately transmit lessons on grammar, style, and rhetoric but transgress disciplinary boundaries if they raise questions about the quality of the assertions writers make.

The syllabus for "Writing about Difference" celebrates students and teachers by inviting them to conduct sustained rhetorical inquiry into a topic that troubles many people in this country—difference. And to our minds, any writing course that positively values the intellectual labor of students and teachers goes a long way toward celebrating the field of composition itself. An ad hoc group of faculty and graduate students worked on the syllabus during the summer of 1990. Membership in what became known as the Ad Hoc Syllabus-Writing Group was open to anyone scheduled to teach the course in 1990-91 and consisted of the director of lower-division English (Linda Brodkey), four other faculty members (Susan Sage Heinzelman, Sara Kimball, Stuart Moulthrop, and John Slatin) of the Lower Division English Policy Committee, which proposed implementing a common syllabus on the topic of difference for one year, six graduate-student instructors (Margaret Downs-Gamble, David Ericson, Shelli Fowler, Dana Harrington, Allison Mosshart, and Rick Penticoff), and Maria Villalobos, the administrative assistant for the program. We make a point of mentioning these names because our weekly, sometimes twice-weekly, meetings produced the syllabus as well as experience of collaboration akin to what we hoped to recreate in the course itself. The collaboration not only shaped the syllabus but continues to shape the intellectual issues that are raised by the syllabus and were ruthlessly ignored by administrative fiat on July 23, 1990, when the dean of liberal arts sent the English department a memo announcing his decision to postpone the implementation of "Writing about Difference" in order to address "misunderstandings about the course expressed within the university community" (Meacham 1990).

As the title suggests, "Writing about Difference" is a syllabus with a focused topic, *difference*. Writing about and discussion of the topic are oriented by four kinds of readings: essays that discuss the issue of difference (e.g., Martha Minow's *Making All the Difference*); U.S. District, Circuit, and Supreme Court opinions on cases involving disputes over specific kinds of difference (race, gender, physical ability, bilingualism, sexual orientation); essays that discuss issues raised in court opinions (e.g., freedom of association); and federal laws invoked in the court opinions (e.g., the First and Fourteenth Amendments to the Constitution; Title VII of the Civil Rights Act of 1964; Title IX of the Education Amendments of 1972). In a series of linked reading and writing assignments, student texts as well as published texts sustain rhetorical inquiry into the topic of difference.

"Writing about Difference" is a syllabus written for English 306, the first-year writing course at the University of Texas at Austin. Credit for English 306 is required of all students at the university. More than half the entering students (about three thousand) take the course each year. Others take an equivalent course elsewhere or place out by passing a standardized grammar and usage test. Students in the course generally come from the top 25 percent of their high school classes. Most are white and middle class; there are slightly more males than females. Despite long-standing and widespread local suspicion, English 306 is neither a "basic" nor a "remedial" writing course, as those who teach open-admissions students would understand the term (see Shaughnessy 1977). Special sections of English 306 are offered only to students, generally foreign nationals, for whom English is a second language. Fifty-plus sections of English 306 are offered during each of the two regular semesters of the academic year (some twenty more during the summer); about 95 percent of these sections are taught by graduate-student instructors, who must take a full load of courses (three every semester) in order to be employed. English 306 is the first course most graduate students teach in the department, and few begin their service with any teaching experience, let alone knowledge of composition research or pedagogy.

We provide these details to give some picture of the institutional context out of which "Writing about Difference" emerged. The department has a responsibility not only to the undergraduates who take the course but also to the graduate instructors who staff the vast majority of sections. Responding to the needs and desires of these sometimes conflicting constituencies required some compromises in the syllabus design. For instance, we decided against portfolios on the grounds that we could not reasonably expect graduate-student teachers to increase their workload at precisely the same point that their own course work is due. Even so, we aimed for solutions that would be pedagogically sound and intellectually defensible for University of Texas students and teachers alike. No doubt the problems and solutions would be different at other institutions.

Most graduate-student instructors of English 306 study literature. The syllabus for "Writing about Difference" attempts to build on the strengths that literature majors are likely to bring to the classroom while at the same time inviting them to participate in teaching composition as an intellectual enterprise in its own right. It positively values their abilities as close readers, yet asks them to work with texts outside their usual purview. Though they are not literary analyses, court opinions work very like interpretations, and literature students are likely to find themselves in familiar territory since both jurisprudence and literary studies are founded on intertextual interpretive practices. Yet to think like a writer—to shift from reception to production—is to accept that the consequences of writing texts, including taking responsibility for the potential violence of words, are different from those of reading them. Michael Calvin McGee, for instance, argues that rhetorical acts that aim at persuading inflict a kind of violence because the persuasive act aims at changing people's thoughts, attitudes, or behavior. Legal opinions strike us as excellent illustrations of this kind of rhetorical power and violence. As Robert Cover so eloquently puts it: "Legal interpretive acts signal and occasion the imposition of violence on others: A judge articulates her understanding of a text, and as a result, somebody loses his freedom, his property, his children, even his life" (1986: 1601). We take Cover to mean that the language used by the court invariably changes people's lives. We mean that the language used by students and teachers in classrooms and essays is, if not equally consequential, as potentially violent, and we want students and teachers to learn that what they say to one another and what they say about texts matters.

Some current work in literary studies will make it easier for students of literature to recognize in the writing of court opinions what rhetoricians know as invention, a process of finding or discovering materials for topics. Jerome McGann's work on textual studies, for instance, though focused on publication, opens up the issue of textual production by questioning the notion of an author's "final" intentions. McGann argues that authors' intentions toward their texts can best be seen as a social process of interaction and negotiation with editors, publishers, copyists, and readers. In jurisprudence, legal briefs, court transcripts, and discovery evidence all contribute material to the court's opinion, visible testimony of a public and protracted invention process. These legal texts also make available a more expansive, ontological view of rhetorical invention—the view that language constitutes social reality. This is a view that James Boyd White argues for in his discussions of both literary and legal texts. From this perspective, one might argue that every decision handed down by the courts, and the Supreme Court in particular, invents democracy anew. In this sense, then, even we who are not judges but citizens who read and interpret and evaluate legal opinions are writing commentaries in the margins of American history.

Many teachers of English 306 are new to composition as well as teaching. New teachers often question the source of their classroom authority, and some deal with their uncertainty by resorting to pedantry. The course intentionally channels interest and enthusiasm for current literary theories into a pedagogy fairer to students than most inexperienced teachers are likely to create on their own. Difference is a notion familiar to most graduate students and dear to some, but the syllabus requires instructors and students alike to examine difference critically, allowing a forum for neither ex cathedra pronouncements based on theories unknown to students nor conclusions based on unverifiable personal experiences. The syllabus, with its common reading and writing assignments and methods of evaluation, initially shifts authority from individual teachers to the program. Hence responsibility for the topic, materials, and assignments is returned to the institution, leaving relatively inexperienced teachers some much needed time to learn how best to teach writing practices—inventing, drafting, evaluating, revising, editing. Finally, the detailed syllabus lessens instructors' anxieties about whether they "know" enough to teach writing even as it encourages them to acquire a common body of knowledge—lore, research, and scholarship—to be generated, applied, and transformed by teachers themselves (see North 1987). Instructors thereby contribute to a larger intellectual enterprise, at the very least one more productive to them and to students than the more usual exploitative one in which they are virtually forced to rationalize teaching writing on the side while they build up cultural capital for a later, more respectable life teaching literature.

Similarly, the syllabus seeks to build on the strengths of the undergraduates who take the course. Most eighteen-year-olds come to college hoping to leave high school behind; older students enter or reenter college already considering high school a closed chapter in their lives. This being the case, we can see no reason to treat any of them as thirteenth graders. "Writing about Difference" breaks decisively with high school by, among other things, using Stephen Toulmin's language in *The Uses of Argument* to talk about writing. While similarities between thesis and claim and evidence and ground enable students to bridge their high school and college discussions of writing, Toulmin's notion of warranting leads most of them into uncharted, but crucial, intellectual territory.

In addition to building on undergraduates' desire for intellectual challenge, the syllabus resituates ongoing campus conversations. Racially directed incidents involving several fraternities during both the spring and fall 1990 semesters, detailed proposals for curricular and administrative reform from both African-American and Chicana/Chicano student groups, and "coming-out" rallies on the part of gay and lesbian groups have established difference as a topic of conversation and, on occasion, shouting matches. Local violence amplifies a national intolerance of difference. Consider the voter showing on behalf of gubernatorial candidate David Duke in Louisiana or the anti–affirmative action ads that Senator Jesse Helms ran in the last weeks of his 1990 reelection campaign. One way or another, people are talking about difference—at home, in the dorms, and on the streets as well as in voting booths and on talk shows—and most of the talk suggests a deep, layered, and conflicted consciousness of the issue. "Writing about Difference" attempts to take an issue in which there is already heated interest and make it an occasion for intellectual inquiry rather than forensic spectacle.

Finally, many students enter the classroom with a desire for an experience that is more participatory than is usually afforded by the standard lecture hall with one hundred–plus students and an instructor pronouncing from on high, behind a lectern. The syllabus puts writing groups of four to five students at the intellectual and logistical center of the course. Each group is responsible for teaching its court case to the rest of the class. Scholastic success relies on the collective as well as individual work of students. We are betting that these intellectual interactions will, in some instances at least, foster friendships outside the classroom and are hoping that they will counteract the fragmenting and alienating experiences that seem increasingly to characterize undergraduate life at large state universities like the University of Texas at Austin (see Wilson 1991).

Such are some of the local circumstances that influenced the formation and design of the syllabus for "Writing about Difference." We tried to take account of the fact that two of the most vulnerable groups at the university, first-year students and first-time graduate-student instructors, are most affected by this course. We tried to be responsible foremost to them in meeting the already stated curricular goals with a common syllabus that supports teaching writing. Our initial goal was to engage students and instructors in intellectual inquiry. The topic of difference poses some risk to this goal, for it is a "hot" issue. But we think it a risk well worth taking because students and instructors need to learn how to discuss political issues in pedagogically and intellectually responsible ways. Teachers and students live outside as well as inside classrooms, and many feel keenly their responsibilities to their families and communities. To the extent that writing classrooms are sometimes also constituted as communities, however temporary and fragile, we do not see difference as an incidental means of engaging in written inquiry, but as a positive way for students and teachers to contribute to civic life.

Scholarly inquiry does not arise out of a historical, social, or political void, but is instead generated and sustained by published texts, many of which exert near-canonical power over most students and some teachers. Yet teachers must afford student texts the same privileges as professional ones in writing classes if they expect students to see their own writing and that of peers as contributions to ongoing intellectual conversations. Efforts to value student and professional texts equally, however, more often than not create conflict between intellectual and pedagogical imperatives. Making professional texts the center of a classroom is often taken, by teachers and students, as a sign of fealty to the intellectual tradition represented by the text. Making student texts the center of a classroom is taken as a sign of the teacher's commitment to writing pedagogy. When intellectual imperatives predominate, there is the temptation to offer professional texts as models: of stylistic features, of structural or rhetorical principles, or of proper moral or political content. In our view, the pedagogy of imitation sets up a textual hierarchy in which student texts are invariably devalued. When pedagogical imperatives predominate, there is the temptation to ban professional texts altogether from the classroom. The ostensible rationale is that students will find their own voices or discover their most creative thoughts only if the more powerful, and hence oppressive, published texts are absent.

We have tried to balance the intellectual and pedagogical imperatives in our syllabus by putting student and professional texts in conversation and contention with each other. "Writing about Difference" begins by trying to interrupt the authority of published texts. We don't ask students to directly model or imitate any of the professional texts in their own writing, but we do create situations in which students can themselves gain sufficient scholarly authority to "talk back" to laws, court opinions, and academic essays. We focus on a common topic for the semester because we reasoned that the more familiar students are with a set of published texts on a topic, the less likely they are to assume that publication itself guarantees that any argument is invulnerable. We also reasoned that students are more likely to gain sufficient scholarly authority to challenge professional texts when they are not repeatedly required to build up wholly new knowledge bases, as they must when topics change with each writing assignment. We teach students scholarly practices—analysis, research, synthesis—that build expertise. And we set up classroom situations in which expertise gained by an individual can be shared with the group. We expect that by the end of the semester, whatever intellectual home the professional texts may have offered initially will be rebuilt or abandoned by students and teachers who work from the pedagogical blueprints offered by the syllabus.

What complicates our attempt to achieve reciprocity between student and professional texts, between intellectual and pedagogical imperatives, is the topic: difference. The topic, and hence the texts representing it, is disturbing. The texts provoke because they sometimes question received wisdom. For example, Judge McMillian's dissent to the majority opinion in *Chambers v. Omaha Girls Club, Inc.* casts doubt on the very idea of a role model. Some texts may also provoke because they ask us to consider the lives and views of people different from most students and instructors at the University of Texas. Peggy McIntosh, in "White Privilege and Male Privilege," for instance, notes homologies between the privileges males have in relation to females and those white people have in relation to people of color. The syllabus asks students to perform a similar imaginative exercise for themselves in relation to those whose vision or hearing is impaired.

No doubt the topic will make some students uncomfortable, particularly those who were taught to believe that laws literally prevent discrimination or that privilege is necessarily deserved. Other students may see raising the topic as a violation of a politeness convention; that is, problems may exist but polite people don't talk about them. We have staged an educational scene that may well distress some students. While writing classrooms need to be safe places for students, we take that to mean safe from gratuitous judgments of their writing, not safe from intellectual life. It is at least arguable that intellectual discomfort gives a point to writing in a way that intellectual comfort cannot.

When instructors are confronted with reluctant or rebellious students, they often resort to "explicating the text" in order to ensure that students "get the message." Instructors can then claim they have at least done right by the text (or the message or the author or the group represented by the author), if not by the students. In a writing class, resorting to explication seems both unfair and antithetical to the aims of pedagogy. Learning to teach writing is learning to do right by the texts students write. No text, professional or student, can be treated as sacred. The syllabus for "Writing about Difference" discourages students from making pronouncements about issues based on personal experience (which is what most first-year students have to go on), and teachers from making pronouncements about texts based on theories (which is what most graduate-student teachers have to go on). Pronouncements from either quarter stifle the pedagogy of writing as inquiry. Rhetoric of inquiry relies on students and teachers talking with rather than talking at one another.

Many students have been taught that finding a position is the intellectual task in a writing course. For these students, once a position is stated there's really not much interesting work left to do beyond marshaling the requisite three pieces of evidence smartly on the page. We hoped to interrupt this version of argumentation on parade with Stephen Toulmin's language of claims, grounds, and warrants. One of the singular advantages of Toulmin's terms is that they encourage us to examine the positions we take as claims. Claims make it easier to treat positions as partial and provisional statements about the world, rather than as unarguable and immutable truths with which readers either agree or disagree. And when the conversation shifts from thesis statement to claim, we become less concerned about the position as a position and more interested in where an argument for it would position us—in relation to both other people and other arguments. In other words, Toulmin's lexicon offers students and teachers alike a view of argumentation as a prologue to further inquiry, which we see as an antidote to viewing arguments as debates, as performances that invariably end with winners and losers, and, ultimately, in silence.

In Toulmin's model, argumentation begins with a claim made about a problem or a state of affairs. A writer asserts that such and such is the case. When a reader responds to this initial claim with the question "What do you have to go on?" the writer offers some data as grounds for the assertion. Just offering these grounds, however, may be insufficient to make the assertion convincing. One might well ask "How do you get from here to there, from ground to claim?"—that is, how well is the relation between ground and claim warranted? Further, one might challenge the rule, principle, custom, or law that is used as a warrant. One may ask, in other words, about the grounds for the warrant itself by asking whether the backing for the warrant is sufficient.

The concepts of claims, grounds, and warrants have a number of features that are important to our pedagogical aim of generating and sustaining inquiry in writing. Claims are provisional statements, a way of staking out an intellectual territory. In *An Introduction to Reasoning,* Toulmin, along with coauthors Richard Rieke and Allan Janik, compares making a verbal claim to "staking a claim" for mining rights (1984: 30). Territorial claims are subject to dispute and need defending, certainly legally, but often physically as well. We are less concerned here with the analogy drawn beween physical and intellectual property, and more intrigued by the notion of territory or position. Any claim stakes a position in an intellectual field, which then circumscribes the kinds of arguments that can be made from that position. By way of example, some readers of *Fricke v. Lynch,* a case in which a male high school student sued to overturn his principal's prohibition against bringing a male escort to the prom, may claim that homosexuality is wrong. These readers will find, however, that such a claim positions them in an intellectual field not considered by the court. The plaintiff argued that the principal's prohibition was a violation of his First Amendment right to free expression; the defendant argued that the prohibition was made in the interest of public safety. Homosexuality itself is not an issue for either the litigants or the court. To make it an issue, one has to shift the grounds of the dispute from civil liberties to personal conduct, and, in some states, from civil to criminal law.

The provisional nature of claims can be seen in the way the issue is, in fact, framed in *Fricke v. Lynch.* One could say that two acknowledged rights are in conflict: the right of free expression and the right to enjoy public order and safety. Historically, federal courts have defined neither right as absolute. Students may well find during their inquiries that the courts shift position on the issue of free expression. A district court argued for the primacy of this right in *Fricke*, but the Supreme Court denied its supremacy in *University of Pennsylvania v. Equal Employment Opportunity Commission,* unanimously finding against the university's claim that confidentiality is necessary to protect the First Amendment rights of those who write tenure reviews. Students may not readily accept our assertion that claims are provisional, but the writing assignments developed for the syllabus require all of us to make public the grounds on which we state such and such to be the case.

For purposes of pedagogy, the key concept in Toulmin's model is warranting. Warrant is complex because it refers both to things (principles, rules, customs, laws) and actions (warrants *license* the relation between claims and grounds). The chief feature of warrants is that they are field-dependent. In warranting the relation between claim and ground, at least three conditions must be met: (1) the grounds must be relevant to the claim; (2) the grounds must be sufficient to substantiate the claim; and (3) the argument must be rhetorically appropriate to the situation. The criteria of relevance, sufficiency, and appropriateness link argumentation to the contingencies of context and loosen its connections to the determinant laws of logic.

The notion of warranting is particularly useful in assessing the merits of majority and dissenting opinions—especially so in *Chambers v. Omaha Girls Club, Inc.* Crystal Chambers, a single black woman employed as an arts and crafts instructor by the Omaha Girls Club, was fired when she became pregnant. The defendant argued that employees were expected to be role models for the predominantly African-American "members" of the club, that pregnancy outside marriage is a harmful behavior to model for this membership, and therefore that Chambers's pregnancy was grounds for dismissal because it modeled harmful behavior. In this chain of arguments, one strand that becomes an issue among the judges is as follows: claim—girls will emulate Chambers's behavior and get pregnant; ground—Chambers is a role model for the girls; warrant—people will emulate the behavior of role models. The majority opinion accepts this chain of reasoning as valid. Judge McMillian's dissenting opinion, however, takes issue with the warrant:

> The district court, and now this court, accepts without any proof OGC's [the Omaha Girls Club's] assumption that the presence of an unwed pregnant instructor is related to teenage pregnancies. . . . OGC failed to present surveys, school statistics or any other empirical data connecting the incidence of teenage pregnancy with the pregnancy of an adult instructor. OGC also failed to present evidence that other girls clubs or similar types of organizations employed such a rule. OGC instead relied on two or three highly questionable anecdotal incidents to support the rule. (*Chambers* 707)

The dissent disputes the backing for the warrant, the evidence used to support the behavioral law or principle that predicts that people emulate the behavior of role models. Note that the dissenting opinion does not question the ground of the argument, that Chambers was employed to function as a role model, but challenges instead the relevance of the ground to the claim. McMillian reasons that if there is no empirically verifiable evidence to support a necessary cause-effect relation between the behavior of a role model and that of her clients, then Chambers cannot be fired on the grounds that she was a negative role model. Being a role model might be a part of an employee's job description, but in this case one cannot say, if one's test is empirical evidence, that the job either is or isn't being done.

This example illustrates how context-dependent—or "field-dependent," to use Toulmin's language—warranting is. The judges writing the majority opinion are willing to accept anecdotal evidence for the efficacy of role models because, we presume, it is commonsense and customary knowledge that such a relation exists. In fact, the majority is even "uncertain whether the role model rule by its nature is suited to validation by an empirical study" (*Chambers* 702). The dissenting opinion, by contrast, takes a view of the role-model principle more characteristic of what one has come to expect in, say, experimental psychology, namely, that an assertion can be applied generally as an explanation of human behavior only if it has been empirically validated. The opinions in *Chambers* are thus arguments drawing warrants from two competing fields, custom and science. We realize that the very notion of warranting is highly complex precisely because it is field- or context-dependent. One obvious reason to make it a critical part of the course, however, is that we see warranting as a way of teaching students that providing three pieces of evidence does not "prove" a claim, if only because data are themselves problematic.

Seen in terms of pedagogy, Toulmin's terminology also gives us a way to make the daily activities of the course internally coherent to students and teachers. Claims, grounds, and warrants are the terms in which all readings are analyzed as well as the invention principles by which all writings are generated. Toulmin would not himself argue that these analytical terms generate arguments, since logic, unlike rhetoric, is not concerned with invention. But standard heuristics, such as Young, Becker, and Pike's tagmemics (1970) or the adaptations of Burke's pentad (1969), which focus on gathering data, are by themselves not sufficient for invention because they do not easily transform data into information. Data cannot be seen to ground a claim without an explicit procedure for determining their relevance to a particular argument. The criteria for warranting allow us to sift through data and "find" those that are relevant, sufficient, and appropriate to the argument at hand. Students can use Toulmin's language to analyze and evaluate their own arguments as well as those they read. As may already be apparent from the discussion of warranting, Toulmin's language redefines form and content as mutually implicated in argumentation, making it apparent that both must figure in evaluation. Organizational and stylistic choices in a text are taught as part and parcel of warranting. This means that organization and style are treated as intrinsic features of a particular argument, crucial for judging its effectiveness, not as empty and interchangeable containers into which content is poured.

We designed "Writing about Difference" to encourage students to conduct intellectual inquiry in writing. For those of us who worked on the syllabus, such inquiry is made possible in the academy by sustained intellectual dialogue in which positions are grounded by research and warranted by relevant, sufficient, and appropriate arguments. Teaching inquiry is not simply a matter of providing students with tools: scholarly texts and strategies of argumentation. Nor is it a matter of putting the tools to work through assignments that ask students to reproduce what they read. Such approaches employ students and teachers alike as day laborers who produce piecework in return for the academic equivalent of a paycheck—grades for students, credentials for graduate-student teachers. The very possibility of intellectual inquiry entails imagining students and teachers as intellectuals, fully capable already of doing, or developing the ability to do, independent intellectual work. To this end, we designed the syllabus with two structural principles in mind: (1) the course activities had to be both sequential and cumulative; and (2) the course activities had to revolve around a common topic for all participants through the entire semester.

The first structural principle animates the teleology implied by our notion of intellectual inquiry. In other words, what students write at the end of the semester depends on what they have written throughout the term. We see the syllabus as differing from similar writing courses we are familiar with mostly in terms of ends rather than means. We are not trying to influence cognitive or psychological maturity (see Flower 1985; Axelrod and Cooper 1988). Nor are we trying to lead students through a process of self-creation (see Coles 1988). While we would not necessarily exclude these other ends, we view students as intellectuals, and we hoped that the course might even encourage some students to see themselves as transformative intellectuals, people who, in the words of Stanley Aronowitz and Henry Giroux, can make "the pedagogical more political and the political more pedagogical" (1985: 36). We are perhaps not as convinced as Aronowitz and Giroux that transformative intellectuals are necessarily in opposition to a "dominant" society, since our understanding of a democratic society—as individuals and groups whose multiple and sometimes contradictory interests intersect differentially—suggests that the hegemony of those in power is vulnerable to internal as well as external critique. We wholeheartedly agree, however, that intellectual activity is potentially transformative, personally and socially. We hoped, then, that after a semester of reading and writing arguments about discriminatory employment and educational practices, students would come to see themselves as reasonably well informed on the topic of difference and entitled, therefore, to participate in the ever more intense public debate about civil rights.

The teleological structure is premised on four conceptual nodes. In the first node, Toulmin's language of argumentation frames the topic of difference. Students read from Martha Minow's *Making All the Difference* and are asked, in several informal scripts and one formal essay, to identify a central claim she makes and the grounds she offers in support of it. They next read Peggy McIntosh's essay "White Privilege and Male Privilege" and are asked to use it as a springboard for library research into stereotypes (these stereotypes come from the court cases considered later in the course). Minow's conception of difference as relational rather than inherent underlies both McIntosh's insight into the nature of privilege and students' understanding of stereotypes. The relational notion of difference also helps open up the practice of argumentation by showing that intellectual positions are not fixed to immutable truths encased in prefabricated structures but are constructed for particular purposes from local materials.

The second node of the course uses the Supreme Court opinion on *Sweatt v. Painter* and "The Spurs of Texas Are upon You," a chapter from Richard Kluger's *Simple Justice,* as a practice case that the whole class does together. We chose *Sweatt v. Painter* in large part because it is a local case. In 1946, under the separate-but-equal ruling, the University of Texas law school refused to admit Heman Sweatt, a black male. He sued and lost at all three state court levels, but eventually won the case in the United States Supreme Court in 1950. The writing assignments ask students to compile a class lexicon of legal terms (used in this and subsequent cases) and to distinguish and analyze the arguments made by the plaintiff, the defendant, and the court in the published opinion.

The work of the third node relies on student writing groups. Each group reads a court opinion and a scholarly essay discussing some issue of difference relevant to the case. Group members write a review of the scholarly essay and an analysis of the court opinion. But here, instead of just identifying and summarizing claims and grounds, students also evaluate arguments in the article and opinion. Evaluating arguments, in this course, means evaluating warrants. Assessing warrants invoked or implied by the court, litigants, and scholars in their respective texts is also likely to require students to unpack notions of difference at work in these texts. The time set aside for each group to present issues and arguments raised by their case to the class is critical, for taking the time publicly values the reading, thinking, and writing students do in the course.

In the last node, students take a set of materials—legal briefs and laws—and write an "opinion" finding in favor of either the plaintiff or the defendant in the case. This is obviously a cumulative assignment because it asks students to use what they have learned from analyzing and evaluating judicial opinions, and from the group presentations, to write their own. Semester-long experience with the topic and terms and opinions and essays teaches student writers the absolute value of giving due attention to the arguments made by plaintiffs and defendants, which is after all the basis of our faith in law and argumentation alike.

The second structural principle, a single topic, supports the implementation of the cumulative syllabus. We realize, nonetheless, that single-topic writing courses have an uneasy relation to the rest of the university as well as to the history of rhetoric. Historically, rhetoric (and written composition as a branch of rhetoric) has most often been viewed as a methodological study, codified in ancient Greek theory as a *techne* or art. As Aristotle put it, "Neither rhetoric nor dialectic is the scientific study of any one separate subject: both are faculties for providing arguments" (1984: 2156). There have been periods, however, when learning rhetoric was considered almost an end in and of itself because eloquence was thought to define the telos of human social existence. For Gorgias and Isocrates in Greece, Cicero and Quintillian in Rome, and Petrarch and Salutati in Renaissance Italy, civic life (*paideia*) *was* the topic of rhetorical study. But this formulation of rhetoric, where technical proficiency cannot be distinguished from a person's civic or social identity, is abandoned when the state prevents citizens from having an effective voice in its affairs or when academic disciplines artificially rationalize the study of language by segregating language users from language use, form from content, intentions from effects, grammar from rhetoric, rhetoric from philosophy, and philosophy from social life.

Modern English departments, formed in the late nineteenth century around the study of literature, retained responsibility for one branch of rhetorical instruction—the teaching of writing. And so long as English departments have been responsible for it, writing has been largely conceived of and taught as a methodological and instrumental art. This conception of writing has proven to be the source of many conflicts because English departments must forever fret about whether they should teach writing as a service to the rest of the university or as a service to their own discipline. In the university-service model, writing is usually taught as instrumental to the discovery and propagation of knowledge. Instruction focuses on formal features, whether they are considered "universal" (e.g., organizational patterns or punctuation) or particular to a discipline (e.g., research proposal or technical manual as genres). In the intradisciplinary-service model, writing is taught as the instrument of literary style or as the conveyor of literary content through textual explications. When writing is taught as a university service, one can ask why composition necessarily "belongs" to English departments. When it is taught as a service to English majors, one can ask why students across the university are required to learn it. Neither conception of composition makes a persuasive case for the practice of writing in and of itself.

"Writing About Difference" is grounded in an alternative conception of rhetoric that reconfigures disciplinary boundaries. In our version of rhetoric, which some scholars have already labeled "the rhetoric of inquiry" (see Nelson, Megill, and McCloskey 1987), form and content jointly construct social reality, and topics are hardly incidental to learning and teaching. Despite recent reconceptualizations of rhetoric embodied in such programs as the University of Iowa's Project on Rhetoric of Inquiry, a topic-driven writing course remains problematic in the modern university because it is presumed that topics, with their established content and approved methods for studying them, already "belong" to some discipline. Topic-focused writing courses make some discipline-oriented academics anxious because students will not be learning the disciplinary representations of those topics. As David Bartholomae and Anthony Petrosky point out in the introduction to *Facts, Artifacts, and Counterfacts,* students in these kinds of writing courses "can only approximate the work of professional academics; they can only try on the role of the psychologist or anthropologist or sociologist. They will not 'get' the canonical interpretations preserved by the disciplines, nor will they invent that work on their own" (1986: 38). Despite these limitations, they go on to say, students can "learn something about what it means to study a subject or carry out a project" (38). Along with Bartholomae and Petrosky, we would argue that topic-driven writing courses, ours included, that refuse an instrumental relation either to the English department or to the university as a whole require students and teachers to actually "invent" a discipline.

Inquiry invents disciplines. To paraphrase John Dewey, inquiry transforms an indeterminate situation into a determinate one. The purpose of inquiry is to construct "warranted assertions" about a disturbed, troubled, ambiguous, confused, conflicted, or obscure "existential situation" (Dewey 1986: 108). What could be more disturbed, troubled, ambiguous, confused, conflicted, or obscure than existential situations evoked by difference? It is inquiry, then, more than the acquisition of any content or skill, no matter how valuable, that justifies the subject matter and pedagogical activities of "Writing about Difference." It may seem that the course is about law, given that most of its texts are laws, court opinions, or articles framed by legal issues. But the course is only incidentally about law. It may also seem that the course is about writing as rhetorical skills, given that the writing and reading assignments teach traditional rhetorical strategies. But the course is only incidentally about rhetorical skills. When students explore in writing an indeterminate situation like difference, they transform seemingly determinate disciplines like law and composition into new, yet-to-be-determined disciplines. Inquiry thus secures students both the right to enter "disciplinary" conversations in the classroom and the right to contribute to public debate—as citizens whose authority to speak out rests less on having an opinion than on being willing and able to lay out a case in support of it.

Every writing program articulates a project. If a project is meant to be intellectually transformative, however, it must deal with what law sometimes calls hard cases. Hard cases in law complicate a court's ability to reach facile rulings because human contingencies prevail over legal precedents. Difference is one of those contingencies. At the University of Texas we hoped to use law's hard cases to foreground some hard cases for writing pedagogy. A hard case for students is learning to use writing to conduct rhetorical inquiry. In turn, the hard case for teachers is teaching themselves and convincing students that learning to conduct rhetorical inquiry takes precedence over learning to produce more examples of what Janet Emig once called the "Fifty-Star Theme" (1971: 97). Hard cases for students and teachers add up to a hard case for research in composition, namely, how to study what is taught and learned about writing arguments in courses where rhetorical inquiry into difference grounds writing pedagogy.

Theory can generate a syllabus, but theory only imagines what can happen rather than what does happen to students and teachers. It is research that links theory and practice, for it interrupts the excesses of theorists and practitioners alike by asking the hard questions that might be called the cui bono questions. We hoped "Writing about Difference" would interest more students and teachers than other courses teachers might have designed and taught. And we hoped that their interest would be justified by what they learned about writing during the semester. While we had good commonsense reasons to think a single topic would be a more viable approach to writing pedagogy than changing the topic with every assignment, our reasons for teaching argument as rhetorical inquiry are more theoretical than practical. Yet, whether one reasons from experience or from theory, only a full-scale empirical study could have even begun to broach the kinds of pedagogical issues we hoped to redress with the syllabus.

To the extent that classes can be seen as mounting cultural scenes at which students and teachers stage cultural events, a writing class would be the site at which students and teachers produce literacy. What does and does not count as literacy is played out in a series of literacy episodes in the course of a semester. The syllabus for "Writing about Difference" stipulates a definition of literacy that is premised on rhetorical inquiry. Defining literacy as largely a matter of exploring arguments by identifying, analyzing, and evaluating their claims, grounds, and warrants leaves little room for what students call personal opinions. While personal opinions may be based on reasons, the reasons are usually of considerably less interest to the claimant than the claim itself. In this course, however, we hoped to shift attention from claims to the ways grounds and warrants qualify opinions. Research could tell us something definite about what happens to students and teachers whose literacy scripts narrowly define writing and reading in the classroom along these lines and expressly prohibit more familiar scripts that count for a good deal elsewhere.

The syllabus discounts personal opinions as irrelevant to the practice of conducting rhetorical inquiry, however important they may or may not be in a writer's own experience. No writing assignment, for instance, solicits a personal opinion or personal narrative from students. This was a deliberate decision made in the interests of pedagogy. Given that some students and teachers understand "everybody has a right to their own opinion" to be the sine qua non of classroom democracy, however, it's hard to imagine that some would not see the privileging of argument as a violation of free speech. Like the courts, we do not believe free speech to be an absolute right and consider it instead to be contingent on other rights and responsibilities in the classroom. We take seriously the potential violence of language, and so would not encourage students and teachers to state claims they do not intend to argue. (Patricia Bizzell, following Mina Shaughnessy, characterizes this assertion of a right to personal opinion as "the ethos of the honest face" [1978: 353].)

The decision to prohibit personal opinions comes from practice, specifically from remembering that displays of personal opinions too often preface a decision among students *not* to argue, commonly signaled by the invocation of "everybody has a right to their opinion." Yet, had we taught the course and conducted surveys and interviews and observations and talk-aloud protocols indicating that our injunction against personal opinions was inhibiting the writing of arguments, we would have revised the syllabus to accommodate those findings. In the absence of data, however, the theory and practice out of which we produced the syllabus for "Writing about Difference" stand aloof from any but the most speculative criticism about our understanding of writing and writing pedagogy or our motives for asking students to read and write about difference or for selecting discrimination suits or for assigning particular essays.

The course was designed to examine legal decisions as literate events at a time when many people profess to believe that discrimination is a thing of the past. The court cases testify that not everyone believes this to be so, and the decisions clarify, as little else would, that the arguments in court opinions are profoundly contingent on circumstances. We can think of no more important dimensions of culture to study than laws prohibiting discrimination and the strategies of argumentation employed in suits brought before the courts. Law is one of the few places in this society where arguments are evaluated as arguments. We would like to think that the academy is another. But convincing students and teachers that the academy is such a place requires that pedagogical conditions transform classrooms into cultures wherein people use arguments to raise more interesting intellectual questions than they resolve. Only when these conditions obtain will we have a society that is as gratifying to inhabit as it is to study.

AN AUTOETHNOGRAPHY IN PARTS

PART I: THE OFFICIAL LINE

A Report from the Superintendent of the Denver Public Schools

Denver Schools Respond to Judge Doyle's Decree

December 11, 1973: District Court Opinion determined the entire Denver School District to be a "dual" school system and that a system-wide plan of desegregation "root and branch" was therefore required under Supreme Court mandate.

December 17, 1973: Federal Court Judge William E. Doyle ordered that plans for desegregation of the Denver Public Schools be submitted to the District Court.

January 23, 1974: Desegregation plans prepared by the defendants (School District No. 1, Denver) and the plaintiffs (Wilfred Keyes, et al.) were submitted for consideration to the United States District Court. After hearing arguments concerning desegregation plans of the parties involved and having considered aspects of various other plans, the Court found the desegregation plans to be inadequate. Based on this determination, Judge William E. Doyle directed Dr. John A. Finger, Jr., court appointed consultant, to devise a desegregation plan for the Court's consideration.

PART II: THE LINEUP

Second grade. I loved riding the bus. When I started voluntary busing, I felt very grown up waiting on the corner to be picked up while the rest of the neighborhood kids walked to the local elementary school. The bus, to me, looked like a yellow blimp with its round edges and large print running down the sides advertising "Denver Public Schools" instead of "Goodyear." All by myself I got to choose which of the fat green seats to slide onto. I bounced three times on the generous springs at every bump or dip in the street. The window was mine to lift or close as I watched outside—I knew how to sit still from riding the city bus with Gram and let the passing cars or people or buildings lull me into imagining a little story in my head as the engine comfortably hummed through the floorboard under my feet. When it

snowed sometimes we slid a little on the ice and everyone said "whoa!" or "yaaah" at the same time. When it really snowed we were late to class, but no detention.

The worst part of the day was getting off the bus and walking the short distance to the front of the school. It was a long wait for the first bell most days because I was scared of a group of fifth-grade girls who yelled. They'd crowd around one of us and use words that baffled me at first: white patty, cracker, hoe, cow. But I knew what honky meant. I sensed that if I cried it would make things worse but once I did. The biggest girl pushed me hard and my head cracked against the wall and I woke up in the nurse's office and Mom took me to the doctor. After that the big girl hunted me but I never cried.

I liked my teacher very much and I liked my class friends. This school had a jungle gym on the playground that I climbed to the top every recess.

That year Mom and I drove to many other neighborhoods some evenings and walked four blocks at a time—up one side and down the other—ringing people's doorbells. She talked to them and I gave them folded sheets of paper I got to carry in a mail bag. She told the people that my sister Laurel, who was in junior high, and I both rode the bus to school.

At the end of the year my parents got the form in the mail and so asked me if I wanted to continue riding the bus. I said I didn't know. They said there was time to think about it. I liked doing what my sister did and I liked walking the precincts with Mom. I thought of the fifth-grade girls. Finally, I said no. As I grew older I regretted the decision. When Dad would have his friends from politics over he'd talk about voluntary busing. He'd tell them about Laurie. He never mentioned my name.

PART III: THE (HOME) FRONT LINE

February 18, 1994

FATHER:

We were always pro busing. We thought then, as we do now, that desegregation was a desirable social objective. Having grown up in segregated society we were awakened, you might say, during the 1960s by the Black Power movement which began in the Unitarian Church and spread quickly to many other institutions, especially political. People like Mom and me came to realize that there was a tremendous amount of inherent institutional racial prejudice and bias which we, to a large extent, were unconscious of. Our black friends brought the awareness to us—pretty much had to impose it upon us. We felt considerable guilt and a strong desire to end segregated society and do what we could to achieve racial equality and secure civil rights and achieve racial justice. So we were very much in favor of integration. We favored voluntary busing in the late sixties and continued to be supportive after the school board election of '69 (before I quit politics) when Benton and Pascoe, the pro-busing candidates, were defeated. After the election, the majority of the board was then anti-busing and voted to stop voluntary busing. That led to the filing of the case in federal court.

So, we encouraged you children to engage in voluntary busing and supported you when you did. Then, after the court order, you experienced the effects of involuntary busing and, you know, a lot of the experiences were rough. [My brother] Huck was the victim of endless harassment. His lunch money was stolen every day, we found out later. He was afraid to tell us at the time for fear of retribution. The upshot of it is that we finally realized that we were in effect using our own children to do penance that we felt should be done in this issue. After it was too late, we realized. You guys were sacrificial lambs for our own collective guilt—not just Mom and me but a whole generation of white Anglo-Saxons' guilt for unknowingly condoning and supporting a system that dealt injustice to racial minorities. To do penance for that injustice, we used you children in the trenches of integration, to bear the brunt of that effort. We had manipulated you and your generation unfairly, made you pay the price for our own inadequacies.

DAUGHTER:

I've never heard you say this before. Would you do things differently in retrospect?

FATHER:

I don't know how I'd do things differently. I'll have to think about it, it's a very tough question. Would I do differently? Hmm, it would take a lot of thought and I haven't thought it out. Many of our black friends ended up opposing busing and feeling that the system as it was implemented had failed and was detrimental. First of all, the prejudiced white parents in Denver just moved to the suburbs—there was a flight to the suburbs. You see, the Supreme Court ruled in such a way that it did not apply across school districts, and the suburbs were, and are, mostly white. So segregation was impossible to address and resegregation occurred. Parents of black children resented the great inconvenience of shipping their children off into hostile environments and felt it was not beneficial. And then they pointed out how resegregation happened in the schools because of the separation of supposed advanced students and nonadvanced. You know, how there are "honors" courses and the "regular" track and the "lower" track. It fell heavily along racial lines—and still occurs—that minority children were put into the lower tracks. So many liberal and radical black families felt busing was a failure and began to oppose it. In the local Democratic Party, for example, there was strong opposition from black members as time went on.

I felt after the experience and today that from your standpoint, comparing your experience to ours, that on balance you benefited in the long run, difficult or painful as it was. We grew up in neighborhood schools that had no black people throughout our young adult lives. We were ignorant, insensitive, and simply lacking in understanding of race relations in the U.S. until later in life. I came away believing that on the balance it was still beneficial to you.

DAUGHTER:

How did you and other people you knew [who were] supportive of busing talk about why it was important?

FATHER:

We believed then that encountering people different from you, not in an academic sense so much as a social–human relations sense, was important. It would prepare you for life after school in society—this is what people talked about then. Public school experience was defended on those grounds. And it does prepare you for life—the more it relates to real life, the better. The principal reason we never pushed you to go to private schools was because of this. In that sense, it was considered educationally beneficial. Not until much later did I come to realize the benefit of cross-cultural contact academically.

DAUGHTER:

Were there limits to these beliefs? I mean, where did they stop?

FATHER:

Some of our white liberal friends and acquaintances, not Mom and I, felt that integration was fine but drew the line at intermarriage. Unfortunately, there was a heightened fear of racial mixing that accompanied desegregation.

Part IV: The Official Line

Honorable William E. Doyle
Judge, U.S. Court of Appeals
Denver, Colorado

April 5, 1974

Dear Judge Doyle:

I hereby submit to you my recommendation for the desegregation of the Denver Schools. I believe that the procedures proposed are feasible, workable and educationally sound. You should anticipate that there will be considerable opposition from the citizens of Denver, but I know of no way to implement your responsibilities without such opposition. It is lamentable that no one speaks of the important outcomes to be achieved through the integration of schools, although I think most citizens really believe in the American ideal of equality and equal opportunity, it is understandable that that ideal gets in conflict with the desire to provide for one's children and one's own self fulfillment through one's children. I don't think most people want to condemn some children to poverty or an unfulfilled life, but few people want to pay a price at the expense of their children to bring this about.

Despite the widespread opposition to busing, there is no evidence that it hurts anybody. The facts are that many children enjoy it. Others view it as just a thing one does like driving to work in one's car. One just does it. Some children don't like it, but that usually is because the bus is unsupervised and the children are teased or assaulted.

Everyone knows that without effective planning and sometimes with it, there will be problems of confrontations among students. Difficult as these are to deal with, students do eventually seek and find accommodation. I wish that the citizens of Denver would know and believe that the bringing of people together is better than the alternatives of keeping them apart. The research does seem clear on one point, and that is that Anglo students attending school with minority students do just as well as their compatriots in predominantly Anglo schools. . . . Thank you for inviting me to be your consultant.

Sincerely,
John A. Finger, Jr.

Part V: The Lineup

Dr. John A. Finger, Jr.
Court Appointed Consultant
Denver, Colorado

April 5, 1994

Dear John Finger:

I hereby submit to you my recommendation for the desegregation of the Denver Schools. I believe that the procedures you proposed were lovely, but you should have anticipated considerable opposition from the people involved. It is lamentable how many administrators thought busing was about riding a bus to school. Although I think most of those who determined bus routes and calculated acceptable percentages of white and black really believed in the American ideal of integration, it is incomprehensible that the ideal provided an opportunity to ignore the desire to help children through a turbulent transition. I don't think most people wanted to leave children on the curbside to figure out how to deal with differences that have condemned some to poverty or an unfulfilled life, but few people want to pay a price at the expense of their own procedures and ideals.

The widespread opposition to the way busing was implemented grew because of the evidence. The facts: children don't drive to work in cars, "just do it" is a Nike commercial, children have been assaulted, and children have assaulted each other.

Everyone knows that effective planning sometimes is a way to avoid problems and confrontations, difficult as these are to deal with. Students do eventually seek and find survival strategies that don't accommodate the plans. I wish I believed procedures were about bringing people together rather than keeping them apart. And let me clarify—you predominantly attended to Anglo students, compatriot. I've invited myself to be your consultant, thank you.

Sincerely,
Kate Burns

Part VI: The (Home) Front Line

February 21, 1994

MOTHER:

Well, the liberal white parents I knew didn't object to dating and romance and marriage because they didn't like blacks, but because they didn't want the kids to suffer by society. They didn't want them persecuted. In those days the black community didn't accept a mixed couple any more than the white community did. We had several mixed couples at the Unitarian church because it was the only place they were accepted in Denver.

I remember an incident—do you remember Evone? The girl you wanted to invite home for lunch? Well, I called up Mrs. Daniels—she and I had been working together quite a bit to start a dialogue between the white and black kids—and asked if Evone could come home with you. I was shocked; it was then that she told me that black parents didn't want their kids to mix with the white kids because they were afraid the white kids would get them on drugs. And here it was the white parents who thought it would be the black kids to bring in drugs. But it made sense, I mean it was the upper-class white kids with the money. They had the money to buy drugs. It's so funny looking back. [laughs]

At Hill it was a class issue more than a race issue. The blacks who came in were poor, from north-central Denver. Hill was full of wealthy white kids. It was economic contention at the heart of it.

DAUGHTER:

What did you and Mrs. Daniels do to start a dialogue?

MOTHER:

We fought the Hill administration. Rose and I went to the school counselors and tried to set up places where three or four kids could get together and talk, get to know each other. They [the counselors] were scared to do that, they never did it. The administration resisted our efforts to do anything to get kids to get along. The principal . . . was scared to death. So we organized very few things in the end but we'd get parents and students together for a softball game. We had a picnic. Only twenty to thirty people would show up—out of a school of six hundred students or something. But one time we had a potluck dinner event and asked everybody to bring food. I invited my clown friend and she did tricks for everyone. We were so shocked because so many people showed up. Three hundred or three hundred and fifty people came—kids, parents, families. Rose had arranged to have a black choir sing, and they got up there and sang the black national anthem. The room almost exploded. Those wealthy whites were thinking, "It's bad enough that these people come to our school, but to sing the black national anthem *instead of* our *national anthem . . ." They were all ready to get out their guns and kill a few people. It was really funny, the look on a lot of those white parents' faces. Rose practically started a revolution.*

DAUGHTER:

That's great. I remember that. I didn't know what was going on with the parents, I mean, but I remember the choir. And the clown.

Didn't you and Mrs. Daniels also have a group or an organization or something?

MOTHER:

Yeah, we called it the Human Relations Council. We realized it was partly the busing culture itself that kept up the turmoil. Rose said it was where the older kids taught the younger ones not to take guff off the whites. But it got out of hand and became a contest. We rode the buses trying to keep the kids calmed down. The black mothers rode over with them and the white mothers drove [the black mothers] home.

We didn't get anything much done. Who knows what effect we had. We quit by the time you got to Hill.

It was a terrible position to put the bused kids in. They came with a chip on their shoulder and had a reason to. And the white kids were so inexperienced with people. It was so painful for the kids. The black kids—the system just shredded their self-esteem, and [so did] the white kids and teachers. It did very harmful things to them.

DAUGHTER:

Do you think anything positive happened?

MOTHER:

It's hard to say with things in such a mess as they are now. I don't know whether it made things worse or helped. I always thought that if you know one person from another race or country, it would be harder to be violent to the group. But I just don't know if that's true.

Overall it was worse when the black kids were segregated—the black schools were terrible. The white parents had the clout to get the schools into shape—and they finally wanted to once their own kids were bused in. Before, the black parents couldn't get the school board to do anything. That was one good impetus behind busing, to put the screws on the school board. Back then it was mostly white. There was one black but he couldn't do anything by himself. And the administrations were all white. That has changed in time with busing too. . . . There are more people of color now.

PART VII: THE OFFICIAL LINE

Findings by the U.S. Commission on Civil Rights, June 1973

1. Desegregation doesn't result in poorer quality education as many people fear. Often, desegregation contributes to substantial improvement because:
   a. administration takes a "new look" at schools.
   b. federal money is available for special instruction and teacher training.
2. Careful and sensitive desegregation preparation is necessary for parents, students, teachers and community.
3. "Busing" problems can be minimal. Added community cost and time is slight. Safety has been NO problem.
4. Many school administrations have tended to consider only the white community when desegregating. Burden has fallen on minorities. At first, minorities were willing to go along in order to get better schools. Now minorities want to equalize the "burden."
5. Reactions by news media, school administration, and civic leaders to disruptive incidents can either preserve calm or heighten tension.
6. Sharp contrast between reactions of community members to own personal experience with desegregation and to expressed feelings concerning desegregation in general. Most parents interviewed by Civil Rights Commission were satisfied with desegregation as it affected their own children.
7. Controversy and confusion at the national level concerning busing have had effects on communities.
8. Common Problems:
   Teacher adjustment.
   Displacement of black officials.
   Resegregation of students within schools by ability grouping.

Unfairness in student discipline, real or imagined.
Community anxiety.

9. Keys to Success:
Determination of the School Board and administration to carry out the plan.
Support by the media, local officials and civic leaders.
Fair and equitable distribution of the burden of desegregation among total community.
Involvement of parents as active participants; keeping them informed and soliciting their advice.
Development of procedures to assure full student participation in school activities.
Firm, fair and impartial discipline.
Efforts to improve the quality of education.

Findings by the U.S. Commission on Civil Rights, August 1976

1. While many school districts lost significant numbers of white students between 1968 and 1972, there are no significant differences between those districts that desegregated, either under H.E.W. [U.S. Department of Housing, Education, and Welfare] or court pressure, or voluntarily, and those districts that did not desegregate. Average loss of white students was 6%. However, loss of white students was greater (average 15%) where black enrollment exceeded 40%.

2. Vast majority (82%) of school districts desegregated without serious disruption. Ninety-four percent of disruptions were in southern or border states.

3. There has been a marked change in community attitudes. White communities changed from 20% to 50+% positive; black community now 79% positive.

Part VIII: The Lineup

Hey, how you doing, folks? Thank you, thanks very much. How's everybody doing tonight? Good? Good. It's great to be here. You look good there, buddy, with your California tan, yeah. You a surfer? I never went for surfers, nope. I'd see 'em on TV, all buff and blonde but it didn't do me. Until I came to San Diego and found out that women surf too, hey. I bet my girlfriend's board is bigger than yours. No really, you see I come from mountain people, not sea people. Anyone here from Colorado? Denver? Yeah? All right! Give her a hand, folks. Where'd you go to school, honey? Oh, I remember that

school. They had a great girl's basketball team—bunch a baby dykes, yes ma'am. Why are you blushing? Did you play basketball? Oh shit, does your boyfriend there know? Hey, buddy, don't get upset. Why do you think she wanted you to take her to see a queer comic? If you don't use your head, you might as well have two butts—that's what they say where I come from. Yeah, think about it.

Anywaaaaaay. I didn't play school sports until high school. No, actually we didn't have athletics in junior high—they were canceled, yeah canceled. I went to Hill Junior High, affectionately referred to as Hell Junior in teaching circles. It was during integration, you know, when school busing started back in the early seventies. Anybody else go to school during that time? You too? It was hell, forget the junior. Wasn't it? Hellllp! Helter skelter. They canceled team sports after the riots during field day. Yeah, I'm tellin' the truth, it was my first year in Hell. Hey, what do you expect when they throw together a bunch of upper-class white kids and working-class black kids for the first time and they want us to solve racism by putting a giant rubber band around our ankles to run the three-legged race? Come on! Yeah, and the white kids were disappointed because they thought the wheelbarrow race was when they got to tell the black kids where to haul the manure to put on their parents' landscaped gardens. And the black kids thought the obstacle course was about walking through the halls without getting questioned by the security guards. Kinda makes you want to throw a brick or start a riot or something. Unbelievable.

Well, you see, I had it tough—I was born a privileged white child. I know, it's sad, isn't it? A sacrificial lamb, as someone once said. But seriously, it *was* sad when I went to the dances. First of all, they announced the school dances in such a way as to make sure white girls and boys didn't mix with black girls and boys. We were allowed two dances a year: a sock hop and a soul train. Guess which one I was supposed to go to? The sock hop depressed me because I thought, "Fuck the hair bows and bobby sox." I wanted to grease my hair back and roll a pack of cigarettes in the sleeve of my brother's smelly T-shirt I used to wear. Anyway, my boyfriend at the time—yes, I had a boyfriend once. But hey, he was pretty and shorter than me, the femme to my butch until I got the guts to come out. Anyway, he was cool and we decided to go to the soul train dance. Well, Murray was a slight, skinny kid with a Yiddish accent and I was so uncomfortable with my body that was sprouting womanly things when I still had a tomboy soul—it would be kind to just say we couldn't have emulated Ward and June Cleaver if we wanted to. So we crashed the soul train and sure enough, we were the only white faces there. It was scary at first, let me tell ya, because the racial tension at this school was sky high. And there were no teacher-chaperones there, either. I guess they were scaredy-cats too. But somehow it broke the ice when we got out on the dance floor. Murray was doing this retro new wave Hava Nagilah thing and I was religiously avoiding any bouncing movement so I could remain in denial of my breasts. You know the stereotype that white folks can't dance?—we definitely reinforced it that day, people. The black kids surrounded us and howled with laughter. We started laughing. Eventually the novelty wore off and we just danced together. It was nice.

I tell you, folks, they did everything short of labeling the fountains "white" and "colored" to keep us apart. No coed sports, separated dances, and the only classes where races mixed were the gender-role classes like shop or home ec. They wouldn't let me take shop and my theory is that even back then they had a phobia of the Bobbitt solution. Get those girls around table saws and carving knives and they might get ideas! Anyway, the way I see it is that they weren't counting on me and Vyronda in all their heterosexist fear of miscegenation. 'Cause it was right around that time that my friends were getting heavy into the drugs and I had already decided to save my body for science. No really, speed, coke, and LSD scared me to death at the tender age of fourteen—I guess I was immature. So I started hanging out by myself during lunch hour and Vyronda was kinda hanging out by herself in the same spot a lot . . . she was left out of her circles too for whatever reason. I usually brought some reading material and when we were talking one day she asked what *Rubyfruit Jungle* was about. You know that book? Yeah, that woman in the audience who played on the basketball team knows that book I bet. So we understood each other somewhat, we had a place where we connected. Well, I wish I could tell you a romantic story of two young women who turned the straight white system on its ass. But alliances between outcasts in junior high, let alone in Hell, were often tenuous. She did eventually put her hand under my shirt, but in a fist full of slop from the trash can that she smeared on my chest and face. It was the initiation rite that her new potential friends required of her before they would let her "in." Even then I understood that it was much more dangerous for her to have a white friend than for me to have a black one. She had to ride the bus home. But it still broke my heart, and as Molly Bolt said in *Rubyfruit,* "I hauled off and belted her one." What are you laughing at, buddy, this isn't the funny part of my routine. Yeah, shut up. I fought her like I hated her. No, not like. We hated each other suddenly.

Luckily, hate between friends only lasts a minute or so and we let our fists down. But in Hell, man, children lust for blood. They smell it from a mile away, too. We were instantly surrounded by the mob circle—and no one would let us out until one of us was down for good. You see, the mob was our way of finding student-only space in the midst of all that surveillance and discipline. Creative, huh? The security guards and the tough teachers would start to peel brown and white bodies away from the circle and some kid would yell to the others where to fill in the gap. Hey, we knew how to work together when we wanted to! I don't know why they didn't understand how we *did* "just get along"—we showed them our cooperation and industriousness every day.

So the security guards finally got through and it took four grown men to pull us apart. We didn't get any fame from that because the record was still five—but four was a decent showing, nothing to be ashamed of. You know, the security guards were an important part of our school family. I realized just how much when I looked back through my old seventh-grade yearbook a while ago. We had six security guards and their pictures took up three pages of the yearbook. Their photos came before the faculty, I'm not kidding. And they got full body shots—head to toe, in uniform—while the faculty only got mug shots, twelve to a page. Really!

As I was sayin', the guards took Vyronda off somewhere—probably the state prison—and the vice principal backed me in the corner. Have you ever noticed how all vice principals look alike? They're all ex-football coaches and they've got that dent in the bridge of their noses like they've been punched one time too many. You know what I'm talking about? Well, this guy was Mr. Jones and I swear his twin was the v.p. when I went to high school, Mr. Smith. Anyway, Mr. Jones, he wouldn't touch me because my hair was all clumped in knots and stuck to my face from the blood and snot and tears. I couldn't breathe or stand straight because of a blow to the solar plexus but his number one security guard kept yanking me upright to look at Jones respectfully while he lectured. "Not very ladylike," he kept saying, "we should send you to charm school." Yeah, like he was a charmer himself. "I expect it of them, but you?" Them? You talkin' about my Vyronda? I didn't have any fight left in me so I threw up on his shoes instead. It got me three days suspension instead of one, but I look back on it as a moment of triumph.

You see, we all wanted to get together somehow; I mean, the desire to mix was generated and fueled by the forced separation at such close quarters. So there were some good times, but mostly we opted for the easiest kind of cooperative resistance we could figure out. We found a shared motivation powerful enough to fight for: the intimacy of tearing each other apart.

I remember my grandmother taught me a saying that you chant if you've been holding hands with someone and you have to let go because a pole or a fence or something comes between you. If you say "bread and butter" then no harm will come until you can bring your hands together again. Yeah, well, "bread and butter," Vyronda. I actually saw her at a women's bar when I passed through Denver last year. I don't know if she saw me. Maybe next time I'll say hello.

Well, that's it for tonight, folks. Thank you very much. Thank you folks, you've been a great audience tonight. Drive safe when you go home tonight, OK? Hey, "bread and butter" everyone. Until next time. Thank you. Good night!

Sources: Parts I and IV: The Superintendent Reports (Denver: Superintendent of Denver Public Schools, 1974), 1. Part VII: Composite View of Denver's School Desegregation (Denver: League of Women Voters, 1974, revised 1976), 11-12.

The Spirit of Literacy

I have to admit that I totally bought into those notions of literacy as something liberating, and even when I started to realize that what I teach in school is steeped in personal and institutional politics, I maintained this image in my head of literacy—*true literacy*—as a process of enlightenment, an emergence up from the dark depths of ignorance. Describing this vision now I begin to see that there are problems with it, the relative values assigned to images of *light* and *dark*, the notion of moving up toward literacy, even the belief that *true literacy* is something I would recognize. Still, I want to describe this vision in a little more detail. I imagine someone engaged in studies based entirely on her or his interests with empathetic teachers and mentors directing and assisting the student. This student would, of course, have the desire, time, space, and resources to conduct her or his studies. In this vision, I recognize ideas from my long-ago readings of John Holt's work as well as my studies of Plato in graduate seminars. In many ways this vision is about the kind of education I believe would have been ideal for me—in which case I should add that the mentor is a radical feminist.

However, I'm now aware that my vision does not take into account several facts. For instance, while there would be few if any restrictions on a person's potential literacy explorations, my vision does not include the vast majority of people in the world whose dream this could or would never be: people whose economic conditions are too restrictive, people who learn differently, people whose lives are ordered by very different sorts of priorities, and people with entirely different thoughts on literacy. I'm not sure why I have maintained this belief in a *true literacy* until now. My own experiences should have suggested otherwise to me, with all the discussion of "getting back to the basics" and preparing students adequately for the competitive global world market of the future. Advocating literacy that does not embrace the politics, economics, and religion of the American mainstream is generally perceived as pointless at one extreme, and subversive and dangerous at another.

I'm surprised I didn't realize the conservative politics and cold-blooded pragmatism of American mainstream literacy sooner, given my early training in Molokan literacy. (The Molokans are a sect of fundamentalist Christians who united to oppose some of the practices of the Russian Orthodox Church in the 1700s.) Now I'm guessing that this is *why* it didn't happen sooner—Molokan literacy was presented to me as being entirely different from anything (but especially education) that was clearly part of the World. Raised to believe that I wasn't part of the mainstream, I knew by the time I was ten that whatever I learned at school was only of secondary importance compared to what I learned at home and in church. Outside of school, I learned this secret literacy, based in the beliefs, teachings, and separatist lifestyle of the Molokan religion, which does not proselytize or accept outsiders. You have to be born one to be one—and then you're always one. Because Molokans claim that aspiring to worldly wealth and fame is a waste of time—some even go to great lengths to return to the "simple" lifestyle of their Russian peasant forefathers (many of whom were actually intellectuals, I think)—they teach their children early, before sending them to school, what not to believe, who not to trust, how not to act. The most fundamental fact I learned about the world was that I must live in it but not be a part of it. I learned I wasn't better than others, but Jews and all Dark-Skinned People were damned (not for the same reasons) and Catholics were part of the Antichrist. Others were spiritually uninformed, or religious in some well-intentioned but faulty way; none were to be trusted.

Years later I finally acknowledged the limited and bigoted framework of this form of literacy, but that didn't make it much easier for me to see through the assumptions and goals of more publicly respected literacies that I've since accepted and worked to excel in. I thought I was leaving bigotry and exclusivity and snobbery behind and moving toward something more progressive and humane. But as Michael Warner, who was raised a Southern Pentecostalist, argues in "Tongues Untied: Memoirs of a Pentecostal Boyhood," maybe shedding selves is not really like shedding skins; that is, maybe one cannot shed ingrained and essential parts of oneself. It's just possible that the pure literacy I've been after is really a secular version of Molokanism. In other words, maybe you can learn to recognize and question the assumptions you use to construct reality, but you can never become a new person despite what some people will tell you about the possibility of being "born again." While Molokan literacy certainly seems suffocating and self-serving from my present vantage point, I'm starting to wonder if academic literacy is any less oppressive or more rational and beneficial to society than Molokanism.

Academics, at least those who are religious about their lives as academics, who know and act as if their knowledge of the world and themselves is the Truth, these academics damn—and silence and marginalize—lots of the same people that Molokans don't have much fondness for; and they're not so big on fundamentalists, either, I've found, although recovering fundamentalists are okay if they don't talk about their "former lives" too much, except to make it clear that they have shed that part of themselves. I suppose it's possible within academia for a small number of the Damned to become part of the ranks of the Saved, but we know who they are, don't we?

When my family moved with a few other Molokan families to Australia, following the prophetic words of one church member that, during the(se) last days, Australia was the chosen refuge for our people to wait for the Second Coming, the pressure to follow the laws, to live the life, to become better, purer Molokans became intense because we had to prove our worth to ourselves, and we were actively engaged in trying to entice other Molokans from California to follow us there. We were concerned for our families and friends still in the United States who were going to be caught in the middle of a major catastrophe soon, we believed, and we needed more of our people to join us to legitimize and sustain us in our Movement. I say "we" and "our" like I had something to do with all the decision-making and reality-forming processes that were going on. In truth, I was only ten years old, so I was powerless to decide how or where I was going to grow up; but I have to say that I was a willing participant in what seemed like both a huge adventure and a secret mission for several years. It felt good to be told that I was Special with a Purpose in life to match; it was appropriate that I was being taught lessons and secrets that I believed only Molokans could understand, appreciate, and act upon. I understood absolutely that I shouldn't talk about any of this to outsiders because they wouldn't understand and would probably make fun of me and my beliefs. Even those who might be interested in my religion, I learned, would inevitably soil and damage it because there would come a time when they would want to change something or question something that shouldn't be questioned. To protect my religion, to protect myself, I had to maintain my silence, I believed.

To entrust a child with a secret is really to be able to control and isolate that child. Even big, glorious secrets may make a child feel alone, wanting, as she does, to prove she is worthy of the trust placed in her by adults, and not understanding any of the rules about secrets. Because adults often aren't really very good at keeping secrets. They know that they can share whatever it is with their significant other, or a trusted friend, and they know that they haven't actually broken the trust of the secret as long as it doesn't become general knowledge. Children, on the other hand, don't understand this and may view the secret and their knowledge of it in a much graver manner than an adult.

This is not to say that I didn't love the secrets that filled my life. I did, absolutely. I loved the carefully nurtured sense of being different and took my lessons in Molokan literacy very seriously. I was the kid who, whenever possible, hung out with the adults—well, actually with the men who officially held the power in our church—to hear their discussions and debates over what they thought was happening or going to happen "back home." Their interpretations of riots, earthquakes, and fires excited and terrified me, in fact, as they and I watched and waited for the moment that would clearly signal the Beginning of the End. I wanted to be as close as possible to what I recognized as the center of power, not out of envy or desire for something I couldn't have, but to understand how it functioned, to see how they—men who were barely into their thirties, I realize now—discovered the truth. My curiosity was also fueled by what I thought at the time to be very pragmatic desires; I wanted to know if I was going to have a chance to grow up or if my life on earth was about to be cut short. While life in heaven promised to be splendid, I wasn't sure I was ready yet to give up what I knew and liked well enough. So I had very little patience for the conversations of my mother and the other women, who sometimes entered the male realm (as peacemakers, usually) but for the most part stayed in the kitchen, where they would clean up after a big meal and then sit around the kitchen table and talk about more domestic issues. Now I suspect that they actually did talk about some of the same issues that the men were discussing but in more oblique and less authoritative ways. Maybe their way was harder for me to understand at that time, or maybe they were more cautious than the men in their predictions and convictions, not so dramatic and, therefore, not so riveting for a young child with a hungry imagination.

Impatient to understand what I was devoting my life to, maybe even giving it up for, I was even responsible for initiating a short-lived little game that involved me and the handful of other Molokan kids there who were about my age. I called the game Big Ears, and the point of it was for one of us to spy on these adult conversations and then to report back to the rest of the group with as much information as possible about what we had heard. Thinking about it now, I'm sure that my friends and I must have misinterpreted much of this illicitly gained information since it would have been over our heads. And it wasn't always easy to get the information because there were limits to what they wanted us to know. In some ways, my parents (and the others) expected their children to think and act like adults, but I also know that they didn't want to frighten us, and they still believed that we should basically live the lives of children, just children with special responsibilities and very heavy secrets. But because a good part of what they were discussing was scary and difficult to understand, I wanted all the more to know it, to be able to mull it over in my brain, to store it in that place that added evidence to my belief that I was Special. I needed this knowledge, more and more as time went by, to remind myself that I was Different, to explain why my life was different.

This kind of literacy is a powerful hook, a powerful incentive to be good, to shut up and do one's bit. And the longer you're in it, the harder it is to imagine not being in it. I occasionally still say "we" and "our" even now as if I were living the life that my parents planned for me. It's hard to drop this "we" that I treasured as a kid, but where it was a pronoun that I proudly embraced as a child, it's now one that weighs on me, pulls on me even though I've been straining to move on for more than ten years. And I suppose that, as much as anything else, it is this internal battle over a simple pronoun that makes me resist the enticements to be Born Again into this or that academic sect.

Literacy really is that possessive, that jealous, I think. People teach children what they want them to know so they'll grow "the right way," and they teach them the cautions they think will keep them going that way. And people mean that training to stick—it's a privilege that can become a solemn duty. Hence literacy practices always include, exclude, even punish in ways that they might not mean to. To be literate is to be part of an exclusive club—the Molokan club, the Marxist club, the Foucault club, the queer club, the feminist club. What you know makes you who you are. Moreover, as I have been suggesting throughout, religious literacies are every bit as empowering, as intellectual, and *as restrictive*, as academic literacies are. Michael Warner says that religion supplied him with experiences and ideas that he's "still trying to match." At this point in my life, however, I want to try to fight my desire to match those experiences; I want to become more aware of the implications of the kind of living and working I choose. I can't claim not to be a little nostalgic for the days when everything was clear and life was laid out and there was a Right and Wrong Way, but I like the fact that I am developing some sense of history. I mean, after waiting for Jesus for ten years, what could possibly match that for a theory? How could I give my soul to another theory? And why would I want to?

Still, I do get tripped up, because the training keeps me looking for something else that will satisfy, that will replace the part of me that I keep working to uproot, even though I don't believe I'll be entirely successful in either endeavor. And my parents, who didn't want me to get an education beyond high school, since my main goal in life should have been to snag a husband and become a good Molokan wife and mother, ironically instilled in me a desire to know and understand much more than they thought necessary or good for me. Now I see their point, although my curiosity and ideals about literacy keep me going.

The critical thinking skills that I learned as a child, the same skills that I watched my father and the other men exercise with vigor and joy, have served me well in my academic pursuits. Those discussions in the living room and on the porch weren't always about the Signs of the End hovering over "the States." Often they would discuss biblical passages, and by their disagreements, their earnest and heated arguments over a single word or phrase, I learned that words have shades of meaning, ambiguous meanings. And I learned, as they compared Russian, Hebrew, and various English interpretations of the same crucial passages, that the true meaning of anything important is hard to settle on. It became obvious that politics is involved in interpretation and translation, and that even "my side" engaged in this less-than-holy business. The Catholic Bible, for instance, was not consulted at all because of the close alliance that Catholics supposedly had with the devil. Listening to those debates over biblical passages taught me, in part, what I know about critical thinking. Eventually I learned to wonder how anyone could ever know what was really meant. This is still my question.

Russ Cunningham

A Literacy of Silence

> The world is too public. Freedom can only be secured through privacy . . . through the fact that nobody knows.
>
> —Ian Fleming, *Doctor No*

In the hillside suburb of Los Angeles where my nuclear family closed out the remainder of its unbroken years, the rigid demarcation of public and private space was a fundamental aspect of our cultural literacy. Established and upheld in an atmosphere of procedural efficiency, restrained emotion, and tacit understanding, this demarcation served to prevent our loose confederation of white middle-class households from becoming "too public." Within these households, each set back from the curb by sharply cut lawns and cleanly swept driveways and decisively separated from one another by wooden fences or concrete walls, curtained windows, and the orderly arrangement of street addresses, intimacy sequestered itself from the public domain and secured its "freedom"—from censure, from ridicule, from punishment—through privacy.

And judging from my own experiences in one such household, the distinction between public and private space often extended *into* the home as well. While my own family drew away from the public sphere and collectively *in* upon itself, much like the night-blooming jasmine in our yard did every morning at the first hint of sunrise, it seemed that each one of us—my mother, my father, my younger sister, and I—retreated still deeper into the even more private realm of individuality. Although my family *was* considerably bound by the ties of kinship (though not in all cases by the ties of love), it was also a modular unit, one comprised of four separate personalities. Inside the home, these personalities not only shared communal space, they also staked out individual spaces for themselves. My sister and I had our upstairs bedrooms and our "secret" spot in the attic. My mom had the entire house when my sister and I went off to school and my dad went off to work, and she also had her bathtub every night for an hour after dinner. My dad had his job, which none of us (including my mom) seemed to know very much about. We came together as a family around the dinner table (except when my dad worked late), at IBM family picnics, Little League games, and other public gatherings, and during my sister's periodic medical emergencies. But even in the midst of our deepest crises, even in our most celebratory moments, we were never completely consolidated by a spirit of oneness. We all played for Team Cunningham, sure enough, but we were also free agents in the community at large, and as such we had to follow the rules of a game that neither began nor ended within familial confines. So, while the family could be separated from the communty, the community could not be separated from the family. Inside or outside the home, the same rules applied.

For the *private* free agent in our community, then, family space was, in many ways, *public* space; and as a nine-year-old very much governed by the collective superego of my community, a consciousness of restraint and correctness that permeated even the most intimate levels of human interaction, I did my best to adhere to the strict delineation between public and private space by, among other things, cloaking the knowledge of my parents' divorce within a literacy of silence.

When the inevitable was finally set into motion, I can't recall the word *divorce* ever being spoken in my presence, at least not until several years after my parents' insipid marriage of ten years had officially ended. While the "D" word may have reached my ears now and then during the protracted legal death rattle of my parents' life together, it did so entirely by accident. Only an adult's slip of the tongue would have let that forbidden word fall in my presence. As I remember it, the word *divorce* was studiously avoided when my parents sat me down, one evening about a week before my ninth Christmas, to inform me that they weren't "going to stay together anymore." The family had just finished dinner—I had just choked down, under orders, my last lima bean—and my little sister and I were settling down in front of the television to watch *Santa Claus Is Coming to Town*, a tired piece of animation that kept showing up at about this time every year. Feeling somewhat smug in my knowledge that Santa Claus wasn't a real guy, I took great pride in being able to keep this enormous secret from my four-year-old sister. My parents, having recently fessed up to Santa's nonexistence, continually admonished me not to "spoil" Christmas for my little sister by betraying this secret to her, and as I was rarely inclined to test the extent of parental forgiveness, I grudgingly complied.

On this night, my parents believed they had another secret to let me in on, this one being not quite as innocuous as the sham of ole Saint Nick. But what they had to tell me came as no real surprise. While I never would have said so to anybody, I knew my parents were about to call it quits. I knew it was just a matter of time. Over the last several years, my parents' union had become as illusory as the image of Santa Claus parking his sleigh on our rooftop. The odd thing was that I seemed to have come to this realization even before they did. When they finally decided to end the illusion, I only wondered why it had taken them so long.

Yet, while I was prepared to see my parents go their separate ways, I wasn't prepared, on this night in December, to hear them *announce* such a decision. But that announcement was made, meekly and awkwardly, as the saccharine strains of "Santa Claus Is Coming to Town" droned on in the background. It happened something like this: after dinner, my mom and dad lingered conspicuously around the dinner table, engaged in tense, hushed conversation. As this was not the usual after-dinner procedure, I suspected something was going on. What I *didn't* anticipate was being asked to join their conversation; the edgy, hesitant tone of voice coming from the dinner table sounded mostly like grown-up talk. Usually, when my parents talked to me, they talked in explanations. When they spoke to each other, they frequently spoke in questions. On this night, they seemed to be asking each other a lot of questions, questions I was quite sure I didn't have the answers for. So when they quietly, politely called me back over to them, my first impulse was to run the other way. My immediate second thought, however, sent me straight in their direction. My little sister, uninvited and seemingly uninterested, stayed glued to the television set. (She would remain relatively excluded, for the next two years or so, from all subsequent conversations on this particular topic, but she came to know far more about the situation than my parents would have liked.) Once I'd sat down between the two of them, my mother, smiling cautiously, began with a trademark preface: "Sweetheart, your dad and I have something to tell you." When my parents opened conversations with such superfluities I knew there was trouble on the horizon. In this case, I knew instantly and precisely what the trouble was, and I was certain that I didn't want to hear it. When the words started to spill slowly from their mouths, muddied by euphemism and thick-tongued apology, I grew quite distressed. To me, the lousy thing was not that my parents were going to get divorced; it was that they were *admitting* to such a thing. Their confession seemed so undignified. Why did they have to *tell* me about it? Why didn't they just do it? "No!" I howled, interrupting my father in midsentence. Feeling incredibly claustrophobic, I pushed away from the table and flung myself upstairs to my bedroom.

For the next two years, the word *divorce* banged around constantly inside my head. But it never left my mouth. In 1976, divorces in our white middle-class community still did their utmost to keep to themselves. Most of my friends' parents were still together, and those who weren't, well, we just pretended not to notice. The growing phenomenon of divorce in our community was a silent one; it metastasized without much public acknowledgment. In fact, it seemed that as the incidence of divorce increased in our community, it became more assiduously confined to the privacy of the homes in which it occurred. Like all children my age, I was expected to know the word *divorce*, and I was expected not to utter it. Thus, my parents didn't have to admonish me to keep our new secret. I had no intention of telling anyone that I had become a child of divorce.

I do not, however, think of my parents' divorce as a tragic episode in my life. I didn't at the time, and I don't now. I'm no more a victim of divorce than one is a victim of being born into white middle-class suburbia. These days, divorce comes with the territory. My parents may have been among the first young couples in our neighborhood to get divorced, but they certainly weren't the last. In fact, when I think back on it now, the only frightful consequence of my parents' divorce that seemed to regularly preoccupy my nine-year-old mind was that it (the divorce) made me, in some strange way, *different* from my peers. I was ashamed of being different, primarily because I was unable to distinguish between *difference* and *deviance.* As I saw it, to be different was to be wrong. But it seemed I was the only one who noticed my deviance, or at least the only one who cared anything about it. Nobody ever bugged me about my parents' divorce. Nobody teased me. Nobody looked at me askance. But I assumed this was because nobody knew, and I wasn't going to be the one to tell them. Outside of my imagination, my trajectory of becoming didn't change all that much as a result of the divorce. My life moseyed on, relatively uninterrupted, and I continued to enjoy all the advantages of being a much loved and well-provided-for youngster. After the divorce, my mom and dad remained the same warm and supportive parents they'd always been to my sister and me. So, I share this experience of white middle-class divorce not because of its pathos, but because I think it reveals many of the cultural codes of conduct that governed both collective and individual behavior in our community.

When I speak of cultural codes of conduct, I refer particularly to the unspoken rules of propriety designed to keep community members from living out their private lives in the public domain. These unspoken rules, constructed chiefly by silence, coalesced around one fundamental admonition: *Do not violate your own privacy.* In discussing one's personal life, it was far better to say nothing at all than to say the wrong thing. In a community where there was a time and a place for everything, it could be quite dangerous to get these well-established times and places mixed up. As a nine-year-old, I came to recognize this danger not only through my personal interactions with family members, neighbors, friends, and teachers, but also through the almost always solitary practice of reading.

As my parents made no real attempt to teach me how to read, my introduction to the joys of literacy didn't come until the first-grade. Embarrassingly, I discovered that most of my first-grade classmates had already met Dick, Jane, and Spot. As they proudly read aloud in class, I marveled at their ability to turn letters into words, words into sentences, sentences into stories. I was horribly ashamed that I couldn't follow along and steadfastly determined to enter the ranks of the six-year-old literati as quickly as possible. By the time my parents parted company, I was nearly three years into my ferocious attempt to make up for lost reading time. Next to listening (religiously) to California Angels baseball games on AM radio (710 KMPC), reading was my favorite thing to do. And while the Angels were only around from April to September (they never did make the playoffs), books were around all year. I could turn to a "Great Brain" story, a "Sports Legends" biography, or a Stephen King thriller almost whenever and wherever I wanted to. In my world, books (and magazines) seemed to be everywhere: on the coffee table at home, on the bookshelf at my grandparents' house, in the library at school, at the bookstore on Foothill Boulevard. While I didn't see many people, children or adults, doing much reading outside of school, I had every indication that it was, generally, a much-admired activity. My interest in reading frequently earned me commendation from the various adults in my life. As a child who craved approval, I discovered that reading was one great way to get it.

Around the time of my parents' divorce, I learned that reading could also give me space. I learned that reading could isolate me, at least for a while, from the rigorous unpredictability and courteous brutality of the veritable world. Reflecting back, I cannot think of my reading experiences during this time as transporting me somewhere else, into, say, a world of fantasy; I can only think of them as fencing me off from everything and everybody around me. I'd like to say I read to inspire my imagination, but I think it more accurate to say I read to inspire my separation from social practice. Mostly, I read to escape from interaction with other people. When I wasn't playing sports—the one endeavor that made me feel comfortably and actively connected with the symbolic order—I usually wanted to be alone. Often, the only way to remain unmolested in my solitude was to press a book up to my face.

I very much liked being alone, because being alone was the *safest* way to be. I came to believe that solitude, and the silence that accompanied it, kept me from violating those cultural codes of conduct that seemed so apparent to everybody else and yet so nebulous to me. By the third grade, I was turning out to be a reasonably intelligent kid, and my precociousness began to instill in me a great sense of caution. The more I learned about the world, and the rules that administered my engagement with it, the less confident I became in the public sphere. Every newly acquired bit of knowledge suggested there was much, much more that I *didn't* know. I was extremely concerned with getting things right, horribly afraid of getting things wrong, and rarely inclined to test my luck in the company of others.

Reading was an activity I associated primarily with my mother; she was one adult who appeared to take reading as seriously as I did. And she never seemed to be more alone than when she was sitting quietly behind a book. Consequently, it didn't take me long to consciously equate the act of reading with the solitude and silence I so treasured. I soon discovered that reading could provide me with the perfect excuse to remain out of the social scheme of things. Reading became for me a form of hiding, a way of putting the present, and the self, on hold. Thus, I never thought of my engagement with a text as something active. For me, reading was a retreat into the passive and invisible role of spectator. I wasn't at all conscious of the creativity in turning words into images and ideas. I likened reading to listening to the Angels' games, during which I registered no distinction between the announcer's verbal descriptions of the game and the actual occurrences on the field. Because I didn't feel like I was *doing* anything while I was reading, I never felt on the spot. If I couldn't define a particular word, or if I grossly misread a passage, there were no serious consequences. Books were forgiving. They were *safe*. They offered vicarious participation in narratives that I could make as much (or as little) my own as I wanted.

Not long after my parents' announcement of divorce, I discovered one particular narrative, strewn across a series of books, that came to captivate me as no other had before. While picking through my grandparents' bookshelves one afternoon, I came across the dashing character of Bond. James Bond. *Doctor No* was the first of nearly a dozen James Bond novelettes I would devour, one after another, over the next several months. So voracious was my appetite for these fast-paced accounts of the courageous, charismatic, and superbly competent master spy, I would sometimes gobble up an entire book in a single sitting. James Bond became my secret hero, and when I wasn't reading about him, I was involved in my own surreptitious acts of make-believe espionage, giving me a secret life that certainly rivaled that of the legendary Walter Mitty.

But these stories did more than just spark my naive imagination; they also presented me with a daunting version of the symbolic order as an exclusive, competitive, and chaotic realm where my survival and success depended on keeping my secrets well concealed from those who might use them against me. These stories told me that my relationship with the symbolic order was a necessarily problematic and unstable one, likely to betray me if I wasn't careful. The trick, I learned from Agent 007, was to say very little, and when obliged to speak, to always say the right thing. When I discovered how well deception paid off for the likes of James Bond, I was further reinforced in my belief that it was best to keep quiet about such things as my parents' divorce.

I knew that language was necessary for engagement in the symbolic order, but I also knew that its slipshod use could bring embarrassment and alienation. Frequently punished for passing notes in class—notes that I rarely wrote myself—I soon came to appreciate that *writing* could be a very risky business. Once, I made the mistake of telling a female classmate, in writing, that I "liked" her. After the contents of my amorous missive were (purposefully) revealed to the entire third grade, I was subjected to great derision for several weeks. Regularly punished for talking during class, I also learned that *speaking* could be a censurable act. After hearing me brag about my solo hiking expeditions in the mountains adjacent to our community, my fifth-grade teacher began to question my mom and dad's parental fitness, suggesting that no good parents would let their child go hiking alone. I felt that I had gravely betrayed my parents by being so free with this information. More subtly, I learned that listening, too, could bring reproach; a nine-year-old was not to listen in on adult conversations unless expressly invited to do so. When adults were talking, particularly in hushed tones, youngsters were to keep their distance. In keeping with official school policy, when my parents conferred with my grade-school teachers about my performance in school, I was expressly forbidden to attend. It was much more difficult for adults to reprimand me for reading, but it did happen. Unable to put a book down, I would often read under my desk while the teacher held forth in front of the class. When I was detected in these clandestine acts of reading, I was often reprimanded for "poor citizenship" and obliged to stay after school.

Did Bond have these same problems when *he* was a kid? I suspected that he did, and that he had learned his lessons well. While they showcased many of the literate skills I thought were necessary to operate successfully in the symbolic order, the stories of Agent 007 also suggested that such verbal operations were invariably risky and dangerous. What I learned from Bond was that I needed to be extremely restrained and selective in my use of language. When Bond gets into trouble in *Doctor No,* it's because he says too much. When the sinister doctor meets his demise (at the hands of Agent 007, of course), it's because he has divulged (to Bond) too much about his evil operations. Doctor No's greatest defense is his privacy, and once he allows Bond to violate this privacy, his secret, diabolical scheme is doomed.

The Bond stories displayed language as a potentially useful vehicle for making one's way in society, but they also suggested that language is not always to be trusted as a transparent signifier of reality. The Bond stories taught me to be forever suspicious of language's claim to represent the truth. From the first pages of *Doctor No,* Bond is repeatedly confounded by language. Throughout his mission, Bond constantly encounters characters and situations that spitefully hide their true identities and intentions. Those he meets either lie to him or refuse to tell him anything at all. As the story unfolds, the island paradise of Jamaica becomes, for Bond, a tropical hell. Ultimately, what he was told would be "a holiday in the sun" turns out, instead, to be a grueling fight to the death with a powerful and ruthless enemy. When all's said and done, however, Bond proves that he can be an even craftier liar than his deceitful foe, and he ultimately prevails in this deadly game of chicanery.

Language may have brought me into being as a subject in the first place, but it was constantly outrunning my grasp when I tried to pin it down and make some sense with it. I didn't mind not being able to understand something I read (as I mentioned earlier, I saw no real consequences to misreading), but I was terrified of not being able to understand when communicating through speech or writing. Though I could not have articulated this at the time, I was acutely aware, in my often futile attempts as a nine-year-old boy to say what I meant and to mean what I said, of the problematic relationship between signifier and signified. But the symbolic order appeared to be functioning under the assumption that language *was* capable of mirroring reality, and so I came to believe that my difficulties in attaching the right words to what I had in mind were, for the most part, my own problem. I got the feeling that the text of the real world was, indeed, readily decipherable, and that I often was simply not making the right verbal connections. The "pool of language" in which I saw myself reflected seemed a murky and turbulent one; its churning surface of significations didn't seem to be mirroring my self-image or my actions with much coherence or consistency. Adults were constantly demanding that I explain why I did the things I did, and I found myself frequently unable to provide a satisfactory answer. For instance, when I quit my Little League baseball team in sixth grade, my coach and many of my former teammates hounded me for weeks, calling me on the phone and coming by the house to ask "Why'd ya quit?" I didn't know how to respond. I had myriad reasons for quitting, reasons that seemed clear enough in my own head, but I was entirely unable to articulate them. I don't know that I could articulate them much better even today, fifteen years later.

Generally speaking, Bond didn't have much trouble explaining himself. And when his rhetorical skills weren't enough to bail him out of a particulary sticky situation, he could always resort to his fists, his 25 mm Beretta, or some other (gentlemanly) form of violence to escape from what always appeared to be a certin demise. When, in the climactic scene in *Doctor No,* Bond drops several tons of guano on the evil doctor's head, his lethal actions speak, quite succinctly, for themselves. Regarding my own dilemmas, however, violence never seemed to be a very practical option. A gun was certainly out of the question, and when I did fight with my fists, I usually got in a lot of trouble. The thought of dumping a lethal dose of guano on some people's heads did occur to me on a few occasions, but such an opportunity never presented itself.

Like so many other of the characters I came across in my reading at this time, James Bond was an ideal figure residing in a world that seemed tailor-made to suit his talents and encourage his success. And when competence wasn't enough to bring about a happy ending, a pinch of good luck was always available. Somehow, Bond always got the job done. More impressive to me, however, than his stunning success and good fortune was how firmly rooted in the world (at least in the world of the narrative) Bond always appeared to be. His ego was so clearly established, so well delineated from the deviant otherness of his foes. In an utterly Manichaean world, so explicitly divided between good and evil, it seemed there could exist only two states of being: Bond, and the *absence* of Bond. As I read, fantasized, and tried to relate the world of fiction to the world where *I* lived, I could never figure out where I fit into this dichotomy of being. Surely, I was no James Bond. But could I be, on the other hand, allied with the likes of Doctor No? To be neither of the above presented me with a troubling existential problem: Who *was* I? When I looked up from my reading, the same Manichaeism seemed to be functioning in the world around me, though the distinctions between right and wrong were far more equivocal than those I encountered in the world of fiction. Because right and wrong in our tight-lipped community were so often assumed and so rarely stated, and because it seemed so inappropriate to inquire as to which was which, I found it easiest to keep my nose in a book and, as I saw it, do nothing. When I *did* participate actively in the world, I did so through athletics, where the rules and parameters of play were totally unambiguous: three strikes and you're out, ten yards to a first down, two steps after the dribble. As I read the Bond stories, I sensed that my *literate* and *oral* language practices were going in separate directions. Bond, in the midst of great peril, could turn to a character like Honeychile Rider (his love interest in *Doctor No*) and suavely say, "I like the way you do your hair." While it sounded great when *he* said it, I knew that if *I* were to toss out such a line, under any circumstances, I would probably be sent directly to a child psychologist. When it came to the language of efficiency, of protocol, of *cool,* what worked for Bond would almost never work for me. While these stories filled my head with lots of sophisticated vocabulary, very little of it did me any good in my own social interactions. Bond's language wasn't, and couldn't be, my own; consequently, it couldn't empower me or keep me out of harm's way as it could for Agent 007.

In short, the Bond stories showed me how dangerous the world could be, but they didn't provide me with the means—verbal or otherwise—to overcome these dangers. They offered little more than this vague admonition: *Watch what you say, and how you say it.* And these stories weren't alone in suggesting to me the dangers of language; many of the narratives I read during these early years of literacy, from the fairy tales of the Brothers Grimm to the police dramas of Joseph Wambaugh, evinced similar doubts about language as an able signifier of the swirling confusion of objects and events that comprised the symbolic order. Weaving between their lines of written text a literacy of silence, these stories warned against the indiscreet use of language.

I find that the following scene from *Doctor No,* in which Bond comes to the end of the doctor's sadistic (and, for anyone but Bond, inevitably lethal) obstacle course, serves as a fitting metaphor for the dangers of such indiscretion. Walking through a metal shaft toward what he assumes is his freedom, Bond gets careless:

> The shaft was beginning to slope gently downward. It made the going easier. Soon the slope grew steeper so that Bond could almost slide along under the momentum of his own weight. It was a blessed relief not to have to make the effort with his muscles. There was a glimmer of grey light ahead, nothing more than a lessening of the darkness, but it was a change. . . .
>
> Suddenly, Bond realized that he was slipping down the shaft. He opened his shoulders and spread his feet to slow himself. It hurt and the braking effect was small. Now the shaft was widening. He could no longer get a grip! He was going faster and faster.
>
> Bond's body crashed into a bend and round it. Christ, he was diving head downwards! Desperately Bond spread his feet and hands. The metal flayed his skin. He was out of control, diving, diving down a gun barrel.

Bond, of course, survives this mistake. *Only he could.* For a mere mortal like me, however, it was imperative to avoid such mistakes in the first place. Such mistakes could be irreparable. Unfortunately, like the gentle slopes of the shaft, the difference in our community between a good movie and a bad one was often barely perceptible. So, I would have to go slow. I would have to walk, and not run. I would have to think, and not react. I would have to whisper, and not yell. I would have to listen, and not speak. If I wanted to play it safe, I would have to stagnate in my own indecision.

What I remember most about my mom and dad's ten years together is how unsettlingly quiet they were. Muffled flurries of verbal skirmishing would only occasionally punctuate the interminable, cancerous silence that existed between them. My parents spent the last several years of their marriage in a monotony of silence that seemed a perverse deepening of the silence that the community at large demanded of us in all of our social interactions. While I didn't recognize this at the time (and thus my attempt to keep the "secret"), their decision to divorce did much to break this harmful silence, by openly revealing the failure of their intimate lives together in the hope of more fully reconciling themselves, and their two children, with the future. Although I suppose I could look upon my parents' divorce, and the public admission of private failure that it entailed, as a tragedy, I now prefer to view it as an incentive to one who has found it so difficult to comfortably integrate his public and private selves.

Michel Foucault suggests that the individual (private) body is "the irreducible element in the social scheme of things," and that, as such, it functions as our most fundamental site of power in our struggles against the forces of repression, socialization, and punishment that continually act upon us in society. In the community where I grew up, this fundamental site of power was believed to be best secured by one's reticence. Thus, in the company of others—family members, close friends, and total strangers—one's store of personal knowledge was dispensed carefully, reluctantly. As a youngster, I emulated the adults around me by keeping this individual site of power firmly under wraps, scrupulously out of view, tenaciously away from those who might trespass against it. As a reader, I generally viewed literacy as something to store away, as something to invisibly and silently nourish my intellectual metabolism. I seldom viewed it as something to put to use. I exercised my literacy primarily as a means of (quietly) observing the world around me, and rarely as a way to actively engage with it. It seems that, as a white male in middle-class America, I could easily afford to hold up this private and passive notion of literacy. From my position of relative privilege in society, I could afford to keep quiet.

But my silence has implied a deep complicity with those forces of repression, interpellation, and punishment that feed upon the quiet desperation of the middle class; my silence has indicated a tacit acceptance of those structures of domination that maintain the distance between have and have not by representing speech and writing as precarious practices in the spaces in between. Hushed and inhibited, convinced of the dangers of too much language, and content to express itself (solely) through its commodity consumption, the middle class silently holds the line. I believe it is the silence of the middle class that most deeply implicates us in the ongoing colonialist project, in institutionalized forms of racism, in the reification of gender dichotomies, in the ruthless delineation of socioeconomic boundaries, in the false promise of meritocracy. Our keeping quiet has done much to keep things firmly in place. All talk of a (November 1994) middle-class "revolution" aside, it has been our customary retreat to the quiet recesses of the political private sphere that has most completely registered our political (un)consciousness as a class.

In its tendency to conflate literacy with (enforced) silence, solitude, privacy, and safety, in its penchant for linking the act of reading to the (obligatory) quietude of libraries and classrooms and studies, the middle class has done much to turn activism into anathema and thereby establish itself (through its inertia) as a formidable defender of the status quo.

So, while I'm learning that it might benefit me, and those for whom I advocate, to clear my throat and make a bit more noise, I suspect that until the middle class can find some genuine, motivating stake(s) in progressive political action, few with the power to change things will feel inclined to listen.

Catholic Boy: An Account of Parochial School Literacy

I trace my conscious awareness of involvement in an "educational process" to two incidents in the fifth grade. The first was a realization toward the end of the school year, sometime shortly after the class had mastered fractions, that I had learned everything in school that I needed to get by in life. A short time later, the teacher asked during class if anybody had ever heard of some far-off geographical place. I had. I raised my hand and matter-of-factly reported what I knew, which brought turned heads and stares of incredulity, and one indicting question from a classmate: "How did you know *that?*"

I had read it in *The Golden Book Encyclopedia*, which had been acquired by my mother, one volume at a time, from Kroger's, as had the *Funk and Wagnalls Encyclopedia* she was then currently collecting, and the *Golden Book History of the United States* from which I learned everything I knew about American history. *Funk and Wagnalls* was pretty dry, but I had started reading *The Golden Book* in the first or second grade and knew the contents of each volume intimately. Each one had a different-colored spine, and on the front was a still-life drawing of some of the contents of that particular volume. I would thumb through pages for hours, reading an article here, an article there, and some favorites—like the one on goldfish—many times. Although I knew the articles were arranged alphabetically, I preferred instead my own system of finding an article by looking for its picture on the cover of a volume and then searching through the pages until I found the article. In that way I was sidetracked a lot, and read even more, until I had read most of the sixteen volumes. It was a game to me, systematically desultory, and remains to this day my "method" of doing library research, shopping, driving cross-country, making friends, and building a career.

I had many other informal experiences of formal literacy. On family vacation trips to my grandparents' home in Florida, I was appointed navigator and charged with the task of plotting the family's course southward by calculating mileage and ETAs for cities along the way. We watched TV at home with an almanac and atlas within reach, and although I was only five years old at the time, I can recall my father's explanation to me of the 1960 presidential election. *Life* was my window to a much larger, richer world. I did not read the articles, but I pored over the photographs of Vietnam, the civil rights marches in the South, and the movie stars "on location." When the magazine did a six-part essay on the Roman Empire, I cut out the pictures and saved them; a year later they came in handy for a school project on ancient Rome, for which I also wrote a play, made costumes, and constructed cardboard sets, all inspired by the photographs.

In these ways I had acquired a great deal of formal information completely outside the formal educational process, and I assumed that my classmates had been doing the same. Apparently they hadn't, and now I had been separated from them and could feel them closing ranks in silent censure. I also felt myself shrinking, not understanding clearly the social reasons for their reaction, but still sensing them.

Nothing very tangible changed that day, or during the rest of the school year. As I walked home with the same kids as always, we talked the same talk, but more warily. I believe now that the reason it took me until the fifth grade to notice the signals by which people indicate the topics and tenor of the conversations they are ready to have is a function of the very total way in which my peers and I were "ability" grouped in fully self-contained classrooms, beginning in the second grade and continuing in a more refined and even more isolating manner in the third and fourth grades.

For what must have been extremely practical economic reasons that were no doubt supported by some wild educational rationale, the fifteen "brightest" students in my second-grade class were combined with the fifteen "brightest" students in the same year's first-grade class. Our classroom was in the parlor of the former priests' residence (picture the rectory from *Going My Way* and *The Bells of St. Mary's*), a place that was utterly cold and apart from the rest of the school. The following year, space opened up in the actual school building, on the second floor at the end of a very long hall across from the outer wall of the gymnasium. There it was considerably warmer, but we were no less apart. An experienced, creative teacher might find some potential in these extraordinary circumstances; she might experiment with small groups and peer tutoring; she might take the virtual impossibility of teaching two curriculums with different materials to two groups at the same time as her excuse to scrap both curriculums and develop her own. But I did not have experienced, creative teachers. We were divided, one grade three rows wide on the left side of the room; the other grade three rows wide on the right. Assignments to be done while the teacher attended to the other grade were written on our side of the blackboard; then, theoretically, she gave the other grade seatwork while she attended to us. But second and third graders are more dependent than third and fourth graders, and I was an upperclassman. Consequently, I spent most of two school years laboring in a work sheet sweatshop.

When I remember that time I am sitting in my desk along the windows in the afternoon. I look up from some seatwork I am doing and I see some swallows, dark and sharp against the sky, swoop down straight into the chimney of the building next door at full speed. Two, three, four, I count them, and I wait and I stare at that chimney, which is almost at eye level and very close, and I wait, and I stare, and I think to myself, what are they doing in there? Isn't that dangerous? How long can they stay in there? Don't blink—you'll miss one. Without warning they shoot out as fast as they entered, like they'd never stopped moving, but there are *more* of them than went in! How could that be? I needed to watch longer, maybe. Contemplation of this mystery gave me hours of quiet, secret, desultory meditation.

All the work sheets in the world could not keep us busy forever. Between assignments we talked to each other, and sometimes even during assignments we talked, which led to my first extended writing assignment: lines. Much has been written about the destructive effect on students' attitudes toward writing that lines have (and as a teacher I hardly endorse the practice), but I never thought of writing "I must not talk in class" as writing. In fact, my classmates and I saw getting them all done as a challenge and would help each other with them to kill time. Then I hit upon the idea of doing them in advance of the assignment, and my first extended writing assignments became my first overt acts of opposition. Our seatwork routine was punctuated by occasional special projects and assignments, and it was these that I cared most about. There was a Christmas play in which I had a supporting role, and I wrote a report on Egyptian mummies in which I described in sensational prose how the brains of the deceased were ripped out through the nose by a device that looked like a crochet hook. My information came, of course, from *The Golden Book Encyclopedia*, as the structure of the report probably did also, although I clearly remember wondering how to organize my ideas and holding the conviction that this was *my* work, and I must make it original.

On rare occasions when we had actual class discussions, a premium was placed on the possession and sharing of information relevant to the topic at hand. Instant celebrity and status were conferred upon the student who could supply an interesting fact or tell a story that would add to the general pool of knowledge in the discussion. We were the children of professionals, of doctors and CPAs and airline pilots and nurses, people who were expected to know things and to share their expertise in useful, productive ways. We students quite clearly saw ourselves as the children of professionals and, by extension, as sharers in their expertise. Molly, whose mother was a nurse, was our resident expert on first aid and health-related issues; John, whose father was an engineer, knew about buildings. In the course of two years of self-contained isolation, we came to know each others' parents' occupations and to respect and defer to each others' specialized knowledge, as we expected others to defer to ours. Our reified little "speech community" became a think tank in which it was implicitly recognized that knowledge conveyed power and authority.

My membership in that particular group was suspended during the fifth-grade. My aunt was going to teach the split-grade fifth-grade class, and she did not want the special pressures of having her nephew for a student. I was placed in the "B" group, with kids whom I knew from the playground and my neighborhood, but not "professionally" as students. That made little difference, however, because these new classmates did not regard themselves as professionals. We did less seatwork, but we spent more time on the clerical task of correcting it together as a class. We talked a lot, but our discussions seldom strayed from topics in which everyone shared a common knowledge base, such as TV shows, local amusement parks, and plans for decorating the windows for the holidays. We had no play that year and did no special projects, except for the plaster of paris poinsettias we painted for Christmas presents. Who was I to complain, or at first even to notice? Life at school was suddenly much less stressful, and I was enjoying myself a lot more.

It is tempting to look for similarities between the situation I have described and the situation Shirley Brice Heath describes in *Ways with Words* and suggest that it was sociolinguistic differences in child-rearing practices and the ways of speaking at home that accounted for the differences that I experienced between going to school with the children of professionals and nonprofessionals, but this presents some major difficulties, because it does not appear on the surface that there were any dramatic differences among us in our ways of speaking. Heath's three groups had very separate social and cultural histories, had different traditions in their religious practices, and lived in separate localities; all of my classmates were Roman Catholic descendants of German and Irish immigrants to this country around the turn of the century, who lived with both their natural parents in single-unit, three-bedroom, usually brick homes with attached garages and two maple trees in the front yard, in a very socioeconomically homogeneous town.

There were, however, significant differences in the content of things we talked about with each other in school, and in the ways that my peers in the fourth grade and I used language as the vehicle to negotiate for our teacher's and each others' attention and thereby gain influence and authority in the classroom-workplace, compared to the way that language was used by my peers in the fifth grade to scrupulously avoid gaining hegemony over others in that work environment.

Heath also argues that it was the incongruence of the ways of using language in the homes of the children of Roadville and Trackton with the ways of using language in the classroom that led to their eventual poor performance in school, but it makes no sense to me to suggest that the school curriculum I endured until that time was more congruent with the cultural values of professionals than with those of nonprofessionals. On the contrary, my fifth-grade classmates were quite successful and quite happy with a routine of seatwork that emphasized decontextualized rules of grammar, spelling, and reading "skills," and other tasks that never asked more of students than that they get the job done. Their ways of working were in perfect congruence with the agenda of the classroom and their lives. I was the one who was out of step.

What accounted mainly for the differences I experienced, and I think also for the differences that Heath describes—and that she herself would have had to acknowledge had she, as her critics have suggested, spun her causal analysis out to its logical conclusion—is economic history, and more specifically the history of the relationship and underlying tensions between labor and management, that is, between those who direct and those who are directed.

For us children of professionals, knowledge about the world was highly empowering. It gave us status, which conferred on us the power to manage others, and it was the instrument by which we intended in the future to make a living.

For the children of nonprofessionals, however, knowledge was the means by which they experienced being controlled in order to make a living. Demonstration of knowledge quickly marked the demonstrator as someone who might be looking for the verbal authority to manage them. For example, I had a very good friend in high school and college whose father was a pipe fitter and a high school dropout. From Bill's birth, his parents' oft-stated dream was to see their son become the first college graduate in the family. We entered the same college together, and for a while, Bill prospered. But near the end of our sophomore year, I began to hear stories about real tensions in Bill's home, which eventually built to near-brawls between father and son. The fights began, according to Bill, whenever he brought up any point of information, however slight, during a conversation with his family. His father accused him of being "too big for his britches" and "a know-it-all," in response to which Bill complained to me, with all the condescending invective of management toward labor, "You can't tell them anything!" Neither side had anticipated how a college education might alter the filial relationship and threaten to destroy the family. Within a year, Bill had left college; today he drives a delivery truck, bowls three times a week, and lives at peace with his family.

Catholicism helped to create and to sanctify a hierarchical social order within the school and the community. The theme of the *Baltimore Catechism*, simply put, was: know your place. We understood that the "greatest blessing in life" was to be called by God to serve as a priest or a nun. I seem to have absorbed the chain of command from the laity to the pope, and by similar means acquired a working knowledge of the major religious orders and their vocational niches, or "charisms." I developed a sense of their rank order as well. At the top of the list were, of course, the Jesuits, who were the toughest order to get into and had the most rigorous and lengthy methods of training in medieval techniques of rhetoric and logic, which enabled them to come up with the tightest arguments in support of Catholic dogma and to defend the Church against its enemies, both internal and external. They took a special vow to serve the pope, but eschewed membership in the episcopacy. In all my childhood and adolescent years, among my family and at school, the Jesuits were never referred to except in tones of the utmost respect and reverence. Their power was sacred; they had saved us during the Reformation. They were the Church's lawyers, whose "charism" was to mediate, through carefully chosen words and carefully crafted arguments, God's will for man on earth through the control of public and private Catholic visions of social reality. Early in my mass-going career, I had learned to kill time by browsing through my missal and reading the blurb about the saint whose feast day it was. I developed a ghoulish taste for the hagiographies of martyrs and delighted in the succinct but suggestive descriptions of their deaths. Many years later I realized that sainthood was almost always reserved for those who died for being exemplary "company" men and women.

I was moved back into the "A" group in the sixth grade and stayed there through the eighth, but there were some significant changes in the curriculum by that time. The split-grade arrangement had ended, and although we were still grouped hierarchically, the teachers had partially departmentalized themselves, so that in the morning we moved from room to room for math with one teacher, English with another, and so on. Life in the classroom began more and more to resemble life at the office. We spent more time working in small groups rather than individually and worked jointly on tasks that were less constraining than work sheets. Our homeroom class resembled work the most; when we went to other teachers' classes the desks were still in rows and it was apparent that the "slower" students were still working on their "skills."

A single exception to this rule was the teacher of the sixth grade "C" students, Mrs. Brinkmann, who was exceptional for a number of reasons. First, she liked and respected the "Cs" and refused to label them as defectives and potential delinquents the way their previous teachers had. Second, she was Protestant. She had been hired during a teacher shortage in the late 1960s, and she did not yet realize what a near sacrilege it was to express her opinion. Third, she smoked in the boiler room and took it to be her right to do so, since there was no faculty room. I don't recall that she was an especially fine instructor, but I certainly admired her individuality and her spunk, and intuitively sympathized with her position as an outsider.

To enter high school, I crossed an alley on the school grounds and entered the building next door.

In the ninth grade the quality and quantity of my written language exploded. I had always been a competent and confident writer on demand, but now I began to produce for the sheer joy of sharing what I had written with an audience. I wrote puerile, vulgar serials lampooning my teachers and my classmates, and I shared them with selected puerile friends. I had a dream and when I woke up in the morning I wrote it out as a story. I took the same characters from that story and wrote two more episodes; soon I had a family saga going. I had also seen Hal Holbrook's performance *Mark Twain Tonight!* on television, and now I tried to copy Twain's style. For the first time in my life, I began to really *work* at something, to consciously hone my skills. My newfound persistence and dedication to craftsmanship sprang from the same sentiments as those once expressed by Kurt Vonnegut about writing, that any fool could get the words right if he just stuck to it long enough. Well, *I* was Any Fool; *I* could do this. The great attraction of writing for me was that if people got to know you by the words you wrote, then you still had a chance to convince them that you had a smooth, witty intellect and were an insightful observer of the human condition rather than the dull little twerp you appeared to be in person.

The most important experiences of the production and power of written words were those I had as a staff member of the student newspaper, the *Reflector.* Oddly enough for someone who considered himself the next Twain, the content of each issue was of little importance to me at first; it was form and the production end of each issue that were the challenge. We did not send our paper out to an offset printer, as most schools did, but produced it entirely in-house using wax stencils and an ancient, temperamental mimeograph machine. Each page had three columns of print; a line was twenty-six characters wide, and there were sixty lines to a column. To justify the right-hand margins, we typed all copy in columns and then filled in the missing characters on each line with "¢234" to make each line twenty-six characters long. The copy was then laid out on boards and headlines were written to precisely fit the space allotted them, using a calculation between the size of the letters, their width, and the width and height of the space for the headline. We then typed the copy on wax stencils, leaving gaps between individual words on each line according to however many "¢234" spaces we had filled. Headlines and drawings were etched in with a stylus. Small mistakes were fixed with a waxy correction fluid; for larger errors we learned to cut and cement patches on the stencils with surgical precision. We ran off five hundred copies on both sides of eight and a half- by eleven-inch paper and then collated each copy and stapled it twice on the left side.

Such intense effort, not surprisingly, created intense camaraderie, and it is not surprising either that every staff member at my grade level had also been in the third and fourth grades together. After seven or eight years of contact, we had developed an intimate understanding of each others' talents and weaknesses, and learned to balance them automatically when we worked together.

Gradually, some of us began to feel we needed to "get a life," and that meant getting a job. The most driven of us, Sue, began by working a few hours a week, but she soon stretched that to twenty to thirty hours, while she was going to school and participating in a half dozen extracurricular activities. Sue was at the breaking point and wondered if other students were in the same situation. The *Reflector* ran a survey of the student body; response was heavy, and what we learned was not pleasing to the administration or to many of the teachers.

Essentially, the students believed they were learning more at work than they were at school. They were prouder of their paychecks than of their report cards, and they felt that teachers were jealous of the time they spent working when they "should have been studying." They were no longer "preparing for life." They were already living.

The day we tallied the surveys, Sue and I went to a local coffee shop to discuss the writing of the article for the *Reflector*. She could not write it, she said; it would look bad since she had a job. But I was not yet working. It made more sense for me to write the article, but I must do it objectively; we'd lose credibility if we sounded immature.

So I wrote the article, and became a sort of temporary hero among the working students, a voice of reason against the unreasoning and false assertions of teachers and administrators that the high school curriculum was an adequate preparation for life. It felt great. I was a writer, and I had been stroked by my public.

A month later the principal decided that it would be very educational if the whole school went to see *Fiddler on the Roof* together. A lot of the students thought this was a ridiculous waste of time and money. These were the incorrigible "C" and "D" students whose educational experiences had long since recentered them in activities far removed from petit bourgeois educational amusements. Sensing a terrific opportunity to resist authority, they refused to buy tickets. If they were left behind, what would they do all afternoon?

The civics teacher thought he had a terrific idea. He had some friends who were members of TRAIN (To Restore American Independence Now), a subcommittee of the John Birch Society. Their goal and motto was "Get US out of the UN . . . NOW!" They had a film in which geopolitical experts like Martha Raye, Bob Hope, and John Wayne spoke movingly of the capitulation to a communist point of view that the United Nations was slowly forcing the U.S. government to accept. Take Vietnam, for example, they said.

The film would be shown to students who did not go to *Fiddler on the Roof,* and speakers from TRAIN would hold a "panel discussion." I learned of this through my history and English teachers, who were shocked but powerless, they said. That was my cue. My fellow, now crusading, editors and I approached the civics teacher and asked to borrow the film, since we would otherwise miss it. The following afternoon we decided to scrap that month's editorial about the prom and rush a special edition of the *Reflector* to press with my editorial that challenged the ethics and educational value of the planned program.

We had never been required before to submit any copy for prepublication review, and so we distributed the edition in classes before lunch, as we always had. I went to lunch, then to class, and then in the middle of my next class, typing, I was called to the principal's office.

She was livid.

Who did I think I was? How could I be so irresponsible? It was not my place to question what was and was not educational.

I only told the truth, I protested.

I had betrayed my school. I had taken advantage of my freedom. I was an embarrassment. And what about that survey? I was undermining everything she and the teachers and the parents had worked for.

I was doing what I believed in, I said.

Who was I to involve the school's reputation in what I believed in? This school had a good reputation, but didn't I know there were people in the community who didn't like us? I was helping the school's enemies. This sort of thing could ruin the school's good name. This was a Catholic school, and my behavior did not reflect Catholic values.

If people were doing things that would ruin the school's name if they got out, then maybe they shouldn't be doing them, I said.

Exactly, she said. She would be watching me. And from now on, she wanted to see what we had written before we handed it out.

The film was shown anyway. My parents, and in particular my father, were scandalized that I had questioned authority, and especially in its own terms. Had I been caught smoking or drinking or spraying graffiti on the school walls, they could have understood that. Working-class acts of resistance and defiance of authority by adolescents are expected, even cherished as rites of passage in our society. But I had assaulted authority itself using the same instruments by which it legitimated its control over us. I had challenged, through carefully chosen words and carefully crafted arguments, God's will (as mediated through the school) for our lives on earth. I had dared to challenge the school's right to control our public and private visions of social reality.

My interest in school waned shortly thereafter. I learned to drive, I got a job, I began to date, and I quietly disconnected my identity from my schoolwork. I increasingly looked forward to college, where I hoped things would be different.

The process of separating laborers from managers that had begun in primary school was concluding for me, as my disillusionment with the ends, but not the means, of management began to grow. Since then I have wandered, in a desultory search for more satisfying things to do.

Leslie K. Yoder

Resisting the Assignment

Theory, including critical theory, without research on practice is dangerously abstract.

—Linda Brodkey, "Writing Critical Ethnographic Narratives"

I write this late at night because this is all the time I have all the time.

If I only had time
to write
I'd write
about
not having time
to write.
—Beverly Slapin, *The Magic Washing Machine: A Diary of Single Motherhood*

A "literacy event is any occasion in which a piece of writing is integral to the nature of participants' interactions and processes of interpretation" (Heath, quoted by Brodkey).

September 1989. I'm trying to write my thesis and getting nowhere, so my adviser tells me to just make something up, pretend. I produce a six-page draft titled "Free Fall: What I Might Write about My Thesis if I Knew What I Was Doing, or What if I Did." It begins

> Wren rock, rock, rocks in her swing, totally taken with lifting and falling, lifting and falling, rocking to the rhythm of ca-click, ca-click, ca-click as the handle turns around. I, too, am mesmerized by the swinging, the clicking; I sit, slowly turning my computer chair back and forth, matching beat for beat the music of Wren's swing. I don't know, exactly, what I will write about in my thesis, but I know that swing well: the handle makes thirty-six clicks each time it goes around, taking slightly under a minute for a full revolution—that's an average; the swing rocks more quickly at the beginning of a cycle, more slowly at the end. Even Wren knows that;

her cries remind me to wind up the swing before it runs down.
Something about the body.

Chaos theory, like a fractal, branches off into many directions . . .

What I am trying to do in 1989 is make an argument that everyone's thought/composing process is "chaotic"—sometimes it shows up in the work, sometimes not. I use French feminists, Lyn Hejinian, and chaos theory from physics. I use Wren. The paper shifts back and forth between passages on theory and passages on Wren. What I am trying to do is justify my life. If I can prove that what I'm doing is "universal" (my adviser likes universals), then I won't be insane.

> It is a way of saying, I want you, too, to have this experience, so that we are more alike, so that we are closer, bound together, sharing a point of view—so that we are "coming from the same place."
>
> —Lyn Hejinian, *My Life*

My adviser delicately pencils in the margin of the first section about Wren, "Your poetry is lovely," meaning "this is not thesis material."

The narratives available to describe experience inscribe experience.

May 1989. Nonlinear narratives seminar. Same professor, different assignment, similar project. Read aloud your draft for feedback. The title is "Rupture." I go last.

> Pregnancy paints pictures in black and white: rest good, stress not; healthy milk, dangerous alcohol; take vitamins, not drugs; sit up straight, don't slouch; sleep well, avoid caffeine; breathe deep, don't smoke; keep clean, shun cat shit; don't worry, be happy.
>
> Neils Bohr says that these dyadic distinctions are merely semantic . . .
>
> *Worried about the effects of stress, the woman took a break from cleaning up cat shit in the yard. Sitting stiffly in the chair, she washed down her vitamin, bought at the drugstore, with a White Russian made from milk and vodka, then lit a cigarette, took a drag, and breathed deeply. As she slid down in her chair, she felt rested, happy, and knew that she would sleep well that night although it would take three cups of coffee to get her going in the morning.*

Silence. Uncomfortable shifting in seats. Wren kicks me from the inside. "Oops! Looks like we're out of time. Thank you everybody."

When I get my paper back, delicately penciled in the margin is "These aren't really dyads."

Fall 1990. First quarter in a Ph.D. program at The University. Wren is one year old. I write my first real live Ph.D. seminar paper on *Ruth Hall* by Fanny Fern. *Ruth Hall*, written in the mid–nineteenth century, begins with the death of the title character's husband and traces her struggle to make a living, finally as a writer, as the single mother of two small children. All I can think as I read this book is "nothing has changed"—an admittedly not very historicist place to start, but that's what I do: using close textual analysis, I trace out Fern's argument about the cultural forces bearing on single mothers in the nineteenth century and compare them to now, drawing on popular culture texts (women's magazines, commercials, etc.) and my own experience. When I do a presentation of an early version of my project (sans the personal experience stuff), the professor humphs, but several of the women in the class come up to me afterwards to say how much they liked it. When I get the final draft back from the professor, I see that he has written three barely legible sentences in response. He characterizes the essay as "essentially, as you intended it to be, a personal piece."

Are we political yet?

> Time and time again I, too, have felt so full of luminous torrents that I could burst. . . . And I, too, said nothing, showed nothing; I didn't open my mouth, I didn't repaint my half of the world. I was ashamed. I was afraid, and I swallowed my shame and fear. I said to myself: You are mad!
>
> —Hélène Cixous, "The Laugh of the Medusa"

C., married, full-time academic, mother of one: "I'm going insane!"

A., married, part-time writing instructor, mother of two: "I'm going insane!"

D., divorced, undergraduate student, mother of one: "I'm going insane!"

K., married, graduate student, mother of one: "I'm going insane!"

M., divorced, full-time junior college instructor, mother of one: "I'm going insane!"

L., single, graduate student, TA, mother of one: "I'm going insane!"

N., married, graduate student, TA, mother of two: "I'm going insane!"

O., married, graduate student, TA, mother of two: "I'm going insane!"

Child's interpretation of lyrics to Blues Brothers' song "I'm a Soul Man": "I'm sooooooo mad!"

Am I mad or am I mad?

You are so generous, they told me, allowing everything its place, but what we wanted to hear was a story. (Hejinian)

December 1991. A bad quarter. I'm broke, paying over $500 a month on child care just to cover the hours I'm on campus. After over two years of haggling, the campus child care center has finally admitted that I will never get in on a subsidized basis unless I quit my job and go on welfare or have more babies. I'm taking a cultural studies seminar for which the instructor has assigned approximately $200 worth of reader (two volumes) and books. I buy the reader but not the books. I read some of the reader. The area of the course is the history of cultural studies and topics related to cultural studies—subcultures, working-class culture, that sort of thing. Everyone is very hip. I say very little.

During the sixth week of the course, the instructor turns to me during a pause in the discussion and asks quite innocently, "Are you in this class?"

I write my final paper, "Are You in This Class?" in one sitting. I am *pissed,* in deep shit and know it, but I just don't care anymore. I am *so* sick of listening to people talk about "the other" while they sip their $2.50 cappuccinos that I could puke. But I make sure that my essay is "theoretically informed":

> The question "Are you in this class?"—asked explicitly a few weeks ago—is one that has plagued me for some time. This "paper," such as it is, is a partial attempt to answer that question within some sort of theoretical and cultural framework. Because the "you" addressed in the question is the "me" who is writing the paper, and because the answer, for "me," involves specific material conditions of my life (but which are by no means limited to my self and are pertinent to many single, or in some cases, partnered, working mothers within the academy), I run the rather obvious risk of producing what will be read as "a merely subjectivist rebellion against monolithic modes of thought" (Smith 102) or, as one of my first pieces for a professor here was criticized, "essentially, as you intended it to be, a personal piece." Questions of intention not entirely aside, I take up this position in order to examine the subject positions (un)available for working mothers (or other "nonsanctioned" "others") in general and more specifically within the academy. It is not my intention to provide an exhaustive account of the limited social construction of motherhood in mass culture but rather to explore a particular intersection/relationship between mass/popular cultural representations of working, single mothers, the ideology reflected there, and its manifestations within the university.

I then launch into a discussion of interpellation as modified by Paul Smith in *Discerning the Subject* (a book not on the reading list). Hailing:

Hence, the importance of "Are you in this class?" as a rhetorical question. . . . I agree with Smith that "current conceptions of the 'subject' have tended to produce a purely *theoretical* 'subject', removed almost entirely from the political and ethical realities in which human agents actually live" and that this "subject" needs to be "discerned."

Professor's red-inked comment at the end of this section: "Smith is too psychological; use Therborn instead."

Surprised by the light, the lions dragged the porter's body off into the bush. The drag marks and blood spoor were easy to follow when Brian took up the trail a few minutes later, attended by an unhappy gunbearer who aimed the flashlight beam over Brian's shoulder. "Came up with them after only fifty yards," he said. "Could have followed them on those tearing sounds alone. Came round a bush and there they were, ten feet away. The lioness had already disembowelled him: she raised her head up and I gave her the first bullet in the chest and she slumped right down." (Matthiessen, quoted in Yoder, "Rupture")

MOMMY!!! GET ME SOME MILK!!!!!!!

Dan Quayle is right about some things. The absence of fathers is one of the central pathologies of the underclass.
—Eleanor Clift, "The Murphy Brown Policy"

If the message is that family disintegration and the dramatic rise of single-parent families are a major social disaster for this country, then the message is clearly correct.
—John Leo, "A Pox on Dan and Murphy"

I think of all the words I wanted to put down on paper, but I was too distracted and too interrupted even to jot them down, and now those thoughts are forever lost. . . . (Slapin)

The body of data leads to the inescapable conclusion that single parenting is harmful to children.
—Amitai Etzioni, quoted by Leo

We must all live with the consequences of children who are not brought up properly. . . . They mug the elderly, hold up stores and gas stations, and prey on innocent children returning from school. . . . Several bodies of data strongly indicate that infants who are institutionalized at a young age will not mature into well-adjusted adults. As Edward Zigler puts it, "We are cannibalizing children. Children are dying in the day care system, never mind achieving optimal development." —Amitai Etzioni, "Children of the Universe"

The nuclear family has emerged as the most important matrix of the child's emotional development. . . . The SPOC [single parent, only child] group showed a higher degree of disturbance than did the control group. . . . All the SPOC mothers manifested personality disorders without overt psychiatric symptomology. Their lifestyles were unstable and characterized by frequent changes in location, work, and world outlook. . . . These mothers give the impression of being adolescents who are still struggling with their developmental tasks. —Bayrakal and Kope, "Dysfunction in the Single-Parent and Only-Child Family"

I got fired today, sort of, and they did it so smoothly I didn't even know what was happening until I was out the door. What happened was, I fainted at my desk again, and they said they couldn't stand to see me coming to work looking so sick, so I should go home and rest and come back after the baby is born, unless, of course, they will have hired a replacement, which, I understand, they'll have to do. (Slapin)

The family is an organization, and it is consistent with all known patterns of animal behavior, including that of man, that the male should be the head of the family. . . . When environmental factors prevent the man and woman who make a family from living out the qualities with which

Nature endowed them and from maintaining a family unit, serious consequences follow. . . . The cycle of sick or broken families keeps repeating itself, the effects spread from one generation to the next and slowly but surely the sickness tears down the best traditions of mankind which made our society strong.
—Harold Voth, M.D., *The Castrated Family*

MOMMY!!! GET ME SOME GLUE!!!!!!!

Mommy. This is a love rock and it has all my love for you in it and when you touch the rock my love will come out and go over your whole body and you should take the rock with you all the time so you can have my love all the time.

The problem with a good or "natural" story is that it seems uncannily powerful and persuasive, with pretense to being an accurate transcription of events. It performs a kind of tyranny in its narrative power, in forestalling and blocking off alternative stories. Indeed, it makes them seem unimaginable.

—Jeffrey Williams, "Packaging Theory"

I find that even when I'm telling the truth, I feel guilty, like I'm lying. My stories do not have "the ring of truth" about them. "I'm sorry, I couldn't get my paper in on time because my child kept waking up." *Oh sure.* "I'm sorry I'm late. Wren kept stalling and threw a tantrum just as we were leaving." *Yeah right.* I'm sorry I'm sorry I'm sorry

TA meeting, Winter 1991: An instructor reveals her concern that one of her students, a single mother, may be exploiting their shared maternal status by using her child as an "excuse" for repeatedly turning in work late or missing class. I cringe, bracing myself for the blow that I know is coming. The Person in Charge declares, "You'll simply have to tell her that if her child gets sick again, she'll just have to drop the class." I want to scream, "HOW DARE YOU! YOU OF ALL PEOPLE SHOULD KNOW BETTER THAN THAT!" but I just slide down in my seat, wincing, thinking "I'm dead."

3
And here is one more poem
for the woman at home

with children.
You never see her at night.
Stare at an empty space and imagine her there,
the woman with children
because she cannot be here to speak
for herself,
and listen
to what you think
she might say.
—Susan Griffin, "Three Poems for Women," quoted by June Jordan in
"Who's Rocking the Boat?"

A "literacy event is . . ."

Summer school 1993. The most hellish class I have ever taught. Two big-mouth bigots take over the discussion in a group that consists of two women (who never talk) and twelve men (mostly various "minorities," who rarely talk). After a few initial attempts, I do not urge the quiet students to do battle with the big mouths. I hear one student near me mumble in response to Big Mouth #l's claim that racism is no longer an issue in this country, "Jesus, all you gotta do is turn on the TV," but when I encourage him to repeat what he said, he just shakes his head and looks down. I don't blame him; under any other circumstances I wouldn't waste my time with or expose myself to these assholes either. But here, I am the PC Queen and I can do anything.

BM#l homework excerpts	*PCQ comments*
On Patricia Williams: Williams is very quick to offend her audience and to promote her obvious hatred for men.	who *is* her audience?
On Audre Lorde: I was disgusted by this author's disregard for the children who grow up in lesbian environments. It makes me sick. . . . Why not discuss the issue of the children? . . . She discredited herself in my eyes when she said she was a lesbian.	I thought she *was* discussing the children
On Harold Voth, M.D.: What a wonderful book. I agreed with everything in it. What a relief to read	agreement $\neq$ analysis. By lauding those who share your views and bashing the rest, you've neglected to

something from the right side. His style is very professional. . . . It is clear that his beliefs are parallel to those of the Bible. That says something good about the Bible.

address the rhetorical strategies that they use.

Later: Voth's appeals are universal, transcending the interests of class, race, and gender.

You have *got* to be kidding.

BM#2 homework excerpt

On Lorde: Lorde makes me sick. She and everyone like her are freaks! . . . We shouldn't have to read this shit.

This is really offensive.

When BM#l shows up the following quarter, predictably, to challenge his grade, he whines, "I don't think you care about my *feelings*. I felt *silenced* in your class." I don't know whether to cry, fall down on the floor laughing, or just punch the guy out. He announces that he's starting a crusade with his similarly free-thinking buddies against the PC conspiracy at not only this but also the other writing programs on campus.

Through what sleight of hand does Lorde, do I, become hegemonic?

How To: The Amazing Reversal of Power Magic Trick (works best for female magicians with a white, straight, middle-class male audience):

1. Get some institutional authority—a TAship is fine.
2. Dress for success! Costuming is very important: old jeans, no makeup, a baggy sweatshirt—you get the picture.
3. Find some counternarratives (stuff written by black women works really well; if they're lesbians, you've really got it made).
4. Photocopy them for your reader.
5. Make your students buy and *read* the reader. (You can ensure this by giving a homework assignment on the aforementioned counternarratives: "Identify a rhetorical strategy in . . . " or better, "Write a brief response to . . .")
6. Return to class and say the magic words: "What is Author X arguing?" or better, "What did you think of . . .?"
7. Voila! The words "I'm oppressed!" will come out of rich white boys' mouths.

8. Repeat as often as you can stand it.

Now we're political.

A "literacy event is any occasion in which a piece of writing is integral to the nature of participants' interaction and processes of interpretation" (Heath, quoted in Brodkey 1987c).

> Still, it was a message, and it was in writing, forbidden by that very fact, and it hadn't yet been discovered. Except by me, for whom it was intended. It was intended for whoever came next.
>
> —Margaret Atwood, *The Handmaid's Tale*

In *The Handmaid's Tale* there's a pivotal scene where Offred finds, scratched into the paint at the bottom of a closet, the Latinate-sounding phrase *Nolite te bastardes carborundorum.* It translates to "Don't let the bastards grind you down." This moment is important for Offred both because writing and reading are strictly forbidden in Gilead and because it marks a point of connection for her to the woman who came before her; the woman is no longer present, but her coded scrawl reminds Offred that alliances can transcend distance and absence. Offred imagines that the woman has freckles. Offred and the woman who came before are breeders.

Spring 1991, 2:00 A.M. In my kitchen there's a pivotal scene. I am working on a paper dealing with the cultural, economic, and ideological factors involved in the decline of breast-feeding around the turn of the century. I pick up one of the books that I have checked out from the library for this purpose, open it, and on one of the opening pages find, in red pen, a circular scribble characteristic of a child about fourteen to sixteen months old. Its presence translates to "I'm trying to do work, but my kid keeps getting into my stuff and demanding my attention and I don't think I'll ever get this project done and Baby is scribbling in the library book and I'm too tired to care anymore." This moment is important for me both because reading and writing are nearly impossible for women with children and because it marks a point of connection to the woman who came before me; the woman is no longer present, but her child's scrawl acts as a coded reminder that alliances can transcend distance and absence. I imagine this woman with the scribbling baby, stare at the red circles until they are burned into my brain; I will recall them whenever I lose hope: someone else has been here, silent affirmation that I am not alone, that we are not alone.

Summer 1992. My friend Alex returns from a trip to San Francisco with a late birthday gift she picked up in a little bookstore in Berkeley: Beverly Slapin's *The Magic Washing Machine: A Diary of Single Motherhood.* It's a short book, and when I finally get around to reading it, I stay glued to the spot on the floor where I was sitting when I opened it:

> *How many other women have had to lie here, just like this, uncomplaining, looking at the exact same spot on the ceiling? How many hands in how many vaginas? How many gallons of pee stored in how many bladders full to bursting? . . . Why did I allow myself to feel only self-hatred, when I knew it would have been much more healthy to feel the anger, and direct it where it belonged? And the other women in the hospital, and in the clinic, why didn't we all get together, and pull the walls down to reclaim our stolen dignity? . . . How do you put a scream into words? Why don't we talk about the anger and rage and frustration and loneliness and fear and pain and helplessness of being tired when our babies want to play, and their being hungry when we want only to sleep, and when strangers and friends say, "how cute" and then walk away, leaving us with dirty diapers and vomit on our clothes? . . . What it was, was that I never knew that I was one of those disempowered people I was fighting for, for all these years.*

I read all seventy-two pages, holding my breath, thinking ohmygod, she did it, she really did it and it's published, and ohmygod, terror, if Alex hadn't bought me this book I never would have found it. I sit in that spot on the floor and cry until it's time to go pick up Wren.

> November 10, 1978
>
> I made a list today of all the things I had to do; later I crossed off the things I had done. It looked like this:
>
> ~~SHOP~~
> ~~COOK~~
> ~~CLEAN~~
> ~~LAUNDRY~~
> ~~FORMULA~~
> READ
> WRITE
>
> (Slapin)

This is why you hear about us but rarely from us.

My friend Diane teaches basic writing part time at a local community college. She estimates that a fifth of her students there are single mothers. They are very quiet, she says. My friend Diane also teaches writing part time at a private Catholic university. She estimates that her students there are 99 percent "free-thinking" assholes; none are single mothers (unless you count the Virgin Mary). They won't shut up, she says. Meanwhile, two of the single mothers have already dropped out.

> You cannot alter consciousness unless you attack the language that you share with your enemies and invent a language that you share with your allies.
>
> —June Jordan, "Who's Rocking the Boat?"

> How did I get through it? . . . Maybe it was the knowledge that everywhere there is suffering, there is resistance. Maybe something was pushing me outside myself, to meet other single mothers, to find out I was not alone, to write down these words, and somehow, to become part of the resistance that will one day take back our power. (Slapin)

So this is what I wrote.

WORKS CONSULTED

Academic Questions. (1987). Transactional Periodicals Consortium. Transaction Publishers. New Brunswick, N.J.: Rutgers.

Ackerman, Todd. (1991). "Effort to Include Bias in UT Class Aborted." *Houston Chronicle,* 5 Feb.: A1.

Almanac. (1992). "Attitudes and Characteristics of Freshmen, Fall 1991." *Chronicle of Higher Education,* 26 Aug.: 13.

Almanac. (1994). "Attitudes and Characteristics of Freshmen, Fall 1993." *Chronicle of Higher Education,* 1 Sept.: 17.

Anyon, Jean. (1983). "Workers, Labor and Economic History, and Textbook Content." In *Ideology and Practice in Schooling,* ed. Michael Apple and Lois Weiss, 37-59. Philadelphia: Temple University Press.

Apple, Michael, and Lois Weiss. (1983). "Ideology and Practice in Schooling: A Political and Conceptual Introduction." In *Ideology and Practice in Schooling,* ed. Michael Apple and Lois Weiss, 3-33. Philadelphia: Temple University Press.

Aristotle. (1984). *Rhetoric. The Complete Works of Aristotle.* Ed. Johnathan Barnes. Vol. 2. Princeton, N.J.: Princeton University Press.

Aronowitz, Stanley. (1981). *The Crisis in Historical Materialism: Class, Politics and Culture in Marxist Theory.* South Hadley, Mass.: Bergin.

______, and Henry Giroux. (1985). *Education under Siege: The Conservative, Liberal and Radical Debate over Schooling.* South Hadley, Mass.: Bergin & Garvey.

Atwood, Margaret. (1985). *The Handmaid's Tale.* New York: Fawcett Crest Ballantine.

Axelrod, Rise, and Charles Cooper. (1988). *The St. Martin's Guide to Writing.* 2d ed. New York: St. Martin's.

Balibar, Etienne, and Pierre Macherey. (1980). "On Literature as an Ideological Form." In *Untying the Text: A Post-Structuralist Reader,* ed. Robert Young, 79-99. Boston: Routledge & Kegan Paul.

Baron, Dennis. (1991). *The English Only Question: An Official Language for Americans?* New Haven, Conn.: Yale University Press.

Barth, John. (1967). *The End of the Road.* New York: Doubleday.

Bartholomae, David. (1980). "The Study of Error." *College Composition and Communication* 31: 253-69.

______. (1985). "Inventing the University." In *When a Writer Can't Write,* ed. Mike Rose, 134-65. New York: Guilford.

______, and Anthony Petrosky. (1986). *Facts, Artifacts, and Counterfacts: Theory and Method for a Reading and Writing Course.* Upper Montclair, N.J.: Boynton/Cook.

Bayrakal, Sadi, and Teresa M. Kope. (1990). "Dysfunction in the Single-Parent and Only-Child Family." *Adolescence* 25 (Spring): 1-7.

Beach, Richard, Judith L. Green, Michael L. Kamil, and Timothy Shanahan, eds. (1992). *Multidis-*

ciplinary Perspectives on Literacy Research. Urbana, Ill.: National Council of Teachers of English.

Bell, Derrick. (1987). *And We Are Not Saved: The Elusive Quest for Racial Justice*. New York: Basic Books.

Belsey, Catherine. (1980). *Critical Practice*. New York: Methuen.

Bereiter, Carl, and Marlene Scardamalia. (1982). "From Conversation to Composition: The Role of Instruction in a Developmental Process." In *Advances in Instructional Psychology*, ed. Robert Glaser, 1-64. Hillsdale, N.J.: Erlbaum.

Berger, John. (1980). *About Looking*. New York: Pantheon.

Berger, Joseph. (1988). "Conservative Scholars Attack 'Radicalization' of Universities." *New York Times* (national edition), 15 Nov.: A22.

Berlin, James. (1987). *Rhetoric and Reality: Writing Instruction in American Colleges, 1890-1985*. Carbondale: Southern Illinois University Press.

Bernstein, Richard. (1990). "The Rising Hegemony of the Politically Correct." *New York Times* (national edition), 28 Oct. sec. 4: 1.

______. (1991). "Nonsexist Dictionary Spells out Rudeness." *New York Times* (national edition), 11 July: C13+.

Bizzell, Patricia. (1978). "The Ethos of Academic Discourse." *College Composition and Communication* 29: 351-55.

______. (1982). "Cognition, Convention, and Certainty: What We Need to Know about Writing." *PRE/TEXT* 3: 213-43.

Bourdieu, Pierre, and Jean-Claude Passeron. (1977). *Reproduction in Education, Society and Culture*. Beverly Hills, Calif.: Sage.

Bowles, Samuel, and Herbert Gintis. (1976). *Schooling in Capitalist America*. New York: Basic Books.

Boyd, Michael. (1983). *The Reflexive Novel: Fiction as Critique*. Lewisburg, Pa.: Bucknell University Press.

Brannon, Lil, and C. H. Knoblauch. (1982). "On Students' Rights to Their Own Texts: A Model of Teacher Response." *College Composition and Communication* 33: 157-66.

Braverman, Harry. (1974). *Labor and Monopoly Capital: The Degradation of Work in the Twentieth Century*. New York: Monthly Review.

Brecht, Bertolt. (1965). *The Mother*. 1931. New York: Grove.

Britton, James, Tony Burgess, Nancy Martin, Alex McLeod, and Harold Rosen. (1975). *The Development of Writing Abilities (11-18)*. New York: Macmillan.

Brodkey, Linda. (1986a). "Tropics of Literacy." *Journal of Education* 168: 47-54.

______. (1986b). "Writing Critical Ethnographic Narratives." Paper presented at the Eighty-fifth Annual Meeting of the American Anthropological Association, Philadelphia, Dec. 4.

______. (1987a). *Academic Writing as Social Practice*. Philadelphia: Temple University Press.

______. (1987b). "Modernism and the Scene(s) of Writing." *College English* 49: 396-418.

______. (1987c). "Writing Critical Ethnographic Narratives." *Anthropology and Education Quarterly* 18: 67-76.

______. (1987d). "Writing Ethnographic Narratives." *Written Communication* 4: 25-50.

______. (1989a). "On the Subjects of Class and Gender in *The Literacy Letters." College English* 51: 125-41.

______. (1989b). "Transvaluing Difference." *College English* 51: 597-601.

______. (1992a). "Articulating Poststructural Theory in Research on Literacy." In *Multidisciplinary Perspectives on Literacy Research,* ed. Richard Beach, Judith L. Green, Michael L. Kamil, and Timothy Shanahan, 293-318. Urbana, Ill.: National Council of Teachers of English.

______. (1992b). Interview transcript: Amelia. 27 Dec.

______. (1993). Interview transcript: Amelia. 1 Jan.

______. (1994a). "Making a Federal Case out of Difference: The Politics of Pedagogy, Publicity, and Postponement." In *Writing Theory and Critical Theory,* ed. John Clifford and John Schilb, 236-61. New York: Modern Language Association.

______. (1994b). "Writing on the Bias." *College English* 56: 527-47.

______. (1995). "Writing Permitted in Designated Areas Only." In *Higher Education under Fire: Politics, Economics, and the Crisis of the Humanities,* ed. Michael Bérubé and Cary Nelson, 214-37. New York: Routledge.

______, and Michelle Fine. (1988). "Presence of Mind in the Absence of Body." *Journal of Education* 170: 84-99.

______, and Shelli Fowler. (1991). "Political Suspects." *Village Voice* 23 (April): 1.

______, and Jim Henry. (1992c). "Voice Lessons in a Poststructural Key: Notes on Response and Revision." In *A Rhetoric of Doing: Essays on Written Discourse in Honor of James L. Kinneavy,* ed. Stephen P. Witte, Roger Cherry, and Neil Nakadate, 144-60. Carbondale: Southern Illinois University Press.

Brown, Wendy. (1991). "Feminist Hesitations, Postmodern Exposures." *differences* 5 (Spring): 63-84.

Burhans, Clinton S. Jr. (1983). "The Teaching of Writing and the Knowledge Gap." *College English* 45: 639-56.

Burke, Kenneth. (1969). *A Grammar of Motives.* 1945. Berkeley: University of California Press.

Caplan, Cora. (1986). *Sea Changes: Essays on Culture and Feminism.* London: Verso.

Caputo, John. (1993). "On Not Knowing Who We Are: Madness, Hermeneutics, and the Night of Truth in Foucault." In *Foucault and the Critique of Institutions,* ed. John Caputo and Mark Yount, 233-62. University Park: Penn State University Press.

Chambers v. Omaha Girls Club, Inc. (1987). 834 F. 2nd (8th Circuit): 697-709.

Chatman, Seymour. (1978). *Story and Discourse: Narrative Structure in Fiction and Film.* Ithaca, N.Y.: Cornell University Press.

Cheney, Lynn. (1995). "Mocking America at U.S. Expense." *New York Times* (national edition), 10 Jan.: A15.

Chodorow, Nancy. (1978). *The Reproduction of Mothering: Psychoanalysis and the Sociology of Gender.* Berkeley: University of California Press.

"Civil Rights: Theme for a Writing Course." (1990). *New York Times* (national edition), 24 June, sec. 1: 31.

Cixous, Hélène. (1980). "The Laugh of the Medusa." In *New French Feminisms: An Anthology,* ed. Elaine Marks and Isabelle de Courtivron, 245-67. Amherst: University of Massachusetts Press.

Clift, Eleanor. (1992). "The Murphy Brown Policy." *Newsweek,* 1 June: 46.

Cohen, Carol. (1987). "Sex and Death in the Rational World of Defense Intellectuals." *Signs* 12: 687-718.

Coles, William E. Jr. (1988). *Seeing through Writing.* New York: Harper & Row.

Collison, Michele N-K. (1993). "Survey Finds Many Freshmen Hope to Further Racial Understanding." *Chronicle of Higher Education,* 13 Jan.: A29+.

Colvin, R. J. and J. H. Root. (1978). *Tutor.* Syracuse, N.Y.: Literacy Volunteers of America.

Colvino, William, Nan Johnson, and Michael Feehan. (1980). "Graduate Education in Rhetoric: Attitudes and Implications." *College English* 42: 390-98.

"Conservative Professors Cry: 'Reclaim the Academy.' " (1988). *Campus Report from Accuracy in Academia,* Dec.: 1+.

Cover, Robert M. (1986). "Violence and the Word." *Yale Law Journal* 95: 1601-29.

Crawford, James, ed. (1992). *Language Loyalties: A Source Book on the Official Language Controversy.* Chicago: University of Chicago Press.

Crenshaw, Kimberle. (1989). "Demarginalizing the Intersection of Race and Sex: A Black Feminist Critique of Anti-Discrimination Doctrine, Feminist Theory and Anti-Racist Politics." *Chicago Legal Forum:* 139-65.

Crowley, Sharon. (1985). "writing and Writing." In *Writing and Reading Differently: Deconstruction and the Teaching of Composition and Literature,* ed. Douglas Atkins and Michael L. Johnson, 93-100. Lawrence: University Press of Kansas.

______. (1990). *The Methodical Memory: Invention in Current-Traditional Rhetoric.* Carbondale: Southern Illinois University Press.

______. (1991) "A Personal Essay on Freshman Composition." *PRE/TEXT* 12: 155-76.

Cunningham, William. (1990). *Presentation to Parents' Convocation.* 27 Oct.: 1-12. Jenny Huang's copy.

______. (1991a). "UT Excellence Began with Constitution." *On Campus* (University of Texas), 1 April: 2+.

______. (1991b). Letter to Professor Ellen Pollak. 8 March.

Curtis, Gregory. (1990). "Behind the Lines: The Bring-Something-Texan-That-You-Want-to-Burn Party." *Texas Monthly,* May: 5-6.

de Cani, John, Michelle Fine, Paul Sagi, and Mark Stern. (1985). "Report of the Committee to Survey Harassment at the University of Pennsylvania." *Almanac* 32 (24 Sept.): ii-xii.

DeGraffenreid v. General Motors Assembly Division, St. Louis. (1976). 413 Federal Supplement: 142-45.

Dennis, Donna J., and Ruth E. Harlow. (1986). "Gay Youth and the Right to Education." *Yale Law and Policy Review* 4: 448-78.

Dewey, John. (1986). *Logic: The Theory of Inquiry. John Dewey: The Later Works, 1925-1953.* Vol. 12: 1938. Ed. Jo Ann Boydstone. Carbondale: Southern Illinois University Press.

Donald, James. (1983). "How Illiteracy Became a Problem (and Literacy Stopped Being One)." *Journal of Education* 165: 1+.

Douglas, Wallace. (1976). "Rhetoric for the Meritocracy: The Creation of Composition at Harvard." In *English in America: A Radical View of the Profession,* Richard Ohmann, 97-132. New York: Oxford University Press.

Duban, James. (1990). Letter to Joseph Kruppa, chair, Department of English, University of Texas, accompanied by his syllabus for E 306. 31 Aug.

Durrell, Lawrence. (1957). *Justine.* New York: Dutton.

______. (1958). *Balthazar.* New York: Dutton.

______. (1959). *Mountolive.* New York: Dutton.

______. (1960). *Clea.* New York: Dutton.

Eagleton, Terry. (1983). *Literary Theory: An Introduction.* Minneapolis: University of Minnesota.

Ehrenreich, Barbara. (1989). *Fear of Falling: The Inner Life of the Middle Class.* New York: HarperCollins.

ELPAC: English Language Political Action Committee. (1992). Undated letter (received in late Oct. or early Nov.) addressed "Dear California Voter," signed by Steve Workings, executive director.

Elsasser, Nan, and Patricia Irvine. (1985). "English and Creole: The Dialectics of Choice in a College Writing Program." *Harvard Educational Review* 55: 399-415.

Emig, Janet. (1971). *The Composing Processes of Twelfth Graders.* Urbana, Ill: NCTE.

Etzioni, Amitai. (1993). "Children of the Universe." *Utne Reader,* May/June: 52-61.

Faigley, Lester. (1992). *Fragments of Rationality: Postmodernity and the Subject of Composition.* Pittsburgh: University of Pittsburgh Press.

Fern, Fanny. (1986). *Ruth Hall (and Other Writings).* Ed. Joyce W. Warren. New Brunswick, N.J.: Rutgers University Press.

Fine, Michelle. (1986a). "Contextualizing the Study of Social Injustice." In *Advances in Applied Social Psychology,* ed. Michelle Fine and Len Saxe. Vol. 3. Hillsdale, N.J.: Lawrence Erlbaum.

______. (1986b). "Why Urban Adolescents Drop into and out of Public High School." *Teachers College Record* 87: 393-409.

______. (1987). "Silencing in the Public Schools." *Language Arts* 64: 157-74.

______. (1990). *Framing Dropouts: Notes on the Politics of an Urban High School.* Albany: State University of New York Press.

Fingeret, Arlette. (1984). *Adult Literacy Education: Current and Future Directions.* Columbus, Ohio: ERIC Clearinghouse on Adult, Career and Vocational Education.

Fiore, Kyle, and Nan Elsasser. (1982). " 'Strangers No More': A Liberatory Literacy Curriculum." *College English* 44: 115-28.

Flower, Linda. (1985). *Problem-Solving Strategies for Writing.* 2d ed. San Diego: Harcourt Brace Jovanovich.

Flower, Linda, and John R. Hayes. (1981). "A Cognitive Process Theory of Writing." *College Composition and Communication* 32: 365-87.

Foster, Frances Smith. (1991). "Postponement of Course Raises Academic Freedom Issues." *Modern Language Association Newsletter* 23 (Spring): 6-7.

Foucault, Michel. (1972). *The Archaeology of Knowledge.* New York: Harper Colophon.

______. (1973). *Madness and Civilization: A History of Insanity in the Age of Reason.* New York: Vintage.

______. (1976). "The Discourse on Language." In *The Archeology of Knowledge,* 215-37. New York: Harper & Row.

______. (1977). "What Is an Author?" In *Language, Counter-Memory, Practice: Selected Essays and Interviews,* 113-38. Ithaca, N.Y.: Cornell University Press.

______. (1979). *Discipline and Punish: The Birth of the Prison.* New York: Vintage.

———. (1980a). *The History of Sexuality.* Vol. I: *An Introduction.* New York: Vintage.

———. (1980b). *Power/Knowledge: Selected Interviews and Other Writings, 1972-1977.* Ed. Colin Gordon. New York: Pantheon.

Freedman, Sarah Warshauer. (1984). "The Registers of Student and Professional Expository Writing: Influences on Teachers' Responses." In *New Directions in Composition Research,* ed. Richard Beach and Lillian S. Bridwell, 334-47. New York: Guilford.

Freire, Paulo. (1970). *Pedagogy of the Oppressed.* New York: Seabury.

Fricke v. Lynch. (1980). 491 F. Supp.: 381-89.

Gartman, Bill. (1992). "Yesteryear's Work." *New York Times* (national edition), 3 Aug., sec. 4: 16.

Giroux, Henry A. (1983). *Theory and Resistance in Education: A Pedagogy for the Opposition.* South Hadley, Mass.: Bergin.

———. (1988). *Schooling and the Struggle for Public Life: Critical Pedagogy in the Modern Age.* Minneapolis: University of Minnesota Press.

Gitlin, Todd. (1993). "The Left, Lost in the Politics of Identity." *Harper's* (Sept.): 16+.

Goodman, Paul. (1970). *New Reformation: Notes of a Neolithic Conservative.* New York: Random House.

"Good Riddance." (1991). *Houston Chronicle,* 6 Feb.: 16A.

Goffman, Erving. (1981). "The Lecture." In *Forms of Talk,* 160-96. Philadelphia: University of Pennsylvania Press.

Goody, Jack, and Ian Watt. (1968). "The Consequences of Literacy." In *Literacy in Traditional Societies,* ed. J. Goody, 27-68. Cambridge: Cambridge University Press.

Gramsci, Antonio. (1971). *Selections from the Prison Notebooks.* New York: International.

Gribben, Alan. (1989). "English Departments: Salvaging What Remains." *Academic Questions* 2 (Fall): 89-98.

———. (1990a). Letter to Anne Blakeney. June.

———. (1990b). "Politicizing English 306." *Austin-American Statesman,* 23 June: 5.

Gross, Paul R., and Norman Levitt. (1994). *Higher Superstition: The Academic Left and Its Quarrels with Science.* Baltimore: Johns Hopkins University Press.

Gutierrez v. Municipal Court of S.E. Judicial District, County of Los Angeles. (1988). 838 F. 2nd (9th Circuit): 1031-54.

Habermas, Jürgen. (1981). "Modernity versus Postmodernity." *New German Critique* 22: 3-14.

Hairston, Maxine. (1991). "Required Writing Courses Should Not Focus on Politically Charged Social Issues." *Chronicle of Higher Education,* 23 Jan.: B1+.

———. (1992). "Diversity, Ideology, and Teaching Writing." *College Composition and Communication* 43: 179-93.

———, and John J. Ruszkiewicz. (1988). *The Scott, Foresman Handbook for Writers.* Glenview, Ill: Scott, Foresman.

Hall, Stuart. (1986). "On Postmodernism and Articulation." *Journal of Communication Inquiry* 10: 45-60.

Halloran, Michael S. (1990). "From Rhetoric to Composition: The Teaching of Writing in America to 1900." In *A Short History of Writing Instruction: From Ancient Greece to Twentieth-Century America,* ed. James J. Murphy, 151-82. Davis, Calif.: Hermagoras.

Haraway, Donna. (1988). "Situated Knowledges: The Science Question in Feminism and the Privilege of Partial Perspective." *Feminist Studies* 14: 575-99.

______. (1994). "A Game of Cat's Cradle: Science Studies, Feminist Theory, Cultural Studies." *Configurations* 1: 59-71.

Harding, Sandra. (1988). *The Science Question in Feminism.* Ithaca, N.Y.: Cornell University Press.

Hartouni, Valerie. (1991). "Containing Women: Reproductive Discourse in the 1980s." In *Technoculture,* ed. Constance Penley and Andrew Ross, 27-56. Minneapolis: University of Minnesota Press.

Hartsock, Nancy. (1985). *Money, Sex, and Power.* Boston: Northeastern University Press.

Hartwell, Patrick. (1985). "Grammar, Grammars, and the Teaching of Grammar." *College English* 47: 105-27.

Heath, Shirley Brice. (1983). *Ways with Words: Language, Life, and Work in Communities and Classrooms.* New York: Cambridge University Press.

Hejinian, Lyn. (1987). *My Life.* Rev. ed. Los Angeles: Sun and Moon.

Henson, Scott, and Tom Philpott. (1990a). "E 306: Chronicle of a Smear Campaign: How the New Right Attacks Diversity." *Polemicist* 2 (Sept.): 4+.

______. (1990b). "English 306: Reading, Writing and Politics." *Austin Chronicle* 10 Aug.: 8.

Hirsch, E. D. Jr. (1987). *Cultural Literacy: What Every American Needs to Know.* Boston: Houghton Mifflin.

Holmes, Steven A. (1995). "Programs Based on Sex and Race Under Attack." *New York Times* (national edition), 16 March: A1.

hooks, bell. (1989). "Representing Whiteness: Seeing *Wings of Desire.*" *Z Magazine,* Feb.: 36-39.

Horkheimer, Max. (1972). *Critical Theory: Selected Essays.* New York: Seabury.

______. (1974). *Critique of Instrumental Reason: Lectures and Essays Since the End of World War II.* New York: Seabury.

Hull, Gloria. (1982). *All the Women Are White, All the Blacks Are Men, But Some of Us Are Brave.* New York: Feminist Press.

Hunter, Carmen St. John, and David Harman. (1979). *Adult Illiteracy in the United States: A Report to the Ford Foundation.* New York: McGraw-Hill.

"Is the Curriculum Biased? A Statement of the National Association of Scholars." Advertisement. National Association of Scholars, Princeton, N.J.

Jameson, Fredric. (1971). *Marxism and Form: Twentieth-Century Dialectical Theories of Literature.* Princeton, N.J.: Princeton University Press.

Jay, Martin. (1973). *The Dialectical Imagination: A History of the Frankfurt School and the Institute of Social Research.* Boston: Little, Brown.

Jordan, June. (1994). "Who's Rocking the Boat?" *Ms.*, March/April: 70-73.

Kafka, Franz. (1948). "In the Penal Colony." In *The Penal Colony: Stories and Short Pieces* (1919), trans. Willa Muir and Edwin Muir, 191-227. New York: Schocken.

______. (1961). *The Castle.* 1930. Trans. Willa Muir and Edwin Muir, with additional material translated by Eithne Wilkins and Ernest Kaiser. New York: Knopf.

Kamler, Barbara. (forthcoming). "Towards a Critical Writing Pedagogy in English." In *Constructing Critical Literacies: Teaching and Learning Textual Practices,* ed. Peter Freebody, Sandy Muspratt, and Allan Luke. Cresskill, N.J.: Hampton.

Kazemek, Francis E. (1985). "An Examination of the Adult Performance Level Project and Its Effect on Adult Literacy Education in the United States." *Lifelong Learning* 9, no. 2: 24-28.

King, Robert. (1989). Letter to William O. Sutherland. 26 Jan.

______. (1991). Letter to Joseph E. Kruppa. 26 June.

Kinneavy, James L. (1971). *A Theory of Discourse: The Aims of Discourse.* New York: Norton.

Kluger, Richard. (1975). "The Spurs of Texas Are upon You." In *Simple Justice: The History of Brown v. Board of Education and Black America's Struggle for Equality,* 256-84. New York: Vintage.

Kohl, Herbert. (1993). "Over the Rainbow." *Nation,* 10 May: 631-36.

Kolodny, Annette. (1988). "Dancing between Left and Right: Feminism and the Academic Minefield in the 1980s." *Feminist Studies* 14: 453-66.

Kozol, Jonathan. (1980). "A New Look at the Literacy Campaign in Cuba." In *Language and Thought/Language and Reading,* ed. M. Wolf, M. K. McQuillan, and E. Radwin, 466-97. Cambridge, Mass.: Harvard Educational Review Reprint Series No. 14.

Kuhn, Thomas S. (1977). "Second Thoughts on Paradigms." In *The Essential Tension,* 293-319. Chicago: University of Chicago Press.

Labov, William. (1972). *Language in the Inner City: Studies in the Black English Vernacular.* Philadelphia: University of Pennsylvania Press.

Lacan, Jacques. (1977). *Ecrits.* London: Tavistock.

Landau, Miša. (1984). "Human Evolution as Narrative." *American Scientist* 72: 262-67.

Lanz by Lanz v. Ambach. (1985). 620 F. Supp. (D.C.N.Y.): 663-67.

Lazere, Donald. (1988). "Conservative Critics Have a Distorted View of What Constitutes Ideological Bias in Academe." Point of View. *Chronicle of Higher Education,* 9 Nov.: A52.

Leo, John. (1992). "A Pox on Dan and Murphy." *U.S. News and World Report,* 1 June: 19.

Levine, Judith. (1994). "The Heart of Whiteness: Dismantling the Master's House." *Voice Literacy Supplement,* Sept.: 11-16.

Lévi-Strauss, Claude. (1973). *Tristes Tropiques.* 1955. New York: Atheneum.

Lewis, Magda, and Roger Simon. (1986). "A Discourse Not Intended for Her: Learning and Teaching within Patriarchy." *Harvard Educational Review* 56: 457-72.

Lionnet, Françoise. (1990). "Autoethnography: The An-Archic Style of *Dust Tracks on a Road."* In *Reading Black, Reading Feminist,* ed. Henry Louis Gates Jr., 382-413. New York: Meridian.

Lorde, Audre. (1988). "Turning the Beat Around: Lesbian Parenting 1986." In *A Burst of Light: Essays by Audre Lorde,* 39-48. Ithaca, N.Y.: Firebrand.

Malamud, Bernard. (1971). *The Tenants.* New York: Farrar, Straus & Giroux.

Mangan, Katherine S. (1990). "Battle Rages over Plan to Focus on Race and Gender in U of Texas Course." *Chronicle of Higher Education,* 15 Nov.: A15.

Mann, Thomas. (1954) "Tonio Kröger." In *"Death in Venice" and Seven Other Stories* (1903), trans. H. T. Lowe-Porter, 76-134. New York: Vintage.

Marcus, George, and Michael K. Fischer. (1986). *Anthropology as Cultural Critique: An Experimental Moment in the Human Sciences.* Chicago: University of Chicago Press.

Marcus, Jane. (1989). Afterword. *Not So Quiet . . . ,* Helen Zenna Smith. New York: Feminist Press.

Martin, Emily. (1987). *The Woman in the Body: A Cultural Analysis of Reproduction.* Boston: Beacon.

______. (1994). *Flexible Bodies: Tracking Immunity in the American Culture—From the Days of Polio to the Age of AIDS*. Boston: Beacon.

Matthiessen, Peter. (1981). *Sand Rivers*. New York: Viking.

McCarthy, Cameron, and Warren Crichlow, eds. (1993). *Race, Identity, and Representation in Education*. New York: Routledge.

McCarthy, Lucille. (1985). *A Stranger in Strange Lands: A College Student's Writing across the Curriculum*. Ph.D. diss., University of Pennsylvania, 1985. Ann Arbor: UMI. 8515414.

McGann, Jerome J. (1983). *A Critique of Modern Textual Criticism*. Chicago: University of Chicago Press.

McGee, Michael Calvin. (1982). "A Materialist Conception of Rhetoric." In *Explorations in Rhetoric*, ed. Ray E. McKerrow, 23-48. Glenview, Ill.: Scott, Foresman.

McIntosh, Peggy. (1988). "White Privilege and Male Privilege: A Personal Account of Coming to See Correspondences through Work on Women's Studies." © Peggy McIntosh. Wellesley, Mass.: Wellesley College Center for Research on Women.

Meacham, Standish. (1990). Memorandum to the English Department. 23 July.

Memmi, Albert. (1955). *The Pillar of Salt*. Trans. Eduoard Roditi. Chicago: O'Hara.

Miller, Susan. (1991). *Textual Carnivals: The Politics of Composition*. Carbondale: Southern Illinois University Press.

Minow, Martha. (1990). *Making All the Difference: Inclusion, Exclusion, and American Law*. Ithaca, N.Y.: Cornell University Press.

Mooney, Carolyn J. (1988). "Conservative Scholars Call for a Movement to 'Reclaim' Academy." *Chronicle of Higher Education*, 23 Nov.: 1+.

Moore v. Hughes Helicopters, Inc. (1983). 708 F 2nd 475 (9th Circuit).

Moynihan, Daniel P. (1965). *The Negro Family: The Case for National Action*. The Moynihan Report. Washington, D.C.: U.S. Department of Labor.

Murray, Marge T. (1986). "A Radical Pedagogy of Composition." *Writing Instructor* 5: 85-95.

Myers, Greg. (1985). "The Social Construction of Two Biologists' Proposals." *Written Communication* 2: 219-45.

______. (1990). *Writing Biology: Texts in the Social Construction of Scientific Knowledge*. Madison: University of Wisconsin Press.

"NAS Impact, Texas." (1990). *National Association of Scholars Newsletter* 3 (Fall): 5.

National Association of Scholars. Suite 244. 20 Nassau Street. Princeton, NJ 08542. (609) 683-7878.

Nelson, John S., Allan Megill, and Donald M. McCloskey. (1987). "Rhetoric of Inquiry." In *The Rhetoric of the Human Sciences: Language and Argument in Scholarship and Public Affairs*, ed. John S. Nelson, Allan Megill, and Donald N. McCloskey, 1-18. Madison: University of Wisconsin Press.

Nelson v. Thornburgh. (1983). 567 F. Supp.: 369-84.

North, Stephen M. (1987). *The Making of Knowledge in Composition: Portrait of an Emerging Field*. Upper Montclair, N.J.: Boynton/Cook.

Northcutt, Norvell. (1975). *Adult Functional Competency: A Summary*. Austin: University of Texas Press.

Ohmann, Richard. (1985). "Literacy, Technology, and Monopoly Capitalism." *College English* 47: 675-89.

Olenick, Arnold J. (1992). " 'Free Trade' Means No Jobs and High Prices." *New York Times* (national edition), 3 Aug., sec. 4: 16.

Olson, C. Paul. (1983). "Inequality Remade: The Theory of Correspondence and the Context of French Immersion in Northern Ontario." *Journal of Education* 165, no. 1: 75-98.

Ong, Walter J. (1982). *Orality and Literacy: The Technologizing of the Word.* New York: Methuen.

"Over 12 Percent of Adults Illiterate, Census Says." (1986). *Education Week*, 30 April: 4.

Parker, Frank, and Kim Sydow Campbell. (1993). "Linguistics and Writing: A Reassessment." *College Composition and Communication* 44: 295-314.

Payne v. Travenol Laboratories, Inc. (1982). 673 F. 2nd 798 (5th Circuit).

Penley, Constance. (1992). "Feminism, Psychoanalysis, and the Study of Popular Culture." In *Cultural Studies,* eds. Lawrence Grossberg, Cary Nelson, and Paula Treichler, 479-500. New York: Routledge.

Penn Harassment Survey. (1985). Philadelphia: Office of the Vice Provost for Research, University of Pennsylvania.

Penticoff, Richard, and Linda Brodkey. (1992). " 'Writing about Difference': Hard Cases for Cultural Studies." In *Cultural Studies in the English Classroom*, eds. James A. Berlin and Michael J. Vivion, 123-44. Portsmouth, N.H.: Boynton/Cook.

Perelman, Chaim, and L. Olbrechts-Tyteca. (1969). *The New Rhetoric: A Treatise on Argumentation.* Notre Dame, Ind.: University of Notre Dame Press.

Perl, Sandra. (1979). "The Composing Processes of Unskilled College Writers." *Research in the Teaching of English* 13: 317-36.

Piatt, Bill. (1990). "Toward Domestic Recognition of a Human Right to Language." *Houston Law Review* 23: 885-906.

Pratt, Mary Louise. (1977). *Toward a Speech Act Theory of Literary Discourse.* Bloomington: Indiana University Press.

______. (1985). "Scratches on the Face of the Country; or, What Mr. Barrow Saw in the Land of the Bushmen." *Critical Inquiry* 12: 119-43.

______. (1986). "Fieldwork in Common Places." In *Writing Culture: The Poetics and Politics of Ethnography*, ed. James Clifford and George E. Marcus, 27-50. Berkeley: University of California Press.

______. (1991). "Arts of the Contact Zone." *Profession* 91: 33-40.

______. (1992). *Imperial Eyes: Travel Writing and Transculturation*. New York: Routledge.

Pratt, Minnie Bruce. (1984). "Identity: Skin Blood Heart." In *Yours in Struggle: Three Feminist Perspectives on Anti-Semitism and Racism,* ed. Elly Bulkin, Minnie Bruce Pratt, and Barbara Smith, 11-63. New York: Long Haul Press.

Rabinow, Paul, ed. (1984). *The Foucault Reader.* New York: Pantheon.

Radway, Janice. (1984). *Reading the Romance: Women, Patriarchy, and Popular Literature.* Chapel Hill: University of North Carolina Press.

Rajchman, John. (1985). *Michel Foucault: The Freedom of Philosophy.* New York: Columbia University Press.

Rendell, Ruth. (1981). *A Judgement in Stone.* 1977. New York: Bantam.

Resnick, Daniel P., and Laura B. Resnick. (1980). "The Nature of Literacy: An Historical Exploration." In *Language and Thought/Language and Reading,* ed. M. Wolf, M. K. McQuillan, and E. Radwin, 396-411. Cambridge, Mass.: Harvard Educational Review Reprint Series No. 14.

Rhode, Deborah L. (1989). "Association and Assimilation." In *Justice and Gender: Sex Discrimination and the Law*, 274-304. Cambridge, Mass.: Harvard University Press.

Robertson, Claire, Constance E. Dwyer, and D'Ann Campbell. (1988). "Campus Harassment: Sexual Harassment Policies and Procedures at Institutions of Higher Learning." *Signs* 13: 792-812.

Rorty, Richard. (1982). *The Consequences of Pragmatism (Essays: 1972-1980)*. Minneapolis: University of Minnesota Press.

Rosenthal, A. M. (1995). "Losing Money and Nobels." *New York Times* (national edition), 10 Jan.: A15.

Rothenberg, Paula S. (1988). *Racism and Sexism: An Integrated Study*. New York: St. Martin's.

Ruszkiewicz, John. (1990). "Altered E 306 Format Compromised by Ideological Freight." *Daily Texan*, 24 July: 4.

Scotch, Richard K. (1988). "Disability as the Basis for a Social Movement: Advocacy and the Politics of Definition." *Journal of Social Issues* 44: 159-72.

Scott, Joan W. (1991). "The Evidence of Experience." *Critical Inquiry* 17: 773-97.

Scribner, Sylvia, and Michael Cole. (1981). *The Psychology of Literacy*. Cambridge, Mass.: Harvard University Press.

Shaughnessy, Mina P. (1977). *Errors and Expectations: A Guide for the Teacher of Basic Writing*. New York: Oxford University Press.

Shor, Ira. (1980). *Critical Teaching and Everyday Life*. Boston: Seabury.

Simon, Roger, and Donald Dippo. (1986). "On Critical Ethnographic Work." *Anthropology and Education Quarterly* 17: 195-202.

Slapin, Beverly. (1983). *The Magic Washing Machine: A Diary of Single Motherhood*. Mesquite, Tex.: Ide House.

Smith, Paul. (1988). *Discerning the Subject*. Minneapolis: University of Minnesota Press.

Snowe, Ted. (1985). "Literacy Has Many Happy Returns." *Philadelphia Inquirer*, 3 Dec.: A11.

Soja, Edward. (1989). *Postmodern Geographies: The Reassertion of Space in Critical Social Theory*. New York: Verso.

Sommers, Nancy. (1982). "Responding to Student Writing." *College Composition and Communication* 33: 148-56.

Sontag, Susan. (1973). *On Photography*. New York: Farrar.

______. (1981). *Under the Sign of Saturn*. New York: Vintage.

Spillers, Hortense. (1987). "Mama's Baby, Papa's Maybe: An American Grammar Book." *diacritics* 17: 65-81.

"Statement of Academic Concern, A." (1990). Advertisement. *Daily Texan*, 18 July: 2.

"Statement of Principles and Standards for the Postsecondary Teaching of Writing." (1989). *College Composition and Communication* 40: 329-36.

Steichen, Edward. (1955). *The Family of Man*. New York: Museum of Modern Art.

Stubbs, Michael. (1976). *Language, Schools and Classrooms*. London: Methuen.

"Students' Right to Their Own Language." (1974). *College Composition and Communication* 25: 1-32.

Sullivan, Francis Joseph Jr. (1986). *A Sociolinguistic Analysis of the Distribution of Information in University Placement-Test Essays*. Ph.D. diss., University of Pennsylvania, 1985. Ann Arbor: UMI. 8603710.

Sweatt v. Painter. (1950). U.S. Supreme Court: 629-36.

Szwed, John. (1981). "The Ethnography of Literacy." In *Writing: The Nature, Development, and Teaching of Written Communication,* ed. Marcia Farr Whiteman, 13-23. Hillsdale, N.J.: Lawrence Erlbaum Associates.

Time of Change: 1983 Handbook of Women Workers. (1983). Washington, D. C.: Government Printing Office.

Toner, Robin. (1995). "Rifts Emerge inside G.O.P." *New York Times* (national edition), 16 Jan.: A15.

Toulmin, Stephen. (1958). *The Uses of Argument.* Cambridge: Cambridge University Press.

———, Richard Ricke, and Allan Janik. (1984). *An Introduction to Reasoning.* 2d ed. New York: Macmillan.

University of Pennsylvania v. EEOC. (1990). *United States Law Week,* 9 Jan.: 4093-98.

United States Department of Education. (1986). *Update on Adult Illiteracy.* Fact sheet in letter sent May 22.

Voth, Harold M. (1977). *The Castrated Family.* Kansas City: Sheed, Andrews and McMeel.

Warner, Michael. (1993). "Tongues Untied: Memoirs of a Pentecostal Boyhood." *Voice Literary Supplement,* Feb.: 13-15.

Watt, Ian. (1978). "On Not Attempting to Be a Piano." *Profession* 78: 3-15.

Weiner, Jon. (1988). "A Tale of Two Enclaves: Campus Voices Right and Left." *Nation,* 12 Dec.: 644-46.

Wheeler, John Archibald. (1982). "Bohr, Einstein, and the Strange Lesson of the Quantum." In *Mind and Nature* (Nobel Conference XVII), ed. Richard Q. Elvee, 1-30. San Francisco: Harper.

White, James Boyd. (1985). *Heracles' Bow: Essays on the Rhetoric and Poetics of the Law.* Madison: University of Wisconsin Press.

Will, George F. (1990). "Radical English." *Washington Post,* 6 Sept.: B7.

Williams, Jeffrey. (1994). "Packaging Theory." *College English* 56: 280-99.

Williams, Patricia. (1991). *The Alchemy of Race and Rights.* Cambridge, Mass.: Harvard University Press.

———. (1992). "A Rare Case of Muleheadedness and Men." In *Race-ing Justice, Engendering Power: Essays on Anita Hill, Clarence Thomas, and the Construction of Social Reality,* ed. Toni Morrison, 159-71. New York: Pantheon.

Williams, Raymond. (1977). *Marxism and Literature.* New York: Oxford University Press.

———. (1983). "The Tenses of Imagination." *Writing in Society.* London: Verso. 259-68.

Wilson, Robin. (1991). "Undergraduates at Large Universities Found to Be Increasingly Dissatisfied." *Chronicle of Higher Education,* 9 Jan.: Al+.

Wimsatt, W. K., and Monroe C. Beardsley. (1954). "The Intentional Fallacy." In *The Verbal Icon: Studies in the Meaning of Poetry,* 3-18. Lexington: University of Kentucky Press.

Winkler, Karen J. (1993). "Scholars Mark the Beginning of the Age of 'Post-Theory.' " *Chronicle of Higher Education,* 13 Oct.: A9.

Woolf, Virginia. (1927). *To the Lighthouse.* New York: Harcourt.

———. (1929). *A Room of One's Own.* New York: Harcourt.

———. (1939). *Three Guineas.* London: Hogarth.

______. (1942). "Professions for Women." In *"The Death of the Moth" and Other Essays,* 235-42. New York: Harcourt.

______. (1953). *A Writer's Diary.* Ed. Leonard Woolf. New York: Harcourt.

______. (1971). *The Waves.* 1931. New York: Harcourt.

Worsley, Peter. (1968). *The Trumpet Shall Sound: A Study of "Cargo" Cults in Melanesia.* 2d ed. New York: Schocken.

Yoder, Leslie. (1989). "Rupture." Unpublished manuscript.

Young, Iris Marion. (1989). *Justice and the Politics of Difference.* Princeton, N.J.: Princeton University Press.

Young, Richard, Alton Becker, and Kenneth Pike. (1970). *Rhetoric: Discovery and Change.* New York: Harcourt, Brace, and World.

Zuber, Sharon, and Ann M. Reed. (1993). "The Politics of Grammar Handbooks: Generic *He* and Singular *They.*" *College English* 55: 515-29.

INDEX

Linda Brodkey is the director of the Warren College Writing Program and associate professor in the Department of Literature at the University of California, San Diego. She is the author of *Academic Writing as Social Practice* (1987) and of articles on writing, narratives and literacy. She has also contributed essays to numerous books.